T0244279

MURDER IN A MILL TOWN

MURDER IN A MILL TOWN

SEX, FAITH, AND
THE CRIME THAT
CAPTIVATED A NATION

BRUCE DORSEY

OXFORD

UNIVERSITY PRESS

OXFORD
UNIVERSITY PRESS

Oxford University Press is a department of the University of Oxford. It furthers
the University's objective of excellence in research, scholarship, and education
by publishing worldwide. Oxford is a registered trade mark of Oxford University
Press in the UK and certain other countries.

Published in the United States of America by Oxford University Press
198 Madison Avenue, New York, NY 10016, United States of America.

CIP data is on file at the Library of Congress

ISBN 978–0–19–763309–0

DOI: 10.1093/oso/9780197633090.001.0001

Printed by Sheridan Books, Inc., United States of America

For Martha, forever

What think you of Ephraim K. Avery? Is he guilty, or not guilty? Read, try, judge and determine for yourselves.

Aristides, *Strictures on the Case of Ephraim K. Avery* (1833)

CONTENTS

MURDER IN A MILL TOWN

New England towns where Sarah Maria Cornell and Ephraim Avery lived and worked.

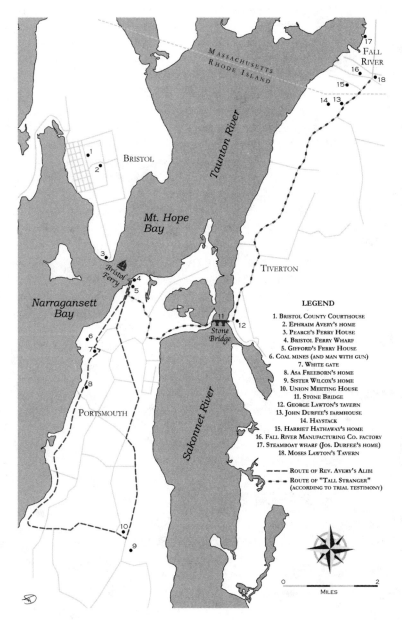

Disputed routes taken by Ephraim Avery on December 20, 1832.

Prologue

Before the Curtain Rises

LONG BEFORE THE DOORS OPENED, a crowd gathered outside the theater. Noisily, they bustled in, country folk and urban dandies alike, to find themselves good seats. The old mansion's walls reverberated with their footsteps on the hardwood floors, spirited greetings, idle gossip, and talk of politics.

The playhouse had once been the country home of Aaron Burr, who nearly thirty years earlier returned across the Hudson River to his Richmond Hill estate from the New Jersey palisades after his notorious duel with Alexander Hamilton. As Burr's fortunes waned and the growing city encroached from the south and east, John Jacob Astor purchased the mansion, lifted it and rolled it a few blocks closer to the center of Manhattan, and converted it into the Richmond Hill Theatre.

Earlier the same summer a teen-aged Walt Whitman had described feeling mesmerized by the dark green curtain of a New York theater. Transfixed when it lifted, with "quick and graceful leaps, like the hopping of a rabbit," Whitman knew that behind the drapery lay a "world of heroes and heroines, and loves, and murders, and plots, and hopes." As the Richmond Hill's curtain rose this September night, a cotton factory at sunrise came into view. Young women conversed as they commenced their work, beginning the night's feature, *Sarah Maria Cornell: or, The Fall River Murder*.[1]

Surely the audience erupted as Matilda Flynn entered as the title character. Playing opposite drama's biggest male stars the previous autumn in New York, the twenty-something actress found herself now headlining a company full of amateurs and unknowns.[2] As Sarah Maria Cornell, she breaks into the factory-floor gossip of her co-workers:

> "Good morning sisters. I have been a lazy girl; you have got a-head of me."
>
> "What detained you Sarah? You are not usually behind us at work."
>
> "I have had such a dreadful dream . . ."

As Cornell relays her premonition that she will die a violent death at the hands of another, the girls gather around, occasionally interrupting her to remind the audience that, no matter her fate, Cornell is a "good, virtuous, and industrious" woman.[3]

And so an onstage whirlwind began, carrying the audience from a cotton mill with its "factory girls" to a farmhouse of guileless Yankees—familiar stock characters—to an isolated, wooded glade where a camp meeting and a Methodist minister evoked chaos, sex, violence, ambition, and greed, before drawing to a close at a haystack with the killing foretold in the play's title.

None of this surprised the Richmond Hill audience. Entering the theater, they passed enormous posters depicting in graphic detail the scene of a man strangling a woman. They had seen similar images in handbills plastered on street corners, with smaller versions adorning their playbills.

They knew the characters and the story before the curtain rose because it mirrored a real-life drama that played out in newspapers for months in 1833. By summer's end, the factory girl and the preacher had become cultural celebrities, immortalized in at least two plays and in songs about the affair that were performed in Broadway revues for months on end.

Young America had little experience yet with a phenomenon that would one day be a defining feature of popular culture in the United States: sensational criminal cases that garnered the label "crime of the century"—no matter how frequently such crimes occurred. Here was the nation's first spectacular trial, and Americans couldn't get enough of it. Theatergoers had come that evening—and would return night after night—to experience a scandal performed in accelerated time.[4]

When theatergoers purchased a ticket in the 1830s, they expected a smorgasbord of entertainment—Shakespeare plays, farces, a medley of popular songs, circus stunts, equestrian troupes—sometimes all on the same night. Or they might be hoping for a melodrama, a play depicting a morally polarized universe of good and evil, of innocent virtue and depraved villainy. Audiences sought out melodramas because, as Herman Melville observed, they wanted performances that offered "more reality than real life itself can show." Yet in Cornell's story, real life itself resounded with the unmistakable qualities of melodrama. Passion, virtue, seduction, a vulnerable young woman, a hypocritical villain, dark plotting, and irrepressible urges to speak incessantly in order to leave nothing unsaid, all were on full view in this scandalous murder case.[5]

Still, *Sarah Maria Cornell* at the Richmond Hill was not a typical melodrama. It borrowed from comedies and Gothic horror, and most important, its virtuous heroine neither triumphed over nor escaped from her villainous, seducing foe. Instead, this protagonist met her demise through rape and murder.

The real-life demise of Sarah Maria Cornell and all that followed illuminate the very essence of a transformative moment in history, unveiling what anthropologists call a social drama. Such a drama begins when normal and peaceful means of redressing a crime fail to satisfy longings for more complete explanations. Social dramas prompt two questions: *Why did this happen?* and *What does it tell us about who we are?* An ensuing scandal reveals deep cleavages emanating from the struggle to come to grips with a world seeming to change before one's very eyes. Public fascination with the crime exceeds the bounds of normal curiosity surrounding everyday gossip and news. In search for answers people look to cherished beliefs about politics, religion, and family. They turn to familiar stories and plots to make sense of human actions and their repercussions. Collectively, they participate in an enveloping drama that, in turn, transforms the world they sought to comprehend.[6]

Audiences flocked to the theater or purchased popular reading about the factory girl and the preacher so they could take part in a scandal rich in personal meaning. In the stories of the saga's key characters they saw the experiences of their neighbors and families, sensing keenly that issues that mattered in their own changing lives were being played out in a legal thriller. They understood that women in a new workplace called the factory had uncharted opportunities to live independent lives, but they could also be exposed to sexual threats and to rumors and gossip, threatening their livelihoods and reputations. They knew too the disparity of power brandished in sexual violence and its double standard of culpability. Long before organized movements to confront sexual harassment and sexual violence, Americans understood and explained these real dramas with their own ideas about vulnerability and coercion.

Those who were captivated by this story sensed too what was at stake when evangelical religion began to take center stage in their culture and politics. At a dizzying pace, religious beliefs and personal identities were becoming intertwined with the economic marketplace and partisan politics of a young democracy. Even if they couldn't foresee the long history of a politics that construed personal choices and a changing society as contests over moral values, Americans knew the cultural battles exposed by such a scandalous case. They sensed especially that fast-changing new forms of communication—an explosion of new print media—mirrored the incessant movement of individuals into new communities and new professions.

If this shocking tale of a preacher and a factory girl constitutes a social drama, it is a drama with a multitude of narrators, scripts, and performers—a contest over stories and storytelling. Stories reveal what mattered most to people in the past; how they lived their lives; how they explained their own actions and the behavior of friends, neighbors, and strangers; and how they communicated their most deeply prized values. Stories expose as well how little people understood the historical transformations that shaped their personal lives, their society, and their culture.

As the curtain rises on the pages that follow, a real rather than an imagined drama of the preacher and the factory girl begins. It is a tale in which violence and storytelling expose the personal histories of two complicated people whose lives intersected amid an ever-changing world that each of them tried to embrace but could not control. Although they lived in an exceptional time, they were not themselves exceptional human beings. Their personal histories survive as narratives of ordinary people whose experiences embodied the spirit of a new world taking shape right before their own—and our—eyes.

ACT I

Murder

I

The Haystack

STEPPING OUT OF HIS FARMHOUSE, John Durfee noticed a chill had set in. The earth crackled under each step of his boots. It was the first day of winter: December 21, 1832, a Friday. The previous day had been a seasonably pleasant autumn afternoon, with clear skies and a full moon rising early in the evening. Overnight the temperature had dropped to near twenty degrees, and a steady wind blew from the west.

Durfee's farm lay along the main road in the sleepy village of Tiverton, Rhode Island, where Durfee and his neighbors made the most of farming small plots of coastal land. They toiled for generations, supplementing their modest income by fishing and by exchanging paid labor with one another. Tiverton sat a quarter mile south of the Massachusetts state line. Across that line stood the bustling textile manufacturing town of Fall River.[1]

Durfee walked to the barn, hitched up his team of horses, and set off downhill toward the Taunton River. It was nine o'clock in the morning.

He got no farther than a few hundred yards when he saw a woman's body hanging from a fence post inside his haystack yard. Approaching the figure, uncertain if she were dead or alive, he parted the hair that had fallen in front of her face. One look must have sent a shiver through the farmer's already cold body. A rope stretched six inches above the woman's neck, securing her rigid form to the stake. No longer was it a typical winter morning. Glimpsing two men within view, he shouted out to them.[2]

While the farmer waited, he observed that the woman wore a calash (a bonnet in the shape of a pleated hood), and that her cloak was fully fastened down the length of her torso, except for one hook open at her breast. Her arms rested awkwardly underneath. Her shoes had been removed and set aside to her right. Her body hung with her knees bent at a right angle, her toes resting on the ground.

Within moments Durfee's two neighbors arrived, along with his elderly father, Richard, who heard his son's cry from the farmhouse door. The four men gazed at the woman for a moment, examining just how she was hanging. Then John Durfee climbed over the fence into the stack yard and tried to hoist her body so that he could slip the rope off the top of the pole. Unable to lift the body with one arm and slip off the rope with the other, he heard his father's impatient holler: "Cut her down." Handed a knife, Durfee cut the rope near the top of the stake and laid the body on the ground. Then he ran to get the coroner.[3]

News spread quickly. Within minutes a young constable from Fall River named Seth Darling arrived, along with a crowd of onlookers. Darling surveyed the grass surrounding the stack yard and observed—and others agreed—that there appeared to be no evidence of a struggle. No one in the small crowd knew the young woman. She must surely be, Darling thought, one of Fall River's "factory girls," as workers in the textile mills were

Durfee farm and haystack, Tiverton, Rhode Island, where a farmer found Maria Cornell's body hanging. From Catherine R. Williams, *Fall River, An Authentic Narrative* (Boston, 1833). Courtesy of the Huntington Library, San Marino, California.

commonly called. A young woman's violent death, no matter the cause, signaled trouble for a factory town.[4]

Within the next hour, Fall River's Methodist minister, Ira Bidwell, made his way to the scene and identified the woman as thirty-year-old Sarah Maria Cornell. He had no idea that she had gone by several different names during her brief life. For most of her adulthood she called herself Maria. Only two months earlier, she had moved to Fall River, found work in the mills, and been admitted as a probationary member of Bidwell's church.

By the time the coroner, Elihu Hicks, arrived, he had already selected six men for a jury of inquest, the customary procedure for investigating sudden, unexpected, or violent deaths. This remnant of English common law placed full responsibility for determining the cause of death in the hands of ordinary men. The most important qualification for serving on a coroner's jury was to be a "freeholder," a property owner. While Cornell's body lay at their feet, Hicks gave the jury its charge, administered their oath, and ordered that the corpse be moved to Durfee's farmhouse for further examination.[5]

As people began to talk on the streets of Fall River that morning, Dr. Thomas Wilbur overheard that a woman named Sarah Maria Cornell lay dead at John Durfee's Tiverton farm. The doctor hurried to the scene. Unlike the gawkers, Wilbur bent down close to the body, opened the cloak, and placed his hand on the woman's abdomen.

When the hastily convened coroner's jury was ready, they summoned Wilbur into a room where they had laid out Cornell's body. One juror struggled to remove the rope from her neck using only his hands, but it was too deeply embedded in her skin. Another man wielded a knife to cut the rope loose. No one asked the only physician in the room to intervene.

The jury instead asked Dr. Wilbur what he knew about the young woman, casting him as the first in a long line of storytellers in this mystery. Cornell had visited his office several times, Wilbur told the jury, and he suspected that she was pregnant. That's why he opened her cloak while her body lay on the ground, to observe whether "she was fuller about the abdomen than women generally are," as he put it. During her visits to the doctor, she confided to him that the father was a Methodist preacher named Avery from nearby Bristol, Rhode Island, a married man with children.[6]

What's more, she had told him that Avery forced her to have sex at a religious camp meeting in Connecticut in August, that she'd relocated to Fall River to seek Avery's financial support, and that she'd spoken and exchanged letters with the preacher. When she informed Avery of her condition, Cornell explained, Avery advised her to take a large dose of oil of tansy to induce an abortion. She then asked the doctor whether ingesting tansy would be safe, and when Wilbur warned her that it could be fatal, she promised not to take it.[7]

While the inquest jury continued its work, John Durfee was busy searching for other clues. Early that afternoon Durfee went to the home of Harriet Hathaway, where Cornell had boarded for the past few weeks. The women of his family had instructed him to retrieve Cornell's belongings so they could dress the body for burial. Durfee also understood from Dr. Wilbur that Cornell had letters in her possession that might incriminate the Bristol preacher. Mrs. Hathaway handed over all of Cornell's possessions—a locked trunk and a small bandbox—informing the farmer that Cornell always kept the trunk's key in her pocket. Back home, the women found three letters in the trunk. Opened but unsigned by their author, they were addressed to "Sarah M. Connell." Durfee also noticed a slip of worn and dirty paper in the bandbox, and a pencil near it. His wife stored the bandbox under a bed.[8]

That afternoon a gathering of women laid out Cornell's body. They followed long-standing customs that assigned healing and burial duties to women, with younger women deferring to the experience of their elders. These women alone witnessed the corpse undressed, and they talked among themselves about suspicious marks and bruises that neither the coroner, nor any physician, nor the inquest jury had seen. As they speculated about acts of violence and motives, the women coalesced into another band of witnesses and storytellers.

For their part, the coroner's jury read the unsigned letters in Cornell's possession and found vague allusions to meetings in Fall River, instructions for letters to be sent to Bristol, and requests to "keep your secret." Still hesitant to draw a conclusion, they arranged to meet again the next morning. On Saturday, the men of the jury became the next group of storytellers, offering up a written verdict stating that "the said Sarah M. Cornell committed suicide by hanging herself upon a stake," and that she "was influenced to commit the crime by the wicked conduct of a married man, which we gather from Dr. Wilbur together with the contents of three letters found in the trunk" of the deceased.[9]

With no further clues, these men embraced a story line familiar to nearly every reader in early nineteenth-century America. A seduction tale was a plot repeated across decades in hundreds of novels and magazines. The particulars mattered little in the familiar saga of a fallen woman—a "love-ruined female." The men of the jury assumed they knew how to complete a tale that began with an unmarried pregnant woman seduced by a married man and found hanging from the end of a rope. And this explanation was expedient: If the cause of death was suicide, the married man need not even be identified.[10]

Once the jury declared its decision, the coroner gave permission for Cornell's body to be buried.

It was still Saturday morning when Fall River's Congregational minister recited a funeral prayer over Maria Cornell as she was buried in the Durfee family's cemetery on their farm. As John Durfee helped lower the coffin into its grave, he remained unsettled by the previous day's events. After the burial, his wife, Nancy, prepared Cornell's personal effects to be sent to her family. Combing through the bandbox stowed under the bed, Nancy came upon the rumpled sheet of paper that John had seen the day before and saw that it was a note—it seemed to have been written hastily—dated the day of the woman's death. It read:

> *If I am missing inquire of Rev. Mr. Avery Bristol he will know where I am gone.   S. M. Cornell. Dec. 20th*

Suddenly, vague details in the unsigned letters seemed less a mystery, and assumptions about suicide less convincing. Combined with Dr. Wilbur's story and the suspicions of the women who laid out the body, the note suggested more plainly that an act of violence had been committed by the Rev. Ephraim K. Avery of Bristol.

Handwritten note found among the possessions of Maria Cornell, dated the day of her death, December 20, 1832. The wording and spelling in this facsimile, produced ten months later, differ slightly from the text given in all trial reports and newspaper accounts. From David Melvill, *A Fac-Simile of the Letters Produced at the Trial of the Rev. Ephraim K. Avery* (Boston, 1833). Courtesy of Harvard Law School.

Those few spare words suggested a tale that might easily have been buried along with Cornell's body. Over the next year and beyond, though, that note would incite endless stories from countless storytellers, rippling outward from Fall River and New England to enter the national consciousness. From the moment a farmer discovered Maria Cornell's lifeless body, people turned to an assortment of labels to describe her. She was a Methodist, a prostitute, a crazy woman, a pious female, a wayward daughter. But most of all she was a "factory girl," which carried its own array of preconceptions.

As tragic as the end of Maria's life would be, her life began amid a fateful family drama.

2

A Troubled Marriage

ON ANOTHER COLD, WINTER DAY, twenty-eight years earlier, Maria's grand-father recorded in his diary:

James Cornell his wife & 3 children arriv'd in the Evening.[1]

It was February 1805, a few months before Maria's third birthday. The cryptic, one-sentence entry unmasks little of the family crisis precipitating their arrival or the further troubles that ensued. Yet this would prove to be the defining moment of Maria's childhood.

James Cornell and Lucretia Leffingwell Cornell arrived in Norwich, Connecticut, in the dead of winter, unannounced. They had trekked south from the western foothills of Vermont's Green Mountains, a nearly 200-mile journey, pushing onward through snowstorms. Even if the weather had been more temperate, the trip would not have been pleasant. The Cornells arrived at her father's home to declare that their marriage was over.

Lucretia's father didn't reveal what he learned of his daughter's failed marriage that night; indeed he mentioned only his son-in-law by name. And it soon became apparent that James's appearance was closer to a departure than an arrival. He had escorted the children and Lucretia—pregnant with a fourth child—to Norwich as the final act of abandoning his family.

Even if Americans thought they knew something about Maria Cornell as the era's most notorious "factory girl," few would have suspected that her maternal grandfather had built and owned factories rather than worked in them. Maria's mother was the daughter of Christopher Leffingwell, a merchant who established some of Connecticut's earliest manufacturing enterprises.[2]

Christopher Leffingwell inherited a merchant's occupation from his father, who exported local produce up and down the North American coast and imported European and Caribbean goods to distribute throughout the New England countryside. In his father's time, all trade between Britain and its colonies contributed directly to the British empire's burgeoning wealth. This was mercantilism, and colonial merchants from New England to the Carolinas had little reason to object, for it made them wealthier men.

When his father died in 1756, Christopher inherited a double portion of the estate at the headwaters of the Thames River in a Norwich neighborhood called "the Landing." By then the American colonists' relationship with the British empire had already started to fray. Christopher didn't see it coming at first. When the Seven Years' War began, he recognized that Britain's repeated wars for empire offered a boon to colonial merchants, allowing them to trade with the sugar colonies in the West Indies and to provision British troops.[3]

Over the next decade Christopher purchased more wharf property in Norwich and New London and expanded his Caribbean trading ventures, often resorting to clandestine smuggling to evade British customs enforcement. By 1765, however, Christopher's mercantile fortunes collided headlong with the maelstrom caused by what he called that "Damnable Stampt Act," Britain's first direct taxation on the colonies. Parliament's desire to tighten imperial oversight and raise revenues precipitated a crisis that ended in a revolution; but before that, these policies wreaked havoc on colonial merchants' trading.[4]

In the midst of this crisis Christopher had the audacity to try manufacturing goods that colonists had always imported from across the Atlantic—even though Parliament prohibited manufacturing by the colonists, who were supposed to be importers of European goods rather than Europe's competitors. At first Christopher built small industries near his home, a short walk from the falls of the Yantic River. Within a few years he had erected a stocking-weaving shop and Connecticut's first paper mill. Soon his paper mill produced ten sheets a minute for writing, printing, and wrapping; it supplied the paper for the *Connecticut Gazette*. A few years later he constructed the colony's first mill to manufacture chocolate.[5]

Each new expansion of his enterprises made Christopher Leffingwell into a more ardent American patriot, determined in the struggle for freedom and independence. He joined Norwich residents in protests against threats to their liberty, and when Parliament shut down the port of Boston in 1774 in retaliation for the destruction of tea, Christopher was one of five men chosen for Norwich's Committee of Correspondence. He soon deployed his well-honed skills in distributing supplies for what he called "so Glorious a Cause": the war to achieve American independence.[6] Like other commercially minded New Englanders, Christopher embraced both patriotism and economic opportunity as the colonists shed the grasp of the British empire.[7]

When the American Revolution ended, Christopher swiftly expanded his manufacturing operations. Since paper was essential for a new republic that expected its citizens to be both readers and writers, his paper mill reaped great profits, supplying newspapers that aspired to a nationwide readership. Hearing that Alexander Hamilton was soliciting information for his "Report on Manufacturing," Christopher tried to convince the treasury secretary that there was no "better place in the United States than Norwich" for a large-scale cotton manufactory. Little would he have expected that one day his own granddaughter would labor in a cotton mill.[8]

Meanwhile Christopher devoted his attention to the kind of small-scale local enterprises that brought James Cornell to Norwich as a young man. Any eighteenth-century man who considered himself a manufacturer was still thinking about goods made with human hands. After all, this was the original meaning of the term: *manual* meant "by hand" and *factoring* meant "to make." The word "factory" didn't yet denote a large building where machines turned out consumer goods but referred instead to an establishment where a trader gathered laborers to craft items for local or global markets.

Christopher opened a set of small workshops called Leffingwell Row within sight of his home. For generations, New England farm families had been more fertile than the scarce farming lands they wished to pass on to their children. A plot of land could be divided only so many times across generations before nothing remained. As more and more men faced poor prospects of becoming land-owning farmers in southern New England, they accepted an agreement offered by Christopher: he would provide the shop, materials, and younger laborers, and they would produce finished goods. He then used his merchant networks to distribute the products to retailers and consumers throughout the Northeast. Over the next decade, a handful of stocking-weavers, tailors, potters, bookbinders, and hatmakers found employment at Leffingwell Row.[9]

Most important, Christopher Leffingwell remained the "master" in these one- and two-story shops. To call someone a master craftsman meant that he was not only the owner of the shop and its tools but also the master of the dependents in the household and shop alike—the young adult men, known as journeymen, and the boys called apprentices. The young boys who arrived to learn a trade before they reached manhood were apprenticed not to the shop's senior craftsman but to Christopher, the master.

Sometime in 1791, seventeen-year-old James Cornell arrived in Norwich to become one of Christopher Leffingwell's apprentices. At No. 5 Leffingwell Row, James learned to cut and process beaver and muskrat furs and to felt wool from a hatmaker named Roswell Gaylord. Gaylord promised to furnish Norwich's ladies and gentlemen with hats "of the best quality," manufactured "in the newest and most approved taste." James hoped that one day he would be a master hatmaker and advertise a similar offer.[10]

The young apprentice slept at the shop, a stone's throw from the big Leffingwell house down the street. James had to work in his master's other enterprises too. Christopher recorded in his diary in 1793 that "Jim C" carried a load of "rags to mill." The next year he noted, "at Mill in Morning took Jim & waggon" with a load of paper to New London. Young James would have remained an apprentice until he reached legal adulthood on his twenty-first birthday in 1795. By the time his apprenticeship expired, references to the diminutive "Jim" had disappeared from Leffingwell's diary, replaced by the earliest mentions of "James Cornell." Sometime around then James started up a romance with the boss's daughter.[11]

Lucretia Leffingwell and James Cornell, Maria's parents, left behind no records of their own thoughts or feelings in letters or diaries. No court testimony registers their voices. In the records of history, they exist only in the shadows of Lucretia's illustrious father and their own infamous daughter.

The sixth of Christopher's twelve children, Lucretia was a stereotypical middle child: unnoticed, with fewer restrictions or expectations. As is true of so many eighteenth-century women, her daily life remains hidden. Her diary-keeping father rarely scratched out a word about his unmarried children's lives, the paper from his mill eliciting greater expressions of pride than the activities of his offspring.[12]

Nonetheless, Christopher apparently wanted the best education for his daughters. After arranging to send his eldest, Betsey, to a prestigious school run by a widow in Wethersfield, he hinted at sending a younger daughter to follow. Lucretia was next in line, but she apparently never attended Hancock's school. Her younger sister Joanna was known to be clever, once impressing a brother's Yale classmate as "a smart girl." Perhaps all the

Leffingwell daughters were smart girls who received exceptional educations, or perhaps Lucretia shone less brightly than her sisters.[13]

Certainly Lucretia absorbed the conflicted values that pervaded the Leffingwell household. A Calvinist heritage valuing hard work and ascetic piety hung in uneasy tension with the worldly pleasures and fashions that accompanied their rising mercantile fortunes. Christopher was himself something of a dandy, attracted to fine clothes and public displays of gentility, even as he was tightfisted. Though he once wrote "I want a good Handsome Chaise," he eventually settled for a cheaper "Second Hand" carriage. Another time he advised a daughter to "make yourself perfectly contented and satisfied" without the "extravagant" indulgence of buying a new outfit for the winter.[14]

By the time James Cornell was completing his apprenticeship, Lucretia was nearly twenty-five and wondering about her future. Her older brother William had recently moved with his wife and children to New York City to establish himself as a financier. It was certain that Betsey, nearing thirty, would remain a spinster in her father's home, while two younger sisters— first Lydia at age nineteen, then Joanna at age twenty-one—had already married young men with strong prospects for careers in commerce and law.

Without the blessing or notice of her family, Lucretia and James commenced a relationship. Only imagination can conjure what kind of endearing words they shared, what forms of secret courtship sealed their love, or who felt the most awkward in this match—the younger apprentice whose clothes and education reminded them both of the chasm between their upbringings, or the boss's older daughter who had not yet caught the eye of appropriate suitors and wasn't "the smart girl" doted on by her father.

In the autumn of 1795, five months after his twenty-first birthday, James appeared again in the pages of Christopher Leffingwell's diary. No longer Leffingwell's "boy," James had become a cog in the wheel of the manufacturer's enterprises. When Roswell Gaylord set out on his own, James became the new hatmaker in Leffingwell's shop. A month later, Leffingwell set out in his chaise, son William beside him, with James following on horseback, for a trip west to Albany to trade hats and other goods. The journeyman hatmaker was learning the retail side of the business, observing how to negotiate with country merchants. A week after that trip, Leffingwell recorded in his diary: "Paid Thomas Lathrop my bill & James Cornell's proposition."[15]

Proposition? Never in ten years of diary-keeping had Leffingwell recorded anyone making him a proposition. The manufacturer never explained, but eight weeks later he noted succinctly:

*Sunday 17 January at Meeting forenoon & afternoon Snowy in Evening
Lucretia was married to James Cornel.*[16]

Hardly anyone understood the American Revolution to mean that
apprentices could now marry the daughters of wealthy men, for social
standing and class difference hadn't disappeared. Parents still hoped for a
proper courtship and suitable marriage for their children. But new ideas
emanating from the Revolution aligned with century-long trends to alter
drastically how parents and children negotiated when and whom a young
person married.

Traditionally, a young couple could not "go to housekeeping"—this, not
the wedding, was the most important act of making a marriage—until they
were financially able to establish an independent household. As many young
men watched all possibility of inheriting land disappear before their eyes, it
was no longer necessary to postpone marriage. Parents, then, began to lose
their power to dictate the terms of their children's marriages.[17]

Americans also began rethinking their understanding of marriage, seeing
it as a metaphor for the bonds of affection (a "more perfect union") that
tied together a republic of citizens. Novelists joined with political writers
to depict tyrannical parents as the greatest threat to young people's independence. Thomas Paine, after all, called the English King a "Royal Brute"
and an unfeeling "pretended" father who made war on his own children.
Challenging a father's authority at every turn, Americans elevated affection
over patriarchal authority for the family and nation alike—a young couple's
choice and their love, not the parents' decree, mattered most.[18]

An unexpected pregnancy, of course, could accelerate plans. Lucretia and
James reached adulthood at a time when premarital sex was much more
common than more prudish descendants wished to remember. Indeed,
one out of every three New England brides was pregnant on her wedding
day. It was not vanishing inheritances alone that freed young people to
question the rationale of waiting until they were married to have sex. The
youth of James's and Lucretia's generation took advantage of greater privacy
afforded by houses built with more rooms and closed doors, and they began
socializing unchaperoned in taverns and homes. Their so-called late-night
frolics gave them greater opportunities for sexual intimacy.[19]

But if local gossips assumed that pregnancy sealed Lucretia's mismatched
marriage to James, their whispered tales were mistaken: the couple's first
child, James Jr., arrived more than nine months after their wedding day.

With parental authority in doubt and a young couple's love accentuated, it was Lucretia's pleas and actions—her freedom, choice, and independence—that surely carried the day with her family. The unnoticed middle daughter and the aspiring former apprentice might have been love-struck, or they both might have simply wished to get away from the Leffingwells.

James, like many young men of his generation, set his sights on economic independence. Not wishing to wait until he could establish his own shop or chafing at the prospect of drumming up local clientele while competing with the town's established hatmakers, he proposed an alternative plan to his wealthy father-in-law. Both his proposition and his relationship with Lucretia reflected an eagerness to establish his manhood. He was considering what it would take to become a breadwinner, master craftsman, manufacturer, and citizen. In the wake of the Revolution, political citizenship for white men still required landownership. "Marrying up," though, would be a sure step toward independence for an aspiring tradesman.[20]

Within months of their marriage, the key to James's proposition became clear: the newlyweds were moving to frontier Vermont to start a new life. He planned to establish himself as a hatmaker in the frontier North, giving him closer access to Canadian furs, allowing him to supply markets near Albany and southern Vermont, and then reinvesting his profits to become a landowning farmer. James's "industry and enterprise" impressed his father-in-law, who saw promise in his inventive plan to extend the market range of Leffingwell's manufacturing enterprises.

This was not a scheme to live off the largesse of Christopher Leffingwell, whose tight-fisted nature was well known to his son-in-law.[21] Although Christopher possessed enough frontier property rights to gift the newlyweds a landed estate, he sent them only a few small monetary gifts. For Christopher this was a business proposition, and he expected a fair return. With a clear design, James intended to transform himself into both a man and a citizen.[22]

James and Lucretia soothed her parents' unease by moving to the town where her uncle Hezekiah Leffingwell had recently emigrated. In these years, Connecticut residents caught emigration fever, bidding adieu to friends and relatives and heading west to Ohio or north to Vermont, hoping to find the kind of prosperity they thought improbable at home. Ten years younger than Christopher, Hezekiah had never prospered in Norwich like his older brother, and after becoming a widower with six children and remarrying a younger bride, the fifty-five-year-old Hezekiah relocated his large family to Arlington, a farming village in Vermont's southwestern corner.

If for James this move promised success and independence, for Lucretia it was a dreadful downward fall, for she lacked the necessary skills for this new life. Hatmakers frequently relied on their wives' assistance to prepare fur or wool, or to cut and assemble hats, but Lucretia had no such experience. Even though daughters of prosperous merchants learned some housekeeping skills, nothing had prepared her for the fatiguing labor expected of rural women in frontier Vermont: raising chickens, milking cows, churning butter, tending gardens, and spinning, weaving, and dyeing wool and linen to make clothes. Living in a place so austere, Lucretia could no longer balance pious frugality with the pleasures of fashion. Instead, she found herself among country women, their skin darkened by the incessant smoke of log-huts, as one traveler recalled, their "dress coarse, & mean, & nasty, & ragged" with "nothing to eat" and their lives "all work."[23]

Lucretia could easily have shared feelings similar to those of her aunt Cynthia, whose family thought she had married beneath herself. A flirtatious young belle, Cynthia staved off a spinster's life by becoming stepmother to Hezekiah's six children, but a move to the frontier hadn't been part of the bargain. Perpetually homesick (I "have the dumps," she wrote), she felt "secluded from all Society" and ill at ease among her Vermont neighbors, whose manners were "so very different" she could never feel at home. What's more, Lucretia couldn't even complain to her mother that she was stuck in "an old Cold dirty house" where her "courage begins to fail," since her mother had died just months after Lucretia's move to Vermont.[24]

In the midst of his own widower's grief, Christopher hoped to maintain his business arrangement with James. Yet while he kept sending supplies of wool for his son-in-law to finish as hats, something had gone amiss between the two men. At some point James stopped picking up packages and mail sent by his father-in-law, and when Christopher didn't hear from James, he complained to family and friends. Over the next few years, the two men communicated only sporadically. James was working toward a new state of independence. Getting free of the Leffingwells seemed to be part of that plan.[25]

Meanwhile, James moved the family fifteen miles north to the town of Rupert. Set at a geographical crossroads, surrounded by mountains, its waters flowing north toward the Saint Lawrence River and Canada and west toward the Hudson River and New York, Rupert offered the hatmaker access to a wealth of consumer markets. In January 1800, Lucretia gave birth to the couple's second child, a daughter she named after herself. By March, James achieved his dream of independence when he purchased a thirty-seven-acre farm. Six months later he took the oath of a freeman to become an eligible voter in the fall elections.[26]

But if James achieved his objectives of landownership and political citizenship—the measure of manhood—he relinquished them a mere two years later. Although he owned a farm, he was not a farmer. He was a fashion-based craftsman where all other village artisans labored in the traditional trades of a farm economy—blacksmiths, house carpenters, stone masons, gristmill or saw-mill operators. James needed the moxie of a peddler or the discipline of a shopkeeper, yet he possessed neither. His restless ambition evidently made him unwilling to buckle down to the arduous work of Vermont farming. Nearly two years to the day after buying his farm, James sold it. Six weeks later, his third child, Sarah Maria, was born.[27]

Sometime after that, the Cornell marriage disintegrated. Eight months after Maria's birth, James took out a newspaper advertisement announcing that he was establishing a new "hat manufactory" near Troy, New York, forty-five miles to the southwest along the Hudson River. He promised his former Vermont customers that they could "once more obtain HATS of CORNELL'S MAKE." But this would be one of the last records of James Cornell as a hatmaker, husband, or father.[28]

Lucretia filed for divorce in Connecticut's Superior Court a year and half after James delivered her and their children to Norwich. Divorces invite storytelling; indeed, although Connecticut and Vermont had the nation's most lenient divorce laws, the courts required stories before approving a disunion. The woman's tale was what they heard most often, since wives initiated most divorce petitions. According to Lucretia's plea, James deserted her in February 1804, before Maria was two years old, having committed adultery and fathered a child out of wedlock, and now resided with this unnamed woman somewhere in Quebec.[29]

Yet the actual details are more shadowy and don't square with Lucretia's divorce story. If James had deserted his family and absconded to Canada with another woman, how could he travel back to Norwich with Lucretia and their children? And when and by whom had Lucretia become pregnant? To satisfy Connecticut's strict legal requirements—a divorce could be granted only if a husband had willfully deserted his wife for three years or had committed adultery—Lucretia streamlined a more complex reality of adulterous affairs and unwanted pregnancies into a tidy, believable story to meet the deadline for the court's next session. The judges granted her plea.[30]

Maria entered the world just as her parents' marriage began its free fall from contemporary standards of respectability. Over the next two years that marriage collapsed completely, and Maria landed on the steps of her grandfather's home in Connecticut.

The failed marriage of Maria's parents was no anomaly in the decades after the Revolution. Like thousands of others, young Maria's family disbanded when a market economy made lives more mobile and ties to traditional towns more tenuous. The family's dissolution left an indelible mark on Maria's life. In letters she wrote to family or in conversations with co-workers or church friends, Maria never once mentioned her father.

3

Native Sons

ON SUNDAY, DECEMBER 23, AFTER a restless night, John Durfee awoke earlier than usual. The previous day he had buried a young woman he'd never met, only to discover that she had left a clue: *If I am missing inquire of Rev. Mr. Avery*. Durfee hurried off to show the note to the coroner, and together they went to see Dr. Wilbur, hoping to obtain more information about both Cornell and Avery.

Although the coroner promised to commence another inquest the next morning, John Durfee and Seth Darling, the Fall River constable, decided not to wait for these legal proceedings. With new evidence in hand, the two men caught the ferry to Bristol on Sunday afternoon to apprehend Avery and deliver him to authorities in Tiverton. They went directly to John Howe, a Bristol justice of the peace, and told him that "it was generally believed there had been a murder, and that Avery was implicated as the person who had done the crime, or was accessary."[1]

In their eagerness to nab their leading suspect, Durfee and Darling hadn't even bothered to find out the preacher's full name. Howe thought Darling said that they had come for a Daniel Everett or Averill, but knowing that their suspect was a Methodist minister, the judge issued an arrest warrant based on Durfee's sworn complaint, and the three men went to find the preacher's home.[2]

Ephraim Avery already knew there would be accusations. On Friday night, Ira Bidwell, Fall River's Methodist minister—after identifying Cornell's body and hearing Dr. Wilbur's suspicions—had hurried to Bristol to inform

Avery that the doctor was alleging that he'd had "illicit intercourse" with Cornell. Bidwell spent the night at Avery's home, listening to his denials, learning of his past history with Cornell, and agreeing to accompany Avery on Monday to Lowell, Massachusetts, where the two men might gather evidence about Cornell's character. Avery believed this information would "rebut any assertions she might have made." For the accused preacher, it was important to rally his Methodist brethren around him. On Saturday, Avery summoned Samuel Drake, the Methodist minister from Portsmouth, Rhode Island. Explaining what he had learned from Bidwell, Avery offered Drake an account of his whereabouts on the night of Cornell's death.

By the time the three men arrived with an arrest warrant, Avery had informed his wife of the troubles brewing and asked Rev. Drake to preach for him that morning. Once Durfee and Darling declared their intention to take him to Tiverton, however, Avery objected to being removed from Bristol County. Judge Howe then ordered him to remain under house arrest, awaiting an "examination," or pre-trial hearing, there in Bristol. Durfee and Darling's bold plans to bring him into custody near Fall River had been foiled.[3]

§

Who was this man charged with murdering Maria Cornell? We have almost no stories in Ephraim Avery's own voice. He left behind no diary, personal letters, or autobiography. He wrote nothing about his childhood and upbringing in rural Connecticut. Nothing about his work. Nothing of how he chose his occupation or met his spouse. No narrative of his conversion, his call to preach, or the reasons he abandoned the Calvinism of his hometown churches. When given the chance to make a statement in his own defense, before and after the trial, he spoke only of events that began once he encountered Maria Cornell in Lowell.

Methodists were too much of a storytelling people for Avery not to have recounted his life story and faith journey at prayer meetings, class meetings, or camp meetings. Yet, throughout this saga, no one professed themselves to be his friend or intimate. Among a people renowned for observing the most intimate details of one another's lives, Ephraim Avery somehow rose to become a successful preacher with few knowing much about him. Not one person came forward to attest that they knew him well.

Yet people from all walks of life seemed to think they understood Ephraim Avery. Whether they prejudged him to be innocent or guilty, they assumed they knew his tendencies, personality, and "character," even if they had never seen or met the man. Tales began circulating at the first hint that he was a suspect. From all over the region rumors emanated from ordinary residents and from parties interested in his defense or prosecution. The most imaginative yarns came from the pens of newspaper editors, who had no qualms speculating and readily peddled preconceived notions about a married man—a clergyman at that—who had seduced and murdered a "factory girl." Avery was at once a stereotype and an enigma.

Stories that circulated about Ephraim Avery—while less numerous than those surrounding Maria Cornell—offer a different window into how the country was changing during these times. A Methodist preacher's life story brings into focus the new experiences for men and new expectations about masculinity at the historical moment when market forces redefined the American economy. Historians attach labels to explain such transformations—the "transition to capitalism," "from farm to factory," the "market revolution"—but people who lived through these changes often experienced them as a confusing push and pull of older values and newer expectations.

Tales of the gallant and heroic masculinity of the previous generation— the patriots of the Revolution—had a formative influence on the upbringing of boys in the early nineteenth century. In Coventry, Connecticut, young Ephraim surely heard those stories. His hometown took pride in its claim that no man ever needed to be drafted to fill its quota of soldiers during the war for independence. Ephraim's grandfather, father, and several uncles and cousins all served during the war. Months before the conflict turned bloody, the men of Coventry were already praising the "happy Unity" and "noble Fortitude & manly Resistance (of *Despotism*), universal throughout America." When news arrived that war had begun on April 19, 1775—the Lexington Alarm—116 Coventry men joined the first call for troops to defend Boston. Ephraim's grandfather, Amos Avery Sr., already a sergeant in the local militia, marched east with his town's brave volunteers.[4]

Local legends, though, often hide a more complicated story. The lore of selfless sacrifice for the patriot cause concealed a more ambivalent dedication, with few men truly ready to commit to a protracted war. Throughout the war years Connecticut soldiers repeatedly squabbled over pay and provisions, walked away from their units, and fell short of meeting troop requests from the Continental Congress. While Ulysses S. Grant remembered stories he had heard of his grandfather, Captain Noah Grant of Coventry, who "fought gallantly" in battles from Bunker Hill to Yorktown, records show that Noah stayed home for the duration of the war. Similarly, Ephraim's grandfather served for a grand total of three days in response to the Lexington Alarm, content to leave the fighting to the next generation. With each passing year, embellished valor blurred accurate memories.[5]

Young Ephraim surely heard stories not only of his family but of his hometown's most famous son, Nathan Hale. When George Washington asked for a volunteer to slip behind British lines and scout out the strength and designs of General William Howe's troops in New York City, Hale alone stepped forward. Once discovered by the British in his disguise as a school-teacher, with maps and plans hidden in his boots, he was executed, but not before uttering his now-famous words: "I only regret that I have but one life to lose for my country." Yet Hale was a confusing role model for young men to emulate. His heroism was premised on being a spy, which many considered to be a disreputable, even unmanly, undertaking. No true man of valor would willingly resort to duplicity and deceit or sidestep the proper rules of military conduct. Young Ephraim surely puzzled over the ambiguous lessons of manly heroism surrounding his hometown's famous spy, even as he contemplated his own family's story of Revolutionary War adventures.[6]

Ephraim's father, Amos Jr., was too young at seventeen to volunteer when the fighting began, but he eventually enlisted in the Continental Army, rising to the rank of sergeant. In 1778, Amos saw action in one of the largest single-day conflicts of the war, the Battle of Rhode Island, an unsuccessful effort to drive the British out of Newport. With intense fighting from both sides, 5,000 patriot forces repeatedly beat back their foes. France's Marquis de Lafayette called the combat "the best fought action of the war."[7]

For men of Ephraim's father's generation, who by their own will fomented a revolution and created a new republic, it seemed plausible that they could pass along to their sons the example of independent manhood from their own lives. J. Hector St. John de Crèvecoeur, the French soldier turned New York planter, who after the war penned the famous *Letters from an American Farmer*, sketched an image of himself tilling the land that ensured "all our rights . . . our freedom" and "our power as citizens." On top of his plow he sat his young son: "I am now doing for him, I say, what my father formerly did for me" so that "he may perform the same operations, for the same purposes, when I am worn out and old!"[8]

What Crèvecoeur could not imagine was the coming transition to market capitalism in the New England countryside, a transformation that prompted a dramatic reconsideration of manhood during Ephraim Avery's lifetime. Even if Ephraim's father and grandfather shared similar expectations with Crèvecoeur at the war's end, the harsh reality of farming in industrializing New England was already destroying those dreams for many fathers and sons. Ephraim's family story occasioned a familiar contrast between the many who floundered and the few who succeeded in this new economy.[9]

When Ephraim's grandfather, Amos Avery Sr., moved his small family to a neighborhood north of Coventry in 1761, he was a recently remarried widower with a young son (Ephraim's father, Amos Jr.). He relocated there along with his first wife's brother, Ephraim Kingsbury, and the two men shared a home while Amos Sr., a skilled carpenter, built houses for each of their families a half mile apart.

North Coventry was not a place where the future boded well for the post-revolutionary generation. Second Parish lay on the town's outskirts, near uncleared woodlands. Town folk referred to the residents there as the "woods people," and, as a Congregational minister recalled, the inhabitants there faced the deprivations and threats of poverty that came with settling a new community.[10]

Both Kingsbury and Avery started out as landowners in this hardscrabble village. Owning a reasonable-sized farm, they believed, made a man independent and ensured him of a "competence"—a comfortable livelihood that could be passed along to his children. For Ephraim Kingsbury, all this came true. He became a local justice of the peace, adding the suffix "Esq." to his name; was elected a dozen times to the state assembly; and served on committees at the Congregational church. His eldest son became state treasurer of Connecticut and his youngest graduated from Dartmouth College before becoming a lawyer and a clerk in the U.S. District Court of New York City.[11]

The fortunes of the Avery men were more mixed and therefore more typical. Ephraim's grandfather and father experienced the declining fortunes common to New England farmers in the early republic. For decades each generation of farm families had put extreme pressure on an already limited supply of viable land. By the 1790s these pressures became more acute. Independence from the British empire plus revolution and wars in Europe induced more farmers to turn to livestock or dairy production, or to growing a single crop for distant markets. As market forces reshaped this rural economy, farmland became far scarcer, and families became consumers of many of the items they had previously produced for themselves or bartered for with their neighbors.

Young men in Connecticut's rural villages now faced several disturbing possibilities: they could become tenants rather than landowners, they could sell their own labor or rely on their children to work for wages in manufacturing, or they could pick up and head west or north to the frontier in search of land. Ephraim Avery's father certainly considered these choices. Since Amos Sr. needed to keep the farm for his own survival, Ephraim's parents, Amos Jr. and Abigail Loomis, didn't wait for an inheritance and, like countless other New Englanders, conceived their first child before their wedding.

Amos Jr. never owned any land. He raised sheep as a tenant farmer and purchased his family's grain from other farmers while his daughters eked out a meager income by making goods at home. Even if he had inherited a tiny fragment of his father's small farm, it could not have supported his family. It was an act of hopeful thinking for Amos and Abigail to name their seventh child and second son, born December 18, 1799, after his prominent great-uncle: Ephraim Kingsbury Avery.[12]

Boys of Ephraim's generation raised on New England farms found that their fathers' and grandfathers' ideals of manhood were rapidly becoming a phantasm. Connecticut's native sons—like those of Massachusetts and Rhode Island—watched a traditional farming economy vanish before their eyes. Rural villages throughout southern New England ceased to be places where most white men could rely on landownership and agricultural self-sufficiency to support their families. Men like revivalist Charles Finney, sex reformer Sylvester Graham, abolitionists Theodore Weld and John Brown, educator-philosopher Bronson Alcott, and showman P. T. Barnum—all raised in rural Connecticut like Ephraim—each headed off in search of a new kind of success story. Legions of other Connecticut Yankees followed similar ambitious paths but flamed out in failure, including Maria's father, James Cornell.

By the time he reached adulthood, Ephraim Avery peered into a future that threatened landlessness, wage labor, and all-too-certain migration. He had no chance of becoming a person of importance, a man of respect and honor like his great-uncle and namesake—that is, unless he could discover a different way to succeed as a man, unless he could find a people who not only overlooked his poverty but exalted it as evidence of God's favor. A new birth, a new faith, a new church in which God called men to be ministers regardless of their wealth or their education offered Ephraim an alternative future.

4

Useful in This World

FAILING TO ARREST REV. AVERY and return him to the scene of the crime, residents of Tiverton and Fall River realized that they needed to gather more credible evidence to build a case for the prosecution—and a key piece of evidence was Maria Cornell's body. Monday morning, the coroner returned to Durfee's farm with an order from a Tiverton magistrate to disinter the corpse and conduct another inquest. Knowing that two of the original inquest jurors were not legally qualified to serve because they were not property owners, or "freeholders," the coroner added two new men to the jury and ordered John Durfee to dig up Cornell's body. Durfee loaded it on a wagon and placed it in the family's barn.[1]

Dr. Wilbur, along with another Fall River physician, Foster Hooper, examined Cornell's body while the coroner's jury looked on. Twenty-seven-year-old Dr. Hooper took the lead. Together the doctors measured how deep a mark the rope had left in Cornell's neck, noted how it remained the same around its full circumference, and confirmed that her neck had not been broken. There were bruises, scrapes, and grass stains on her legs and knees, as well as a dent on her face where it had pressed against the stake. The doctors removed a female fetus from Cornell's uterus, and measured it as eight inches long. This was as much of a dissection as the jury men wanted to observe, and they all retreated to the farmhouse.

Doctors Hooper and Wilbur, though, were dissatisfied with the extent of their autopsy. Wanting to know the condition of Cornell's stomach and lungs, they returned to the barn and made a deeper incision in the abdomen, finding that her stomach looked healthy, but her lungs were engorged with black blood.[2]

At no point that morning did any of these men bother to consult the women who had laid out Cornell's body for burial. Had they asked, the women could have told them about bruises and distinct marks that they thought looked like handprints on her back, pelvis, lower abdomen, and genitals. Even without that information, though, the doctors were convinced that someone had committed a violent act that led to Cornell's death. Wilbur was sworn as a witness and asked to record his recollection of Cornell's office visits, especially anything she may have said about Avery. The second coroner's jury then issued a new verdict claiming that Cornell had been strangled to death by a cord around her neck and her body hung on a stake in Durfee's yard. In this new story, the Rev. Ephraim Avery of Bristol "did kill and murder or cause to be killed and murdered" Sarah M. Cornell.[3]

§

The Leffingwells had to decide what to do for Lucretia and her children once James Cornell had abandoned them. Christopher quickly addressed the family crisis. Summoning his favored daughter, Joanna, and her attorney husband, Charles Lathrop, to his home the next evening, they discussed what steps to take—legally and financially—for Lucretia's family. Nine days later Christopher recorded that he had made an arrangement with Simeon and Lucy Abel from the nearby town of Bozrah "to board Mrs. Cornell & Maria" for ten shillings a week. The Lathrops themselves took in Maria's older brother and sister, despite having five young children of their own. Maria, everyone assumed, was too young to be separated from her mother.[4]

The aptly named Abels were a good choice when it came to a delicate matter of family reputation. Well respected by their neighbors, Simeon had for decades served as a deacon in Bozrah's church, and Lucy was Christopher's niece. Moving Lucretia to live with them would surely deflect attention from her abandonment and pending divorce, not to mention keep her pregnancy out of sight of Norwich's gossips. Four months later, her father recorded matter-of-factly, "Daughter Cornell's Child died this day."[5]

Maria and her two siblings—James Jr. and young Lucretia—spent the rest of their childhoods separated from one another, farmed out to different relatives and neighbors, missing the milestones of one another's lives. By the time Maria reached the age of twelve, her mother and siblings all resided in separate households in different towns. Her sister Lucretia was the farthest afield, taken in by relatives in Providence, Rhode Island. "We have been so long separated that we should not know each other by sight," seventeen-year-old Maria wrote to her sister. A year later, on the eve of a visit, she again wrote, "Oh shall I behold the face of my beloved sister which I have never seen—or have no recollection of."[6]

When she was about eleven Maria moved in with her aunt Joanna and uncle Charles. For the rest of her childhood, the successful Lathrop family served as a reminder of how far her own family had fallen. As objects of family charity, pity, or judgment, Lucretia and her children were never equals in the Leffingwell family.

Christopher Leffingwell died a wealthy man in 1810, with an estate valued at close to $40,000. Five of his six surviving children, along with the children of his deceased daughter Lydia, received equal shares of his property, worth more than $6,000 apiece. But Christopher deliberately excluded Lucretia, instead setting aside $1,500 to be kept in a trust, administered by her brother William, that would pay her only the annual interest. Even with a generous return, her yearly income would be about half of what a struggling American working man earned to support his family. William, meanwhile, had retired at the age of forty-five from his merchant and stockbroker firm in New York and moved to a mansion in New Haven, becoming the town's richest citizen. In his final act, Christopher Leffingwell left a punitive reminder that Lucretia had not lived up to his expectations and that her children must endure the consequences. From this point on, they would be poor Cornells rather than wealthy Leffingwells.[7]

By the time the Cornell children reached their mid-teens, each went to work in the expanding market economy. Soon after her seventeenth birthday, Maria wrote to her sister that she was "learning the Tailors trade." This declaration underlined that her young life would hereafter be defined by her labor. In one sense this was hardly unusual. Women labored hard at home every day to sustain their families. Yet in another sense, this marked a critical moment: Maria was joining hundreds of thousands of other women as the nation's first wave of wage-earning employees outside the home.[8]

Before the industrial age, farm families relied on an informal exchange of their daughters' household work: hours of spinning, weaving, dyeing, and sewing that went into making clothes, and countless days assisting in the never-ending tasks of housekeeping, vegetable gardening, and cooking. With each passing decade after 1790, as more and more goods were produced outside the household, young women were increasingly pressed to look beyond their homes for ways to contribute to the family income or survive on their own.[9]

Young women like Maria faced limited choices. Some farmers' daughters living near newly thriving industries stayed at home and stitched shoes, braided straw bonnets, or wove milled yarn into cloth. This was called "putting out" work; the worker earned a "piece rate" for each finished item rather than an hourly wage. As more white women acquired better educations, some secured seasonable employment teaching children, but school teaching remained unsteady work. Far less desirable was working as a maid, cook, or washerwoman, where pay was minimal and free time beyond the watchful eye of one's employer almost non-existent.[10]

Since Maria couldn't afford more schooling and her family wasn't involved in "putting out" work, she looked favorably on an opportunity to learn a trade, entering a two-year apprenticeship with a Norwich master tailor. Tailors stood near the bottom of the hierarchy of trades, since tailoring didn't call for brawn, capital, or family connections, but needle trades could occasionally offer a woman a chance to one day open her own shop. Women with aspirations did become tailoresses and dressmakers—a unique group of independent female entrepreneurs—in cities like Boston, New York, and Philadelphia.

Maria landed her first employment not in a city but nearby in the rural outskirts of Norwich. By her nineteenth birthday in the spring of 1821, she was delighted to describe her "pleasant and happy situation" near a cotton factory, a few miles west of her mother's residence at the Abels' in Bozrah. "I am the only Tailoress for two miles each way," she explained to her sister, expecting to be busy with work.[11]

Maria's residence near a cotton mill meant she could earn her living by making clothing for factory workers and their families. Women factory workers needed cheaply made clothing and had little time to make their own. Factory wages in turn made women into new consumers, who wished to adorn themselves inexpensively but fashionably. Even young needle workers like Maria, with dressmaking skills, coveted the latest fashions.

There was a difference between making women's clothing—the work of a dressmaker—and men's clothing—the occupation of a tailor. Because custom-made men's clothing demanded greater skill and offered more opportunities for high fashion and top prices, male craftsmen dominated the trade. In time, some master tailors began to "put out" the less-skilled work of trimming or sewing garments to journeymen or women needle workers. Yet master tailors had no incentive to teach young apprentices, particularly women, the specialized skills (known as "cutting") that went into making a man's jacket, vest, or pantaloons.

Maria never received the complete training necessary to establish herself as a fully independent dressmaker or tailor. In later years, when deliberating between factory employment and "opportunities to work at my trade," she explained that needle work in Boston was confined to "shops where tailors hire fifteen or twenty girls to make coats and nothing else." Back when she had completed her apprenticeship, though, she had no idea of the challenges of becoming a self-supporting dressmaker, nor how often women needleworkers were exploited as semi-skilled, low-paid laborers. Instead, when she began to earn an independent living for the first time, she declared herself "thankful to God for placing me in so pleasant a situation."[12]

She chose her words carefully: God and religion mattered as much to Maria as her new work. During her youth, amid anxieties of family dissolution, Maria expressed her budding religious sentiments in letters to the older sister she barely knew. Near her seventeenth birthday, reflecting on another year's passing, Maria offered Lucretia some spiritual advice: "My sister," she wrote, "the time is coming when we shall prize time better than we do now, when we shall improve every moment of the short space allotted us." Maria had absorbed a common refrain of New England's Puritan heritage: time on earth was brief, before facing God's imminent judgment.[13]

Like millions of Americans at the time, Maria delighted in the intense spiritual experiences of religious revivals, a phenomenon that historians have called the Second Great Awakening. Over the course of her brief adult life, Maria's religious experiences and thinking would change dramatically. Her personal transformation took the form of a new kind of religious identity: a bold affirmation of individuality that Americans also displayed in their politics and business dealings.

At first, Maria held tight to traditional religious beliefs she had imbibed from the Lathrops and in Bozrah's factory village. From the arrival of the Puritans in the 1630s until nearly the end of the eighteenth century, most New England churches adhered to Calvinist doctrines about God and salvation: Everyone possessed a corrupt and sinful nature ("in Adam's fall, we sinned all," the *New England Primer* taught generations of children). God alone possessed the power to save a person. According to Calvinism, God predestined the salvation of his chosen people ("the elect") while foreordaining the rest of humanity to damnation. Churchgoers called these doctrines total depravity, divine sovereignty, predestination, and election, and these beliefs echoed endlessly from the lips of clergy and parents alike.

Calvinism proved a powerfully appealing psychology, offering the comfort of an all-powerful God when plentiful epidemics and early death exposed the fragility of human life and the mysteries of the universe. Yet Calvinism also fomented a great deal of anxiety—how could people know for certain they were among God's elect and be confident of salvation?[14]

Not surprisingly, Maria's earliest religious thoughts fixated on the imminent possibility of death and the impossibility of knowing anyone's eternal fate. "The solemn bell has just summoned another fellow-mortal into eternity," she wrote to sister Lucretia, "but what is to be his fate in another world God only knows." Several times Maria drew her sister's attention to the deaths of young people. "When we see one and another of our friends dropping into eternity it ought to remind us, that this is not our home or abiding place," she lamented. "It naturally leads us to enquire was they prepared to meet death and the judgment?"[15]

Filled with anxious thoughts about impending death, Maria believed that she held little power to change her own destiny. Wishing she could "bid defiance to death, and meet Jesus with a smile," she confessed that "my heart is hard, and I am as prone to sin as the sparks that fly upwards." On another occasion she wondered, "Sometimes I think *why am I spared* perhaps it is to commit more sin." No Calvinist preacher could have better expressed beliefs in human depravity and the absence of human agency in salvation. It was God alone who did the work of saving a person's soul.[16]

Maria was looking for answers, and, like generations of evangelical-minded Protestants in America, she came to speak of a religious change of heart with words like conversions and revivals. Conversion didn't mean changing from one religion to another (a Christian, for example, converting to Judaism); rather, it referred to the specific moment when a Christian believer became convinced that she must turn away from profane, worldly concerns and let her soul be saved by a personal encounter with Jesus Christ—this was her "new birth." When many people in a local community, all at the same time, began to display these kinds of heightened concerns about personal salvation, the churches in Connecticut called this a revival.

When Maria heard of Lucretia's conversion, she described it not as a decision made by her sister but as "the change the Lord has wrought in your heart." Casting herself as, at best, the passive recipient of divine actions, she added, "Oh my sister pray for me, that God in his infinite mercy" might "pour the sweet refreshings of his grace on my soul," pleading for God to "condescend to visit your poor sisters heart."[17]

Throughout her time as an apprentice and her first job as a tailoress, Maria's thoughts frequently turned to the state of her soul, and at age nineteen she joined the Congregational church in Bozrah, to the delight of her Norwich family. Her conversion illustrated well this phase of the national religious awakening. In Connecticut's revivals, a God-changed heart was not an invitation to assert one's individualism. Those who were redeemed, these converts heard repeatedly, would show their usefulness in pious good works.[18]

Indeed, Maria's understanding of this Calvinist-inflected evangelical religion came directly from the Lathrops. Enamored of her "dear cousin Harriet," six years her senior, Maria portrayed her as a shining "example of Christian piety." At age twelve, Harriet Lathrop began reading books on "the new birth" and attending several church meetings a week. Soon converted, she convinced her parents to join the church with her. Harriet's letters and diaries sounded the same Calvinist themes that Maria expressed a decade later: God held "all power in heaven and on earth," and despite "feeling that there is no good thing in me, that all my thoughts and actions are sinful," she remained grateful that God "condescended" to draw her near, since "he only can make me holy." The consequence of Harriet's new birth was a lifetime of usefulness. "Let me not live for myself alone," she pleaded to the Lord. "Enable me to be useful to all around me." Before she turned twenty, Harriet had founded a Sunday School and a society to benefit widows and poor children, taught a Bible class for adult people of color, and distributed religious tracts to the unconverted. At twenty-three she married Miron Winslow and the couple set sail for Ceylon to labor as Christian missionaries.[19] Maria wanted to be just like her cousin Harriet. It was her prayer, she told sister Lucretia, that they might both be "useful in this world, and happy in the world to come."[20]

Maria's early religious sentiments also bore the imprint of David L. Dodge, owner of the Bozrahville factory village where she lived and worked as a tailoress. The antithesis of Maria's own father, he briefly became for her a father-figure. Dodge's merchant fortune permitted him to join with Manhattan financiers to build a cotton factory that doubled as "a moral and religious establishment." A thorough-going Calvinist, Dodge was a player in revivals as well as Bible, tract, and missionary societies. Laymen like Dodge helped ensure that revivals in Connecticut remained steadfastly sober and Calvinist.[21]

Maria knew that the pleasures and fashions she found so attractive as an independent working woman clashed directly with her new evangelical "change of heart." She first developed a "passion for dress" while a tailor's apprentice, and once out on her own, she was known to join her female friends in "scenes of innocent amusement and pleasure." When she got serious about religion during the revivals, though, she resolved to leave behind the things of the world "and all its glittering toys," she wrote, "and devote the rest of my life to service of God."[22]

Here was the essence of what it meant to be an evangelical convert: to be "useful in this world" required the rejection of worldly pleasures. If she heard at times David Dodge's voice in her head—he thought idle recreations bred "habits unfavorable to business and devotion" and remained "always dangerous to youth"—Maria would never find it easy to reconcile the consumer pleasures that her wages permitted with her conviction that those "glittering toys" diminished her devotion to God and her usefulness in the world.[23]

During Maria's childhood, even as Calvinism maintained its hold on many New Englanders, a new brand of evangelical Protestantism on both sides of the Atlantic encouraged people to question these deterministic doctrines. But Maria had not arrived there yet.

5

Factory Girl

ON MONDAY EVENING, CHRISTMAS EVE, four days after Maria Cornell's death, Fall River residents called a mass meeting. The hundreds who gathered at Lyceum Hall all knew about the note that Cornell left behind, and they had heard the suspicions regarding the Methodist preacher in Bristol. They knew as well that Rev. Avery had rebuffed their efforts to bring him back to Tiverton. No one that night acted as if Cornell had committed suicide.

More clues were emerging too. Two days after Cornell's death, a couple of men stumbled on a woman's broken hair clip near a livestock trail about a hundred yards from the alleged crime scene. They took the comb to John Durfee, who showed it to Cornell's landlady and the jeweler who had recently repaired it, and they confirmed that it belonged to Cornell. Some wondered: did a violent struggle first take place away from the haystack? Then a steamboat engineer from Fall River came forward to state that back in November a man had asked him to deliver to Maria Cornell one of the unsigned letters found in her trunk.

With great haste the Fall River community rallied to redress a dangerous threat to the town's well-being and reputation. No factory town could afford to let a young woman's violent death go unpunished, no matter the cause. Like other New England industrial towns, Fall River made an implicit compact with rural families: Manufacturers promised them a safe place to send their young daughters to become the pioneers of a newly mobile, wage-earning, industrial workforce. Mill towns could succeed only with the continued willingness of young women to fill the need for labor. Rumors of violent crime, sexual license, or lack of moral supervision could spell the downfall of a manufacturing city, even jeopardize the whole experiment of an industrial economy.[1]

At the Christmas Eve meeting, the townspeople of Fall River appointed a committee of five men to assist with "investigating the cause" of Cornell's death, tasking them with unearthing evidence that could lead to the prosecution of the person responsible. Bypassing local elected leaders, town citizens chose these men because they seemed best suited to finance and carry out the investigation: two wealthy factory owners (Nathaniel B. Borden and Jesse Eddy), a newspaper editor (James Ford), a physician (Dr. Foster Hooper), and a deputy sheriff and auctioneer (Harvey Harnden). Borden would be the group's principal financier and organizer, but all would at different times play the roles of detective, politician, and journalist.[2]

These men were all "strivers," or "men on the make," the type of self-made men who flourished in the new economy and emulated the kind of go-ahead ethos that characterized new ideals of manliness. Men, they well knew, manifested their manliness by action. The youngest, and most eager to serve, were Dr. Foster Hooper and Harvey Harnden.[3]

Local folks were not surprised that Fall River authorities acted with greater urgency and efficiency than their rural Tiverton neighbors. From the deputy sheriff's prompt arrival at the crime scene to the skillful establishing of a committee to assist the prosecution, Fall River's men were eager to conduct a swift and thorough investigation into a young woman's violent death. Yet the Fall River men were also caught in a bind: they couldn't directly prosecute the crime, since Cornell's dead body had been found across the state line in Rhode Island and in a different county from where the lead suspect resided. Curiosity inflamed a restless impatience, as Cornell's words rang in their ears: *If I am missing inquire of Rev. Mr. Avery.*

§

By 1822, after completing her apprenticeship, Maria Cornell had secured employment in her trade, joined in a religious revival, and found new friends in Bozrahville. Then suddenly, just a few months later, she gave up her tailoress work, moved thirteen miles away, and took a job in a cotton factory. What's strange about this decision is that Maria didn't need to leave Bozrahville to work in a mill. Indeed, the factory there was even more profitable and employed more workers than her new employer. She already had affordable housing and belonged to the local church that the mill owner,

David Dodge, and his family attended. After moving, Maria lamented how she missed "the society" in Bozrahville, complaining that "there is no revival of religion here." Clearly something troublesome prompted her to leave her tailoring position for a factory job in Jewett City, Connecticut, but Maria remained silent as to why.[4]

Americans were anything but silent about a young woman's decision to work in a factory. They developed a kaleidoscope of stories to explain the phenomenon, and when Maria's life became the topic of national conversations following her death, myriad storytellers latched onto ready explanations for why she became "a factory girl."

One account insisted that she had been dismissed for socializing too much with female friends until she became "negligent of her needle," hinting that she'd violated the mill company's rules or the state's strict Sabbath laws. Yet her behavior never prompted her Bozrah church to reconsider her good standing. If, on the other hand, Bozrah's religious revival had succeeded in discouraging pious workers from spending too much on fashionable clothes, Maria would have felt it in her pocketbook. Or she could have thought she needed to move farther from her Norwich family, knowing they would disapprove of her social slide from tradesperson to factory laborer.[5]

What matters most is that Maria became a factory worker out of necessity at a time when cotton mills began offering plentiful new work opportunities. In Maria's lifetime, thousands of young women stepped through factory doors. Every woman's decision to work in a factory originated in a singular story of adaptation and survival. Sometimes the choice brought success, other times failure. Women left farms where they could no longer produce goods by traditional skills, and they left farms to make money to purchase goods now made in factories.

When Maria took her place at a machine that spun cotton into yarn, she may have considered the work "very pleasant at first" and "nothing but fun"; or she may have found that the "buzzing and hissing and whizzing of pulleys and rollers" made it all "tiresome" and "disagreeable." Either way, she was in good company among the first generation of wage-earning women who would soon learn the push and pull between opportunity and survival. Maria's working life teetered along the edges of necessity, coercion, and choice, much like her ideas about God and religion.[6]

Like weeds, textile factories popped up all over southern New England during the first twenty years of Maria's life. This new era of cotton manufacturing began in 1790 when English machinist Samuel Slater immigrated with a firsthand knowledge of patented technology and partnered with a family of wealthy Providence merchants to transplant British-style manufacturing in America. After Slater's success in building the first water-powered mill in Pawtucket, Rhode Island, most of the early cotton mills erected for the next two decades emerged from the firm of Almy, Brown, and Slater, or from local mechanics who left the company to establish their own factories.

In these early mills, factory workers spun cotton into yarn, and the companies relied on the "putting out" system to arrange with local households to weave that yarn into cloth. Scattered along the waterfalls of Rhode Island and nearby Massachusetts and Connecticut, these earliest mills soon became known as the Rhode Island System. By 1815 there were more than 160 cotton factories within a thirty-mile radius of Providence, causing a Connecticut newspaper to wonder, "Are not the people running *cotton-mill mad?*"[7]

This new industrial economy seemed particularly unstable to many Americans. "Manufacturing is a very unsteady business," wrote one young man, "sometimes up, and sometimes down, some few gets Rich, and thousands are ruined by it." The whole affair, he concluded, was populated by "Rogues, Rascals, Knaves and vagabonds." The Rhode Island System proved that in good times a small cotton mill didn't require a wealthy merchant's fortune. Blacksmiths, weavers, and skilled mechanics could envision the purchase of a cotton factory as the first step toward a better economic future. But the early textile industry seesawed between bursts of expansion and periods of depression. In the words of one father of factory workers, "This is a new meserable business for making money."[8]

Whether the outlook was gloomy or cheery, entrepreneurs erected new mills and started new companies every year. Some soon shut their doors and sold to new investors. The industry was so volatile that observers rarely knew the exact number of cotton mills in operation at any given time. At least twenty-two different textile factories opened in eastern Connecticut between 1814 and 1820, while seventy-four new factories started up in Massachusetts and dozens more emerged in Rhode Island. Workers like Maria understood that, with factories popping up all over the countryside, if they couldn't find good paying work at one, they could seek out another.[9]

Americans remained uncomfortably ambivalent about the new industrial economy. Boosters like Alexander Hamilton trumpeted nationalist goals of economic independence, but skeptics like Thomas Jefferson defended an agrarian order and voiced fears that factories would corrupt the moral character of American citizens. Critics worried that Americans could not imitate British-style manufacturing without also creating British-like cities with all their associated vices. At first, cotton manufacturers did imitate British machinery and labor practices: Samuel Slater brought to America both his knowledge of British technology and a stubborn refusal to think in new ways about laborers. The challenge for Americans, then, was to mimic British textile manufacturing while also inventing a creation story in which manufacturing in the United States was unlike anything known in Europe.[10]

Promoters of manufacturing crafted this origin story around the myth that Americans could create a wholly different moral landscape for factories. They built factories that wouldn't foster those "disgusting exhibitions of human depravity and wretchedness" evident in British manufacturing cities, because American factories didn't need to be "near mines of coal, to be worked by fire or steam." Rather, they chose idyllic sites "by the fall of waters and the running stream . . . where good instruction will secure the morals of the young." In this story, Americans could reap the benefits of manufacturing without an attendant corruption of moral virtue that threatened the traditional social order.[11]

When Maria got hired at the Jewett City Cotton Manufacturing Company, it was still unusual for a young single woman to acquire work on her own in a cotton factory. Mills in eastern Connecticut still relied on children of local families to supply their labor, just as Slater had done in Rhode Island. "Wanted, immediately, three FAMILIES with large Children, to work in a Cotton Factory," read a typical newspaper advertisement. The company would then tender a contract to the head of a household to employ the children. Water-powered spinning machines were simple enough for a child to operate—if a girl could tie a knot, she could do the work. As early as 1801, Almy, Brown, and Slater mills in Rhode Island were already employing over 100 children between the ages of four and ten. Fathers performed seasonal farm labor, mechanical repairs, or construction work for the mill companies or villages, while mothers almost never worked in the factory. Most important, child workers didn't collect their own wages. The mills paid fathers (in cash or credit at the company store) for their children's labor.[12]

These early mills tried to minimize radical transformations. By designing a family system of labor, they hoped to sustain a father's authority and preserve the traditional division of labor. Indeed, mill owners arranged for the labor hierarchy to resemble a family farm, and Slater's first mills looked more like churches than multi-story brick behemoths. Trouble was, New Englanders could see past this façade. They knew that only desperate and landless families, with too many children to support, had to resort to sending their youngest into factories, and they understood that manufacturing boosters compared cotton mills to workhouses for the poor. All of this fueled a prejudice against factories in the minds of many. Daniel Webster declared on the floor of Congress that he hoped never to see "the great mass of American labor" crammed into "unwholesome workshops," dependent on "the mercy of the capitalist for the support of himself and his family."[13]

In time, the mills began to hire more unattached women like Maria. Already plenty of girls and young women worked in the factories, but since companies didn't want to abandon the family system, they required unmarried women to board with an approved family. The difference was that these single women received their own wages and controlled their own earnings. Initially reluctant to grant this kind of autonomy to unmarried women workers, the mills replaced them with family laborers whenever possible, so single women rarely exceeded 10 percent of a mill's labor force. Eventually the mills exhausted the local supply of families, but when Maria was hired at Jewett City, she was still one of those unmarried women most vulnerable to dismissal.[14]

The most revolutionary part of this transition from farm to factory was that families became increasingly dependent on income earned by young women. Women like Maria comprised an unprecedented new workforce. To stem this tide, ironically, popular writers tried to make thousands of new women workers invisible by convincing readers that industry and production were exclusively masculine endeavors, embodied only by men's activity in the workplace. A person described as industrious or productive almost always bore the pronoun "he."[15]

Maria and her mother, Lucretia, experienced these profound changes in startlingly different ways. As single women like Maria took the lead in these new forms of labor, a chasm widened between their experiences and those of their mothers' generation. Married women's working lives began to disappear from view, enveloped by new, romanticized notions. As women became solely responsible for training children in the new nation (which hadn't been true in previous centuries), a married woman's only acknowledged labor was motherhood. Lucretia Cornell, whose children lived in someone else's household from early ages, by no means engaged in unceasing maternal labor after her marriage ended. While the culture expected her principal work to be mothering, a divorced mother with limited income could hardly match this new, glorified vision of motherhood.[16]

Maria had already lived in a factory village, but she had yet to bend her body and senses to the rhythms of this new kind of work. Now she would wake before sunrise to the peals of factory bells, labor from dawn till dusk in summer, and nearly as long by candlelight in winter. The ceaseless clatter and roar of the throstle spinning machines rang in her ears after each workday ended. After a month at the Jewett City factory, Maria spent more than a week's wages on a new pair of leather shoes—a purchase that exhibited neither her carelessness nor fondness for fashionable clothing. Factory operatives discovered that their feet swelled and their shoes no longer fit after standing at their machines for twelve to fourteen hours a day.[17]

In Jewett City, Maria boarded in company-owned tenements with the family of Roger Alexander, whose four children also labored in the mill. She earned twenty-two cents a day tending a throstle spinner. Male laborers for the same company earned two to six times more, depending on their skills and experience.[18]

To focus solely on what it was like for Maria to work in a cotton mill conceals a greater drama: how the choice of factory work became enmeshed in family and community conflict. In fiction and family stories repeatedly told since Slater opened his first mill, a woman's decision to enter a factory was portrayed as a problem that needed to be explained. Readers knew this tale as early as Sarah Savage's novel, *The Factory Girl* (1814), when Mary Burnham's family told Mary it would be a sad day "when you go into the factory." Insinuations that factory work made a woman disreputable held fast over time. Not only did Americans associate factories full of laboring women with moral corruption, but they also tended to connect productivity with masculinity. To this way of thinking, any woman who stepped outside the home as an independent worker signaled social danger. Time and again, the stories that early Americans told one another about "factory girls" (whether real or fictional) turned the decision to enter a factory into a tale of a fallen woman. The factory represented the seducer, the allure of its wages and independence an act of temptation. In these stories, the virtuous young woman must always resist and abstain.[19]

A year after Cornell's death, a labor activist declared that many New Englanders still "look upon employment in a cotton mill with horror and detestation" and consider it great misfortune to be forced "to labor in these 'palaces of the poor.'" A female worker's action, then, was steeped in risk—not only for the woman herself, but also for her family's reputation and even the well-being of the republic. Maria Cornell's decision to enter a cotton factory was imbued with the same risks, further contributing to her family's social decline.[20]

Maria, like countless other women workers, immediately felt her family's displeasure. Her sister Lucretia "murmured at my coming to the factory to work," Maria wrote from Jewett City. Unwilling to impugn her own choice, Maria told her sister "your *pride must have a fall.*" Maria certainly knew the reputation of "factory girls," but she declared anyway that "I do not consider myself bound to go into all sorts of company because I live near them. I never kept any but good company yet, and if I get into bad it is owing to ignorance."[21]

After only three months Maria was dismissed from the Jewett City factory for reasons shrouded in mystery. It was the summer of 1822, and Maria and her mother soon traveled again to Providence to visit her sister and the relatives with whom she was raised. Twenty-year-old Maria was encouraged by her family to try once more to work as a tailoress. She discovered immediately the stiff competition for needle work in Providence, where nearly three dozen women, and even more men, already worked in that trade. Without the self-possession and means necessary to become an independent proprietor, a poorly paid seamstress was the best one could hope to be.[22]

If this extended stay was an attempt to live once more as an unfractured family, Maria shattered those plans. That autumn she was caught shoplifting.

Maria could easily have been astonished by the vast array of consumer goods on display in a big city. In Providence, she discovered the neighborhoods where tradesmen and retailers opened their shops: on Westminster Street west of the river and in a cluster of east-side storefronts near Market Square along a street called Cheapside. These blocks housed the master tailors who took clothing orders and hired needlewomen like Maria for wages or piece rates. Glancing at the back pages of newspapers or strolling by storefront windows, customers like Maria were lured into shops by promises of an ever-expanding assortment of "fancy goods." Fabrics, trimmings, ribbons, bonnets, handkerchiefs, gloves, and "a great variety of other Goods" were unceasingly "just received" and "sold as cheap as can be purchased at any Store in town."[23]

That autumn Maria frequented a "fancy goods" shop on Cheapside, where a young clerk named Charles Hodges assisted women with purchases of fabric and clothing. Hodges recalled that since Maria lacked the money to buy the silk she coveted to make herself a dress, he "trusted her for it." There was nothing unusual in this arrangement, except the clerk's recklessness in extending his merchant boss's credit.

"Did you see anything strange in her conduct?" a defense attorney would ask him years later, at Avery's trial.

Hodges was "somewhat embarrassed" by the question, unsure what the attorney was driving at. Hodges worried that the too-intimate interactions between women shoppers and young salesmen could embarrass his fellow clerks and disturb courtroom audiences.

"She would come into the shop," he recalled, "approach me as if she had something to say . . . putting her face close to mine," even though "she had nothing to say."[24]

Petite, hardly more than five feet tall, with dark hazel eyes and black hair, Maria was described as a "very pretty" young woman, with a vivacious and trusting nature that made her hard to miss or forget.[25]

Maria longed for a silk dress, but Hodges was hinting at a different kind of desire. Mindful of the flirtatious exchanges between customers and clerks that propelled the new world of shopping, Hodges wasn't entirely candid about how Maria's attentions induced him to extend her credit or how that distracted him as she walked out of the store with stolen items. He also kept silent about his own flirtatious behavior, which surely sealed many a deal. Critics were becoming increasingly anxious about these commonplace commercial encounters between female shoppers and male clerks, situations that permitted, as one observer put it, "her fingers to run to a slight exchange with his under a sheet of sarsnet or gingham," so that desires "become settled into passions."[26]

Eventually Hodges noticed items missing, and another clerk caught Maria sneaking out with stolen cambric under her shawl. By January, Hodges and store owner John Carpenter found Maria in Pawtucket and confronted her. Denying at first their charges, she soon confessed that she had stolen from both Carpenter's store and the nearby shop of Samuel Richmond. As Richmond recalled, he and Carpenter visited Maria at home in Providence. When they arrived, she was joined by her sister Lucretia and a woman named Mrs. Thurber, the owner of a boardinghouse or a relative or friend. The two other women initially seemed to speak for Maria.

"They stated that she had taken some goods from my store, and was willing to restore them or pay for those she had used," Richmond said.

That's when Maria admitted that she had stolen some fabric and lace, as well as a shawl and bonnet, all worth about $5, from the two shops. When Maria's relatives assured the men that they would pay for anything she could not return, the shopkeepers agreed to disregard the whole matter. Other poor women, especially Black women, didn't fare as well when caught stealing. Maria's crime could have landed her several months or a year in prison.[27]

This shoplifting incident would have enduring repercussions for Maria, but not always in the ways that storytellers dramatized after her death. Although some thought that reports of this misdeed dogged Maria for the rest of her life and forced her to resort to factory labor, Maria wasn't simply a helpless victim of gossip and rumor. Rather than a temptation that ruined her life, Maria's shoplifting could have been a willful act of independence.[28]

All the shopkeepers who testified about Maria's theft rather oddly observed that she had a sister who "afterwards married Grindal Rawson," even when they had no apparent reason to mention either Lucretia or her husband. Grindal was a journeyman tailor, a year younger than Maria, and three and a half years younger than Lucretia. He was evidently well known among tailors and clerks on Cheapside, who also knew Maria as an aspiring young tailoress. Yet there was more: Maria later told co-workers that Grindal Rawson had courted both Cornell sisters and that "her sister got him away from her by art and stratagem." Might Maria's shoplifting have been somehow connected to the sisters' rivalry in the marriage market? Did she believe that a silk dress and a leghorn bonnet would improve her prospects for courtship and marriage?[29]

If so, Maria's decision to return to factory work might also have been part of her strategy to pursue her own independence rather than the last resort of a disgraced woman. She had, after all, visited the factory town of Pawtucket when Carpenter and Hodges first confronted her about the theft. She became aware of the lucrative wages of factory workers just as she came to understand the dead-end path that needle work offered a woman in the city's sweatshops. Perhaps she had correctly assessed the labor market and the marriage market, and her desire for consumer goods reflected more than a mere temptation that led her astray and made her the victim of gossips.

If factory wages, and a little guile, promised her both a new independence and control over her economic and consumer choices, then Maria's sentiments echoed the thoughts expressed by another mill worker, who wrote: "I am now almost 19 years old I must of course have something of my own before many more years have passed over my head. . . . I have but one life to live and I want to enjoy myself as well as I can while I live."[30]

After the shoplifting incident, Maria left Providence immediately. She would not communicate with her sister and mother for nearly two years. When she did write again, she pleaded, "Whether I ever see you again or not, I want you should forgive me and bury what is past in oblivion," adding, "I hope my future good conduct may reward you."[31]

Maria's scandalous thievery certainly produced a rift within the family, but it's hard to know who resented her misbehavior more: her own mother and sister or her relatives in Providence. Those kin were, after all, her aunts, uncles, and cousins on her father's side. It's ironic that her deadbeat father's family felt so embarrassed that they needed to spurn one of his children. But if their livelihoods also relied on the unsteady wages of the city's needle trades, then they too could have been especially vulnerable to rumors and gossip.

In another irony, Maria's fall from grace ensured her sister Lucretia's place at the center of the family. Until then, Lucretia had been the one family member sent out of state to live with the Cornells. Her life took a decidedly different course from Maria's once she had successfully courted Grindal Rawson. Married in a Norwich church surrounded by Leffingwell and Lathrop well-wishers, Lucretia returned to live in rural Connecticut (first Killingly, then Woodstock) when Grindal settled down as a country tailor. She became known as a mother, not a laborer, and she garnered local respect when her husband served as deacon in the Woodstock church. Her mother, Lucretia Cornell, spent the remainder of her life in their home. Maria's sister's life became the exact opposite of that of a "factory girl."

6

A Methodist Family

CHRISTMAS DAY ARRIVED ON TUESDAY, four days after John Durfee had stumbled upon Maria Cornell's lifeless body. In New England there might be feasting and folk rituals, but stockings, a decorated tree, gifts, and even church services wouldn't take hold until Americans commercialized the holiday later in the century. In Fall River in 1832, it was a day devoted to ordinary business.

Nothing was ordinary, though, in the wake of Maria Cornell's death. Setting type for the first news story about the crime, the editor of the *Fall River Weekly Recorder* concluded, "The excitement in this community" was "prodigious." At the same time, he was also thinking about the orderly selection of the Fall River Committee. The mill town's response to the crime would oscillate repeatedly between collaborative civic duty and "excitement."[1]

Some Fall River men weren't content to leave the investigative work to the town's aspiring elite. On Christmas day they crowded aboard a boat bound for Bristol, joining the steamboat engineer as he went to see if Rev. Avery was truly the same man who had paid him to deliver a letter to Maria Cornell. The tale of this trip would grow with each retelling—the crowd's size ballooning from 40 to 150, for instance, along with a mission to take the preacher "dead or alive." How the Fall River men descending on Bristol on Christmas afternoon were characterized would vary according to the winds of partisan sentiment about Avery's guilt. The mill town's residents thought they were acting honorably in defense of a wronged community. Those on the other side—those who supported the Methodist preacher—thought they constituted a mob.[2]

That same Christmas morning, authorities from Newport County arrived with an arrest warrant, claiming that the county was the proper jurisdiction for the case. Bristol's justice of the peace, John Howe—who had allowed Avery to be held under house arrest—disagreed. Considering this a local matter, Howe set the start of the examination in Bristol for the next day. In the nineteenth century, an examination served as the equivalent of a modern-day preliminary hearing following an arraignment, in which the prosecution and defense briefly present their cases to a judge who determines whether there's sufficient evidence to warrant a trial by jury. Fall River's men wanted to demonstrate to all concerned that they considered the deadly violence against one of their "factory girls" to be "a most foul and abominable deed," but they were forced to rely on courts and judicial decisions outside of their control.[3]

§

Alone and distraught, severed from her family after her scandalous exposure for shoplifting, Maria fled Providence in early 1823. All over New England people faced similar hardships: families rent asunder as kinfolk traveled in search of better wages. It seemed that an entire nation was on the move— pushed and pulled toward new frontiers in woodlands or on prairies (once or still shared by indigenous peoples), on the waterways and through new transportation hubs, sometimes in chains among slave coffles or in industrial towns springing up throughout the Northeast. Maria recognized this movement from her father and brother. James Jr. dropped an occasional line, notifying relatives that he was in Natchez or Port Gibson, Mississippi, or New Orleans, and then he would be missing for months, if not years, at a time. "My own dear brother—where is he?" became a common refrain in letters that Maria exchanged with her sister and mother. In the spring of 1823, it was Maria who ventured off, alone and "friendless," as her contemporaries described a person without family.[4]

As fodder for gossip, Maria couldn't have felt comfortable embarking alone, but as a woman with factory experience, she would be encouraged by the prospects for work within a day's travel of Providence. She tried out a couple of different cotton factories north of Providence before finding reliable work that summer as a weaver at Slatersville, a manufacturing village founded and managed by Samuel Slater's brother John, and designed as an idyllic rural setting for textile production. She arrived there under an assumed name: Maria Snow.[5]

Whether Maria changed her name to conceal her past sins and prevent gossips from spoiling her employment chances, or to hide from her family amid the sisters' falling-out over the courting of Grindal Rawson, one thing was certain: changing one's name was an unusual occurrence. Maria's decision raised suspicions and conjectures that echoed long after her death. At some point, her brother James went looking and found her in Slatersville, revealing her real name. For a while she went by both names, and then she began telling folks that her real name was Maria Snow Cornell.[6]

Maria finally ended her long estrangement from her family when she had a story to tell them: Her life had changed. "Almost two years has elapsed since I have written a letter or hardly a line to anyone," she reflected in 1825, her past misdeeds weighing heavily. "I feel as though I had done with the trifling vanities of this world—I find there is no enjoyment in them and they have almost been my ruin." She longed for reconciliation. "I want you should forgive me and bury what is past in oblivion," she pleaded. "Perhaps you have long since forgotten you have a daughter Maria—but stop dear Mother, I am still your daughter and Lucretia's only sister."[7]

Her anguish and pleas prefaced a story Maria was eager to tell. She had experienced a dramatic transformation. And she had found a family after all—a family of strangers, a family composed of ever-moving members, connected not by blood or law but by the Spirit, united not by natural birth but by a "new birth."

Imagine Maria walking down Slatersville's main street, her feet and muscles aching from a long day at the mill, the imposing spire of the Congregational church built by John Slater casting a moonlit shadow over the village green. Farther down the road, she hears loud voices emanating from a simple wooden structure, and as she inches closer cries of "Amen!, Amen!, Glory be to God!" ring out. Cautiously approaching, she opens the door and with "a trembling, faltering step," she walks in, joining in those "delightful" and "glad sounds" she would later remember with "emotions indescribable."[8]

In Slatersville, Maria joined a group that espoused a new popular form of evangelical Christianity—the Methodists—the young nation's fastest-growing body of believers. Here was the defining moment in Maria's adult life, and she was excited to tell her mother and sister all about it.

"God in mercy has shown me the depravity of my own wicked heart," Maria informed them, offering a candid review of her past failings. Despite a previous profession of faith, her slide toward "the beggarly elements of the world" had "brought reproach upon the cause of God," even "caused Jesus to open his wounds afresh." She had shamed and denied her Lord. "When I look back upon my past life it looks dreary, and I feel like a mourner alone on the wide world without one friend to cheer me through this gloomy vale," she wrote. With poetic flourish, she stopped her retrospection mid-sentence and soared to the climax of her conversion story—"but when I look forward it bears another aspect. I have been made to rejoice in the hope of the glory of God. I feel that I have an evidence within my own soul that God has forgiven me, and I have an unshaken trust in God that I would not part with for ten thousand worlds." Here was her enormous change of heart; as she described it, "my views and feelings were vastly altered." She later summed up this transformation in her favorite Methodist saying: "I was a great sinner but I found a great Saviour."[9]

Far more than a lone wayward daughter finding a way to redress a few misdeeds, Maria's embrace of Methodism was part of a momentous trans-formation in American culture. Her journey from Congregationalism to Methodism paralleled the declining appeal of Calvinist fatalism, as like-minded Americans fashioned a democratic and individualistic faith that corresponded with their new economic and political behavior. Just as Maria shed her Calvinist upbringing, hundreds of thousands of Americans likewise came to believe that they possessed the capacity to work out their own sal-vation, much as they were convinced they could forge their own economic destiny or create a new popular democracy.[10] A fellow New Englander, Rachel Stearns, who also found her home among the Methodists, recorded beliefs and emotions remarkably akin to Maria's. Rachel's daily journal and Maria's letters together illuminate a dynamic new religious identity bursting onto the scene.[11]

Gone was Maria's fixation on impending death and her hopeless uncer-tainty about where she would spend eternity. Her past religion, attached to Calvinist beliefs, "appeared gloomy," like "something I must have, in order to be prepared to die." Her new faith, by contrast, was something "more lovely to me than all the pleasures of this vain world." As she longed to tell her sister and mother, "the religion of Jesus is a fountain" of forever flowing joys; she announced, "I feel as though I could enjoy myself in this life while blest with the presence of Jesus."[12]

The telling phrase "I feel" exposed the distinctive voice of Maria's new-found faith. A single pronoun made for a theological revolution, as "I" far outpaced her references to God as the lone author of her salvation. "*I* feel that *I* have an evidence within my own soul that God has forgiven me, and *I* have an unshaken trust in God that *I* would not part with for ten thousand worlds." As a young Ralph Waldo Emerson quipped, this was "the age of the first person singular." Ordinary Americans felt empowered to democratize Christianity by these personal affirmations of their own ability to effect their salvation. Methodists joined with many other evangelical groups in assuring common folk that they possessed the will and capacity to give up the world, make themselves anew, and feel the presence of their redeemer.[13]

It was this religion of feeling that Maria found so attractive. As she told her family that her "views and feelings" were "vastly altered," they in turn described Maria's letters from that moment forward as "full of Methodism, and relating mostly to her religious feelings."[14] Along with the first-person *I*, it was *feelings* that made the world anew. "The strongest evidence that I am now a child of God," Rachel Stearns declared, "is the change in my feelings, conduct, everything. I have not a doubt now. I feel it in my heart." Stearns scattered twelve different references to feelings in a single day's journal entry, culminating with the declaration, "Thanks be to God for the love I feel in my soul, but I want more. I want more feeling, more ardor, more engagedness, more religion." This was, as Maria called it, "every day's Religion," a felt religion, a lived religion.[15]

What drew Maria and countless ordinary Americans to this faith was a simple interpretation of the gospel, alongside the piety demanded of its believers. Primarily working people and travelers to new frontiers, Methodists spurned the convoluted theologies and highfalutin rhetoric of university-trained ministers. They wanted to hear "the plain & simple truths of the Gospel" preached in "a fervent and earnest strain."[16] Methodists could never be satisfied with a rote attention to duty or doctrine, and they regarded Calvinism's sedate revivals as nothing more than religious formalism. "I have found that a form of godliness," Maria cautioned her sister, "will never make me happy" and "will never prepare a soul for the enjoyment of heaven." She preferred the Methodists' emphasis on spiritual experience, on emotional encounters with a living and present Jesus. A few years later she still steadfastly asserted that "the present witness of an indwelling God fills my soul."[17]

When Maria became convinced of her desire to join the Methodists, she listened raptly as the preacher in Slatersville spoke these words: "You are now admitted a member on trial for six months, and if your walk is consistent, and your belief in our principles firm, at the end of six months . . . the brethren will agree to welcome you to our church." For most Methodists, the joys of a new faith made the six-month probation fly by. Indeed, one

Sunday, Maria was asked to rise again and declare whether she was determined to live this religion despite any opposition she might face. Maria answered with an emphatic yes, embracing with enthusiasm the Methodists' distinctive practices—class meetings, love feasts, and camp meetings—all of which propelled them from a small sect to the nation's largest Christian denomination.[18]

"Enthusiasm" was a barbed accusation flung by opponents at Methodists and any spirit-filled evangelicals. It implied excessively emotional and disorderly spirituality, a kind of religious fanaticism that bordered on insanity. Nothing sparked these epithets more than the reputedly unrestrained gatherings zealous Methodists held in the woods, known as camp meetings. Maria surely pondered these aspersions when she wrote, "Perhaps my friends may think it strange that I chose a people different in their views and opinions" than any of her family. If she wondered whether she was "looked upon by my relations as insane—crazy," she had the comfort that these all-too-frequent attacks united her with her fellow Methodists.[19]

Methodists knew that the hostility of strangers paled in comparison to the scorn often encountered within their own families. Relatives and neighbors were known to gather around the first Methodist they met, "to see what sort of an animal a Methodist was," leading new converts to wonder how they might "look at me, talk about me." From the first expression of interest to the day of conversion, new Methodists faced suspicions, teasing, bitter invectives, and shunning from their own kin. Maria sensed the displeasure of her own mother, sister, and brother-in-law from their refusal to communicate with her.[20]

Maria embraced the Methodists as her surrogate family, clinging to them with a ferocity that only a neglected daughter could know. "Let me tell you my dear sister," she wrote to Lucretia four years after her Slatersville conversion, "the Methodists are my people—with them by the grace of God I was spiritually born—with them I have tried to live." With bated breath she informed her birth family that she had found a connection that eclipsed the ties of blood and flesh. "Though destitute of any natural friends," Maria told her mother ("friends" meaning family), "God has raised up many christian friends" to take their place. She felt "all united heart and hand" with these new kin, bound for heaven together.[21]

This was how the Methodists saw themselves—as a spiritual family. As in other popular evangelical groups, members called one another "sister" and "brother" to remind themselves of the special love of an alternative family and to emphasize their spiritual equality. African American and white Methodists were all brothers; wealthy and poor Methodists likewise were sisters.

This new family eased the painful memories of a broken home, an absent father, an inattentive mother, a sisters' rivalry, and harsh words of familial disapproval. It was a sweet feeling, said Methodist women frequently, to be "addressed by the title of sister," and for years Maria kept letters from her Methodist girlfriends, who addressed her as a "worthy sister."[22]

It was the Methodists' distinctive practices, what they called the discipline, that confirmed what it meant to call this group of believers an alternative family—to choose "God's people for my people."[23] These loving sisters and brothers also maintained a strict watch over one another's behavior. Maria, like all members, was required to join a weekly class meeting, a gathering of twelve to twenty people, where believers developed a unique blend of intimacy and oversight.

In these intimate settings, Maria and her "sisters" told one another of their spiritual journeys, their personal histories of sin and redemption. The listeners monitored whether sisters properly renounced worldly fashions and pleasures, shunned loose talk, and clothed themselves in plain attire. "I am thankful that I have placed myself under the watch-care and discipline of a church," one Methodist woman declared, so that "when I do wrong they will tell me of it." Wayward believers welcomed this inquisitive surveillance, and Maria, who had fallen into the alluring trap of consumer desire, found great comfort in the Methodist discipline. Within a few years, she would begin to view her shoplifting not as her downfall but rather as a moral lesson, as a plot-twist in a personal tale of redemption. She could admonish her blood sister that consistent Christians need to "bid farewell to the world" and never "follow its customs and fashions."[24]

In the intimacy of class meetings, Maria displayed spiritual gifts fitting for this stage. She once boasted that the Methodists "thought her a bright Christian" and that she could pray and speak "as well as any of them." One preacher confirmed this assessment, recalling Maria as a leading member of the classes at Lowell, with considerable talent for eloquence and piety. She had, he added, a "power of touching the feelings," beyond any other woman he knew.[25]

Camp meetings, the defining trademark of the Methodist experience, also came to matter a great deal to Maria. For two consecutive summers, in August of 1825 and 1826, Slatersville's faithful traveled twenty-five miles west to join three or four thousand others in the woods outside Woodstock, Connecticut, for week-long gatherings of prayer, singing, and preaching.

Methodists had started to change the meaning of a revival to an event planned and reproduced at a particular place or time, such as a campsite in the woods or a multi-day meeting in a city. Eventually, other evangelical churches felt compelled to adopt similar "new measures" to work up a revival by human efforts.

Methodist officials liked to emphasize the "good order" at these meetings, but they also spoke of amazing displays of God's "glory and power" during nights of "pleasure and rejoicing." For decades already, Americans had heard or read stories of what happened at camp meetings: people fainting, shrieking, falling into trances. Maria surely witnessed all of the emotional excesses that camp meetings were famous for and that carried innuendos of illicit sexuality.[26]

Though Maria had found a spiritual home, she could not be sure of the permanence of these familial bonds. She joined a family that proclaimed all members to be spiritual equals possessed of free will, while also demanding strict conformity to its rules and discipline. Rejecting Calvinism carried both liberating potential and restrictive liabilities. The same free will that enabled anyone to seek salvation also made it possible for a Methodist convert to fall from grace, what they called backsliding. After her time in Slatersville, Maria would seesaw between experiencing Methodism's welcoming and exclusionary impulses.

For the rest of her life, Maria remained torn between maintaining a connection with her own birth family and her desire to be "united heart and hand" with spiritual kin who were all "bound to one home." She scattered throughout her letters wishes and promises to visit her mother or sister, yet her life among the Methodists always seemed to interrupt these intentions. After mentioning plans to travel from Slatersville to Connecticut, she quickly backtracked and confessed that she'd already asked for too much time off from the factory to attend Methodist meetings. Usually it was when camp meetings were held in the vicinity of her family that Maria penned heart-felt wishes for a reunion, only to cancel at the last minute. Her mother and sister began to recognize this pattern, especially when Maria expressed a wish to visit them before declaring it impossible, since "I have lately given five dollars for the purpose of erecting a new Methodist meeting house in this town."[27]

Maria frequently chose her birthday, May 3, as the occasion to dip her pen into an inkwell and write to her blood relations. At those moments her heart ached with the sense that she was "destitute of any natural friends," even as she was "surrounded by many dear friends who are near and dear by the ties of friendship and grace." Welcomed by Methodists, she expected, "Lord willing," to "spend my days in Slatersville." Yet she also imagined other fates, musing, "Sometimes when I think of leaving Slatersville, it strikes a dread upon me. Can I ever leave this delightful spot, where I have enjoyed so many delightful seasons and privileges, it seems to be a place highly favoured by God."[28]

7

Moving Planet

FEELING SAFE IN HER NEW Methodist family gave Maria the courage to try to mend the frayed relationship with her own biological family. Her conversion to Methodism and her letters from Slatersville initiated a tenuous reconciliation with her mother and sister. During the summer of 1825, Maria visited the Rawsons and her mother in Connecticut. By then, Lucretia and Grindal had married in a church wedding in Norwich and had their first child. "I was truly pleased with my visit at your house, to see you thus happily situated, with your family around you," Maria wrote to her sister that autumn. "I hope dear sister you will never have cause to grieve again on my account," she continued. "I desire to live so that none may reproach me." Maria even expressed affection for Grindal ("Remember me to Mr. Rawson, I can never be thankful enough to him for all his kindness to me").[1]

Still, Maria's true home lay elsewhere. "I can truly say my dear mother," Maria wrote in earnest, "that the year past has been the happiest of my life." She was "comfortable," healthy, and enjoying "all the necessaries of life" in her new mill-town home in Slatersville. "I don't want great riches nor honours," she wrote, "but a humble, plain, decent, and comfortable living will suit me best." Slatersville's wide lanes and old-fashioned colonial appearance captivated her, even if she was too young to feel nostalgic for that lost era. She had fallen under the town's spell.[2]

Having acquired an occupation, she wrote, "my employment has been weaving on water looms." Though she never described this factory work in great detail, knowing her family was not a receptive audience, Maria traced

out a career as an operator of power looms at a time when cotton textile production took another important leap forward in mechanization.[3]

Ten years earlier, wealthy Boston merchants Francis Lowell and Nathan
Appleton financed the building of the first successful power loom in
America, which promised to "put a new face upon the manufacture" of
cotton cloth. When Maria left Providence in disgrace in 1823, Slatersville
was one of the few locations in the Rhode Island System that had invested in
power-loom weaving. John Slater was bullish on the new technology, while
his older brother Samuel remained content for his mills to spin yarn and
leave the cloth-making to hand-loom weavers.[4]

Weaving gave Maria an identity in the new economy with an occupation in considerable demand. "My wages have not been very great," she
admitted, "yet they have been enough to procure a comfortable living,
with economy and prudence." Operating a power loom promised none of
the independence that a dressmaker might achieve in her own shop, but
it expanded wage-earning opportunities for women willing to master the
machine's monotony. Threads of yarn stretched vertically across the loom
(the warp) while a wooden projectile called a shuttle was hammered back
and forth to weave factory-spun thread (the weft) into cloth. A power-loom
weaver's main task was to maintain her concentration amid fast-moving machinery, keeping shuttles filled with thread while tending two or three adjacent looms. Mimicking the human motion of a centuries-old craft, power
looms were dangerous machines to operate. Young women knew that the
hazards extended beyond their swollen feet, or the dust, lint, and grime
that clung to their faces and clothes. When a fast-moving loom intersected
with a slower-moving limb, a distracted woman could lose a finger or even
a hand.[5]

Maria's remark that her wages were not "very great" was more an observation than a complaint. Once she learned to adapt her own pace of
work to the speed of the machine, she could find ample employment.
The agents who ran cotton factories bemoaned the perpetual shortage of
skilled weavers, while male hand-loom weavers throughout the countryside
complained about "all their work done by Girls." Here were the two faces
of industrialization: some workers experienced abundant opportunities for
lesser skilled work, while skilled craftsmen lamented that labor had become
feminized and wages lowered. Female weavers in Pawtucket went on strike
in the spring of 1824, joined by 500 workers and the widespread support of
working families—the first strike in America's textile industry and the first
to center on protests by women.[6]

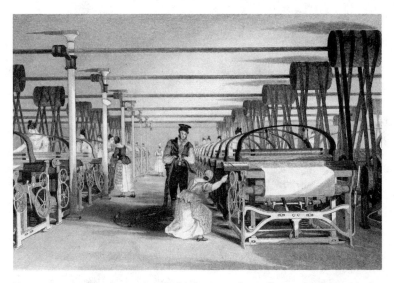

Power loom weaving expanded what textile mills produced—whole cloth rather than merely yarn—and skilled operatives like Maria Cornell could earn top wages for tending up to four looms at a time. From Edward Baines, *History of the Cotton Manufacture in Great Britain* (London, 1835). Courtesy of Bryn Mawr College Library.

Among the "girls" in the weaving room, Maria experienced a new kind of camaraderie. Whether because they shared dangerous work and performed the same repetitive tasks on identical machines or just because they were in high demand, weavers forged a special community in cotton factories. They often found employment in the same room as women they knew well—friends, sisters, or cousins. They conversed with one another, read newspapers, books, and personal correspondence together, watched out for one another's looms, and kept the overseer at bay. When an occasional lull occurred in the pace of work, the women gathered together, "arranged their curls or adjusted their combs, tattled all the gossip, and found out who was who, and what was what," an observer recalled. "Just before the bell rung, I heard . . ."—that's how Maria conveyed the talkative social life generated amid the clatter of flying shuttles. Women weavers would later prove to be the mill town residents who knew most intimately what Maria had said, what she wrote, what she wore, and how she behaved inside and outside the mill.[7]

These women became Maria's confidantes, the "many dear friends" that she drew near to her when the pain of separation from her own family felt most acute. Elizabeth Shumway worked as a weaver beside Maria, and they

Thirty years after Maria Cornell worked in a mill, this photograph (ca. 1860) captures the camaraderie of women weavers with their iconic shuttles in hand. Courtesy of the American Textile History Museum Collection, Kheel Center for Labor-Management Documentation and Archives, Cornell University.

became more devoted friends after Elizabeth joined Slatersville's Methodist church and the two began to call each other "sister."

Maria had stumbled into two communities of sisters—Methodists and "factory girls." Shrouded in stereotypes and myths, both groups were imperfect, flesh-and-blood people. In time, Maria realized that their intimacy was built on fellowship and day-to-day storytelling.

But only six weeks after she had described her contentment in a letter to her mother, in early 1826, Maria and her co-workers awoke before dawn to watch a fire consume the Slatersville mill. It started in the basement furnace; cotton mills, with their wooden floors and beams smeared with machine oil and littered with lint, were highly flammable. The Slaters had no insurance—no firms wanted to insure such structures—and estimates gauged the loss at $50,000. Without a safety net, factory workers listened to John Slater's promises to swiftly rebuild, but in the meantime they were left to their own devices to make a living.[8]

Unwilling to give up her beloved Methodist community, Maria began weaving at the Branch Factory about a mile and a half downriver. She could still attend class meetings in the evenings and church services on Sundays, while keeping an eye on the rebuilding of Slater's mill. Then the vagaries of weather—a summer dry spell lowered the river's water level at the Branch Factory—left Maria searching for work once more. In mid-July, she moved again, this time a couple of miles north, to weave in a woolen factory called Mendon Mills, across the state line in Millville, Massachusetts, where a local paper advertised for "*active industrious* GIRLS," and "those of *fair* character and *only* those," to weave on power looms.[9]

Despite Maria's continued devotion to her Slatersville Methodist community and her determination to stay close, something went awry. Later that fall the Methodists in Slatersville raised accusations against her character. One church member would later remember that Maria had been charged with "lewdness," which could imply a wide range of improprieties. Others recalled that she "kept company" with men, and that she'd been seen "leaving the ground at a Camp Meeting" with a young man who was not a Methodist. Elizabeth Shumway, sister weaver and Methodist, heard the charges read in church one Sunday; she later reported that Maria was dismissed "for bad behaviour, and for having intercourse with men."[10]

Maria's letters shed no light on her sexual desires or the nature of courtship for young women in factory towns. Whatever the truth of the accusations, in the intertwined social circles of mill workers and Methodists people continued to talk about Maria. She stood little chance of staying on at Mendon Mills, given management's insistence on the "fair character" of women employees. Nor had she any incentive to stay. After the fire, her only reason for remaining near Slatersville was her family of Methodist sisters and brothers.[11]

Maria realized that her separation from the Methodists meant that she no longer possessed that all-important piece of paper—a certificate of good standing—that was issued to confirmed church members by either local church leaders or the Methodist minister. Like a letter of recommendation, this certificate could guarantee work in the mills and a place in a respectable boardinghouse. Once she was banned from church meetings, Maria needed to find a new place to earn her living and a new church home.

Just when Maria faced excommunication, a violent crime rattled the peaceful veneer of Slatersville. A local cabinetmaker, in a heated dispute arising from his wife's decision to leave him and take their infant child back to her parents, pulled a knife and fatally stabbed his wife, before also killing a dinner guest who had tried to stop the violence. The murderer then reached for a razor and slit his own throat. The mill community must have felt conflicting emotions when newspapers described the cabinetmaker as a man "of fair character." The murder-suicide would leave a lasting impression on Maria.[12]

Severed from her spiritual family, Maria was on the move yet again. Partly reconciled with her birth family, she stopped first in Providence and Pawtucket to meet her mother, sister, and Grindal and to try to repair the family rift with her Cornell relatives. But Maria had no intention of staying in the shadow of her sister or her Rhode Island relatives. She wanted to strike out on her own and took advantage of news of ample employment near Boston. At Dedham, ten miles south of Boston, she met up with another mill worker from Slatersville (a sister Methodist who apparently left before Maria's expulsion), having heard the promise of the "highest wages" for experienced weavers. "I went to weaving the next day," Maria reported to her mother just after she arrived.[13]

Maria traveled in search of good pay to ensure her independence, but the best wages alone wouldn't satisfy her longings. She was also looking for a fresh start in a new Methodist home. Within four weeks she moved once more, expressing dismay that "there was no meeting at Dedham that I wished to attend." This time she set out for Dorchester, Massachusetts, less than five miles from the vital home of New England Methodism, the Bromfield Chapel in Boston.[14]

Maria gauged a locale's desirability by its access to Methodist preachers, so dear to her since her conversion. Boston was where New England Methodists stationed their most charismatic clergy. Edward Taylor, who became famous as "Father Taylor, the sailor preacher," and John N. Maffitt were both regularly located there. Dynamic, energetic ministers who exhibited that they were filled with God's spirit, these men first attracted Maria to become a Methodist in heart and mind.[15]

In Dorchester she could once again return to the rapturous spell of these men. The first thing she reported to her family was neither her prospects for work nor her wages, but instead her chance to live at the center of the Methodist universe in the big city. "I have spent some time in Boston of late," she reported, attending meetings "there at the Bromfield Lane Chapel," where she took in the preaching of Maffitt, Joseph Merrill, and Timothy Merritt, among others. The preachers made their way to Dorchester as well, and Maria could attend their sermons during week-long camp meetings in the summer months.[16]

In her work, Maria entered the orbit of a new "system" of American textile manufacturing different from what she had left behind in Slatersville. For the first time, she was introduced to the Waltham-Lowell System, established by a group of capitalists (including Francis Lowell and Nathan Appleton) known as the Boston Associates in Waltham, Massachusetts, a few miles up the Charles River from Boston, in 1814. This was the first location in which all of the processes of turning cotton into cloth occurred within the walls of the same building. Gone was the "putting out" work of local farm families, gone was the specialized skill of hand-loom weavers. Instead, bales of cotton arrived at a factory's front gate and exited the mill as bolts of finished cloth.

The corporate factory owners of the Waltham-Lowell mills organized their labor quite differently from the Slaters. Larger factories that included all the operations of cloth-making required far more workers than local farm families could supply. Rather than bargaining with whole families to employ their children, the Boston Associates hired young, unmarried women. Instead of lodging their workers within local households, they built dormitory-like boardinghouses for the influx of young women. Since they were no longer able to ensure the authority of fathers over their daughters' work and wages, the Waltham-Lowell corporations promised parents across the New England countryside that they could trust the company—and the watchful eye of boardinghouse matrons—to take responsibility for the care and moral oversight of farm girls sent to work in the new industrial city.

The factories in Dedham and Dorchester where Maria worked as a weaver were not owned by the Boston Associates, but they were influenced by the Waltham-Lowell model, adopting the same power-loom technology and dormitory-style lodging for their workers. Maria realized the moment she stepped through the door of her Dedham boardinghouse and saw that she had to board with sixty other women—no fathers, mothers, or children—that she'd left behind the family-system of labor she'd known in Rhode Island.[17]

Rather than pursue tailoring work in Boston, Maria chose the better paying work of weaving in Dorchester's cotton factory. In a letter to her mother in early 1828, Maria disclosed some specifics about her work for the first time. "I have been weaving on four looms at the rate of 120 or 30 yds. per day, at 1 half cent per yard," she reported. Experienced weavers like her found that they could earn the most if they learned to operate three or four looms at once—two in front and two behind them. Indeed, mill owners knew they could get maximum production for minimal labor costs if they demanded that weavers tend multiple looms. This was the only occasion when Maria disclosed her earnings. She earned sixty-five cents a day, or about $4 a week before her rent and board were deducted.[18]

The wages in Dorchester were the highest Maria had ever earned—three times what she made at her first factory job in Jewett City six years earlier—and yet they came at a price. "My work has been very hard the winter past," she sighed, "and I have got almost beat out." The factory work was beginning to take a toll on Maria's health. She didn't want to complain or appear ungrateful to God, but she disclosed that "I have never been well enough to work one whole month since I have been here." She worried too about the higher cost of living expenses near Boston, including travel costs to Methodist meetings. Still, as a Methodist she knew better than to dwell too long on worldly matters. She reassured her family that she had "every thing around me to make me contented and happy." "I have no reason to complain," she wrote to her mother. "I have cause to be thankful that it is as well with me as it is."[19]

Meanwhile, Maria continued to discover how fervent a family was Dorchester's Methodist community. These were old-school Methodists—what folks at the time called serious Methodists—close-knit both in physical proximity and in communion of faith. Two deeply devoted converts (Anthony Otheman and Mrs. Elizabeth Simmons) and their families founded the church eleven years before Maria arrived, worshipping in an old carpenter's shop converted into a chapel. Inside a building no larger than twenty by twenty-seven feet, they packed benches onto the ground floor and built a U-shaped gallery along three walls. The space was close enough, old-timers remembered, that people in opposite galleries could nearly reach across and touch hands. By the time Maria came to town, an energetic circuit rider had occasioned a revival, and the congregation had grown to around eighty members, along with dozens of hopeful aspirants.

Like an early generation of Methodists fully dedicated to the stern-
ness of their faith—no drinking, no dancing, no fashions, all spirit, all
the time—Dorchester's faithful had encountered scorn, mocking, and violence from locals who felt threatened by the Methodists' dour rejection
of worldly pleasures coupled with the loud and bodily enthusiasm of their
meetings. Members recalled this time as "the heroic days of persecution,"
when they were "opposed, maligned and assaulted." Young boys and men
apprenticed to a furniture factory across the street frequently threw objects
at churchgoers, broke windows, and burst into meetings, leading the congregation to station two men to guard the door while women led worshippers
in hymns, prayers, and stories of their faith journeys. It must have been a
source of joy for Maria to be addressed as "worthy sister" by this group of
true believers.[20]

Still, from early on, there were signs of trouble beneath the surface
of Maria's attachment to her new spiritual home. The church's founding
matriarch, Mrs. Elizabeth Simmons, was known to be especially rigid in
her expectations of piety and a well-ordered life. In the church's memory,
she criticized "ladies in the matters of dress" and lectured husbands for
not leading family prayers. More particularly, she "objected to the reception into the Church of two women from Dedham on account of
their style." These women must have been Maria and her Methodist
friend who moved together from Slatersville to Dedham and then to
Dorchester. It's unclear what Simmons found objectionable about
Maria's "style." Perhaps Maria adorned herself in the latest fashions or
projected an urban cosmopolitanism characteristic of the new breed of
independent women factory workers. Apparently Mrs. Simmons couldn't
initially sour other Methodists on the "two women from Dedham," because Maria was happy to report that the church folk in Dorchester
"treated me with the greatest respect" and that she retained "a respectable standing" in the church.[21]

Over time Maria would once again find that the watchful gaze of the
Methodist family, deployed to maintain the discipline of the church, could
turn a welcoming space into an arena for gossip, rumors, and mistaken
impressions. To be a serious Methodist, Maria needed to tell the stories of
her past sins, as testimony to God's saving grace in her life. But for the first
time, she became aware that some critical Methodists failed to distinguish
stories of past failings from confessions of present sins. This kind of slippage
would plague Maria throughout her remaining years and linger beyond her
lifetime.

Young Methodist sisters who knew Maria there would later recall that she had confessed to them she'd been guilty of profanity (once calling her fellow Methodists "a pack of damned fools") and pilfering things that were not her own. Her religious sisters assumed these sins had been committed in Dorchester. If they had listened more carefully, these confidants would have known that Maria was reciting former sins, for which she looked to a forgiving God and a forgiving church for redemption. But rumors and misheard confessions turned into present-day accusations when Maria was charged with theft before the Dorchester church, even though no one could produce any evidence that she had stolen anything. Though acquitted of the charges, and despite the certificate of good standing that she retained, Maria no longer felt entirely at home among Dorchester's Methodists.[22]

Within weeks, in the spring of 1828, Maria set off again to find both a new spiritual home and even better wages as a weaver in textile factories. She set her sights on the nation's premier new industrial city—Lowell, Massachusetts.

Contemporary critics of factory work voiced concern about the growing ranks of young people "who leave their friends, and remove from village to village, hiring out themselves, and working as long as it suits their convenience in one place and then at another." Unmoored individuals, "governed by this roving disposition," they feared, were "liable to contract all the worst vices of the whole factory community," and if unchecked, this vice of unrestrained motion could "become a deadly leprosy throughout the land." Defenders of the new factory system, by contrast, saw this mobility as evidence that America, unlike its European rivals, had not succumbed to a "permanent factory population."[23]

Maria was conscious of, even sensitive about, how often she moved from place to place in her young life. In the six years between first entering a cotton factory in Jewett City and her move to Lowell, she lived and worked in at least ten different locations in three states. From Lowell on her twenty-seventh birthday, in May 1829, Maria revealed her family's unease with her constant movement. "I received a letter from mother about four months since in which she mentioned she thought I was a moving planet," she wrote to her sister. Maria's first instinct was to refute the charge, reminding her sister that she had remained in Dorchester for more than a year, and that two weeks hence would mark a full year's residence in Lowell. But her Methodism offered the best retort. "Tell mother she must remember that I am connected with a people that do not believe in tarrying in any one place longer than a year or two years at most at any one time—and I am with them in sentiment believing with the Apostle that we should be as strangers and pilgrims having no continuing city or abiding place, but seek one to come."[24]

Surprisingly, Maria here identified with the expectations of a Methodist itinerant preacher. Certainly the Methodists believed that their true home was an eternal one in heaven, but it was the circuit riders of Methodist lore—not ordinary church members—whom bishops and presiding elders assigned to a different home every year or two, and whose fame was built on their prowess as spiritual men on the move. If Maria was a moving planet, she felt comforted that her experience resonated with her church and the life stories of famed circuit-riding Methodist preachers—men exactly like the Reverend Ephraim Avery.

8

Circuit Rider

WHILE EVERY DAY FOLLOWING MARIA Cornell's death seemed to bring turmoil and clamor for the people of Tiverton, Fall River, and Bristol, it took nearly a week before newspapers began to widely publicize the alleged haystack crime. Word-of-mouth reports moved faster than the newspapers' presses. Still, once rumors spread that a Methodist preacher had been accused of murdering a factory worker, the semi-weekly papers unleashed a flurry of responses. "OUTRAGE AND MURDER" screamed a *Providence Journal* headline. Usually sedate journalists dropped sensational phrases like "extraordinary excitement" and "horrid murder" into their first reports of what Fall River's paper called a "Melancholy Event."[1]

From the start, even the simplest facts of the case were reported inaccurately. Two days after Christmas, the *Providence Journal* reported a minister named Averill as the suspect in the young woman's death and announced that he had been committed to Bristol's jail. The unnamed woman was incorrectly portrayed as a resident and church member in Bristol, with the seducer-minister promising to convey her out of town so that her pregnancy wouldn't tarnish her reputation. Errors and all, the *Journal's* story got reprinted in papers in every New England state plus western New York and New York City. Headlines over the next two weeks referred to the case as the Tiverton Murder, the Rhode Island Murder, the Bristol Murder, and the Fall River Murder.

All the early news stories, in print and by word of mouth, agreed that what made this a sensational and extraordinary case was that a clergyman had been charged with a "most foul and abominable deed." As the reading public became ever more aware of the details of the alleged crime, the frenzy surrounding this "outrage" remained focused on the intersection of religion and wrongdoing.[2]

§

Like Maria Cornell, Ephraim Avery found his home in the spiritual family of Methodists, with their new individualistic faith built on intimacy and intense spirituality. During his childhood in Coventry, Connecticut, Ephraim couldn't help but hear stories about his hometown's other famous son, preacher Lorenzo Dow. Celebrated more for eccentricity than for masculine bravery, Dow became the country's best known and most talked about preacher during those years.

Lorenzo Dow was a sight to behold. With clothes unkempt, long hair draping down his shoulders, a shaggy beard, and a sickly looking physique that belied his boundless intensity, Dow attracted immense crowds of followers and foes alike. "Many were offended at my *plainness* both of *dress*" and manner of talking "about heart religion," he recalled, admitting that most people knew him "by the name of *crazy Dow*."[3]

The "crazy" preacher pioneered two of the most important new forms of communicating with the masses—camp meetings and cheaply published print. Sensing from the start that camp meetings could be revolutionary innovations in a newly democratic age, Dow placed himself at the center of these week-long religious meetings that often attracted crowds into the tens of thousands. And Dow's reach extended well beyond the pulpit. The most prolific self-published writer of his time, he had such a popular following that scores of children were named after him.[4]

Lorenzo Dow tapped into the desire for equality that flourished among ordinary white Americans following the Revolution. Targeting aristocracy and promoting democracy with his voice and pen alike, Dow, like the vast majority of early Methodists, opposed slavery and preached the spiritual equality of Black and white believers. Yet Dow's egalitarian bent showed itself best in his defiant rejection of Calvinist theology. Dissatisfied with the doctrines taught at his childhood church in Coventry, he sought out a people—the Methodists—who preached the free availability of salvation to all. As he was fond of saying: The Bible says Christ died for all, "and A double L does not spell *part*, nor *some*, nor *few*, but it means *all*." When questioned if he really understood Calvinism, Dow offered a ditty that revivalist preachers repeated for decades: *"You can and you can't—You shall and you shan't—You will and you won't—And you'll be damned if you do—And you'll be damned if you don't."*[5]

Despite Dow's renown, the Averys and their North Coventry neighbors appeared to have interacted with Methodists only rarely before Ephraim converted. His family was connected with the Second Congregational Church, the parish's tax-supported church, where ministers had preached Calvinism since the church's beginnings. No one started a Methodist church in his hometown.[6]

Ephraim certainly knew about revivals in Calvinist churches all over Connecticut. In 1814, when he was just fourteen years old, nearly sixty young people from the village, including his older sister, Polly, experienced religious conviction and joined the church. There's no way to know how Ephraim was affected by these stirrings. In both Ephraim's and his father's generation, it was mostly the women of the family who populated the church rolls—seven out of ten members were women. Neither Ephraim nor his father appear in the records of the Second Congregational Church, a result of either their dissatisfaction with Calvinism or their economic straits as tenant farmers and landless men.[7]

By the time he had reached adulthood, Ephraim gave up any hope of a farmer's life. Like many ambitious young men with no prospects of landownership, he set his sights on self-made success in commerce or the professions. So little was known about Ephraim before he became a Methodist preacher that people later tried to remember what occupations he had previously pursued. Some thought he'd worked as a storekeeper, others remembered him as a schoolteacher, and still others thought he'd studied medicine. All these memories point to Ephraim's aspirations to rise above the lowly status of a farmer, to elevate himself in the new marketplaces of business, religion, and the professions. What is certain is that Ephraim left the farm town of North Coventry by the time he was twenty.[8]

While living in nearby Manchester and East Hartford, in 1821, Ephraim fell into the orbit of the Methodists. With various evangelical groups competing for potential converts, and countless people eager to jettison the grim Calvinism they had heard all their lives, Methodists began to reap sizable dividends by preaching a gospel that heralded action and personal autonomy. This gospel of spiritual self-determination attracted Ephraim, as it did so many.

Ephraim heard the message most dramatically from a flamboyant preacher named John N. Maffitt. Five years older than Ephraim, the recent

Irish immigrant became an overnight sensation when he sparked a great revival in Connecticut. With stunning good looks and florid romantic oratory that only an inveterate consumer of novels could produce, Maffitt appeared nothing like the sickly Lorenzo Dow, but the "heart religion" was the same. Maffitt preached all over the region, spurring on other Methodist preachers, including Ebenezer Blake, who kick-started a revival around East Hartford in the spring of 1821. That August "one of the greatest and best" camp meetings in New England convened in the woods outside East Hartford, with nearly 1,000 people camping out during the week, and upward of 8,000 arriving on Sunday. All told, 300 converts joined the Methodists that summer.[9]

Ephraim counted himself among the newly saved. Sophia Hills, a young woman from East Hartford, three years older than Ephraim, also got swept up in the excitement of camp meetings. She, like Ephraim, had been raised under the influence of Calvinists. Ephraim and Sophia fell into a sudden romance that was intertwined with their newfound attraction to Methodism. The next summer they were married by Ebenezer Blake, just a few months after Ephraim was officially admitted to the Methodist conference as a "preacher on trial."

In a whirlwind, Ephraim Avery experienced Maffitt's preaching, camp meetings, romance, marriage, and a new professional status. Ephraim might have shared the sentiments of another young convert who joined the ministry at that time, proclaiming "that camp-ground was nearer to heaven than any other spot on earth." Indeed, it would not be too far-fetched to suspect that Ephraim experienced a wave of human passions and desires—spiritual, sexual, ambitious—that he always coupled with his personal and professional successes. This was all a formative part of his development as a man.[10]

There was a familiar ring to the stories of how men became Methodist preachers, as much alike as the matching clothes they wore on their backs. The tale always began with a young man's conversion and an intensely emotional camp meeting experience, just as it had for Ephraim. Typically, this life-transforming encounter with the divine prompted an insatiable longing to tell others about the experience. Soon the young man was preaching to family, friends, and strangers in his own neighborhood. Then Methodist leaders would ask him to say a few words (called "exhorting") following a preacher's sermon. When other believers began talking about how they too had been awakened to faith by the young man's words, "God and the Church thrust" him "out into the great work of saving souls." It became official when he was appointed a "preacher on trial," a two-year probationary status.[11]

Ephraim Avery joined thirty-six other young men, including John Maffitt, admitted as probationary preachers in 1822, the largest total of new preachers yet added to the New England Methodist Conference. This group of men can best be described as a traveling fraternity—what people then called itinerant preachers, a signature feature of transatlantic revivalism.

Every aspect of the Methodist system depended on men on the move. By the time Ephraim enlisted, circuit riders were one of the most recognizable groups on the American landscape—men who were seen everywhere, on foot or on horseback, traveling down every country lane, fording creeks and rivers, scurrying across farm fields and through wooded forests. In fair weather and foul, rural Americans saw them trudging along from one preaching appointment or house visit to the next. As an old American proverb went, "There's nothing out today but crows and Methodist preachers." Preachers, elders, and even the bishops were all in constant motion. Bishop Francis Asbury traveled more than a quarter million miles during his forty-five-year career, visiting every conference and every state at least once a year.[12]

The itinerant system that defined Ephraim's labors was designed to Christianize a fast-moving populace with a limited number of clergymen. It proved especially effective in frontier areas. Churches that had to rely on one Protestant minister per village, as Congregationalists and Presbyterians usually did, left huge swaths of the country without preachers. Methodists instead assigned one or two men to a circuit, demanding that their preachers travel to dozens of different settlements over several weeks, preaching at two or three different locales a day, before starting the circuit all over again. The farther removed from population centers, the greater distances a circuit rider traversed. A typical itinerant preacher might travel over 500 miles, preaching as many as sixty-three times, in a four-week circuit. Every year or two, the bishop assigned him to another circuit.[13]

It was an ingenious system of religious entrepreneurship, well suited to a new competitive religious marketplace in a nation on the move. Methodist circuit riders blanketed the entire country and established more churches in more settlements than any comparable evangelical group. Starting in the mid-Atlantic states, then spreading rapidly to the South and West, Methodist membership outpaced the growth of the population. With such an efficient system for deploying preachers, Methodists became the nation's fastest growing religious body, expanding from a few thousand followers before the American Revolution to more than half a million in 1830, then

The ever-moving Methodist circuit rider, traveling rain or shine, became a familiar sight to America's growing and mobile populace. A. R. Waud, "The Circuit Preacher," *Harper's Weekly*, October 12, 1867. Courtesy of Swarthmore College Library.

doubling their membership again a decade later. By then, they were easily the country's largest denomination.[14]

By the time they sent preachers to New England, a few years before Ephraim's birth, Methodists found men and women leaving farming villages to try a better life on the northern frontier or in new cotton mill towns. The church sent circuit riders to both, and New England Methodists grew by 400 percent during Maria Cornell's brief lifetime.[15]

Young men learned to be Methodist preachers under the tutelage of slightly older and more experienced preachers, a mode of on-the-job training that combined observation and mentorship with everyday practice. Ephraim began on the Tolland Circuit—the villages north and west of Coventry—under the mentorship of Ebenezer Blake, who was known for stirring the emotions of his listeners when praying or preaching. Their partnership was an immediate success. During Ephraim's first year laboring alongside this circuit's preachers, Methodist membership there grew by nearly 25 percent.[16]

Ephraim impressed his fellow Methodists as a man truly called to preach. The conference sent him ninety miles away in 1822 to Mansfield, Massachusetts, halfway between Boston and Providence. Thus began Ephraim's peripatetic life as a Methodist preacher, moving his family every year or two, unable to call any place home.

In its earliest years, Methodism appealed to people on the economic margins—tradesmen, laborers, and seamen—for whom poverty and a renunciation of riches were badges of honor. Ephraim's role models in the ministry started out as shoemakers, millers, sailors, and farmers. The Methodists' itinerant system opened the door for almost any man, regardless of his limited education, to elevate himself to the professional status of a minister.

Without great resources, this first generation of circuit riders faced severe deprivations in their travels. The physical demands of daily riding and walking, sleeping in barns or flea-infested beds offered by other poor Methodists, while earning the most meager of salaries, instilled a tough-or-die approach to their new profession.

These men prided themselves on their physical stamina and godly strength. The itinerant system required young, physically fit men. One New England preacher referred to himself as "a plain, natural ram's-horn sort of a man." By century's end the circuit rider with his trademark black cloak and saddlebag, with a Bible under his arm, had risen to legendary status. "What a mighty man he was!" recalled a later Methodist, "this man, the Methodist circuit rider, stands the peer of any man, or set of men, who helped to build this republic." Unfortunately, for some young men circuit riding could mean an early grave. It was not unusual for preachers in their mid-20s to succumb to the hardships of this calling.[17]

Among the sacrifices of being a circuit rider was time apart from the companionship of a spouse. Bishop Asbury discouraged the first generation of traveling preachers from marrying (he himself never wed), and George Pickering, long-time leader of New England's Methodists, hardly spent one of every five days at home with his wife during their fifty years of marriage.[18]

Preaching itself became the most important way that circuit riders connected with fellow Methodists. "They came out from the people, and knew how to address the people," one Methodist explained. Like their audiences, preachers had hardly more than a common school education;

they spoke in a plain and informal style that captivated their listeners. Methodists believed that no sermon was truly effective if it didn't touch the feelings (or as their critics said, "excite the passions") in such a way that listeners' bodies reacted. They spoke commonly about melting into tears, even while critics expressed shock at the fainting, shouting, crying, and body-shaking that accompanied this preaching.[19]

It had to have thrilled Ephraim that a landless son of landless farmer could be recognized as the equal of any other clergyman in every town he entered—even if, as the wife of one of Ephraim's peers explained, Methodist preachers "never grew fat in those days." While a typical tradesman might earn $300 in a year, and a Congregational minister $500 to $700, an unmarried Methodist preacher was still paid only a $100 annually when Ephraim first started. But he was fit for the task. By the time Ephraim joined this traveling fraternity, he had grown tall and robust, standing about six feet, with dark wavy hair, a warm complexion, and a high forehead, full lips, and expressive eyes that radiated hardiness and intensity of feeling.[20]

The church's rule book, known as *The Discipline*, had a test for whether probationers were made of the right stuff: Did they possess the gifts for the work? Are any people "truly convinced of sin, and converted to God, by their preaching?" Though almost no listeners' accounts survive of Ephraim's speaking, in his second year as a young preacher a rare record appeared in a description of a camp meeting south of Boston attended by 3,000 people. On the first evening, following a Black preacher's sermon noted for its simplicity, energy, ingenuity, and good sense, Ephraim rose to give an "interesting and powerful exhortation." Those two adjectives don't reveal a great deal, although it was a positive assessment. Ephraim's preaching wasn't described as energetic, spirited, affecting, or persuasive. Nor did it spark signs of God's spirit, like crying and fainting, as other preachers did. Ephraim seemingly had a flair for stormy and hell-raising rhetoric more than deeply personal and heart-tugging eloquence. Even so, church rolls grew on all his circuits, and the Methodists kept promoting him because adding more converts marked a preacher as successful.[21]

Opponents of Methodist circuit riders sometimes focused on the sexual threat posed by these mobile young men who possessed special gifts for touching the feelings and exciting the bodies of female converts. From the start, Methodist preachers were accused of being sexual predators and seducers of women. By arousing spiritual desire with an erotic language of Christ's love, they and their camp meetings whipped up these fears.[22]

Ephraim Avery was aware of the rumors and allegations of sexual improprieties leveled at circuit-riding preachers. As evangelical religion spread across the nation, countless sex scandals involving clergymen threw local churches and towns into turmoil. Two men who joined the traveling fraternity along with Ephraim faced accusations of improper conduct with women, the most famous being the charismatic John N. Maffitt.[23]

One contemporary remembered Maffitt as the "most striking celebrity of my boyhood," eminently handsome "with curling hair and rosy cheeks and brilliant eyes." More than his good looks, what people obsessed about was Maffitt's "exquisitely musical voice" and theatrical preaching style. He could "play on the sympathies of his hearers like an accomplished musician on the strings of his instrument," another preacher observed. Audiences seemed to "yield themselves entirely to his magical power, alternately smiling and weeping." While critics sneered at the "disgusting tenderness of intonation in his speech" or remembered Maffitt's style as "ornate as the tail of a peacock," everyone took note of his appeal to women.[24]

Maffitt became a popular sensation in Providence in 1822, just when Maria Cornell had arrived there, and she had even tried to join a church where Maffitt frequently preached. Crowds lined up hours before he was expected to speak, filling every sitting, standing, and leaning place in the church, while hundreds were turned away. A pamphlet war broke out between his defenders and the numerous critics who mocked his bombastic rhetoric and theatrical affectations.[25]

When a Boston newspaper accused Maffitt of plagiarizing sermons and conniving to get young women alone with him, Maffitt sued the paper's editor for writing a "false, malicious, scandalous and defamatory libel." The case redefined libel law in the United States when, for the first time in an English or American courtroom, the judge allowed the truth of the allegations to be an admissible argument for the defense. As a result, Maffitt lost his lawsuit.[26]

The New England Methodist Conference conducted its own ecclesiastical trial and found Maffitt not guilty of any immorality, even if he exhibited a "want of judgment and prudence," and they maintained him as a favored preacher in good standing. Showing a fierce determination to protect the circuit-riding fraternity when faced with even a whiff of scandal, the conference defended a fellow preacher. Their own report concluded that the preacher might have escaped such criticism "if some females had been a little more reserved in their attentions to Mr. Maffitt." This would not be the last time the conference closed ranks around one of its own—nor the last time it deflected blame onto women.[27]

Ephraim discovered quickly that he too could count on support from the traveling fraternity of Methodist preachers. At various posts over a decade, his combative nature was on display in verbal altercations with other Methodists, several of whom came to understand these incidents as slander. In each case the circuit rider confidently asserted his authority.

After Ephraim completed his first year of circuit riding in Massachusetts, the Averys returned to Connecticut. Located among New England's new factory villages, Ephraim's Pomfret circuit got its name from the mill town that the Slater group established on the Quinebaug River, a few miles south of Thompson. Hardly any time passed in Pomfret before Ephraim provoked a conflict with a local Methodist woman.[28]

Nancy Stanley was staggering from unbearable grief when Ephraim and Sophia Avery made a pastoral visit one autumn day in 1823. Her husband, Sylvester, had fallen from a tree, suffering fatal injuries. Left a pregnant widow with nine children (six of them twelve years old or younger), Nancy recalled the couple's kind words and how brother Avery "gave an affectionate address" at the graveside and offered his family's assistance with whatever she might need. In spite of that, their interactions soured within a matter of days.[29]

Gossip circulated freely in this factory village among workers, families, and Methodist lay persons and preachers. Soon after his arrival, Ephraim surely heard the rumors that Sylvester Stanley had wanted nothing to do with him after he preached his first sermon in town. Nancy recalled that back then Avery started the sermon in a pleasing manner, but ended it "to his shame & to my sorrow." What exactly Avery said, what prompted his fiery sermon, or what caused many in the church to sit in shocked silence remains a mystery. Sylvester was "so disgusted," though, that he told Nancy he would never go hear Avery again and forbade anyone from inviting the preacher into his home.

Not many weeks after Sylvester's accident, Ephraim resorted to his own form of gossip. A neighbor informed Nancy that Ephraim and another preacher on the circuit were "whispering sad stories" about Nancy's eldest daughter. Twenty-year-old Sophronia had married a young man only a week after her father's death, prompting rumors of a hasty marriage to hide a premarital pregnancy. Nancy remained adamant that Sophronia's character was unblemished. Ephraim, on the other hand, "reported her as a bad character" and expelled Sophronia from the Methodist church. In anger and despair

Nancy put her thoughts into verse, declaring that Avery had laid a plan "to slander me, my child also."[30]

Village talk continued through the winter, with locals repeating what Nancy, Sophronia, and the Methodists had to say about one another. By April, Ephraim demanded that Nancy appear before the Methodist church to face charges of speaking falsehoods. "Call a meeting at my house to-night," she answered back, "for I wish the world to know the truth," that my child and I are not bad characters. In fact, Sophronia had not been pregnant at the time of her marriage. "I told him the truth," she recalled, but "Avery was such a stranger to the truth he verily thought it was a lie." Advised by many to take Avery to court for slander, Nancy and her daughter declined, having decided to leave Avery "in the hand of God."[31]

In mere months, Ephraim had found a way to stir up resentments in this mill town. If locals thought his conduct made a case for slander, the Methodist leadership considered it strong-handed discipline and issued no warnings or reprimands to the young preacher. Only a year after the Maffitt scandal, more was at stake than a young woman's sex life: a talkative and defiant widow had challenged the disciplinary authority of Methodist preachers. Ephraim correctly understood where his elders stood regarding his freedom to squelch that challenge.

Once his term at Pomfret ended, twenty-four-year-old Ephraim moved to a factory village near Providence, followed by a year preaching a cir-cuit on Cape Cod. A full member of the conference at twenty-six, Ephraim relocated once again to Scituate and Duxbury, south shore towns along Massachusetts Bay. There he clashed with another older Methodist woman.

When Ephraim arrived in Duxbury in 1826, he found a fledgling Methodist society with a vibrant woman guiding its intimate fellowship: forty-five-year-old Fanny Winsor, the unmarried daughter of a Duxbury sea captain. Fanny, who owned a shop in town, was described by a contemporary as the kind of indispensable woman who holds together a congregation—pious and tireless, whether caring for the sick or offering counsel to the young and old.[32]

It wasn't long before Ephraim's penchant for speaking loosely upset townsfolk. After visiting a man whose wife had recently died, he conveyed the sad news to Fanny Winsor along with an offhand comment that the widower, who had struggled with drinking, "will soon drown his sorrow." Winsor made the mistake of repeating Ephraim's words to family and church friends, stirring up resentments against the preacher for his "un-feeling and ill-timed" remarks. Ephraim resolved then to put Fanny in her place, starting with "sneering remarks" to fellow Methodists, words that struck Fanny like "barbed arrows." Unable to shake the faithful's confidence in her, Ephraim lodged more formal charges, seeking to get Fanny expelled from the Duxbury church.[33]

By Fanny's account, Ephraim accused her of repeating his words indiscriminately and indulging in "unholy and ungodly temper." Although Fanny confessed and apologized for her sin of repeating his remarks to others, telling Avery that "any compensation you requested I was willing to make, even at your feet," he shunned her, speaking behind her back and refusing forgiveness. She denied the other charges, fuming (as had Nancy and Sylvester Stanley): "how can I hear such a man preach that bears such a spirit? No I cannot!"

In Fanny's mind, "character" stood at the center of their dispute. "You seem to lay the axe at the root of my moral and religious character," she wrote. Nothing was more dear, she explained, and defaming one's integrity was a dreadful evil. "Take away our good name from among our brothers and sisters in the Church, and then this world will be a barren wilderness." Fanny's Duxbury neighbors and the town Methodists agreed. They continued to hold her in high esteem and issued certificates of her good standing in the church. Once again, friends of a woman whom Ephraim had slandered encouraged her to file a lawsuit against him. In her last letter to him, Fanny threatened to turn to the law—"putting myself in the way to have justice," as she put it—if he didn't drop his vendetta. At that point Avery let the matter go.

Yet again, Ephraim received neither a tongue lashing nor demotion from his fellow-preachers and Methodist superiors. Both incidents, in fact, seemed to embolden the young preacher's combative style. He moved next to preaching in circuits near Boston. Two years later, in the final weeks of an assignment at Saugus (just south of Salem) in 1830, after hearing that he had landed a plum post at Lowell, Ephraim stepped into the sectarian fray. When the pulpit became vacant at the Congregationalist West Parish across town, Ephraim offered to preach on occasional Sundays. The church politely accepted, though they showed more interest in Universalist and Unitarian ministers. Even worse, in Ephraim's mind, a rival Methodist, Thomas F. Norris, began preaching there, to the parishioners' great delight.[34]

Ephraim's competition in Saugus resulted from an internal dispute among the Methodists about governance. Like the Episcopal Church from which they originated, Methodists entrusted authority in a bishop, who chose presiding elders, who then assigned the traveling preachers to their stations. The bishops and the circuit riders alone made all the decisions and possessed all the power, through their governing conferences. An ordinary churchgoing Methodist had no voice in the church's decisions about doctrine, policy, or finances and had no say over who filled the pulpit at their local meeting.

By the mid-1820s, as Andrew Jackson and his supporters forged a new Democratic Party, some disgruntled Methodists demanded an American-style democracy in their church by drafting petitions, circulating pamphlets, and publishing a journal called *Mutual Rights* demanding democratic representation. When the Methodist leadership expelled these dissidents, they splintered off, so that by 1830 (just as the competition for the pulpit in Saugus was heating up) these democratic-minded Methodists had established a rival body, calling themselves the Reformed Methodists, and numbering as many as 30,000 nationwide. Methodist leaders saw Reformed Methodists as one of several foes, aligning the splinter group with their other competitors like the Baptists and Universalists.[35]

Thomas Norris emerged as one of the Reformed Methodists' leaders. A charismatic speaker, Norris began as a traveling circuit rider at nineteen and gained full standing in the New England Conference before withdrawing to become a local preacher while he raised a family. Similar to Baptist farmer-preachers, Methodist local preachers worked during the week for their own financial support and preached during their off-time. Laboring at a drinking-glass factory, Norris supported his young family, supplementing his wages with occasional fees for performing weddings. Dissidents like Norris provoked both a labor conflict and a political struggle with the powerful Methodist hierarchy.[36]

In Ephraim's last days in Saugus before leaving for Lowell in June 1830, he ascended the West Parish pulpit and accused Thomas Norris of being "a deceiver" and "not a regularly ordained minister." None of the baptisms, communions, or marriages he performed were legal, he declared, and therefore the children of the couples he married were "illegitimate and bastards." None of these claims were true: the Methodists themselves had lawfully ordained Norris decades earlier and he had long been recognized as a Methodist local preacher.

Four months later, Ephraim returned to Saugus with the intent of maligning Norris once again. Three months after that, he traveled again from Lowell to Saugus to impugn Norris. On these latter occasions, Avery accused Norris of criminal behavior. "Thomas F. Norris is a thief and I can prove it," he proclaimed. Norris, Avery alleged, was in the habit of stealing from his employer. Avery spun a tale in which Norris was caught embezzling glassware, called into the manufacturer's counting room where he confessed his guilt, and forced to settle for the stolen goods with money he acquired from other dissident Methodist preachers. Listeners in their pews were as shocked by the charges as they were by Avery's belligerent style: "All this time his face was violent red, and he appeared to be in a great passion."[37]

Unlike Nancy Stanley and Fanny Winsor, Ephraim's rival this time was a man, and Norris did not hesitate to turn to the law. He sued Avery for slander. The civil case was decided by a jury in the state Supreme Judicial Court's fall 1831 session. Norris's attorneys argued that Avery willfully defamed his rival's character with known falsehoods. A jury agreed and swiftly rendered a guilty verdict, ordering Avery to pay damages of $287, a sum that exceeded Ephraim's annual salary. Avery's attorney moved swiftly to try to get the judgment suspended on technicalities, and in the interim, the Methodists settled out of court for $190, plus court costs, before the judgment could become official.[38]

If the Methodist leadership had been dissatisfied with the cost of settling the lawsuit, they were not unhappy with Ephraim Avery's role as a loyal foot soldier. His superiors once again looked away from a court's verdict and supported their fellow minister. They called their own Ecclesiastical Council to investigate Avery's conduct and fully acquitted him of any wrongdoing, even issuing him a certificate of good standing. Ephraim's efforts, in their view, were not self-interested actions motivated by personal competition. Rather, this was the kind of masculine fighting and competitive striving that made him the ideal team player for the Methodists. He was seeking to bring down a rival preacher, but he was also striking a blow at a group of dissident Methodists who threatened the power of the conference. It's easy to understand why Ephraim was assigned to two key locations for Methodists in New England—Lowell and Bristol—where Reformed Methodists had recently established congregations.

Ephraim Avery roamed through New England's industrializing communities in as nomadic a fashion as Maria Cornell, with one important difference: his mobility represented not a desperate search for work but professional success as a preacher. Ephraim Avery's path to masculine success, his move from farm to profession, was accomplished within a religious community that encouraged constant movement and ambitious striving. He observed and learned the lessons of the Methodists' defense of John N. Maffitt: that the traveling fraternity was committed to ensuring that a preacher's indiscretions not be magnified into crimes. While a few people experienced firsthand Ephraim's combative and aggressive style that put competitors—rival preachers and uppity women—in their places, most Methodists and his peers in the ministry knew him as a preacher who successfully promoted revivals of religion. It was that reputation that landed him in the nation's most important industrial city.

9

Moral Police

ALL THE HUBBUB AROUSED BY a murder charge and a Fall River crowd descending on their town on Christmas Day didn't sit well with the residents of Bristol. In a seafaring port town made rich by trading in enslaved persons and Caribbean goods long after northern states had begun abolishing slavery, Bristol folk put a premium on deference and order even as those boom times waned.[1]

On the surface, Ephraim Avery hardly seemed like one of their own, having arrived just six months earlier. Yet two Bristol County justices of the peace—John Howe from Bristol and Levi Haile from nearby Warren—were determined to conduct an examination in Bristol's County Courthouse regarding whether there was cause to try Avery for Cornell's murder. The imposing, three-story stone edifice had loomed over the Bristol commons for a decade, sitting between the Baptist meeting house on one side and a public schoolhouse and Methodist chapel on the other. Providence attorney William Staples stepped in as prosecutor because the attorney general was occupied with the in-session state supreme court. Because neither of the two attorneys retained by Avery had any experience defending clients accused of capital crimes, they enlisted the help of a prominent Newport lawyer.[2]

As crowds gathered the day after Christmas, no one had an inkling of how long the preliminary hearing would last. For a typical felony, it might be an hour or two. Yet after the entire first day was consumed by the testimony of only four witnesses, a Providence paper guessed that the examination might take up the remainder of the week. Four days later the same paper declared that it was "likely to continue, *ad infinitum*." With each new edition, newspaper editors grew impatient for a decision, but none of this stopped the courthouse from being "continually thronged" with spectators every day.[3]

Among the faithful regulars in attendance were members of the Fall River Committee, particularly manufacturer Nathaniel Borden and constable Harvey Harnden, who attended all the days the court was in session. Within weeks the committee had assembled nearly three dozen witnesses across three states to establish a chain of circumstantial evidence that connected Ephraim Avery to Maria Cornell and to the site of her death at the haystack. The Methodists, on the other hand, had just begun to display their commitment to proving Avery's innocence. Initially uncertain, even divided, over how to respond to the terrible accusations against one of their own, the ministers of the New England Methodist Conference wanted both to distance themselves from Avery and to put a swift end to the scandal. By the second week of the examination, it became clear that the Methodist leadership would learn how to marshal resources and manpower to assist Avery's legal team, amassing a mountain of evidence to disparage Cornell's character and cast doubt on the prosecution's narrative.

Tiverton and Fall River spectators were impressed with the public-spirited response of their own citizens. Sure, "the public mind" was "considerably excited," observed the *Fall River Weekly Recorder*, but "it is an honorable trait in the character of our citizens, that their feelings are excited; that they view with abhorrence" a heinous crime.[4]

At the same time, the mill town's citizens couldn't have been pleased with the way the examination played out. By the second day the prosecution's plan to prove that Avery had been in Fall River on the night of Cornell's death backfired when two eyewitnesses incorrectly pointed to a different Methodist clergyman and then to a former judge in the courtroom, rather than to Avery. The justices remained impressed that no eyewitnesses could definitively place Avery near the scene of the crime. It didn't matter to them, as it did to newspaper stories and barroom conversations, that Avery had no convincing explanation for where he had been between two o'clock in the afternoon and nine thirty that evening.[5]

No doubt Fall River residents also felt disappointed that some of the most damning evidence in everyone's minds was inadmissible in court. The justices barred Dr. Wilbur from testifying about Cornell's declarations that Avery had forced her to have sex at an August camp meeting or that he'd advised Cornell to take a deadly drug to induce an abortion. By rule of law no man could be convicted of a crime based on hearsay unless it was a deathbed confession. For the same reason, a letter that Maria Cornell wrote to her sister and brother-in-law in November—widely published in newspapers in the weeks after her death—was never introduced as evidence. There Maria wrote that she had declared her pregnancy to Avery at the four-day meeting in Fall River in late October, and according to Maria, "He owned and denied it two or three times."[6]

In all, sixty-seven witnesses were called to testify as the examination dragged on for twelve days. Together journalists, newspaper readers, mill town residents, and Methodists throughout the region eagerly awaited the decision by the justices of the peace in Bristol. All could see that the central question in the case was to be the respective characters of a "factory girl" and a revivalist preacher.

§

When circumstances worsened for her in Dorchester, Maria became aware of Lowell's ascendancy as America's largest and fastest-growing industrial city. Most important, she had heard that the mills there had an insatiable demand for laborers. "Women with past histories" came to Lowell, mill worker Harriet Hanson Robinson recalled, "to hide their griefs and their identity, and to earn an honest living in the 'sweat of their brow.'" Over the next decade or two, Lowell defined for Americans the cultural meaning of manufacturing, women's work, and the moral reputation of the "factory girl."[7]

Lowell was still a young city when twenty-six-year-old Maria arrived there on a spring day in 1828. Six years earlier, the village of East Chelmsford was no different from any other New England farming community. A few hundred souls, a smattering of farm houses, a tavern, a store, and a couple of gristmills and other local industries completed the town. The Boston Associates were drawn to this site where the Merrimack River made a dramatic thirty-foot descent because they could construct a network of canals to tap this enormous power source.[8]

Those capitalists created the Merrimack Company in 1823 and immediately began erecting the largest textile mills in the country. These brick behemoths were typically 45 feet wide by 150 feet long and five or six stories high, capable of producing, like the Waltham mill before them, fully finished cloth from raw cotton. The pace of growth seemed relentless. By the time Maria arrived, investors had founded the Hamilton, Appleton, and

Lowell, Massachusetts, America's largest and fastest-growing indus-trial city, attracted women workers from all over New England. Its five story brick factories produced an appearance unlike anything young farm women had ever seen. F. H. Lane, *View of Lowell, Mass.* (Lowell: T. Moore, ca. 1835). Library of Congress, Prints and Photographs Division, LC-DIG-pga-07376.

Lowell Corporations and put eleven factories into operation, with two more opening soon. The city's population had soared from 3,500 to 12,000; a decade later Lowell would be home to nearly 30,000 people. By the time of Maria's death, Lowell's factories were taking in about 5 million pounds of cotton each year and producing more than 16 million yards of cloth.[9]

When Maria first stepped off the stagecoach or canal boat that carried her from Boston, she was confronted by novel sights and sounds. Giant red-brick factories loomed over new white clapboard homes with green shutters and a handful of white-steepled churches. Nearly everything was new—newly laid out and newly named streets; young trees planted along the canals; and churches, hotels, and retail shops glistening with fresh paint and new win-dows. The block-long brick rowhouses erected to accommodate the thousands of women workers would have been a strange sight indeed. And the oddest phenomenon of all: at the sound of a bell at sunrise, the streets and lanes filled with the chatter of young people's voices and the sounds of hurried steps, only to be silent for hours when all workers retreated into those brick fortresses. When the clamor ceased, the new city felt almost like a ghost town.

Most of Lowell's female workforce came from rural New England, and they learned about the mills and secured their employment after neighbors, sisters, or cousins hired before them returned home with plenty of cash and new wardrobes. As mill after mill opened over the next two decades, Lowell's corporations began employing men to travel from Vermont to Maine, and everywhere in between, to recruit the daughters of farm families. One woman who worked there in the 1830s recalled that "troops of young girls came by stages and baggage-wagons, men often being employed to go to other States and to Canada, to collect them at so much a head, and deliver them at the factories."[10]

Maria's background and experiences diverged strikingly from those of Lowell's typical mill workers. She was not a farm girl. She had been an independent wage-earning woman for years. She arrived as an experienced weaver, what her contemporaries called an old hand. The work was no less arduous, but Maria's self-confidence was palpable to novice operatives and overseers alike.

75 Young Women

From 15 to 35 Years of Age,

WANTED TO WORK IN THE

COTTON MILLS!

IN LOWELL AND CHICOPEE, MASS.

I am authorized by the Agents of said Mills to make the following proposition to persons suitable for their work, viz:—They will be paid $1.00 per week, and board, for the first month. It is presumed they will then be able to go to work at job prices. They will be considered as engaged for one year, cases of sickness excepted. I will pay the expenses of those who have not the means to pay for themselves, and the girls will pay it to the Company by their first labor. All that remain in the employ of the Company eighteen months will have the amount of their expenses 'to the Mills refunded to them. They will be properly cared for in sickness. It is hoped that none will go except those whose circumstances will admit of their staying at least one year. None but active and healthy girls will be engaged for this work. as it would not be advisable for either the girls or the Company.

I shall be at the Howard Hotel, Burlington, on Monday, July 25th ; at Farnham's, St Albans, Tuesday forenoon, 26th, at Keyse's, Swanton, in the afternoon; at the Massachusetts' House, Rouses Point, on Wednesday, the 27th, to engage girls,---such as would like a place in the Mills would do well to improve the present opportunity, as new hands will not be wanted late in the season. I shall start with my Company, for the Mills, on Friday morning, the 29th inst., from Rouses Point, at 6 o'clock. Such as do not have an opportunity to see me at the above places, can take the cars and go with me the same as though I had engaged them.

I will be responsible for the safety of all baggage that is marked in care of I. M. BOYNTON, and delivered to my charge.

I. M. BOYNTON,

Agent for Procuring Help for the Mills.

Mill owners in Lowell hired men to recruit young women throughout rural New England to work in the mills. As this advertisement (ca. 1859) reveals, their youthfulness was a key to their qualifications. I. M. Boynton, 75 young women from 15 to 35 years of age, wanted to work in the cotton mills! in Lowell and Chicopee, Mass. Courtesy of the Baker Old Class Collection, Baker Library, Harvard Business School.

Despite these differences, Maria forged bonds with her fellow mill workers around missing home and family. One Lowell worker recalled the many young women who left the family farm to "try their fortunes in a great manufacturing town," only to be "homesick even before they landed at the doors of their boardinghouses." Stories written by Lowell workers for the *Lowell Offering* frequently focused on young women's debilitating homesickness. Parents often counted on those feelings to bring back the wanderers, whether at harvest time or after they had tired of mill work.[11]

A typical mill girl was homesick after only a few weeks. By the time Maria moved to Lowell, she hadn't seen her family for nearly two years. It would be another three years before she would again set eyes on them. Her letters home exuded the heartbreaking pain of their neglect. Letter after letter garnered no reply despite Maria's repeated pleas that "I want you should write as soon as you receive this." Maria would have trudged to the Lowell post office week after week, asking a postmaster if any mail had arrived for her. Her humiliation had to have been excruciating.[12]

True, her mother penned an occasional letter, but these hardly proved satisfying. After waiting in vain "for more than eight long months," with neither her mother nor sister responding to her request to visit them in Connecticut, Maria cried out in frustration: "It appears to me if you were in the land of the living and possessed a parent's feelings you would have written before this." Finally, she gave up on visiting, exclaiming, "Enough of this—I will cease to trouble your minds with such painful feelings."[13]

While they traded stories of loneliness, Lowell's mill women liked to talk about family letters, and Maria didn't want to be left out of these intimate conversations. Sarah Worthing, a weaver about Maria's age, recalled that Maria was "frequently in the habit of bringing in letters to the Mill and reading them—from her mother and her brother James." Repeating herself from a handful of rarely received letters, she clearly hoped not to appear "friendless" among her new acquaintances.

In her last surviving letter from Lowell in 1830, Maria admitted the painful truth that Grindal and Lucretia Rawson had never once written to her in the six years since they married. Maria had initiated every attempted reconciliation. She pleaded with her mother to ask them to write and wrote directly to Lucretia requesting a letter, with nary a reply. "I do not know why you or Mr. Rawson have not written me," Maria penned to her sister after arriving in Lowell. She closed her last letter from Lowell promising her mother that she would write to Grindal when she returned from a camp meeting, adding, "I expect my sister's time is pretty much taken up with her children."[14]

Six years seemed far too long for Lucretia and Grindal to still be embarrassed about Maria's shoplifting. Whether ill feelings remained from the sisters' rival courtship or Lucretia felt ashamed of her factory-laboring sister, the consequences for Maria were the same.

Maria's gesture to motherhood to explain her older sister's cruel neglect illustrates how pervasive associations of domesticity were with "true womanhood" in those years. The "factory girl," in songs and stories alike, represented the antithesis of the domestic ideal—the common tale about Lowell's iconic factory girl was that she would one day terminate her venture in the working world when she married and became a mother. The song, "The Factory Girl," included the line "A factory life is a weary life," ending with the pointed verse:

> Now soon you'll see me married
> And settled with a man,
> Then I'll say to all you factory girls
> Come and see me when you can.[15]

Neglected by her own family, Maria the "factory girl" had become part of a cultural phenomenon attracting national and international attention.

For over a decade after Maria joined this first wave of women workers, Lowell's "factory girls" remained the flashpoint for an American cultural conflict over women's economic independence. As one woman wrote back to her family from Lowell in the 1830s, "I am 21 years old today and feel as independent as" any young man. For Maria, of course, economic independence was not new. She had earned roughly as much during her time in Dorchester, but the work in Lowell was steady and reliable—Lowell had more power looms than any other mill town, allowing experienced weavers to earn high wages. A chorus of voices rang out in support of this independence, from the defenders of the factory system to women writers to Lowell's first striking protestors.[16]

Acclaim for white women's independence emerged, from the defenders of the factory system to women writers, just as New Englanders were embracing "free labor" and antislavery principles and also trying to erase memories of the region's own history of slavery. To Lowell's women, their unparalleled wages ensured that factory work was nothing like human bondage. On two occasions after Maria left town, Lowell workers went on strike to protest wage cuts and increased boarding charges. When 1,500 women walked out of the factory, they sang, "Oh! I cannot be a slave,/I will not be a slave,/For I'm so fond of liberty/That I cannot be a slave."[17]

Female independence revealed itself most dramatically in the ability of these women to purchase consumer goods. With each passing season, Maria surely witnessed the steady increase in brightly lit and well-furnished shops that remained open until nine o'clock, attracting women workers with surplus cash. One young woman praised Lowell as "a very busy place and the girls earn a great deal of money and spend more than they earn." Critics were equally quick to censure the extravagant habits and accumulating debts of these newly independent wage earners. For Maria, battling these temptations remained a defining feature of her commitment to her Methodist faith.[18]

Yet for all the anxieties New Englanders expressed about shopping, debts, and labor protests, it was the morals of "factory girls" that primarily obsessed them. And questions of morality never centered on women's consumerism, or even on temptations to drink, swear, gossip, or join unions. The real worries were always and almost entirely about the sexual activity of unmarried women. This was the female independence that parents, mill owners, and moralists feared most. If mill employment gave these women the autonomy of working for their own income, that independence stood precariously against cultural assumptions that imagined a working woman as a public woman—the equivalent of a prostitute.

The architects and defenders of the Lowell system touted their guarantees of moral guardianship for the thousands of young women who sought employment in their mills. Parents of farm families, they well knew, wanted to believe that just because their daughter had become a "factory girl" she had not compromised her morals, jeopardized her chances at marriage, or permanently ruined her reputation. Elisha Bartlett, a Lowell physician, defended the moral guardianship of the Lowell system. Bartlett emphasized the "watchful care and oversight" of the mill superintendents, overseers, and boardinghouse matrons. "The moral police of all the establishments is vigilant, active and rigid," he proclaimed, and "no violations of the excellent and judicious rules of the corporations, and no improper or suspicious conduct" was tolerated.[19]

Moral police? This was a new phrase, invented in Maria's lifetime, and she would soon feel the full brunt of its power. Behind it stood the weight of American gender conventions and evangelical righteousness. Two buzzwords—character and respectability—captured the expectations of moral policing. "It is only by maintaining an unsullied and unimpeachable character that a girl can retain her situation in the mill," Bartlett concluded, "and when dismissed for any impropriety from one establishment, there is no possibility of her getting a place in any of the others."[20]

Lowell was a company town—or more accurately, a town of companies— and the mill corporations worked together to construct and encourage the moral police that disciplined their workforce. To begin with, there were rules. Each of Lowell's corporations published "Rules and Regulations," all essentially the same, that defined the conditions of employment for all mill workers. Without spelling out all possible improper conduct, they insisted that each employee observe the regulations of the overseer in the room where she was employed, board at and follow the rules and curfews of a company boardinghouse, get permission for any leaves of absence, and attend church every Sunday.

The Lowell mills colluded from the start to blacklist undesirable employees. If a laborer abided by the mill's regulations and remained "of good character" for twelve months of employment, she could receive an "honorable discharge," allowing her to be hired again at any of the other mills. But those "dismissed for bad conduct, or who leave the mill irregularly," town historian Henry Miles explained in the 1840s, had their names "sent to all the counting-rooms of the city," and there "entered on *their* books. *Such persons obtain no more employment throughout the city.*"[21]

Lowell's boosters promoted a myth that Lowell women possessed a "very superior" moral character, reflecting the innate virtue of New England women. Certainly there were bad eggs, but they were few and far between. Only in the rarest instances did a young woman get dismissed from a factory because of her "immodest or improper conduct." Nearly everyone had a stake in maintaining this myth. The women who wrote for the *Lowell Offering* saw no reason to question it. And when boardinghouse keepers and mill overseers, some of whom had worked for Lowell corporations for as long as twenty years, were surveyed by Miles, nearly all underestimated the number of workers dismissed for so-called "licentious conduct." One boardinghouse matron claimed that only one of the nearly 500 women who resided with her over the past nineteen years was ever discharged for "bad conduct." Overseers at the Appleton and Hamilton mills with decades of experience likewise asserted they had known either one or two cases of dismissals or none at all.[22]

The truth, Maria and her fellow workers knew, told quite a different story, confirmed by the records of the Lowell corporations. Employee registers for the Hamilton company during Maria's time in Lowell reveal significantly more frequent dishonorable discharges for transgressive behavior. Women were most often dismissed for not abiding by the regulations: for failing to give sufficient notice before taking a leave of absence (usually marked as "short" or "short notice" in the register) and for leaving a company boardinghouse while still employed. Remarkable too is how company records illuminate workers' resistance and overseers' petulance. Overseers described workplace failings like "carelessness," "incompetent for the work," "comes in late," "could not learn," or "neglecting to oil her loom," but when an overseer simply wrote "not good" in the register it's difficult to know whether those women were fired on account of their skills or their conduct.

Criticisms of character, attitude, or personal behavior were commonplace too. The mere suspicion of behavior considered to be immoral was enough to get a factory worker fired. Overseers dishonorably discharged women for "impudence," "on account of her language," for being "contrary," or for "conduct irregular." Weltha Burry was labeled a "notorious thief," and Rebecca Fletcher "stole abominably," while others were marked simply as a liar or thief. Religious passion also sometimes interfered with work: Louisa Eames was dismissed for "Religious frenzy," while a co-worker was fired after having "gone to 4 days meeting."

Equally astonishing is how often overseers cited a woman's sanity as a reason for dishonorable discharge. Augusta Hoyt was dismissed for being "Short & Mad!" Elizabeth Hubbard was labeled "non compos mentis." Another was fired because "spinning and tobacco makes her hysterical," while a co-worker's record stated only, "Gone—crazy." Some factory workers were homesick or had to tend to ill family members, but others were described as "sick of the work." Elizabeth Wilson was discharged after arguing about whether her overseer had given her consent to board with her sister instead of at a company boardinghouse. The mill justified Wilson's dismissal because she gave short notice and was "a devil in petticoats."[23]

Mill agents and overseers were not the only figures involved in Lowell's moral policing. Lowell's boosters liked to trumpet the role that women workers played in disciplining other women; a transgressive woman risked discovery and exposure by her fellow workers. Dr. Elisha Bartlett described mill women's vigilance as a "power vastly more active, all pervading and efficient" than their mill supervisors, manifest in their "jealous and sleepless watchfulness, over each other." The close quarters of weaving rooms and boardinghouses fostered an intimacy that worked against women keeping secrets. One overseer admitted that the facts of sexual misconduct were "usually discovered and made known by the other girls working in the same room, or boarding in the same house." Indeed, more often than not, it was the gossip of fellow workers that brought dismissible offenses to the attention of authorities. Bartlett insisted that "their censorship is despotic," for they might shun a co-worker and refuse to board or work with a woman of unrespectable character.[24]

Maria, of course, was familiar with being watched closely by her sisters in the Methodist church. But she needed their spiritual kinship more than she feared their watchful eyes. Whenever Maria wrote to her family, it was always on a Sunday. That was a mill worker's only day off, but it was also the day when the pull of the Methodists most occupied Maria's mind. She would end a letter quite often with a phrase like, "The bell rings for meeting and I must draw my letter to a close." Maria came to Lowell for the steady and high wages, but what she treasured most was the continuation of her familial bonds with Methodists.[25]

If women workers typically relied on extensive kin networks—sisters, cousins, or neighbors—to facilitate their move to Lowell, Maria turned to her spiritual family. Immediately upon arrival, instead of boarding in Merrimack company housing, she asked the city's Methodist preacher, Abraham Merrill, if she could live with his family. With four children and a paltry salary, Merrill had an incentive to take in boarders. Maria's certificate of good standing from the Dorchester church gained her immediate admittance to the new church on Chapel Hill. But a few months later, when Merrill was assigned to a different preaching circuit, Maria had to move into a company boardinghouse.

Maria's reputation as a devout Methodist sister soared as she settled into the routines of work and worship in Lowell. Methodists who remembered her from this time remarked that she was "always regular in her attendance" at church services and class meetings. The Rev. Abraham Merrill recalled that she possessed spiritual gifts that Methodists highly valued, including "a talent at exhorting and praying." Indeed, Maria heard this praise often from her fellow Methodists. Brother Merrill even remarked that Maria "had the power of touching the feelings, beyond almost any female I was ever acquainted with." While only men could officially become preachers, Methodist women regularly spoke of faith experiences in their testimonies and prayers at meetings. This new popular evangelical faith was a religion of feelings, and Maria proved adept at it.[26]

As Methodism grew more central to Maria's life, she found a renewed infatuation with camp meetings. She returned from a gathering on Cape Cod with over a thousand others, she told her family, "in better health and better spirits than when I left." Knowing that stories about camp meetings might not sit well with her family, she interjected that she'd imagined Grindal Rawson saying, "'Well Maria this is one of your Camp Meeting scrapes.'" "Let me tell you," she informed them, "I love them now as well as I did five years ago. Yea far better—for I have known real good produced by them."[27]

Maria wanted the Methodist church in Lowell to be the intimate, loving family that she had always longed for. For more than two years she immersed herself in the spiritual life of that fast-growing community. Maria filled her letters from Lowell with heart-felt expressions of her beloved Methodist faith, boldly defending her choices even as she suspected her family thought it "strange that I chose a people different in their views and opinions." This was her spiritual home, and "the Methodists are my people," she told her sister. In the summer of 1830, she told her mother that "I have been in Lowell so long that I should feel lonesome anywhere else."[28]

IO

Fornication and Lying

MARIA WITNESSED LOWELL'S METHODIST CHURCH grow considerably during her residence there. A few years earlier, New England's Methodists had hardly given the town—a tiny village of farmers and craftsmen—a second thought. As late as 1827, the year before Maria's arrival, the Methodists assigned Hiram Waldron to the town. Waldron was a junior preacher from an insignificant circuit with a bachelor's salary so meager that he had to supplement it by teaching school. But as Maria and thousands of other women began arriving in droves to labor in the newly opened factories, Lowell quickly became a preaching station for men of ambition and recognized talent. As the city's population soared, one preacher recalled, "Methodism found among them a vast, inexhaustible field for its labors." Starting with Abraham Merrill, and every year after, the conference appointed to Lowell men they hoped would be rising stars in the denomination.[1]

Ephraim and Sophia Avery had to be thrilled with an assignment to the booming young city, a plum post compared to the hardship of a country circuit with hundreds of miles of weekly travel. Instead of the circuit rider chasing migrants on the frontier, an ever-moving population headed toward the Methodist preacher.

Arriving in June 1830, Ephraim set to work with his usual vigilance. As if the eyes of the Methodists were upon him, he penned two updates about his Lowell ministry for the *New England Christian Herald,* the first after six months and the second around the one-year anniversary of his arrival. Writing about himself in the first person plural, he noted that "the prospect at the commencement of our labors was not so flattering as could have been desired." Though he alluded to "some trials" and "embarrassments" facing the church, Ephraim offered his readers no details, except that a firm hand was needed from a preacher known for facing down disturbances. "The principal difficulty we had to encounter," he wrote, "was the long neglect of discipline." Though Methodist "discipline" covered nearly every aspect of believers' spiritual lives, Ephraim could have been alluding here to the expulsion of one or more church members for improper or scandalous conduct. Ephraim had willingly joined Lowell's "moral police."[2]

Ephraim had scarcely settled into his new home near the Methodist church on Chapel Hill when Brooks Shattuck, an overseer from the Appleton mills, approached him. Shattuck informed Ephraim that he had heard credible stories that a Methodist in his employ, Maria Cornell, had engaged in illicit sexual intercourse with one or two men from Lowell. When Shattuck threatened to fire her for immoral conduct, Maria admitted it was true. "She promised if I would let her stay a day or two," Shattuck later recalled, "she would make acknowledgments to Mr. Avery. Being satisfied that she did not do it, I informed him myself."[3]

Ephraim wrote out the complaint—fornication and lying—brought against Maria before the whole church, but he assigned the task of bringing those charges to one of the church's class leaders, Nathan Howard. Warning Maria that the details of a church trial could be embarrassing, Ephraim advised her to return home rather than face the awkwardness of being publicly read out of the church. Maria was devastated. With no intention of returning to her mother and sister as a disgraced woman, she instead ventured that September to her favorite camp meeting on Cape Cod—luckily, she had obtained a certificate from Avery as a member in good standing earlier that summer. It was during her absence that she heard news of her expulsion from Lowell's Methodist church.

From that time forward, the reputations of Maria Cornell and Ephraim Avery veered in opposite directions. Reeling and stunned by her loss of employment, severed from the spiritual family she loved most, Maria left Lowell in search of some way to salvage her life. Lowell's fame as a boom town meant nothing to a factory worker once she had been fired, blacklisted, and excommunicated.

The preacher, on the other hand, proceeded with confidence that his stature was on the rise. Ephraim was soon reporting to the *New England Christian Herald* that despite those initial "embarrassments," the Methodist church was experiencing a considerable revival that autumn.[4] His presiding elder, Joseph A. Merrill, could hardly contain his excitement over the "very encouraging" news from Lowell, where "there is a large congregation and all the seats in the house are taken up." Come summer 1831, Merrill assigned Ephraim to a second year. In just two years, Ephraim Avery doubled the size of Lowell's Methodist church, from 225 to 451 members. As he put it, "On the whole, we think we have much to be thankful for, and much to encourage us in the gracious work of religion." Ephraim had even grander visions: "O that hundreds and thousands may yet be brought to the Redeemer's Kingdom."[5]

Meanwhile, in the midst of her woes, Maria made the most rational of decisions. She moved to the next most prosperous cotton manufacturing site in the Lowell system: Dover, New Hampshire. Investors had been operating cotton mills alongside the Cocheco River at Dover for decades, and during the 1820s, capitalists built brick mills there just as big as the ones at Lowell. Once the Dover company became a leader in manufacturing cloth with calico prints, the construction of cotton factories increased once more, as did the demand for weavers. Maria knew she possessed the necessary skills and spiritual gifts. Yet again she hoped to start anew.[6]

Maria was certainly aware that the Dover company required "strictly moral conduct" from all employees and that gambling, drinking, "or any other debaucheries" would result in a worker's "immediate and disgraceful dismissal." The mill owners also expected their employees to attend "divine worship" on Sundays, and indeed she had her own plans to rejoin the Methodists. Arriving in the autumn of 1830, she approached the Rev. John Dow, presenting him with the certificate of membership she'd received from Avery earlier that year. Even though Dow considered the certificate too old and admitted her only as a probationary member, Maria attended every meeting and every Sunday's worship, her hopes apparent even to those who barely knew her.[7]

Soon, however, Dow received a letter from Avery, informing him that Maria possessed a certificate "which she ought not to have, and that she had been expelled for fornication and lying." Although the Dover preacher seemed willing to listen to Maria with some sympathy, he was ultimately persuaded to deny her membership when Avery sent a second letter explaining the course of actions leading to Maria's expulsion, complete with details about her rumored character. Dow later testified that Avery told him Maria was "a liar and common strumpet," guilty of other immoralities. "Now if you want her in your church, you may have her," Avery concluded.[8]

In Ephraim's mind, Maria was a troublemaker, and he was determined to purge her from the Methodist flock. All evidence indicates that Ephraim initiated this correspondence with Dow after he heard that Maria was in Dover using a certificate signed by him. He even discovered Maria's address in Dover and sent her a letter demanding that she return the certificate, threatening to publish her name and story in the newspapers if she refused. Fearful for her already fragile reputation, Maria immediately returned the certificate.

In Maria's mind, Avery was hounding her in every corner of industrial New England, keeping her out of church and factory alike. When Dow informed her that she had forfeited any chance of being admitted in the Dover church, Maria packed her trunk once more, leaving a well-paying weaving job in Dover-Cocheco's Mill No. 3, to head five miles north to another booming cotton factory town, Somersworth, New Hampshire, where there was another Methodist church to try.[9]

In Somersworth Maria held even greater hopes that she might regain her standing with the Methodists while remaining employed at Great Falls Manufacturing Company. Arriving around New Year's Day in 1831, she found lodgings at the boardinghouse of Mr. and Mrs. Timothy Paul and began attending every church meeting that welcomed non-members. It was at this moment that a fateful truth became apparent to Maria: without a certificate of membership she had no proof of her respectable character, and that meant she was caught in a tragic web of mill town gossip, confessions, and pleas for forgiveness, followed by more gossip, more confessions, and, above all, the Methodists' zeal to protect their church's reputation from wayward members.

Desperate to find a way to enjoy the full "religious privileges" that she so desired, Maria wrote a letter to Avery confessing her sins and pleading with him to forgive her. She wrote twice more, each time unburdening herself until she had made a complete confession of all her sexual sins. Each time, she waited in vain for the Lowell preacher to reply. Meanwhile, Maria's confession to her co-workers prompted them to spread gossip and stories that only further tarnished her reputation. Within two months Mrs. Paul claimed to be dissatisfied with rumors about Maria's character and forced her to leave the boardinghouse.[10]

With some urging from Great Falls' Methodist preacher George Storrs, Maria made a return visit to Lowell in early June. If she could get her Methodist sisters and brothers there to sign a letter stating that they had forgiven her, then Rev. Storrs might offer her a probationary membership.

She took a stagecoach to Lowell at her own expense, making the rounds to friends and former "sisters" seeking their forgiveness. On that same visit, Maria also confronted Avery in person with one more appeal. She would later tell housemates that Avery "did not treat her with common politeness when she went to his house," describing him as "hard hearted and unfeeling." When she asked if he still had the letters of intimate confession that she had written to him, he replied that he did and refused to promise any absolution, admonishing her that "forgiveness from me was nothing" and that she "must seek it of the Lord." Maria insisted on some written statement of forgiveness until Avery finally assented to sign a tepid letter stating that he would not object if Storrs received her on probation.[11]

A few days later, Avery wrote a letter to the preacher at Great Falls, retracting the document he had signed for Maria.

> Rev. George Storrs   Lowell 6th June 1831.
> Dear Brother, It may appear strange to you that I should address a line to you at this time but it is from a sens of duty that I do it— Maria S. Connell called on me Saturday last saying she had come to Lowell on purpose to make an acknowledgement of her fault &c. &c. &c. and after some time I gave her a writing saying that if *you* saw *fitt* to receive her on trial I should not object &c. . . . we were in hopes of haveing evidence of her penitence but alas! alas!! alas!!! this morning derect information was brought to me that she had told a *known willful falsehood*—her standing being as it is I have not taken any paines to inquire into the case, but thought prudent to direct this to you as your name is on the slip of paper she has—we should all of us here be opposed to her joining any where—with this you act *your judgment.*
>   Yours in the bonds of a peaceful Gospel,
>   (signed) E. K. Avery.[12]

The news devastated Maria. Denied membership in a class meeting at Somersworth and refused admittance to the quarterly love feast, she cried out in frustration to her roommates and co-workers, to no avail. By August she had left Somersworth.[13]

So Maria tried her luck in the last remaining location in the Lowell system where she had not yet worked. She moved to Waltham, Massachusetts, the site of the Boston Associates' original mill.[14] Although she took to the work like "an old weaver," Maria stayed only a month, boarding "at three or four different places," because as she told a housemate, her reputation had become so bad that "she was obliged to keep moving about, and that it followed her wherever she went."[15]

Ever the "moving planet," Maria next landed in Taunton, Massachusetts, forty miles to the south. This time she seemed to escape the watchful eyes of co-workers and Methodists who knew of her misdeeds. "I pitched my tent in Taunton last fall," she wrote to her mother in the spring of 1832. "I am now in very good business, and I do not want to lose my place" by going home for a visit. "I am hooking up, and folding cloth, and keeping the weaving room books," she wrote, "and my employer is unwilling I should be absent even for one day."[16]

Then all of it came to a crashing halt once again. For an unexplained reason, Maria remained at Taunton only until June 1832. Free now to see her mother and her sister's family in Woodstock, in northeastern Connecticut, she told them she had arrived merely for a visit. Within a couple of weeks, when it became clear that Maria had no job to return to, she asked for employment as a tailoress in Grindal Rawson's workshop.

She also heard news that a Methodist camp meeting would soon take place just six miles down the road in Thompson. Her fateful encounter with Ephraim Avery there would radically change her feelings about camp meetings. Soon after that camp meeting in late August, where she claimed that Avery had coerced her into having sex, Maria missed her period and began to worry. She confided in her sister, and the next morning Lucretia told Grindal, "Maria is in trouble." With advice from a local lawyer and minister, they decided Maria should move to Rhode Island, ascertain whether she was pregnant and, if so, communicate with Avery. Maria arrived in Fall River in early October and secured employment as a weaver, in search of support for herself and the child she was expecting.[17]

II
<hr>

"If I Am Missing"

IT WAS A THURSDAY, THE last day of autumn, and both Maria Cornell and Ephraim Avery began their daily routines in ways that people expected from a factory worker and a Methodist preacher. Few people around them could perceive the foreboding with which each had doubtless awakened. Both Maria and Ephraim knew that December 20 was going to be a momentous day.

Just as she did every other workday, that morning Maria followed a regimen she did not control. Before sunrise the Fall River Manufactory Company's factory rang its bells, summoning workers like Maria to their machines before the seven o'clock bell signaled the commencement of the mill's operations.

No one directed Ephraim where to go on a Thursday morning. He was a professional man, and on most days his time and movements were his own private business. Whether his two-year-old daughter, sick with a fever, awakened first, or his wife, Sophia, seven months pregnant, rose before the others to stoke the fire, sometime that morning Ephraim said a little about his anticipated excursion that day—but he offered few details.

Fall River and Tiverton residents—farmers and housewives, shopkeepers and stagecoach drivers, tavern-keepers and bar maids, bankers and clerks, laborers and factory workers—awoke to face their daily tasks, all with varying degrees of control over their time and the work they needed to complete. Many observed the comings and goings of people around them as they'd done on most days. No one suspected that this December day would be different from any other day.

By that December Thursday, Maria had resided for nearly three weeks at the home of Mrs. Harriet Hathaway, a forty-seven-year-old widow who lived with her daughter, Lucy. For her first two months in Fall River, she had boarded at the home of Elijah Cole, a shoemaker, who housed many other factory workers. As she became more certain of her pregnancy, Maria wished to escape a house crowded with nosy young women. They would surely notice that she had stopped menstruating, and they were certain to observe her body's physical transformations.

Back on the last day of November, Maria had made an overture to fellow weaver Lucy Hathaway. They had known each other for only a week when, chatting as weavers typically did during slow times in the factory's schedule, she heard Lucy say that she lived at home alone with her mother. During their breakfast break, Maria told Lucy that she wanted to live with a smaller family where she could be "more retired."

"Can I get boarded at your house?" Maria asked.

"I don't know," Lucy replied. "I'll have to ask mama when I go out at noon."

"I will go right up," Maria blurted out, and she hurried over to Harriet Hathaway's to make the inquiry herself. When she returned, she told Lucy, "Your mama says she will leave it to you."[1]

Lucy consented, and Maria moved into the Hathaway home the next day, December 1.

On December 20, Maria marched off to the cotton factory just as she had done every day but Sunday for the previous few weeks. She passed Methodists she knew, and they greeted her fondly with a "good morning, Sister." Her cloak whipped in the stiff breeze, but she didn't mind. The wind helped clear the factory lint from her clothes, and blue skies meant her appointment for that day would not be canceled. She told Lucy the week before that she was nervous about asking the overseer, Mr. Smith, if she could leave work early that Thursday and that she hoped the weather would be fair. Maria was afraid, Lucy remembered, that Smith "would not let her go out on the 20th, and was fearful of losing her place," because she was determined to go "whether he would let her or not."[2]

At her lunch break Maria returned to her boarding house and asked Mrs. Hathaway if she could have her evening supper "ready by or before dark." The landlady agreed, and Maria returned to the factory's weaving room. Having received Mr. Smith's permission, she was in especially good spirits, both Lucy and Harriet recalled. "The afternoon of her departure," Lucy remembered, she was "more lively than usual"—though usually "silent and depressed," on that day "she appeared very pleasant, kind and affectionate." Lucy's mother recalled that on that Thursday Maria "had a pleasant appearance," "did not appear agitated," and seemed "more cheerful than usual."[3]

An hour or so later, on the other side of Mount Hope Bay, Ephraim Avery left his home near the Bristol town common, strode past seamen and dockworkers on their lunch break, and walked briskly toward the ferry wharf at the town's southern tip. At two o'clock he boarded the ferryboat for the half-mile crossing to Portsmouth on the northern end of Aquidneck (or Rhode) Island—what locals just called "the Island."

As William Pearce Jr., the ferryman, recalled, it was a "cold and blustering" morning, but the afternoon became milder. Pearce noticed that Avery wore a brown surtout, a common style of man's overcoat, even though on previous occasions he had seen the preacher wear his cloak. No other passengers crossed with Avery, so the preacher paid a double fare.

"Do you know where the coal mine is on the Island?" Avery asked Pearce.

The ferryman pointed off to his right but offered no directions for how to get there. Pearce stated that a Portsmouth man recently told him that he'd be carrying coal to Bristol by boat if the preacher needed some. They engaged in no other conversation, and Pearce didn't see which direction Avery headed as he left the wharf.

Jeremiah Gifford, the ferryman on the opposite side, also saw Avery arrive and likewise paid no attention to where the preacher walked after disembarking. Within a quarter mile, Ephraim would reach a fork in the road. He could continue south on the Island toward Portsmouth and its coal mines, or he could turn left and head east toward the Stone Bridge that crossed the channel and led northward toward Tiverton and Fall River.[4]

Back in Fall River, Maria engaged in the everyday camaraderie of women in a cotton factory, as she tried to complete her day's weaving. With no clock inside the weavers' room, she listened intently for the bells to toll the hours. Sometime that afternoon, Lucy Hathaway walked over to Maria to borrow eight cents so another "girl" in the room could buy cloth to make an apron. Maria said she wanted an apron too and asked Lucy to buy the same. When Lucy replied that she didn't have any money, Maria gave her enough for all three of them, saying, "We then will wear them all alike next week."

As her workday neared its end, Maria asked Amy Durfee, who worked beside her, to remove her piece of woven cloth before the closing bell—she wanted her loom to be repaired the next day. Maria then asked the overseer if she could sew the aprons on Friday while her loom was being mended.[5]

Maria's interactions with her Fall River co-workers seemed to follow a calculated strategy. Since arriving in town with a suspicion that she might be pregnant, Maria deliberately made others aware that she had recently received three letters and that she'd delivered her own written replies to the post office. Two of the letters—a straw-colored or yellow letter (dated November 13) and a pink letter (delivered by the steamboat engineer on November 29)—arrived while Maria boarded at Mr. and Mrs. Cole's. A third letter, written on white paper (dated December 8, and postmarked Fall River), arrived a week after she had moved into the Hathaways' home. Boardinghouse owners and residents certainly observed when a letter arrived, but there was something more to Maria's actions.

Although the missives entreated Maria to maintain secrecy, to "keep the letters in your bosom or burn them up," she instead held the letters up to be seen, kept them in her lap while sitting in the drawing room at night, and brought them to the mill so other women would notice them. Although she never read them aloud nor let anyone else read them, Maria still wanted others to know about this correspondence.

Both Harriet and Lucy saw Maria sitting by the fire some evenings with all three letters in her lap. They also observed her place the smaller yellow and white letters inside the seal of the larger pink one.

"The pink letter looks like a lady's handwriting," Lucy said one evening.

"No, it is from a gentleman," Maria replied.

Harriet overheard Maria tell Lucy that they were "from a gentleman in Bristol."[6]

On December 20, at about quarter past five o'clock, just as it had turned dark, Maria walked over to the window near Lucy's looms, brushed her hair with a comb—the same hair clip she would wear that evening—and told Lucy that she needed to run an errand to Joseph Durfee's. She asked if Lucy knew where he lived (and repeated the same statement and question to Amy Durfee and Harriet Hathaway that evening). Joseph Durfee, not directly related to the farming Durfees, was a carpenter and shipbuilder employed as clerk at the steamboat company. In fact, Joseph Durfee's home lay in the opposite direction from Maria's boardinghouse and the farm.[7]

It seemed as though Maria was leaving some clues. A visitor from Bristol could arrive in Fall River via one of three means: He could take the stage, entering from the north and alighting at Moses Lawton's Tavern in the town center; he could travel on the steamboat *King Philip* that ran from

Providence to Bristol to Fall River on Thursdays, disembarking at the wharf where Joseph Durfee resided; or he could ferry across to Portsmouth, cross the Stone Bridge, and walk six miles through Tiverton from the south. If Maria wanted to signal that she was meeting an out-of-town visitor, without naming him, what better way than to mention to three different women that she needed to visit a man at the steamboat company.

After leaving the mill around five-thirty, Maria returned to Harriet Hathaway's, ate her early supper alone, then went upstairs to change her clothes and cloak. She quickly grabbed a pencil and scribbled a note on a small scrap of paper—"If I am missing . . ."—and placed it in her bandbox. While her landlady was in the kitchen, Maria hurried back downstairs and headed into the street. Harriet recalled that this was sometime "between candle light and dark." Harriet heard the door slam, but didn't see Maria leave. She would never see her again.[8]

Earlier that afternoon, Ephraim had reached the fork in the road, just south of the Bristol ferry in Portsmouth. Just as the roads divided, two sets of stories would diverge at this juncture. Where he actually went, for many, depended on whose story they would come to believe.

Local residents would tell their tales of passing a male stranger, or spotting him off in the distance, along the route between the Stone Bridge that led north through Tiverton, past the Durfee farm and stack yard, and into the streets of Fall River. The next day, as soon as they had heard of the death of a young woman, they began to connect the sights and sounds from the previous afternoon and evening.

Ephraim Avery told a different story. His alibi was a tale of a southward excursion, heading away from Fall River and toward the coal mines. His outing involved no direct encounters, conversations, or interactions with local residents on the Island. It was also a story that Avery never had to tell in public, since others recounted secondhand what he'd told them about his whereabouts that day.

Maria must have been nervous as she stepped out into the street after leaving Harriet Hathaway's home and pondered her future. Could she become a mother and yet remain an independent working woman? She knew she would need someone's help. She'd rehearsed in her mind how this might work, much as she had in a letter to her family a month before. "I still have hopes and fears," she told them, but she knew not "what the results will be." Recently she'd discovered that "there is a girl here that has had a child, and went into the factory again in six weeks. She gets her child boarded for 50 cents a week." It wouldn't be easy, Maria thought. She expected scandal but told her family (and herself) that "it will not make half the noise here that it would in the country." As she contemplated her immediate future, Maria knew what she needed to do: "I shall try to work till the first of March" and "try to save six dollars a month this winter."[9]

As Maria hurried to her destination, she may have turned over in her mind her conversations with Dr. Wilbur during her office visits these past two months—how she had told the doctor that Avery advised her to take oil of tansy to end her pregnancy; that Wilbur thought it would "destroy her life"; how Wilbur advised her that it was best to meet the preacher in Fall River; and how he thought she should ask for a settlement of $300. She might have remembered the letter she'd written to Fall River's Methodist minister, still sealed, unsent, and stored in her trunk, in which she stated that she couldn't remain a Methodist after what happened at the camp meeting. She hoped that her uncertainties might end that night and the matter would finally be settled.[10]

Hopes and fears: On this night, Maria's last, it would have been easy for fears to loom larger. No moon rose, and the temperature plummeted.

Only two people worried about Maria that evening. Alone in their home, Lucy and Harriet Hathaway stayed up until after ten o'clock, awaiting her return. Harriet had no one that she could turn to for help, so she left the door unlocked and went to bed. "I felt very uneasy about her" and "slept little that night," she later recalled. Lucy's mind too had turned from hopes to fears: she hoped that Maria had gone out with some of her Methodist friends that evening, but when she didn't come home, Lucy began to fear that she might have accidentally walked off a bridge in the night's darkness. When Lucy arrived at the mill the next morning, she asked the other "girls" what they knew. Right around that time John Durfee was startled by the sight of a woman's body hanging from a fence post inside his haystack yard.[11]

12

Manhunt

ON THE AFTERNOON OF JANUARY 7, 1833, twelve days after the preliminary hearing began, Justices Howe and Haile announced their decisions. Their opinions landed like a bombshell. Each justice wrote a separate opinion, but together they ruled that Maria Cornell had committed suicide and that there was no "probable cause" to suspect that Ephraim Avery was involved in her violent death.

John Howe's opinion was the more detailed: a ten-page, 5,000-word journey through his imagined interpretation of the evidence. The forty-nine-year-old magistrate considered himself not just a jurist but a writer and orator as well. His closing statement revealed the literary fashions he had cultivated since his college days. After dispatching the prosecution's "chain of circumstantial evidence," he turned to the crux of the matter: the differences between the reputations of Avery and Cornell. For the Bristol justice, his decision came down to whose character he could trust. Avery's stature, he wrote, had always remained "perfectly unblemished," whereas Cornell appeared to have been "addicted to almost every vice," for years "going about from place to place, and staying but a little while" at any one of them.[1]

He stopped just short of asserting that no respectable young woman would voluntarily work in a factory, but the courtroom audience knew what he was implying. In Howe's mind, the primary difference between the respective characters of the two protagonists was clearly evident in the reasons for their incessant mobility: the preacher's moves from town to town confirmed his "ministerial character," while Cornell's evinced her "bad character" as "an undoubted prostitute."[2]

Howe concluded his opinion with an act of literary fancy. Even if Avery "wrote all the letters imputed to him, and actually received all that are pretended to have been addressed by her to him," and even if he met Maria Cornell on the evening of December 20 at a prearranged site, Howe still wouldn't suspect a man of his character and occupation to be the father of her child, nor "to have taken her off to the stack yard and murdered her." Howe then placed words into Avery's mouth, fabricating a speech that the preacher might have made to Maria:

> "Maria, you have given me a great deal of trouble heretofore, and your late letters, which I wrote you so much surprised me, have given me a great deal more. You are pursuing me, who never did you an intentional injury, with great malignity. I did not know but it might be in your power to do me and my family an injury and bring a scandal upon my profession, when I solicited this interview and promised you aid. I have since thought more of the character of your threats, and the effect of your executing them; and, as it would only be encouraging you to extort from me again, and I could have no security that you would not, after all, do all you could to injure me, I have concluded to retract my promise and set you at defiance. If I thought you had any just sense of future accountability, I would warn you of the sin of thus following up one crime with another."

After a speech like that, Howe concluded, it seemed more plausible that Cornell had decided to "destroy herself" than that Avery had "betrayed and destroyed her."[3]

§

Avery was set free, and the mill town was abuzz. When constable Harvey Harnden returned with the justices' written decisions, 600 people gathered at the First Congregational Church to hear him read Justice Howe's opinion. Residents were aghast and dismayed by what they heard. "Astonished" was how the *Fall River Weekly Recorder* characterized the crowd's reaction. The *Fall River Monitor* portrayed Howe's opinion as "very strange arguments," which, once they appeared in print, were sure to disgust if not "amuse some portions of the public."[4]

That night's crowd was not amused. Mill town folk could see no reason to commence a new search for another suspect. They instructed the Fall River Committee to secure another warrant for Avery's arrest and a proper hearing in Newport County, where the crime had been committed. The next day, with a new arrest warrant in hand, Harvey Harnden set off to Providence to get an order affixed to it by the chief justice of the state supreme court.

Ever since the death of Maria Cornell, Harvey Harnden seemed to be right in the middle of the action. A striving man, he possessed unflagging energy and a nose for the main chance. Harnden was the type of jovial good fellow who succeeded equally well in his auctioneering business and as deputy sheriff in Fall River. At some point too, the thirty-nine-year-old rose to the rank of colonel in the local militia.

While in Providence, the Fall River constable was introduced to the attorney general as well as the chief justice, but he got nothing more than a legal run-around. Growing anxious to return to Bristol, he arrived on Monday, one week after the two justices had released Avery. There Harnden confronted Bristol residents unable or unwilling to assist him. They had heard rumors but knew little of Avery's whereabouts. "Some thought or pretended to think one thing and some another," Harnden mused. The next day, when a Bristol man tried to convince Harnden that he'd driven Avery to a location on the outskirts of Bristol but didn't know where he had gone from there, Harnden investigated and determined that the man's tale was merely a ruse.[5]

Convinced that the preacher had definitely gone into hiding, he questioned the Warren bridge toll keeper, who thought that Avery had crossed the previous Wednesday before climbing into a carriage drawn by two white horses heading northeast toward Massachusetts.

Ten years before Edgar Allan Poe gained acclaim for creating the detective story as a new literary genre, Harnden penned an early forerunner: a thirty-six-page narrative describing his week-long search for Avery across three states. While Poe's hero relied more on sleuthing and deductive acumen, Harnden combined a swaggering display of his powers in divining clues with the adventures of a man-on-the-make, casting himself as the lone detective in search of a fugitive, employing guile, deception, courage, and wit.[6]

With evidence that Avery had left the state, Harnden returned to the state capital and acquired an order of requisition to the governor of Massachusetts authorizing him to retrieve Avery as a fugitive. With a clue to pursue, Harnden began his secretive search. He confided only in men of proven trustworthiness, beginning by testing the honesty of Bristol's deputy sheriff, William Paul, asking him to keep the secret that Avery's arrest warrant was in Harnden's possession, not the sheriff's. "I am now happy to state," Harnden wrote, "that Mr. Paul has proved himself to be a trusty officer." Harnden repeated this test of a man's mettle for every individual who assisted him.[7]

Returning to Avery's last known location, the self-made detective began his search for the carriage with two white horses. He located a tavern in Attleborough where the carriage had stopped on Wednesday night and discovered that the traveling party included two young women (ages eighteen and twenty-five) and two gentlemen (one tall—Avery—and another not very tall). They fed their horses and moved on. The next day Harnden traced the carriage as far as Dedham, ten miles from Boston, where the passengers spent the night.

Posing as a family friend searching for one of the young women, Harnden convinced the landlady to talk by pretending that he had been sent to prevent this female passenger from eloping. In a case already rife with speculation about seduction, Harnden resorted to innuendo to deceive the tavern owners into giving him a physical description of the male travelers, confirming his suspicions that one of them was Avery.

Hurrying on to Boston, where he lodged at the tavern next door to the city's Methodist church, Harnden convinced the barkeeper that he was on a secret errand that prevented him from signing the inn's registry. He deployed the same veil of secrecy when following an erroneous tip that Avery might be in Lowell.

True manhood, Harnden insisted, derived from an unthinking display of public virtue. With a touch of irony, though, secrecy and deception proved just as vital to a "true man's" success in this detective adventure. Much as in day-to-day exchanges in a capitalist economy, men often triumphed by resorting to stealth and deceit. But a democratic society that prized equality and transparency also feared and despised those traits. There was the rub. Deceit and secrecy were necessary for true men like Harnden and his aides to prove their worthiness and achieve their goals, but they were also the signs of the inferior masculinity of the men who "secreted" Avery into hiding.

Meanwhile rumors began to spread about Avery's escape. Newspapers speculated wildly about his whereabouts and designs. Some guessed he'd already been imprisoned in Newport or that he'd posted bail but was keeping away from public officials. Mostly, the papers assumed that he had fled for fear of violence or further prosecution. The most outlandish rumor, published in a Newport paper, claimed that Avery had set sail for Cuba.[8]

With no help from Methodists in Boston or residents of Lowell, Harnden decided to confront a "gentleman" he suspected had joined Avery in his carriage ride to Boston, peppering him with questions about every stop they had made, pausing each time to state with emphasis, "*Ephraim K. Avery* was with you." By the end, the self-fashioned detective threatened prosecution for aiding an escaping fugitive, or at least that he would "publish to the world" the man's name and actions if he refused to reveal Avery's whereabouts. The gentleman relented, admitting that Avery was hiding in the town of Rindge, New Hampshire, where some Methodists resided.[9]

Harnden traveled fifty miles inland from Boston, disguising himself and his quest throughout his journey to Rindge. Upon arrival he collected around him a group of "true" men who could assist him in the final search. Two deputy sheriffs, a local farmer, an attorney with expertise in the state's extradition laws, and a young man Harnden called "the Baker" promised to maintain the secrecy of the manhunt, and Harnden praised them all as "very vigilant men." Like similar narratives of self-made men, Harnden's tale trumpeted his singlehanded heroism, even if he had to admit that his successes required the help of others.[10]

Together they discovered that Avery's likely hiding place was the home of a sea captain, Simeon Mayo, and his wife, Nancy, Methodists who had known him during his previous circuits on Cape Cod. Within no time, Harnden and his four assistants silently surrounded the Mayo house. It was late, nine or ten o'clock at night.

Situating his associates at all the outside doors, Harnden entered the home along with the Rindge deputy sheriff, there to ensure they entered the house legally. To the other lawman, Harnden said he would "do all the talking and fighting if any should be necessary." Inside, Harnden called out, asking if Capt. Mayo was home. A short, stocky man replied,

"My name is Mayo."

"I am here after *Ephraim K. Avery*," Harnden declared.

"*Ephraim K. Avery!*" said Mayo.

"Yes sir."

"I don't know such a man," the captain insisted.

"*I* know such a man," Harnden replied. "I have come a *great* way after him—I came on *purpose* after him and must have him."[11]

With his emphasis on the words *I*, *great*, and *purpose*, readers couldn't miss Harnden's self-important heroism.

Captain Mayo's wife, Nancy, slipped out of the room, and within minutes one of the deputies rapped his fingers on a window, informing Harnden that a woman had just gone upstairs and called to a Mr. Avery. As the detective rushed past Mrs. Mayo on the staircase, she told him he was "after innocent blood." Entering a bedroom he found only an extinguished candle and a rumpled bed. Had he thought to look behind the door, he would have immediately found the preacher, but he thought that space too slight: "I must give the gentleman the credit of having put himself in a position," Harnden wrote, "to require less room than I thought it possible for any *man* to do."[12]

While Harnden continued his search upstairs, the preacher tried to escape out the front door, only to retreat back inside when the detective's men nearly grabbed him. Downstairs, Harnden pressed his hand against a door. Feeling gentle pressure from behind, he concluded that he was "within an inch of the person I had long been looking for." Opening the door forcefully, Harnden shone a candle into the face of Ephraim Avery.

The preacher stood motionless. In the intervening two weeks Avery had grown out his beard, which "very materially altered his looks." The detective, though, emphasized his prey's weakness as much as his disguise, reporting that the preacher couldn't utter a word and that he worried he might faint. Taking him by the hand, Harnden offered these reassuring words: "Do endeavor to overcome this agitation; you need fear no personal violence; you shall be kindly treated." They left immediately, traveling through the night and next morning by stagecoach to Boston, with Avery under arrest.[13]

While Harnden was secretly closing in on Avery, the Rhode Island legislature discussed a petition from Tiverton residents requesting a proclamation offering a reward for the fugitive preacher's apprehension. Legislators who held opposing opinions about Avery's guilt chimed in with various speculations: Did any new evidence exist? Had the public been cheated out of a fair trial? Was the legislature inflaming the popular excitement? Had the preacher actually absconded? Most amazing about this public debate is the fact that key figures in Avery's upcoming trial—a trial that no one yet knew would come to pass—were present and participated in the discussion. The attorney general, Albert C. Greene, and Levi Haile, one of the two justices at Avery's examination in Bristol, felt no compunction about voicing their opinions. Even more, Eleazer Trevett from Newport, who would serve as jury foreman, sat in the chamber listening to whatever rumors legislators threw out. The reward resolution passed with a nearly unanimously vote. To this point, the Tiverton murder had trumped all other legislative business. Only after concluding the debate over Avery did legislators move on to elect their state's next United States senator.[14]

Harnden maintained steadfastly that he had "pursued Mr. Avery and arrested him without the least hope of reward." Still, he found "gratifying" the prospect of recovering his expenses. But when he applied for the reward, Governor Arnold balked, arguing that he hadn't signed the proclamation until after Harnden had apprehended Avery.[15]

Little surprise, then, that Harnden turned to publishing his own account of the manhunt to recoup the considerable cost of his search. If denied the state's reward, wrote a Providence newspaper, the detective should be compensated through the sales of his narrative. For a mere twelve cents readers could purchase Harnden's narrative two weeks after Avery's arrest. Reaching an audience insatiably longing for any story about the preacher and the factory girl's murder, the *Fall River Weekly Recorder* described its appeal: "The language is simple and easily understood by everyone; and there is a vein of humor running through the work—a piquancy and peculiarity in the manner of Col. Harnden's telling his story." The paper recommended it to "all who wish to while away a dull hour" as well as anyone who hadn't yet "felt much interest in the Avery case." The *Providence Journal* agreed: "Few who take it up, will lay it down."[16]

While most newspapers merely summarized the key plot twists surrounding Avery's flight and Harnden's pursuit—that Avery disguised himself by growing a beard, or that fellow Methodist Mayo denied that the preacher was hiding in his house—Harnden's narrative was something greater: a heroic tale of self-made manhood that prefigured the kind of detective stories American readers would find irresistible in the decades to come.

Thirteen thousand copies of the *Narrative of the Apprehension in Rindge, N.H. of the Rev. E. K. Avery* were printed, in at least two editions. What effect would this have on the pool of jurors at the trial, when legions had already read the tale of Avery's flight and Harnden's manhunt, let alone two published editions of the testimony in Bristol?

Rhode Island's attorney general, Albert Greene, was already worried about that before he knew he would be the lead prosecutor.[17]

ACT II

Trial

13

Courtroom Tales

BRIGHT SUNLIGHT STARTLED THE PRISONER'S unprepared eyes. Newport's jailer led Ephraim Avery down the front steps of the jailhouse on a crisp spring morning, directing him to turn right. The preacher had to squint as the sun's rays struck harshly against the white clapboard walls of the Methodist meetinghouse across the street. Some critics may have thought it fitting that Newport's Methodists had chosen to build their meetinghouse on the same street as the town jail. But the first Methodist meetinghouse in America to possess a steeple and a church bell in fact signaled just how far the upstart sect had grown. Earlier Methodists considered such ostentatious displays of worldliness unfitting for their plain and serious piety—a prudent policy when parishioners were mostly poor laborers. But the shiny white spire expressed the yearnings for respectability of a church that three decades earlier could afford only a lot across from the jailhouse.[1]

As the jailer marched the preacher up a slight hill past the White Horse Tavern and alongside a militia common that had hosted no battle training since the War of 1812, he steered him right once again onto Farewell Street. Avery's thoughts surely never strayed too far from the chilling sense that his own life hung in the balance.

Straight ahead stood old Colony House, a three-story Georgian-style brick building, its cupola catching the morning light. Shops all down Broadway were empty, as everyone's attention that day—town folk and visitors alike—was directed toward the courthouse, awaiting a glimpse of the notorious Methodist preacher. Old Colony House, erected nearly a century before,

had been home to the colonial assembly before Independence and continued as the state capitol during the early republic. Avery climbed its stone
steps, under the balcony where the Declaration of Independence was read
aloud in 1776, and entered through the twelve-foot-high double doorway.
The hands of the clock on the courthouse façade pointed to a few minutes
before ten o'clock.[2]

It was Tuesday morning, May 7, 1833, the second day of Avery's trial before
Rhode Island's Supreme Court. A day earlier, the court had begun the trial by
directing the county sheriff to summon men for jury duty. When the preacher
walked the several hundred paces to the courthouse the previous day, it was
the first time he'd been outside in two months—and after less than an hour,
he was ushered back to his dark cell. For three-and-a-half months he had
been confined to a prison cell fourteen feet square, with only a six-by-ten-inch
window, which provided insufficient lighting for reading or discerning human
faces. "My ears assailed with the grating sound of bars of iron and the turning
of keys," he recalled, it was "enough almost to freeze my blood!"[3]

Old Colony House in Newport, the capitol of both the colony and
state of Rhode Island, was the venue for Ephraim Avery's murder
trial. "State House, Newport, Rhode Island," *American Magazine of
Useful and Entertaining Knowledge*, vol. 1 (January 1835). HathiTrust
Digital Library.

An unnerving silence blanketed the courtroom. All eyes fastened on the defendant as he bowed to the three justices and again to the prosecutors before taking his seat at the defense table. Gathered at the bench and bar were the most illustrious legal personages from two states. The public could rest assured, one trial reporter observed, that both sides had counsel of "the highest ability."[4]

At the prosecution table sat Attorney General Albert C. Greene. By his side sat the Newport lawyer who preceded him as attorney general, Dutee J. Pearce, then serving his fifth term in Congress. Next to him was William Staples, prosecutor during Avery's pre-trial hearing in Bristol.

At Avery's side sat defense lawyer Richard Randolph. Hailing from one of Virginia's first families, the Harvard graduate was connected by marriage and business to the most important legal figures in Newport. The star at the defense table, though, was the venerable Jeremiah Mason, the most

Albert Collins Greene, prosecutor in the Avery trial, attorney general for the state of Rhode Island. Courtesy of Rhode Island Historical Society.

renowned lawyer in all of New England. During his distinguished legal career in Portsmouth, New Hampshire, Mason had famously paired with Daniel Webster in the landmark Dartmouth College case. Webster once remarked that if asked who was the nation's greatest lawyer he might say Chief Justice John Marshall, "but if you took me by the throat and pinned me to the wall and demanded my *real* opinion, I should be compelled to say it was Jeremiah Mason."[5]

Mason's talent didn't come cheap. The great barrister in fact always prized compensation above public service, declining judicial appointments because the salaries were too meager. The Methodists, then, hired the region's best and most expensive lawyer to defend Ephraim Avery, whose meager circuit-rider salary could never pay for such counsel. Three other attorneys from Newport and Bristol were retained to assist the defense, but the expectation was that Randolph and Mason would argue Avery's case before the court and jury.

Jeremiah Mason, Ephraim Avery's illustrious defense attorney. Courtesy of State of New Hampshire.

Presiding over the trial were the three judges of the Rhode Island Supreme Court. Chief Justice Samuel Eddy was more of a career-long political office-holder than a practicing attorney. An introvert with a contemplative bent, he nonetheless ran his courtroom with a firm gavel and was known "to delight in exactness—precision." Eddy was joined by two associate justices, Charles Brayton from Warwick and Job Durfee from Tiverton, Durfee being twenty years the junior of his two colleagues. Courtroom observers wondered whether Jeremiah Mason considered these Rhode Island judges lesser legal minds.[6]

After agonizing months of delay, the public was finally getting their trial. Americans watched and waited for what was shaping up to be the most spectacular, headline-grabbing trial in the United States. Their appetite had been whetted during the two-week-long examination in Bristol in early January, followed by the sensational press coverage of Avery's flight and apprehension by Harvey Harnden.

The accused preacher was asked to stand and raise his right hand. The clerk read the indictment, repeating several times the phrase "not having the fear of God before his eyes, but being moved and seduced by the instigation of the devil." Avery was charged with three counts, each one outlining a possible method of killing Sarah Maria Cornell on the night of December 20. First, that he fastened a cord around her neck and choked and strangled her. Second, that he tied a cord around her neck and suspended her body from a stake, thereby choking, suffocating, and strangling her. Third, that he assaulted her by striking and beating her with both hands on her belly, left side, and back, inflicting multiple mortal wounds, after which he affixed a cord around her neck and violently squeezed her neck and throat until she "instantly died." As the clerk spoke, Avery fixed his gaze intently, his lips moving incessantly as if chewing on paper.[7]

"Ephraim K. Avery!" the clerk cried out, "to this indictment you have already pleaded not guilty—what say you now?"

"Not guilty," Avery answered.

"How will you be tried?"

"By God and my country."

"God send you a good deliverance!"[8]

The audience remained silent. Anticipating a swarm of onlookers for the most talked-about case in anyone's memory, the court moved the trial to the Colony House's great hall on the first floor, worried that their regular chamber a floor above, capable of seating a hundred people, would give way under the crowd's weight. The great hall held some 1,500 people, and on the trial's opening days, during which only preliminary business was conducted, it was already teeming with spectators. Ever since the discovery of Cornell's body, and news that a Methodist preacher was accused of her murder, an "unparalleled excitement," as newsmen and court officials put it, had grown unabated.[9]

Crowds of out-of-town visitors were a godsend to Newport. A booming colonial seaport during the era of the slave trade, with three of every twenty persons enslaved, the town's fortunes waned after the Revolution, while neighboring industrial regions, like Providence and Fall River, grew spectacularly. Newport's economy shrank to such depths that not a single new house had been built since the War of 1812. With Avery's trial, taverns, hotels, and stables overflowed with two types of witnesses: the hundreds who came to testify and the thousands who turned up to watch and listen.[10]

The morning before the trial began, passersby in the courthouse square found themselves serenaded by a lone man belting out a ballad of his own composition:

> Ye people all a warning take,
>   Remember Avery's plot:—
> Enough to make your hearts to ache;
>   Don't let it be forgot.
> He killed the mother—then the child;
>   What a wicked man was he!
> The devil helped him all the while
>   How wicked must he be.[11]

The public's excitement was fast becoming a character in the trial's unfolding drama, testing the relationship between public opinion and popular justice in a democracy.

The heightened curiosity brought with it intense scrutiny from the popular media. Before court stenographers and video recordings, the testimony and arguments in high-profile criminal trials were transcribed by journalists or lawyers. Seven men appeared in court the first day requesting to report on the proceedings. Two hailed from leading newspapers in New York City—Richard Adams Locke for the *New York Courier & Enquirer* and Jacob D. Wheeler for the *New York Journal of Commerce*. They were joined by two editors and one reporter from Boston—Richard Hildreth for the

Boston Atlas; Benjamin F. Hallett, who edited the Antimasonic *Boston Daily Advocate*; and Thomas Gill, reporting for the *Boston Morning Post*. To ensure their own faithful version of the evidence and arguments, the Methodists employed a reporter of their own, Thomas Towndrow, a specialist in short-hand. Rounding out this group of scribes was Providence attorney George Rivers, who was also quietly hired by the Methodists. As members of the Rhode Island bar, Hallett and Rivers already had privileges of sitting near the justices. The other reporters hoped for similar access in order to hear both the testimony and the sidebar discussions among the counsel and the court.[12]

Fearing that reports on the trial's content might prejudice the public and possibly the jury, Avery's counsel made a motion to suppress any publication. Since they lacked any experience with what today would be called a media circus, the justices had little precedent for barring reporters from the courthouse, so they made a bargain. In exchange for privileged courtroom seats, reporters pledged to abstain from publishing any of the proceedings until the jury had rendered its verdict. That meant that the media version of the trial, which began immediately after Cornell's death, was paused.[13]

"Let the Jurors be called," declared the chief justice.

Every sentient person in the region had to have been aware of this crime. How was it possible to find twelve white men who stood impartial and un-biased about an event that generated more attention than any other local controversy for generations?

Because the customary call for fourteen men would prove insufficient for selecting a jury, the court ordered the sheriff to summon another forty-eight men before the trial officially started. Attorney General Greene asked the first potential juror the three questions he would repeat to each: Are you related to the prisoner or the deceased? Do you have any conscientious scruples against finding a man guilty of a crime punishable by death? Have you formed any opinion of the guilt or innocence of the prisoner?

The first man was immediately disqualified when he admitted reservations about the death penalty, while a second was excused for ill health. When the third man affirmed a bias, the jousting between opposing attorneys commenced, with Jeremiah Mason objecting to restraints on the questions he could ask.[14]

"Have you formed any bias on your mind against the prisoner?" Mason asked.

"Yes, I have," the juror replied.

"Have you so far made up your mind as not to be able to give the cause an impartial trial?" Greene asked.

"I do not think I have."

Avery was entitled to make up to twenty peremptory challenges to reject any juror he wished, without cause or explanation. With both the juror and Avery standing, the clerk recited:

"Juror, look upon the prisoner; prisoner, look upon the juror. What say you prisoner, will you be tried by this juror; if not, make your objection, and you will be heard."

"I have no objection," said the preacher. Sworn in, the man took his seat in the jury box.[15]

It wasn't always going to be that easy. Not surprisingly, nearly every potential juror already held some opinion about the case. Asked if he had formed an opinion, one potential juror blurted back, "*I have, and that opinion is that he is a GUILTY MAN.*"[16]

The lawyers and justices continued their back-and-forth over how to determine whether a juror's answer constituted bias. The men were pressed to reveal what they had read, whether they had talked about the case, or whether they had expressed their opinions about Avery's guilt or innocence. Some were dismissed as soon as they declared that they had already formed an opinion.

Questioning continued through the morning. By lunchtime only three jurors had been selected, even though Avery had used only three peremptory challenges. During the afternoon, forty-six more men stood for questioning, leading one reporter to lament that the sparring between opposing counsel "appeared interminable." By five o'clock six men had been sworn in, but the entire venire of sixty-two men had been completely exhausted. Exhaustion likely described the court and the audience, too. The court ordered the sheriff to call up another sixty men before adjourning until the next afternoon.[17]

The next day the selection slogged on. A public that loved to read did not make for an impartial jury. Potential jurors had devoured newspaper stories and published reports of the Bristol examination. They had read the content of the letters found in Cornell's trunk and Dr. Wilbur's reported conversations with Cornell, and they had pored over Harvey Harnden's narrative of his manhunt for Avery. After dismissing twenty-five men in a row, counsel and the justices wrangled over how to ensure neutrality when one juror admitted that, although his mind wasn't exactly made up, he thought "that if what was said was true," the preacher "ought to be hung."

Greene was growing frustrated—would they ever be able to find an un-biased jury? If a potential juror read in a newspaper that a certain man had murdered another, and then decided that he ought to hang if the crime was proven, that shouldn't disqualify him. "If it did," Greene argued, "a jury could never be empaneled." Mason countered that, if a juror has read evidence that might appear in the trial and "formed an opinion as to the kind of circumstantial evidence" that would satisfy him, he couldn't be impartial.[18]

Juries were typically selected in a matter of hours, or even minutes, but in this case it took nearly two full days and 108 candidates before twelve were seated. The whole process, a reporter observed, was "almost unprecedented in the juridical annals of Rhode Island."[19]

What happened was also confusing to nearly everyone present. While public sentiment didn't favor the defendant (only one man who had formed an opinion said he thought Avery innocent), the preacher used only nine of his twenty peremptory challenges. Observers struggled to discern a rational basis for Avery's choices—some men had formed opinions, while others had not; some opinions were decidedly against him, while others said their minds weren't made up. Defense counsel declined even to question three of the last six jurors selected, simply taking their word that they had formed no opinion, never asking what they had read. Even more suspect, Avery was observed smiling on several occasions before he asked a juror to stand aside or accepted another without objection.[20]

The court appointed Eleazer Trevett, Newport town councilman and state representative, as jury foreman, and then adjourned until Thursday morning. Overnight a spectacular thunderstorm broke over Newport's harbor, its fort and tall ships standing erect against the blackened sky, prophesying the darkness to be exposed in the days ahead.[21]

On the trial's fourth day Congressman Dutee J. Pearce rose to open the prosecution's case. The courthouse swelled with a crowd "wedged in a mass on the floor." Building the foundation for a case to demonstrate Avery's guilt, Pearce told the jurors that it was not the prosecution's responsibility to prove that the defendant had committed each of the specific methods for murdering Cornell listed in the indictment. The state need only prove one of these charges or a crime analogous to it. Murder, he reminded them, was the taking of life "with malice aforethought," and there was no blurring in this case among manslaughter, accidental death, or murder. If the prisoner was guilty at all, he was "guilty of murder in its worst and most odious features."[22]

Preempting the main thrust of an anticipated defense, Pearce methodically began planting the seed in jurors' minds that Cornell had not taken her own life, insisting that from the moment she was found dead, the details of the scene—the cord around her neck, arrangement of her dress, position of her limbs, bruises on her body, disorder of her hair, even the nearby broken hair clip—all demonstrated that her death came violently, at the hands of another.[23]

This is your starting point, gentlemen, Pearce continued, his rhythm quickening. Your next consideration must be whose hands inflicted this violence. If we show that the prisoner and the deceased had exchanged letters and had an intimacy of long standing, if we show her pregnancy made it expedient for him to wish to remove her out of the way, and if we show that the circumstances surrounding her death strongly presume that he was author of the violence, we shall have presented to you a probability of the prisoner's guilt.[24]

"But, gentlemen, we shall not stop here. We shall present to you a chain of circumstantial evidence as strong as ever presented on a charge of murder to any twelve men in this State or any other."[25] Pearce let that sit with the jurors for a moment before his grand conclusion, "Gentlemen, I need not remind you that this is a case that has created more excitement in this state than any charge of crime ever submitted to a jury of twelve men. Nor in this state alone; it has extended throughout the country." *Why the unprecedented tumult?* Pearce pondered aloud. With the accused being a clergyman in the largest and fastest-growing denomination in the nation, little wonder that its members were anxious to know if one of their ministers was guilty or not. The excitement originated too from anti-religion folk thrilled to see a clergyman charged with hypocrisy and convicted of an odious crime.

"And yet there is still a further cause of this public excitement," Pearce explained, "deriving from the situation of the deceased." Cornell was, Pearce said, "in the parlance of the day, a 'Factory girl.'" It stands to reason, he emphasized, "that for the purpose of protecting this class of our fellow citizens—to convince them that they might, in any outrage or wrong, expect the same protection as others—a great excitement emerged in the flourishing village of Fall River." Then Pearce warned the jury: "But you, gentlemen, must stand aloof from all excitement. You must have no bias," looking to nothing but the law and the evidence to influence your verdict.[26]

The lawyer had taken less than an hour to make "an unassuming but able and entirely candid statement" of the prosecution's case.[27]

The vast audience for Ephraim Avery's murder trial came to know a truth about criminal trials more generally: they derive their organization and logic from storytelling. Allowing two sides to offer competing tales of guilt or innocence to a captive audience—the jury that renders a verdict—trials by their very nature unleash countless tales inside and outside the courtroom. These stories have a singular goal: persuasion. Attorneys and witnesses, judges and court reporters all tell stories to make an argument, to convince audiences that their interpretation of the evidence is plausible, believable, true.[28]

Courtroom rituals make it seem as if the attorneys control the narratives they present to the court, but aside from opening and closing arguments, lawyers must rely on a bevy of independent storytellers called to the witness stand, in hopes of stitching together a coherent narrative. The moment an attorney questions a witness ("Where were you on the night of . . .?"), he solicits the telling of a story, one the attorney never completely controls.

Even before the court called any witnesses, the jury's foreman requested paper so jurors could take notes, but the chief justice denied him, with the curt reply—"It is not usual, sir." Jurors at Avery's trial would have to rely on memory to sort through what the prosecution promised would be at least fifty or sixty witnesses, plus however many more the defense called. Without notes, jurors depended even more on how familiar and persuasive were the stories they heard from each side. Those narratives helped them make sense of the voluminous evidence they would hear.[29]

The trial of Ephraim Avery transpired during an era of persuasion unlike any other that had preceded or followed it in US history. Popular electoral democracy, along with evangelical revivalism, elevated the arts of persuasion to new heights. Ordinary folks could listen for hours to political orators like Daniel Webster, stand all day to hear Abraham Lincoln debate Stephen Douglas, and spend a week in the woods listening to preachers expound all day and night. They were enthralled by spoken words of persuasion and had countless ways to denote the act of speaking—bellow, clamor, prattle, roar, yawp. Courtroom tales, by attorneys or witnesses, were a perfect fit with this cultural phenomenon.

14

Clove Hitch

ATTORNEY GENERAL GREENE CALLED THE prosecution's first witness: John Durfee, the farmer who discovered Sarah Maria Cornell's body in his haystack yard. Durfee's testimony had not wavered since he served as lead witness at the pre-trial hearing in January. The thirty-five-year-old farmer once again recounted how he'd come upon Cornell on that December morning, the frightful hair covering her face. In the Newport courtroom he stooped to mimic the position of her body, with knees bent, heels at right angles, feet tightly together, toes barely touching the ground. Over her dress she wore a cloak that was hooked up nearly from bottom to top, and on her hands she wore gloves. "Her clothes were smoothed back as far as they would reach under the legs," he said. Her shoes had been removed and placed neatly on the ground to her right, her handkerchief lying an equal distance to her left. After calling the coroner, Durfee moved the body from the stackyard to his home, and that afternoon he retrieved Cornell's belongings (a trunk and a bandbox) from Harriet Hathaway's, in part to get clothes for her burial, but also because he heard talk of letters in her possession.[1]

The prosecutor handed Durfee a pile of letters. He identified four that he recalled from Cornell's trunk—one each of yellow, white, and pink-colored paper already opened, along with a letter she had intended to send to the town's Methodist minister.

Asked to describe the cord and the knot that encircled Cornell's neck and bound her to the stake, Durfee admitted that he wasn't familiar with the type of knot around her neck, but the cord tied to the stake with a slip knot was a thin piece of hemp twine, doubled over so that four strands hung off the ends.

Immediately, in cross-examination, defense attorney Richard Randolph tried to cast doubt on the mental picture of Cornell hanging with her cloak nearly all hooked up and her arms underneath. He could not have jurors wondering what kind of suicide looked like that. Seeming uneasy for the first time, Durfee held firm, though he had to admit he wasn't positive whether one of the hooks had come undone while he was taking down the body. Randolph probed further regarding the cord and the knots around Cornell's neck and the stake—what kind of string? how many strands? what type of knot?[2]

Jeremiah Mason pushed back his chair for the first time to interject a question in the cross-examination. As he rose, everyone saw that he was a giant of a man—six foot seven inches in an era when most men stood nowhere near six feet tall; even his large bald head seemed small atop his enormous frame.[3]

"Are you positive that you stated that you cut the cord nearer to the neck?" Mason asked.

"I'm not positive as to what I stated at Bristol as to the place I cut the cord," the farmer answered. In fact, he had consistently said he cut the cord about an inch from the stake. But the strategy for any good cross-examination is to get witnesses to admit uncertainty, even about questions they could never be certain about. Mason had elicited the phrase he most wanted, *I'm not positive.*

"You said that you told Mrs. Hathaway there were letters in the trunk. How did you know?" Mason continued.

"I don't recollect that I have said so. I did not tell her there were letters in the trunk, as I recollect."

"How could you tell then that you saw a pencil mark on the paper in the bandbox?" Mason asked a moment later.

"I did not say so. I said I saw a pencil, in the box, lying by the paper."

It was easier to elicit uncertainty from a witness, Mason was demonstrating, by asking him to recall statements he had never made. Aware of this tactic, prosecutors asked the court to instruct Mason not to mislead the witness by assuming that he had "said what he had not said." Denying any such intention, Mason completed his cross-examination. All in all, the Tiverton farmer proved an able match for the legendary legal giant.[4]

The prosecution then called a series of Tiverton and Fall River neighbors to lay the foundation for the idea that Cornell's violent death was a homicide.

First up was Williams Durfee, one of the six men from the inquest jury. His testimony drew attention to the knot around Cornell's neck: the cord had been wrapped twice around, he explained, and so deeply indented into her flesh that it was difficult to see, and then to remove. Near her right ear it was secured by a little knot.[5]

"The knot is what farmers call two half hitches," Williams Durfee explained, "or a *clove hitch*, as we sailors used to call it."

Greene put out his hand with thumb raised upward, handed the witness a string and asked him to demonstrate. The courtroom crowd watched intently as Williams Durfee made the knot.

"A clove hitch must be drawn horizontally, with both hands, or it will never tighten where the knot is," Durfee said as he finished tying the string.[6]

"Could the knot be tightened if ends of the cord were pulled upwards?" That was the jury foreman, calling out a question, still unsure how it worked.

Williams Durfee demonstrated once more, this time on the foreman's finger, showing that it was an impossibility, since the knot would not tighten unless it was drawn horizontally with both hands. Now the foreman understood. Cornell's body had not been hanged by a slip knot or a noose, allowing her weight to tighten the knot and choke off her breathing. Instead, to kill herself with a clove-hitch knot, she had to strangle herself first, then tie the rope to the stake, or after suspending herself by the rope, pull on both ends to strangle herself.[7]

Seth Darling, the Fall River constable, came to the stand. He confirmed the previous descriptions of the body, rope, knots, and haystack scene. Like Williams Durfee, he too demonstrated for the courtroom how to tie a clove hitch knot. Over the next day and beyond, witnesses for the prosecution added more testimony about the rope and the knots. One more neighbor demonstrated a clove hitch for the courtroom, and the crew of workers who had dynamited rocks near Durfee's farm that day testified that they left behind a cart with bags sewn together with twine nearly identical to the cord around Cornell's neck. When they returned following the crime, one of the bags had been unlaced and the twine removed.[8]

Prosecutors pressed on, knowing their case depended on connecting Avery to the letters in Cornell's trunk and establishing that the two had exchanged correspondence prior to her death. Suspicions raised by those letters—references to Bristol and a member of Avery's household and plans to meet on December 20—would mean nothing unless the letters could be traced to both their hands.

Seth Darling was working at Fall River's post office on November 19, when he heard two letters drop into the mailbox. Having emptied the box just half a minute before, he didn't see who deposited them. One was addressed to the Rev. E. K. Avery in Bristol, the other to Grindal Rawson in South Woodstock, Connecticut. "That is the letter I took out of the box that day," he stated when shown Cornell's letter to the Rawsons, which her family had turned over to the prosecution. Darling identified his handwritten mark of "10" on the outside, for the postage cost, along with a red Fall River stamp.[9]

The Bristol postmaster then testified that a letter arrived for Avery from Fall River that same day, and that the preacher was twice charged the cost of Bristol-to-Fall River postage—for the letter he received that day and also for a letter sent on November 12 (the date that was stamped on the yellow letter in Cornell's trunk).

The Bristol examination should have been a warning, but everyone— from judges and attorneys to newspapermen and spectators—was taken aback by how long this trial was lasting. By the afternoon of the fifth day, attorneys for both sides got testy over the proceedings' glacial pace. Murder trials typically lasted a day or two, and jury selection alone had outlasted a typical trial. One reporter boldly predicted an unprecedented trial of perhaps ten days.[10]

As the trial wore on, the letters grew in importance, although prosecutors had not yet submitted them (or even the penciled note from December 20) as evidence. The point was to establish links in a chain of circumstantial evidence to Avery and Cornell first, while the defense proved equally ferocious in trying to discredit that evidence. Lucy and Harriet Hathaway, followed by boardinghouse-keeper Elijah Cole, his daughter Betsey, and Amy Durfee, a factory co-worker, all testified that they had seen Cornell with the three different colored letters in her possession, both at home and at work.[11]

"I will be there on the 20th if pleasant at the place named at 6 o'clock." Those words, written on a half sheet of white paper, dated and postmarked December 8 in Fall River, became the focus when Harvey Harnden took the stand on the prosecution's fourth day of testimony. Avery had preached in the mill town the night before and was seen with Rev. Ira Bidwell in Iram Smith's store on the 8th, where he asked for a sheet of paper and stood at the storekeeper's writing desk. During the Bristol pre-trial hearing, Harnden returned to Smith's store to retrieve what was left of this very ream of white writing paper. Buried within the bundle, he found a torn half sheet.

"I examined the two half sheets with a microscope," Harnden explained, "and the fibers entered into each other exactly." The watermark matched exactly too.[12]

When it was his turn, though, Methodist storekeeper Iram Smith spoke with deliberate uncertainty. "As to what Mr. Avery did, I cannot say," he began, followed by a string of hesitant responses: "I don't know," "I have no recollection," and "I am not certain." Although Smith confirmed that the torn half-sheet had come from his store, and that Avery had been there on the day the letter was written and mailed, he offered enough help for the defense to sow doubt, even as subsequent witnesses more confidently identified Avery, both with paper in hand in Smith's store and walking away from the post office afterward.[13]

Murmurs surely rippled throughout the crowded courthouse when John Orswell declared, "I have seen that letter in Providence in the hands of a gentleman who afterwards proved to be Mr. Avery." Prosecutors had shown Orswell the pink letter from Cornell's trunk—addressed to "Miss Sarah M. Connell, to be left at Mrs. Cole's."

An engineer of a steamboat that ran regularly from Providence to Fall River, Orswell continued: "Between 8 and 9 o'clock in the morning, a gentleman came down the gang plank, in Providence, and asked me if I could take a letter to Fall River." Not allowed to deliver letters, he told the man to put it in a letter box. When the man persisted, offering a ninepence coin and saying it would be a great personal favor to have it hand delivered, Orswell consented and conveyed it to Mr. Cole. He recognized the pink letter because of sooty smudges he had left on the paper from his work on the steamboat engine. It was a Tuesday in late November, he recalled, when the Methodists held a four-day religious meeting in Providence. (Avery was among the clergymen presiding over those meetings.)[14]

Orswell was certain Avery was the man who had handed him that letter. He had "marked the man" because he wore the typical attire of a circuit rider—black cloak and broad-rimmed dark hat—and "from the delicacy of the man's hand and his manner of speaking" he surmised that he was a minister. On Christmas day, recounted the steamboat engineer, he had gone over to Bristol with a group of Fall River men to identify Avery. Although the preacher's friends showed him into a room with three or four others present, he insisted that the man who handed him the letter was not among them. They eventually brought in Avery, and as Orswell recalled, "The moment he entered the room I recognized him." There in Bristol, Avery countered by asking Orswell if the man he had seen was wearing eyeglasses, since the preacher claimed that he never went out without them. Putting on spectacles, he approached Orswell, asking, "Do I now look as I did?" Orswell replied, "Sir, your glasses do not alter the features of your face." In the Newport courtroom, Orswell remained confident: "I have no doubt in my mind that he is the man."[15]

Observers who turned their eyes toward the Methodist preacher saw a man unmoved. They agreed that Avery exhibited remarkable "composure," "perfect self-possession," and a "great mental firmness," regardless of the up or down swings of the trial. How could any man facing these accusations, one reporter wondered, appear "without betraying either undue anxiety, an affected indifference, or a reckless hardihood"?[16]

Confident that they had tied Cornell's letters directly to the defendant, Attorney General Greene began the trial's eighth day by declaring it time to admit the pink letter as evidence. Randolph immediately objected, and with the jury temporarily dismissed, the attorneys and justices launched into an extended sidebar conference about the letters' admissibility. Sidebar conferences constitute the backstage drama of a trial, more like actors debating their craft among one another than onstage performances for the jury and courtroom audiences. Stories that people longed to tell could run headlong into legal constraints against their telling. Avery's trial abounded with these courtroom clashes—illustrated best by the numerous exchanges about whether Cornell's letters could be entered as legal evidence.[17]

Some proof must be given that this letter is in the prisoner's handwriting, Randolph began. "Surely his delivering the letter, even if we admitted that he had delivered it, would be no proof that he wrote it." Randolph wanted legal justification for admitting the letter.[18]

The prosecution denied any intention of offering it as a letter written by Avery, only that they had a right to present to the jury any item that passed directly from the accused to the deceased. "The contents of the letter are a matter for the jury to judge," Pearce insisted. "If the prisoner is innocent, he can explain the matter to all mankind, and dispel every shade of mystery in which it is involved." The attorney general also argued that if the defense wished to maintain that Cornell killed herself, then the appointment to meet this letter writer on either the 18th or 20th of December could be introduced to rebut the allegation of suicide.[19]

Mason leaned into the contest. In a case of such popular excitement, he began, prosecutors must cite authorities that show this was legal evidence rather than merely resorting to abstract reasoning. "We think this is a vastly important point," Mason emphasized. "The moment they introduce this letter, it is a wedge for introducing another and another letter." Then he offered a glimpse of the defense's future argument—that Cornell might have colluded with another in creating and delivering these letters. Despite Mason's efforts, the justices, after a few minutes' consultation, ruled that the letter should be submitted to the jury, since it had been traced from the prisoner to the deceased.[20]

"Dear Sister," Pearce read aloud. The writer of the pink letter told Cornell, "as I told you I am willing to help you" but "I should rather you would come to this place, viz. Bristol." The letter instructed Cornell to "say nothing about me or my family" while pretending to visit Bristol for another purpose. If she was unwilling to come to Bristol, the writer promised, "I will come to Fall River" on either December 18 or 20 and meet "back of the same meeting house where I once saw you" at a time "before the mills stop work," when fewer people would be present. The letter concluded by directing Cornell to keep their correspondence secret, wear a hooded bonnet, and address her response by mail "to *Betsey Hills Bristol* and not as you have to me."[21]

To any listener it was clear that the writer lived in Bristol with his family, knew where to meet privately in town, and was familiar with evangelical religion, given the salutation of "Dear Sister" and the mention of three different meetinghouses. One detail in the letter pointed most directly to Avery: the name to which Cornell should address her letters. Betsey Hills was the thirty-three-year-old niece of Sophia Avery, described as "lame" ("walks with two crutches"), who had moved with the Averys from Lowell to Bristol. She always received mail addressed to "Betsey E. Hills, care of Rev. E. K. Avery." No one other than Ephraim Avery would have collected mail for her in Bristol.[22]

The battle over admissibility resumed when the prosecution moved immediately to admit into evidence the white letter, the one written on the half-sheet of paper on December 8. Randolph objected that the reasoning used for the first letter didn't apply here. The prosecution hadn't proven anything other than that Avery was in Smith's store on a certain day, and that a witness thought he saw a piece of paper in his hand, which could be true for a half dozen other people. Although prosecutors countered by asserting their right to raise suspicions from circumstantial evidence, they stood on stronger ground when arguing, again, that the letter was valid evidence to disprove suicide. Mason wrapped up the defense's objection with a flourish. "If this is the ground on which evidence is admitted, we may as well forget our law, and burn up all our books." The "warmth of feeling" roused in this sidebar contest and Mason's prowess in legal argumentation notwith-standing, the justices admitted the white letter—not as one written by Avery in his own handwriting, but as evidence with regard to suicide. Pearce then read aloud the white letter from Cornell's trunk, addressed and misspelled again "Miss Sarah M. Connell. Fall River," containing the promise "I will be here on the 20th if pleasant at the place named at 6 o'clock, if not pleasant the next Monday eve. *say nothing*."[23]

The next morning it was time to try to admit as evidence the yellow letter, the third one from Cornell's trunk, which similarly misspelled her name (imagine a New Englander with a heavy accent saying her last name, and the spelling "Connell" will match the sound of it)—and the note from Cornell's bandbox. Although prosecutors had not connected the yellow letter (postmarked November 13) to Avery, they certainly wanted jurors to hear its promise: "I will do all you ask only keep your secrets."

Meanwhile, "I offer the pencil note from her bandbox," Greene announced, "to show the state of mind in which she left the house on the evening of the 20th, to rebut the presumption of suicide." Grindal Rawson had testified that the note that began "If I am missing" was in Cornell's handwriting, so Greene pressed his case for admission, along with the yellow letter. Again, he held fast to the best grounds: "We are bound to show this was a murder" and not a suicide.[24]

Randolph renewed his objections. "Suppose a letter addressed to E. K. Avery was found in her trunk," he said. "Suppose a statement in her hand that she expected to be murdered by E. K. Avery; would that be evidence?" To Randolph it would all be hearsay, not admissible by the rules of evidence. In the end, the defense won the contest to disallow the yellow letter, but they lost when the justices ruled that the penciled note was admissible to show Cornell's state of mind with regard to suicide.[25]

Prosecutors had only one more witness to testify about the letters. Joseph Lesure, a young clerk in Fall River's post office, told the court that he delivered the white letter to Cornell on December 8, and not only that, but he witnessed Avery drop the letter into the letter box. This stunning revelation was mitigated when Lesure admitted under Mason's cross-examination that he had only disclosed this information the previous day, despite attending the Bristol hearing back in January. Mason's powers of cross-examination proved worth their cost to the Methodist Church. The battle over whether the letters could be proven to be in Avery's handwriting would await the rebuttal phase of the trial.[26]

The content of the letters in Cornell's possession, and the types of knots used to hang or strangle the body—these were proving to be all important evidence as the prosecution built its case from one long day to the next in this unprecedented trial. But there was more testimony to come, this time about women, their bodies, and the practice of medicine.

15

Doctors, Women, and Bodies

"I ASSISTED IN LAYING OUT the body. Her clothes were stripped off, and I saw the body entirely exposed," Meribah Borden stated when the court reconvened after lunch on the trial's fifth day. Described by trial reporters as "an elderly woman" and "a respectable matron," Borden gave graphic testimony that troubled the packed courtroom as prosecutors pressed their case for homicide. Their strategy required that they expose Maria Cornell's body—clothed as well as naked—to an intensive gaze. Meribah Borden's testimony took courtroom listeners back to a room inside the Durfee's farmhouse on that December afternoon, a few hours after Cornell was found dead in the farm's stackyard.[1]

After lunchtime, six women had gathered to prepare Cornell's body for burial, just as the inquest jury was wrapping up its initial investigation. Older women, either married or widowed, connected by kinship and social ties, they knew that laying out a body for burial constituted the expected duties of females to their families and community. In traditional villages like Tiverton, women cared for individuals in childbirth, sickness, and death. They practiced this kind of "domestic medicine" when midwives far outnumbered physicians in farm communities. Back in their youth, nearly everyone in America entered and exited this world in the hands and arms of women like those who gathered at the Durfee farm.[2]

Theirs was not generic "women's work" but the labor of specialists. Neither of the two women who lived on the Durfee farm—Patience, wife of the owner Richard, and Nancy, their son John's wife—participated in this burial work. Instead, they called on experienced women who joined in a collective endeavor. Rarely saying "*I* laid out the body" or "*I* stripped off her clothes," Borden and the other burial women preferred descriptions like "I *assisted* in preparing the body for interment." Working with familiarly choreographed movements, experienced hands exhibited techniques for younger eyes—this was how knowledge and customs got passed down. Those taking the lead in undressing, cleaning, and preparing Cornell's body were in their sixties, referenced in the trial reports as "Mrs." or "Aunt" or "respectable matron." Meribah was sixty-four, her sister Hannah Wrightington sixty-eight. The youngest in the room was a thirty-six-year-old widow, Lusanna Borden, sister of John Durfee. She watched and learned but never touched the body.[3]

Meribah Borden was the most experienced, having, in her words, "assisted in laying out many corpses before." She'd even once before seen the corpse of a man who had hanged himself, but a body like Cornell's, "that died by violence," was a sight she'd never seen. When they entered the farmhouse room they saw Cornell's dead body on its back, frozen in the position in which John Durfee first found Cornell at the haystack—legs bent at the knees, right arm raised and bent, with the palm forward as if waving hello or repelling something or someone pressing too close.[4]

They began by removing her garments, knowing their final objective was to clothe her in a clean dress before laying her to rest. As they turned her on her side—Meribah thought she'd "never felt a corpse so cold"—they began to see and react to marks they observed on her flesh. They heated water and applied warm cloths to unfreeze her legs and straighten them. Because Cornell's arm was bent upward from the elbow, they applied hot cloths and tried repeatedly and unsuccessfully to massage her frozen limb to make it lie flat at her side. Two of them held tightly to her arm while Mrs. Dorcas Ford, in her late forties, tried to bend the hand and elbow back into their natural resting positions, to no avail. Some tried to wash grass stains from her knees, also to no avail, while others examined her clothing, discovering feces smashed against her undergarments.[5]

Although Cornell was a stranger to them, they performed the rituals as if she had been their long-standing neighbor or cousin. A personal intimacy of touch guided burial rituals, just as it did early American women's healing and pain-relief practices, especially during childbirth.

Of all the people who first examined Cornell's corpse, the women alone saw her body without clothing. The coroner's jury examined the corpse fully clothed, more interested in the rope and the appearance of her neck than evidence of possible violence elsewhere on her body. Days later, during the first autopsy, the examining physicians left a cloth, about one square yard in area, over Cornell's lower abdomen because members of the coroner's jury objected to its removal, but such modesty was also physicians' common practice at that time when examining women's bodies. None of these men bothered to examine her pelvic area or genitals, despite knowing that she was pregnant and that she had confessed that the man suspected of fathering the child had previously encouraged her to attempt a medicinal abortion. One might expect the doctors, if not the laymen, to question whether another attempt at an abortion might have preceded her violent murder.[6]

The women talked to one another while doing their work. As they washed and handled her corpse, they tried to surmise what might have happened to this young woman. Stories were indispensable to the practice of medicine, as they were to the practice of law. In this setting storytelling passed along traditional knowledge while forging neighborly intimacy.

The stories that women told, though, differed from those spoken by male physicians, and the authority of each remained unsettled. Conversations among women were, in fact, what some folks had feared about midwives for centuries, associating women's healing practices with gossip. Midwives, many felt, were dangerous because of their supposed penchant for loose talk.[7]

When they were asked to retell their stories in a courtroom, the burial women's observations and conversations grew more important in a contest over truth-telling. At the pre-trial hearing at Bristol in January, Meribah and the others were examined in the judges' private quarters, but at Avery's trial in Newport they had to testify in public. Intimate and personal talk from inside a home was forced into public view, leaving them vulnerable to the whims of propriety.

All ears and eyes in the crowded Newport courtroom fixed on Meribah Borden.

"There were very bad bruises down her back," she told the prosecutors, describing the marks she saw throughout Cornell's pelvic area. "Very bad marks," she repeated for emphasis.

"Tell us more about what you saw," Attorney General Greene likely asked each of the four women witnesses, eager for their skillful observations.

"On both sides of her abdomen, low down," they all answered with remarkable consistency, "there was an appearance of a person's hands . . . prints of fingers on both her sides . . . the marks were plain enough to distinguish the fingers and thumbs . . . the thumbs forward, as if she had been grabbed," with the worst marks on the back of her right hip.[8]

"My sister, Hannah Wrightington, applied her hand to the place where there were marks of fingers," Meribah Borden testified, and she too confirmed that the bruises were the size and shape of human hands. "Mrs. Dorcas Ford," she continued, "tried her fingers and said hers would not fay (fit) as aunt Hannah's did."[9]

"I cannot show it on myself," Mrs. Ruth Borden explained, when asked to demonstrate the hand marks, and Mrs. Ruth Cook concurred, stating, "I cannot put them on myself," they "must have been done by some person's hands besides her own." The attorney general then stood for Meribah Borden to demonstrate on his torso, and requested other men to stand for Ruth Borden and Dorcas Ford to demonstrate. Women touching men of authority in this manner did not escape the notice of the packed courtroom.[10]

But discomfort for the female witnesses and courthouse audience had only just begun. The women went on to describe how the entirety of Cornell's lower torso, include her genitals and thighs were "all over a bruise," very dark and black, "not a white spot to be seen."[11]

When Hannah Wrightington saw this as she undressed the body, she lifted up her hands and exclaimed, "Oh, Mrs. Ford, what has been done?"

"Rash violence," was Dorcas's reply.[12]

How exactly these women spoke in public about another woman's genitals can't be reconstructed because even the reporters who recorded their testimony seemed squeamish. Did these women resort to the euphemisms that the newspapermen preferred, like "part of the body" or "her privates" or "her secret," or did they actually speak in more textbook terms, like "pudenda" or "pubis," which reporters also used? Attorneys on both sides knew that in questioning the women closely they were pushing the limits of modesty and propriety that so clearly defined what it meant to be a respectable woman.[13]

Together the burial women came to suspect that Cornell had been abused by someone on the night of her death, but they remained uncertain about the exact nature of that abuse, or what exactly the bruises indicated. In Luke Drury's account of the January pretrial hearing, Dorcas Ford reportedly stated that she thought Cornell "had been very much *abused*" and she didn't mean "attempts to procure abortion, but *violated*." Meribah Borden supposedly agreed that she had "been abused," while Ruth Borden claimed she hadn't formed an opinion, "whether ravished or attempts at abortion."[14]

During cross-examination at the trial, Avery's attorneys pressed to get the women to repeat their speculation that these marks of violence indicated evidence of rape. By suggesting that Cornell had been raped right before her death, the defense hoped to loosen the grip of the prosecution's story about

Avery's motive. After all, Avery had no clear motive for rape compared to his incentive for forcing Cornell to abort in order to prevent exposure of an extramarital liaison and pregnancy. If Cornell died following a rape or attempted rape, then perhaps another man with a different motive might have committed the crime.

Richard Randolph turned up the pressure, starting with Meribah Borden: "Did you not previously say she had been forced?"

"No, that question was not asked me at Bristol," she replied, contradicting the veracity of Drury's report. "I said at Bristol that I thought very harsh means had been used upon her," Borden continued, but she hadn't reached an opinion about rape. "She looked as if she had been shamefully abused. Whether he had done it, or any other man, or what means were taken, it is not for me to say."

Randolph continued to push, in the words of one reporter, "further than was consistent with the lady's ideas of propriety." Meribah finally retorted, "I never heard no such questions asked by no person," abruptly bringing her cross-examination to an end.[15]

Randolph pressed again when cross-examining Dorcas Ford. "Did you give your opinion at Bristol you thought she had been violated?"

"I said she had been dreadfully abused, and I think so still," she said.

Every time Randolph rephrased the question to try to get Ford to say that she thought there was evidence of a rape, she held firm, answering, "I think she was dreadfully abused."

Randolph pleaded with prosecutors to try to get this recalcitrant witness to answer. Greene, Pearce, and the chief justice all posed the same question, and all got the same reply. Eventually asked whether she thought "there had been an attempt by any man at violent connection," Ford replied, "I supposed her life was forced from her, and you must judge in what way yourselves." Digging in, she stated, "I shall give no other answer than I have."

These women had surely internalized the powerful reticence that women of their era felt about making rape accusations—unlikely to be believed, unlikely to bring about prosecution, more likely to bring shame and ruin on female accusers than the men. Randolph finally concluded that he had only two options: move to commit Ford to jail for contempt of court or let her go. "As she is a woman," Randolph decided, "I prefer the latter."[16]

The coroner's jury had left the Durfee's farmhouse early that December afternoon, hours before the women completed their pre-burial labor. No one waited to ask these women what they discovered. Their work and their observations weren't considered germane for the inquest jurors' decision making. Yet the women's observations and stories didn't remain hidden forever. Dorcas Ford, after all, was married to a member of the Fall River Committee; Meribah Borden was mother-in-law to steamboat engineer John Orswell; and Lusanna Borden was John Durfee's sister. Nor would it be long before the competency of medical men would also be brought into question.

Early Americans held no assumptions about the professional medical expertise of coroners when Elihu Hicks took the stand for the prosecution. The seventy-three-year-old Hicks was not a physician; back then coroners seldom were. They were minor officeholders, likely to be also the local fence viewer or fish warden. Coroner jury customs placed full responsibility for determining the causes of death in the hands of ordinary white men, who could call on physicians for assistance if they wished, though they rarely did so. Into the nineteenth century, ordinary folk were still thought to possess the common sense, practical medical knowledge, and observational skills commensurate with those of an educated physician, adequate, therefore, to discern the cause of death. Once Hicks swore in the inquest jury and gave them their instructions, he never again laid eyes on the deceased's body.[17]

At Newport, Elihu Hicks offered a bungling explanation for why there had been two different inquests and coroner's jury verdicts. Everyone in the courtroom quickly realized how "very irregular" the coroner's actions had been. Everyone, that is, except for Hicks, whom observers described as a difficult witness, "being an old man of irritable temperament and rather deaf." The coroner's testimony embarrassed the prosecution, who had to admit that an initial coroner's jury had ruled Cornell's death a suicide and that it fell to a second inquest jury to point toward homicide. As Hicks squirmed to present consistent answers, Avery repeatedly smiled. His supporters were also buoyed; they believed that Tiverton and Fall River residents had conspired from the beginning to persecute an innocent man.[18]

Following the coroner's confusing testimony, the strapping and youthful Dr. Foster Hooper stepped up as the prosecution's next witness. Although Dr. Wilbur's junior, Hooper had taken the lead at the Monday morning autopsy back in December, and at the Newport courthouse he spoke with unwavering confidence, hardly pausing to take a breath. Younger than both Avery and Cornell, the twenty-eight-year-old doctor, a medical school graduate at the University of Vermont, aspired to be a man of importance in the mill town. Beyond his medical practice, Hooper had already been elected to the state legislature, appointed to numerous civic offices, and chosen for the Fall River Committee.[19]

"The indentation passed round the neck above the thyroid cartilage and the spinous process of the second vertebra," Hooper declared, trying hard to sound like a man of science after the coroner's botched testimony.

Together, the two doctors measured how deep a mark the rope had left, Hooper explained, noting that it was drawn in a straight horizontal line across Cornell's unbroken neck. They observed bruises, scrapes, and grass stains on her legs, and an indentation (but no bruises) where her face had pressed against the stake. Hooper described Cornell's face as pale, which he thought was unusual for a person who had been hanged. The doctors then removed a fetus from her uterus, he recounted, measured it as eight inches long, and determined that the sex was female. The physicians came away convinced that Cornell died by the violent act of another, and the official (second) verdict of the coroner's jury agreed. Even at this point, none of the men looked under the cloth that the burial women had placed over Cornell's lap.

Thirty-six days later, on January 26, Drs. Wilbur and Hooper conducted a second autopsy. It was the day after Avery was imprisoned in Newport, following his capture, and the prosecution wanted Cornell's body exhumed again. "The principal object of the second examination," Hooper told the courtroom, "was to ascertain if the rumor was true that her arm was broken."[20]

Hooper was not being fully honest here. By January 26, prosecutors and their Fall River allies knew what the burial women had described at Bristol, so Hooper's and Wilbur's three-hour-long autopsy—it took only minutes to determine that her arm wasn't broken—focused on gathering evidence about Cornell's pelvic and genital areas, which they had not bothered to examine during the first autopsy. Now Hooper could testify to bruises on her hips, back, and groin.

They examined the vagina, cervix, and uterus, which were black as if the result of contusions. Her cervix was open. At this point, Hooper and Wilbur tried the test of washing. In their medical judgment this was the best method to determine if dark spots on human tissue were from bruises or from post-mortem pooling of blood. Since the samples washed clean, both were convinced that what looked like black marks were in fact bruises on her torso and legs, as well as on her vagina and uterus.

Richard Randolph probably began asking his first cross-examination question before he had fully risen to his feet. "What is the circumference of a woman's neck in health?" he asked. It was a preposterous question, akin to, "What's a healthy woman's waist size?" Yet it accomplished his principal objective—to get the doctor's first answer to be "I do not know" (even though Hooper correctly noted that "it depends on the size of the person"). Randolph exposed cracks in the veneer of Hooper's professional confidence. "I never examined any one before who died from hanging," the doctor had to admit; "my impressions are founded on what I have read ."[21]

"Can you tell the precise age of a fetus from its length?" Randolph asked.

"I do not know that I can." Hooper replied.

"You were brought here as a scientific witness, and I should think you ought to know."

"I certainly do not know from my own observation. If you wish me to give the conclusions I arrive at from medical books, I can state that according to Monsieur Béclard, a fetus would be eight inches long in four months."[22]

As a man of science, Hooper felt obligated to be precise, follow the evidence, and express only what could be safely diagnosed from research and prior knowledge. When it came to his conclusion as to whether someone had inserted "a hard substance" into the deceased's vagina and uterus to try to cause an abortion, what observers reported hearing in the courtroom varied. Trial reporters who leaned toward Avery's guilt included both Hooper's statement, "I can draw no strong conclusion" from the fact that her cervix was open and the vagina and uterus blackened, *and* his opinion that the testing by washing proved that these were bruises "produced by contact with some hard substance." Reporters who favored Avery printed only Hooper's admission, "I can draw no strong conclusion."[23]

Lines of combat had been drawn over what Cornell's dead body revealed and who was qualified to be a competent observer and interpreter of that body. The trial's key medical disputes would center on conflicting interpretations over whether the corpse exhibited evidence of external violence, attempted abortion, or death by strangulation rather than hanging, and over a precise date of conception for a fetus. Before the trial concluded, witnesses would also have something to say about Cornell's menstruation, her breasts, and even her sanity.

Thomas Wilbur, a slender soft-spoken Quaker physician, contrasted sharply with the brash Hooper. As he took the stand, the attorney general requested another sidebar. He wished to ask what Cornell had told Dr. Wilbur concerning the father of her child, and he expected the defense's vigorous objection. Beyond the jurors' ears, the attorneys and justices argued over the admissibility of this evidence. Greene insisted that he wasn't trying to present Cornell's statement as proof that the person she charged was actually the father, but just to introduce the fact that "she did make known her situation" and that "she did name a certain individual as the cause of her situation." Randolph insisted that "by no rule of law could such evidence be admitted. These conversations were not dying declarations; they were not made under oath. Her declarations must die with her." The court adjourned for the night. When they returned the next morning, Greene withdrew his question for the present, permitting the cross-examination to begin after Wilbur succinctly corroborated Hooper's testimony.[24]

Wilbur was a difficult witness to crack, even more so because of his quiet and empathetic manner. Randolph's intent of casting doubt on the Fall River doctors' medical acumen and expertise didn't work with Wilbur as it had with Hooper. Avery's counsel repeatedly posed one wrongheaded question after another. Might Cornell, with sufficient resolve, Randolph asked, "have drawn a common slip noose as tight as this was?" (Jurors well knew that she hadn't been hanged by a slip knot or a noose.)

"I should think not," Dr. Wilbur said. "A person would have ceased breathing before they could draw it thus tight." It was as if Randolph was willing to ask a medical expert if a person could at the same time strangle herself and hang herself to a stake, and the doctor shut that door convincingly.[25]

Randolph then gave Wilbur the opportunity to describe what facts had convinced him there had been a violent homicide—the tightness and horizontal indentation of the rope, contusions on Cornell's hips, bruises and scratches on her knees (the ground where her broken hairclip was found, he reminded his listeners, was stony and full of bushes and briars). Although Wilbur never had to say so directly, all of this evidence confirmed that a struggle had taken place. "As I stated before," Wilbur continued, "I have tried since the examination to persuade myself that it was not violence. But I cannot account for it in any other way."[26]

This was not the answer the defense counsel had hoped for. One reporter characterized Randolph's failed line of cross-examination as at best "a multitude of unimportant questions." He couldn't even ambush Wilbur with the question about the usual circumference of a woman's neck. "I measured several females in my family, including my wife," the doctor stated, and healthy females about Cornell's age and size would likely have a neck size from 12½ to 13½ inches.[27]

Day after day, the medical testimony of burial women and local doctors cast a pall over the courthouse, as if to match what one reporter described as the year's "unusually cold" springtime in Newport.[28]

But as Avery's defense team began their full-frontal assault on the women who testified about Cornell's dead body, everything started to heat up inside the courtroom. The women's opinions had been ignored initially by the coroner's jury and the autopsy-performing physicians at Durfee's farm—they had been almost an afterthought at the preliminary hearing in January. Suddenly, they became a central target of Avery's defense.

16

Experts

THE DEFENSE OPENED ITS CASE on the trial's tenth day, Thursday, May 16, calling as their first witnesses five prominent New England physicians, whose sole purpose was to criticize the testimony of the women who had laid out the body and question the procedures and conclusions of Drs. Hooper and Wilbur. Randolph wasted no time in posing his questions.

"Are the dark appearances about the pelvis of the deceased, described by the women who laid out the body, to be expected in a body hung and remaining suspended for 14 to 18 hours?" he asked sixty-two-year-old Dr. Nathaniel Miller, who had been practicing medicine since 1792.

"Yes." Dr. Miller answered.

"Are the women competent to judge whether the marks they saw were appearances of violence, or arising from death by suicide?" Mason asked next.

"I object!" Greene interjected.

Before the justices could sustain the objection, Dr. Miller told the court, "I should suppose that females examining a body may be perfectly competent to describe the marks, but in my opinion women are not good judges of the causes of such marks of supposed violence."[1]

When Dr. William Turner, a physician and surgeon in the US Army for thirty-eight years, testified that afternoon, he too took a jab at the women, stating that dark and livid appearances were very common around the genitals in dead bodies, "and may be mistaken by ignorant persons for bruises."

Dr. Usher Parsons from Providence likewise stated that such dark marks "are often mistaken for bruises by unskillful persons."[2]

Randolph had prepared the jury for this line of attack during his opening remarks for the defense. "Doubtless," he had told them, "the old women of Tiverton . . . actually saw what they thought were bruises," but "inexperienced persons" could easily mistake blood settling in the body for bruises. He also derided "these things the old women called prints of fingers."[3]

More was at stake here than the reliability of certain witnesses. Part of the trial's drama hung upon questions of who possessed the authority to make trustworthy observations and arrive at valid conclusions. This was ultimately a question of democracy—the era's defining principle—made manifest in a conflict between ordinary people and a new professional class. At the time, notions of medical expertise and professional standing stood on precarious footing.

During the preceding Enlightenment-influenced decades, general thinkers and scientists, lay persons and professionals alike, turned to observation, especially visual observation, to arrive at authoritative knowledge. Yet at Avery's trial, professionals like doctors and lawyers remained skeptical, if not downright hostile, to ordinary people's abilities to observe and make judgments, whether about medicine or the law. Lay witnesses were brought into the courtroom and asked to testify about what they saw but told not to give their opinion about the meaning of what they saw. Doctors were asked not only to explain what they observed, but also to judge the observational and interpretation skills of other witnesses.[4]

The gender of an observer was critical. The women in Durfee's farmhouse had no doubts that they had seen recognizable bruises all over Cornell's body. "They looked like bruised flesh, like a person that was bruised," Ruth Cook testified. "They looked black and blue," she continued. "I can state it to the jury. I don't know that I can state it any more. It was bruised flesh." The bruises they saw not only resembled but matched exactly the marks of hands and fingers. These women tried to show the court the kinds of everyday, trustworthy observations that derived from their intimacy with the bodies of neighbors and loved ones.[5]

Despite the defense's efforts to disparage these women's post-mortem discoveries, the women were as keen in their observational skills as the male physicians who conducted the autopsies and even more astute than the farmers who served on the coroner's jury. Meribah Borden's testimony at the pre-trial hearing, summarized as "one of the knees a little darkish colored, a little green; face lightish; neck and arms not black; blood did not appear to have settled in the arms and neck . . . lips very dark; tongue catched between her teeth; not out of her mouth . . ." read as remarkably similar to the summary testimonies of Drs. Hooper and Wilbur.[6]

It was crucial for the defense to undermine the women's testimony. "It is common for persons, after death, to exhibit dark appearances about the privates," Dr. Nathaniel Miller declared. "It is ordinary." He further suggested that the women knew little about the condition of corpses. "Inexperienced people," he stated, "cannot form any correct judgment from such appearances on the body." Inexperienced? It was not clear who had seen more dead bodies in their lifetimes of sixty-plus years—Meribah Borden or Dr. Miller. Nor was it certain that the doctor had seen more deaths from hanging. Miller said that he'd seen only one or two, while the other doctors were no more experienced. Dr. Jabez Holmes had never seen a dead body from a hanging; neither had Dr. William Turner, a surgeon with nearly four decades service in the military. Dr. Usher Parsons had seen only one. Only Dr. Theophilus C. Dunn had observed more, having seen three corpses from hangings.[7]

This didn't stop the doctors from offering authoritative answers and unequivocal judgments about the ways the human body reacted to hanging or strangulation. These five physicians spoke in declarative sentences—"this appearance is very common" or "the reason for this is . . . " Often phrases like "I should think . . ." and "I should expect . . ." served as shorthand for definitive medical professional opinion. When Dr. Parsons declared that "the faces of persons hung are quite often pale as dark colored," listeners were expected to forget that he had just disclosed that he'd seen only one such person. Only during cross-examination—a good one hundred declarative sentences later—did Parsons again admit that his opinions were "founded on my reading and not upon observation, except in one case." The defense's expert witnesses—all male physicians—assumed that, if they had read it in a medical book, they were authorized to state scientific conclusions regarding any aspect of human anatomy, and in turn to discredit those who had merely observed human bodies in life and death.[8]

A medical profession's legitimacy is not natural; it has to be continually sustained and defended. Soon after the nation declared its independence, white male physicians in America wished to lay the foundation for their exclusive authority as a profession. This was not going to be an easy task. Old world traditions that had divided medical men into a three-tier hierarchy—physicians, surgeons, and druggists—never took hold. Americans just called all men who practiced medicine "doctors." Even more challenging, most healing work was in fact undertaken by women in the family or skilled midwives. Within an unregulated marketplace, most patients, rich or poor, turned to women and variously trained men for their medical care.[9]

If physicians hoped to maintain exclusive control of their occupation, they discovered that they would need to establish their own standards of education and certification and form professional societies to license practitioners. Physicians established the Massachusetts Medical Society in 1781 and the region's first medical school at Harvard the next year; by 1825 there were eight medical schools in New England. From the 1780s on, state after state passed laws declaring medical societies the only agencies that could certify and grant licenses to practice medicine, until by the 1820s more than half of the states had laws designed to restrict unlicensed doctors. These exclusionary efforts proved largely ineffective and short-lived. When Avery's trial began, even though elite physicians had for decades aspired to restrict access to their profession, democratic sentiments and alternative medical practices were pushing back. During the 1830s nearly every state began repealing their licensing laws, and regular physicians found themselves competing with other healers to provide health care services for most Americans.[10]

For more than a generation, male medical doctors also endeavored to supplant midwives as their communities' principal healers. They achieved some success by intervening as experts in childbirth, eventually asserting control of the new field of obstetrics, instituting specialized study at medical schools, and using more interventionist tools and drugs. Their new presence arose in part from patient choice—there was greater class status in calling a doctor—and from the willingness of women and midwives to invite male physicians into the traditionally all-female spaces of at-home childbirths. Not until the early twentieth century did the vast majority of women experience childbirth as a hospital-centered event attended by a male physician rather than at home under the care of a midwife and other women. But during the decades prior to Avery's trial, male physicians' role suddenly increased as the demand for paid women midwives declined. Male physicians conceived of their new interventions in childbirth as an important first step in a design to take charge of every aspect of health care.[11]

Since the investigation of Maria Cornell's body centered on sex and reproduction, it was no surprise that the defense turned to men who led this effort to supplant midwives. Walter Channing, Professor of Obstetrics and Medical Jurisprudence at Harvard, became the defense team's star medical witness. Dr. Channing was called on the defense's last day of witnesses, after the other five physicians had finished testifying. His testimony for three hours was one of the trial's longest. Like the other defense witnesses, he found not-so-subtle ways to demean the scientific knowledge of both the Tiverton women and the Fall River physicians.

"It is very common for dead bodies to exhibit dark appearances . . . about the lower parts of the abdomen," Channing stated, just as the person's back would be "discolored, dark, and livid" if laid down horizontally after a natural death. "I think they may be mistaken for bruises by people ignorant of such appearances."[12]

Attorney General Greene focused keenly on this point during cross-examination, asking, "Would women accustomed to lay out dead bodies be familiar with the external discoloration you have mentioned as being common?" he asked.

"I should think so."

"Would a person accustomed to laying out dead bodies be likely to mistake the ordinary appearances in death for bruises?"

"That would depend on their experience."

"Suppose them to be experienced."

"If they had laid out persons who had been hung, I should think they might judge."

"I do not speak of persons who have been hung. I ask whether females, having experience in laying out dead bodies, would be likely to mistake these discolorations, which you say always occur in natural death, for bruises?"

As Channing tried to dodge the question, Greene's frustration mounted. "But, Doctor, my question is simply this. You say that discolorations . . . are always found upon certain portions of the bodies of persons who die a natural death. Now I wish to know whether those who have been accustomed to laying out dead bodies . . . could mistake these marks for marks of violence?"

Twice more Channing tried to avoid the question, at which point the chief justice stepped in, admonishing Channing to answer the question. When Greene repeated it a fifth time, Channing at last admitted that experienced burial women wouldn't likely mistake common discoloration for bruises.[13]

Despite his weak refutation of the burial women's testimony, the mere presence of Channing, the leading figure in a generation-long assertion of male doctors' supremacy in obstetrics must have buoyed the professional aspirations of the other physicians participating in Avery's trial. It was Channing, after all, who penned the most emphatic statements that women should not practice medicine or be admitted to medical schools. In his *Remarks on the Employment of Females as Practitioners in Midwifery*

(1820), he wrote: "It is obvious that we cannot instruct women as we do men in the science of medicine," nor allow them in "the dissecting room and the hospital." The delicate feelings of women would be "destroyed" if they had to "submit to the sort of discipline required in the study of medicine." "Both the character and the education of women," Channing concluded, "disqualify them" from the practice of midwifery.[14]

Women healers were not the only targets of the Avery team's medical experts. They devoted even more time and energy to challenging the conclusions of Fall River's doctors. Randolph set the stage for this line of attack in his nearly four-hour opening statement for the defense, where he also referred dismissively to the "old women of Tiverton." Contempt dripped from his words as he repeatedly characterized Dr. Foster Hooper as "this *young* physician" and "a *young* and inexperienced man," at one point declaring "if he were older, his opinion would be worth more." Joining ageism with sexism, defense counsel conflated old women and young men as the type of "inexperienced persons" incapable of rendering valid medical judgments, especially compared with the "experienced Physicians" the defense had summoned as experts, "men of whose opinion the greatest dependence can be placed."[15]

Defense witnesses wasted no time assaulting the testimony of Fall River's young doctor. Dr. Nathaniel Miller had sat in the courtroom for the testimony of the Tiverton women and Drs. Hooper and Wilbur. Quickly dispatching the observational skills of the women, Dr. Miller proceeded to describe how Dr. Hooper conducted the autopsy.[16]

"This mode of examination is very incorrect," the chief justice interjected. The justices couldn't raise an objection, but they knew that it was highly unusual for the defense to rebut prosecution testimony rather than presenting their own case. The attorney general got the message and rose to object.

Chief Justice Eddy then instructed Randolph to ask questions about the facts and not about previous witnesses' testimony. "The witness has nothing to do with the testimony of Dr. Hooper. The question is, what is his own opinion as a scientific, a medical man, upon a supposed statement of facts." Yet everyone in the courtroom knew that the defense's medical witnesses were there to talk about the Fall River doctors, including Dr. Miller, who kept sliding into criticisms of Hooper and Wilbur's examinations, only to be warned again by the justices.[17]

Besides contending that what looked like bruises were likely natural occurrences, the defense's medical witnesses offered alternatives to the Fall River doctors' conclusions. They testified that the face of a person who had been hanged would commonly be pale, that hanging was a more common form of suicide than homicide, that a cord used for strangulation would leave another set of marks on the neck muscles that a proper dissection should discover, and that violent assaults were more likely to leave internal injuries than visible markings on the skin. Most important, they all stated repeatedly that no reliance could be placed on an autopsy conducted thirty-six days after a person's death—no evidence of bruises or violent force against the uterus could be determined after that length of time.

It would take superhuman strengths of concentration and analytical processing for jurors—especially when they weren't allowed to take notes—to follow all the intricacies of medical testimony over nearly two days. Reporters, who had all the paper and ink they desired, couldn't even record all the answers with precision. It couldn't have helped that physicians relied on a strange scientific language to bolster the impression of professional expertise. They spoke freely of ecchymosis and extravasation (rather than bruises), suggillation and cadaverous lividity (instead of the settling of blood), or catamenia (for a menstrual period).

Defense physicians and Fall River's doctors clashed most extensively regarding the age of the fetus. Maria told three people in whom she confided that Avery had impregnated her at a late August camp meeting. After her death, Drs. Hooper and Wilbur measured the fetus at eight inches long, weighing five ounces, with the sex identifiable only from minute examination.

Everyone in the courtroom understood the significance of the question: could a fetus of nearly four months be eight inches long? It was a crucial link in the prosecution's chain of evidence. If Maria's conversations with Dr. Wilbur were inadmissible as evidence, then maybe the fetus could point toward the fact of a camp meeting sexual encounter. Defense counsel were determined to cast doubt on this by making it a matter of medical expertise.

The defense's eminent physicians landed the blow that Avery's counsel had hoped for when Dr. William Turner stated most emphatically: "Ordinarily, I should think that a fetus would be eight inches after the fifth month. I should expect instances to be rare indeed of a fetus eight inches at three months and twenty days." Four of the five physicians made nearly identical statements. "We think the woman has not stated right," Dr. Miller pronounced during his cross-examination.[18]

But even if they succeeded in weakening the prosecution's case, in the process they also cast doubt on medical expertise itself. When asked to state the probable length a fetus might grow over sixteen weeks, their opinions varied wildly. Dr. Dunn estimated from three to four inches; Dr. Parsons thought four-and-a-half inches; Dr. Turner said five or six inches; and Dr. Miller varied his estimate throughout his testimony.[19]

This entire line of inquiry was riddled with problems that never occurred to the physicians or the attorneys. The defense's experts were citing averages from books that themselves recorded averages, ignoring the possibility of wide variations in length. What's more, researchers had measured miscarried fetuses, with no certainty when a fetus had stopped growing and hence its true age—unless, of course, they trusted the age estimates from the women who carried the fetuses. Yet in the dispute over the age of Cornell's fetus, medical professionals wanted any proof other than trusting the word of the woman who knew best.

The dispute came down to a contest between the authority of book knowledge and that of experience and observation. The physicians cited the books they had read: Béclard, Burns, Dewees, Gardien, Meckel, Chaussier, Carperon, and Beck. At the same time, they didn't want to appear as though they possessed no observational knowledge. Dr. Dunn insisted his opinion derived from "the experience I have, and the authorities I know." Yet no one asked these men how often they had measured miscarried fetuses or performed autopsies on women who died a few months into their pregnancy. Two of them had spent decades as Army and Navy surgeons—unlikely sites for such experience.[20]

When Walter Channing appeared on the last day of defense testimony, Avery's counsel hoped the nation's most renowned professor of obstetrics could seal their argument on the improbability that Avery had fathered Cornell's child at the August camp meeting. The attorney general, however, proved a match for the famous physician.

"Is there any subject," Greene pressed Dr. Channing, where there is greater disagreement and uncertainty among medical authors than "determining the precise age of a fetus by its length?" Channing insisted that the experts in his medical books agree within "a quarter of an inch to an inch." And yet he cited opinions as to the length of a four-month-old fetus that ranged between four and eight inches. Unflustered, Channing felt his profession's scientific integrity remained intact. Yet Greene was suggesting that medical men possessed no general agreement over facts and instead based their conclusions on their own opinions. Earlier, he had succeeded in getting Dr. Miller to admit that "authors differ in medicine as in law."[21]

Here was the rub: physicians aspired to appear in public as men of science who agreed on indisputable facts, unlike lawyers, who lobbed falsehoods and deceptions as they fought over subjective truth. Medical jurisprudence—the science that medical men practiced in courts of law—had come into vogue in the years prior to Avery's trial as a new field of specialization and a duty for physicians. Medical schools began offering regular coursework, beginning with Walter Channing's lectures on the subject at Harvard, and medical periodicals and textbooks, as well as law books, all emphasized that physicians should exert their influence in the courtroom.[22]

Avery's trial proved an important case for the brief flowering of professional medical jurisprudence in America. Where better to perform a new and uncertain professional identity. Yet if the medical witnesses for the defense succeeded in furthering the objectives of Avery's counsel—to confuse jurors and raise doubts about the certainty of a murder—they failed to establish the undisputed superiority of medical school-trained regular physicians as scientific experts in a court of law, or, for that matter, in the court of public opinion. When the attorney general asked, "Can the personal examination of medical men be relied on better than books?," he was insinuating that the prosecution's medical witnesses—Fall River's doctors—could be trusted more than the defense's venerable cast of medical experts.[23]

17

Doctor Visits

AFTER NINE STRAIGHT DAYS AND nights, confined with the same eleven men, jurors like the blacksmith Noah Barker and storekeeper James Easton doubtless replayed testimony in their minds while lying in bed at night, sleepless and homesick. They couldn't rely on their own notes. Instead, to decipher the facts in this trial, they had to make sense of the many stories they'd heard in the courtroom—accounts that directly clashed with one another and seemed to these jury men impossible to reconcile.

Over the previous two mornings, May 17 and 18, they had heard two very different tales of Cornell's visits to a doctor in Lowell.

At this stage in the trial, after the testimony of eminent physicians, the defense began building a case based on a different strategy: to exhibit the immoral behavior and character of Maria Cornell. As the jurors mulled over these two accounts of Maria's doctor visits—first from the doctor himself, then from a factory worker and friend who eerily conjured Maria Cornell's own voice and point of view—the jurors' heads must have ached from the discordant refrains. It was difficult to reconstruct these accounts of the same event without being unsettled and confused. If the jurors tossed and turned, recalling the stories they'd heard, surely they wondered what really happened.

§

Echoing in the minds of the jurors were the words, first of the doctor, then of Maria's factory companion, the witnesses' voices tumbling through their recollections, uninterrupted by the distracting clatter of attorneys' questions and cross-examination.

The Doctor: My name is William Graves. I reside in Lowell, Massachusetts, and I have practiced medicine for over twenty-five years. I presume that I have been acquainted with the deceased, Sarah M. Cornell, but she never applied to me under that name. A young woman calling herself Maria S. Cornell—I spelled her name Connell—called on me for medical advice on August 30, 1830. She arrived at my office after ten o'clock in the evening. She offered as an apology for coming so late that she came from the Methodist class meeting.

She was afflicted with a severe case of *lues venerea*, venereal disease, although not so bad as others I have seen. She called at my office seven times between August 30 and September 20. I furnished her with a prescription, but she was not cured.

When she visited my office the first time, she told me she belonged to the Methodist church. At the time I didn't believe her. Each time that she arrived late in the evening she offered the same excuse, stating that she had come directly from a Methodist meeting. She made a number of strange remarks, which led me to suspect . . .

What's that? You want just the facts, not my suspicions?

As I was saying, while I was mixing up her medicine, she made, I thought, some very strange observations. She felt compelled to tell me that the Methodists considered her a bright Christian, and that she could pray and preach as well as the best of them. These strange remarks led me to suspect that she was somewhat deranged.

At her second visit, she showed me a piece of paper, a recommendation from Rev. Avery to another Methodist church, or I presume it was from Mr. Avery. One time in my office she said "if brother Avery knew what my disease was, he would swear a little." She even said she would rather jump into the canal and drown herself than have him know about it. (Of course, this was just an expression; I never really thought it was her intention to drown herself.) She thought it best to continue in the Methodist church, attend all their prayer meetings and class meetings, because, as she said, if she appeared religious then no one would suspect her of being a bad girl.

At her first visit she asked about a young man, inquired if he was under my care. The young man had treated her improperly and deserted her, she said. Thinking that he was the cause of her malady, she wanted me to speak to him about paying her bills. The young man was not my patient. In later visits Connell also inquired about two other men.

You want me to name the men she asked about? May I ask the court to excuse me from revealing their names. All three men reside in Lowell. They are very respectable men, whose feelings might be wounded if I mention their names in this matter. . . . What? I must . . . then their names are . . .

She wanted me to keep the matter a secret. Due to her strange conversation, and her inquiries about different men, I thought it my duty to communicate all of this to Mr. Avery, despite my profession's rules of secrecy. I had a student at the time who was a Methodist, so I authorized him to inform Rev. Avery. Afterwards, after Connell had left Lowell, Ephraim Avery approached me and we conversed about her case.

The last time I saw her was at Mrs. Howe's boardinghouse where I had gone to treat another woman. Connell was there, and she seemed to be blaming Mr. Avery for turning her out of the church. She called him a rascal and a villain, and said he ought to be hung.

As to whether her conduct indicated anything about her sanity, the truth is my mind was not made up. I was almost inclined to think she was insane. Her language was so different from what I ever heard from a female. I hardly know what to think. I should not be willing to give it as my medical opinion that she was deranged.

When she first came in, she appeared very modest and appeared well. All at once she began to talk in a strange way. I began to suspect she was partially insane. She appeared well until the last time I saw her when she appeared to talk wild and seemed in a great passion. Whether it was passion or insanity, I cannot say.

No, I'm not assessing her sanity merely from the fact that she had such a disease and belonged to the Methodist church. I judged some from her appearance. She talked strange, I thought. It was certainly strange talk for a woman. I recollect nothing but the remark that she could out-pray and out-preach any of them. No, I do not consider that as conclusive evidence she was deranged. It is taken in combination with other circumstances. She kept getting up from her chair and sitting down again, and she took great pains in adjusting her bonnet and wore a handkerchief to conceal her face.

As for Mr. Avery's character as a moral and religious man, I presume it was good. I heard him generally well spoken of. I never prescribed for him for the bad disorder.[1]

A Factory Girl: Maria walked into my room one evening. Her eyes were red and moist as if she had recently wiped away tears. We had once been close, but that was five years ago when we worked together at Lowell. She was boarding at that time at Abraham Merrill's, the Methodist minister there. I suspect that at that time I was the most intimate friend she had.

This was the first quiet moment we'd had to talk since she arrived last week and came to my boardinghouse at Great Falls in New Hampshire. Surely she had a habit of telling stories, but no more than other girls. As she sat down to tell me her troubles, there was a knock at the door. A frightened look appeared in her eyes, and she became agitated. One of the other girls said there was a man at the door asking for Maria.

"Caroline, please go and see who that is for me," Maria said with alarm. She feared it was someone after her for an unfair debt from her time in Lowell. She seemed relieved when I returned to tell her it was the class-meeting leader from the Great Falls Methodist church. He wanted to speak with her about her application for membership.

But when she came back upstairs, her mood had once again changed. The class leader had told her that her name had been stricken from the church books. She threw her arms around my neck and wept so loudly they could hear her down two pairs of stairs.

Rumors about her misconduct in Lowell had followed her here. It was then that Maria confessed to me what had happened. She showed me a letter she had written to Rev. Avery confessing that she had been guilty of lying, fornication, and improper intimacies with men, which led him to expel her from the church. She admitted that she had lied to Avery about having lost her church certificate when she still had it. She used to visit a young man in his counting room in Lowell in the evening, she said, but she spoke of this as a courtship, which she expected would lead to marriage. She did not say that they were engaged, but she admitted improper conduct with him. They even rode out to a tavern in Belvidere one Sunday and passed as husband and wife. Now her reputation as a respectable woman was ruined. "It was all the fault of brother Avery and that old devil, Dr. Graves," Maria exclaimed.

Then she described to me her visits to Dr. Graves.

She had not been feeling well for several weeks when she decided to see a doctor. She took cold, she said, when she was at a camp meeting on Cape Cod in August, and this brought out her bad humors. She went to Dr. Graves to get some medicine for this. Her affliction, she recalled, was severely uncomfortable, making it painful to sit still for any length of time. (I thought about asking her why she had not visited Dr. Kimball, the physician at Appleton Corporation's factory, but after a moment, I reconsidered.)

She tried to see Dr. Graves after the factory bells signaled the end of her workday, but he asked her to return the next evening at ten o'clock. Once she entered his office, Graves locked the door behind her. Then he put his arm around her, kissed her, and told her she was a pretty girl. She hardly knew what to do, but resisted firmly:

"How dare you treat me so! I am a Methodist girl, and I belong to the church here."

The doctor laughed. Her declaration certainly couldn't be true, he thought, based on what he knew of her condition and her willingness to visit at this late hour. She tried to convince him that the Methodists recognized her as a woman with considerable spiritual talents, but to no avail.

She returned again the next day with a certificate of church membership, signed by Rev. Avery, to demonstrate her respectable character. Dr. Graves was not impressed. Again he put his arm around her waist, touched her cheek, and told her that she was a pretty girl. He told her that she did not have bad humors. "You have been intimate with a young man, Mr. W----," he said, "for he told me so himself, and you have got the foul disease." Graves then locked the door, and again expressed his desire for improper intercourse with her. Maria threatened to cry out, but he told her it was no use, no one would hear her or come to her assistance at that hour. If she complied with his wishes, he assured her he would treat her for no charge, but if she refused, he would inform the Methodist minister, Avery, that she had the bad disorder. Despite his designs, she told me, she got away from the old man without incident. Whether she ever received any proper medicine from Graves, I can't say. Maria insisted he had never cured her.

She described the bill for his medical services. Ten dollars! Even in the best of times, that's more than a half-month's wages for a weaver like Maria. She insisted that she didn't owe him more than a half-dollar and refused to pay. "I wouldn't pay the old devil one cent," she said. It was an unjust debt; he had not cured her.

Before she left Lowell, the doctor again demanded payment and now threatened to sue her. He even summoned the sheriff to find Maria and force her to pay. But she said, "Do you think I ain't cunning enough for that old fellow?" She dressed up in another girl's traveling bonnet and dress and walked about the streets of Lowell, passing Graves several times, but he never recognized her. While she boasted of her escape without paying, I could still see, that night in my room, that she remained anxious about these debts following her from Lowell.

Her character, she said, was once as blameless and unsullied as that of any person living, but her life was of no value now. She told me once that she went out in the evening to commit suicide, but her courage failed. When she spoke about the temptation to destroy herself, she looked so wild that I was quite alarmed. On other occasions, she would come into the mill, talk of her troubles, cry exceedingly, but then a moment later she could turn it off with a joke and a laugh.

In the end, Maria complained most about the doctor's unprofessional conduct and meddling talk. She had asked Graves to keep the matter a secret, but he chose instead to talk to other men about her. It's not right for a doctor to treat a patient with so little regard, she insisted, or to disclose her condition to others, including her minister, Rev. Avery. Maria declared she would be a member of the Methodist church in spite of Avery. I told her he would expose her wherever she went.[2]

§

These two courtroom tales from the witness stand—reflecting the accounts by Dr. Graves and Maria Cornell of their encounters in the doctor's office—are both illuminating and contradictory.

Maria Cornell never had the opportunity to tell her story directly. Her story came to life only through the memories and judgments of women like Caroline Tibbitts, who narrated this account for jurors in a Newport courtroom, a tale that veered between gossip and true crime, evoking both pathos and melodrama. Throughout Caroline's narration from the witness stand, the two women remained friends, yet also antagonists. Caroline's recollections of intimate confessions were interlaced with her recounting of Maria's "strange conduct." Jurors like Noah Barker and James Easton must have imagined Cornell's outlook as they mulled over the testimony of a "factory girl."

Concealed by darkness of night and obscured by a closed or locked door, what transpired in that doctor's office no other eyes witnessed. No one other than the doctor and the patient could corroborate how they behaved or the words that passed between them. And neither of them could foresee how consequential that occasion would be.

These two narratives offer an imagining of what was historically possible. Each story was originally told in specific locales and communities, became public in a courtroom, and entered the historical record. Both were gossip, and both storytellers were gossipers, but Graves's status as a professional man made it harder to recognize his words as such.[3]

Both tales were related by people whom literary critics describe as "unreliable narrators." Each is filled with details that make listeners or readers suspect misrepresentations and half-truths. Both storytellers strategically crafted their respective accounts by omitting key facts to mask other motives and hide self-serving interests. The doubts that these stories raised—why, for example, would Dr. Graves have any interest in sexual intercourse with a woman he knew to be afflicted with a sexually transmitted disease?—plagued jurors and the courtroom audience in Newport.

Jeremiah Mason took charge of questioning Dr. Graves as the defense changed its tack. Although he was the sixth physician in a row to be called to the stand as the defense opened its case, Graves was not there to comment on the medical evidence of autopsies, bruises, or fetal length. He was the lead witness for the next stage in Avery's defense, focused on the dead woman's reputation. Graves was followed by thirty-two witnesses—across four days of testimony—summoned to attest to their intimate knowledge of Cornell's disreputable character.

What Maria Cornell knew about the cause and effect between her sexual history and the illness she experienced in the summer of 1830 remains a mystery. Given the cloudy understanding and secrecy surrounding venereal disease, that's not surprising. Germ theory in medicine was still a half-century away. Physicians still thought, even into Cornell's lifetime, that gonorrhea and syphilis were two stages of one disease. It was still common to conceive of venereal disease as a "poison" that began in a woman's womb or a heated imbalance of the body's humors. Hence, Maria Cornell might very well have thought that she was experiencing a disruption of her humors while also fearing that something had gone wrong since her sexual liaison with a young man in Lowell.

Venereal disease had been understood for centuries as a sexual malady—one of the only diseases named for the sinful action that caused it. As the era's most popular book on home medicine put it, venereal disease was "generally the fruit of unlawful embraces." Prior to an understanding of bacteria and viruses, writers discussed it as resulting from the wrong kind of sex. Sometimes that meant too much sex, but most often it meant illicit sex, which meant sex outside of monogamous marriage. This intertwining of disease and sin meant that it always carried a stigma. Shame arose as well from the blame attached to "the pox"—every nation attributed it to their neighbors or enemies, giving it common names like the "French disease" or "Spanish Sickness," while Jews, women, and prostitutes were targeted for blame across many cultures.[4]

Regardless of what she knew ahead of time, Maria Cornell responded to a diagnosis of *lues venerea* as patients commonly did, demanding confidentiality and wishing for a healer of the same sex. Dr. Graves admitted that Cornell "begged me to keep her condition a secret." The doctor also observed that she took great pains to arrange her bonnet and a handkerchief to conceal her face, something he considered "strange" behavior. Yet this was precisely how patients asserted a measure of control over their diagnosis and treatment, including occasionally donning disguises, visiting doctors at unusual hours, and rejecting treatments that couldn't be concealed from housemates.[5]

Dr. Graves, like many others who treated venereal disease, didn't trust his patients or believe their stories. "I did not at the time believe she belonged to the Methodist church," Graves declared from the witness stand, thinking from her remarks that "she was a little crazy." Doctors instead took pride in displaying their superior diagnostic skills and moral judgment by detecting deceit, correctly observing bodies and behaviors, and evaluating their patients' characters. Physicians often resorted to painful treatments for venereal complaints (combining noxious mercury treatments with the bleeding and purges employed for many ailments); if they had any qualms, they could always reassure themselves that punitive therapies suited an immoral disease.[6]

Maria Cornell told Dr. Graves, and then later another physician, that she had "contracted the disorder from a young man" who had "treated her improperly." If she indeed believed that her illness was the product of a sexual liaison rather than bad humors or a cold from her trip to the Cape, as she told Caroline Tibbitts, her choice of treatment options was limited. (And by saying "taking cold," Maria employed a common euphemism for a woman missing her menstrual period. Whether Tibbitts understood that meaning is hard to say.)[7]

Even with fourteen licensed physicians in Lowell, Maria knew better than to seek the assistance of a doctor employed by the mills. She would certainly be dismissed immediately and blacklisted from all the town's factories. If she had known enough about alternative healers, like Lowell's three botanical doctors, their milder medicines might have appealed to her more than the "heroic" practices of regular physicians. Patent medicine sellers might have been another option; they advertised their elixirs and nostrums in Boston, Philadelphia, New York, and a handful of other cities, with promises of venereal cures. None of Lowell's druggists and booksellers, though, advertised for Swaim's Panacea or Dr. Relfe's Botanical Drops, sworn to cure "distressing, dangerous and inveterate Diseases" like "Venereal Taint." Regular physicians dismissed these products as medical quackery.[8]

Maria had heard something about Dr. Graves before heading off to see him late that night after a Methodist class meeting. Graves could have been known to be a specialist, or at least a doctor of first resort, for such treatment.

A whiff of the nefarious hung about Graves's medical practice. In the Newport courtroom, he spoke as if he had treated plenty of *lues venerea*, noting that Cornell's case was not as severe or advanced as others he'd seen. Although Graves tried to raise suspicions about Cornell's morals by alluding to her late-night visits—it wasn't easy for a Lowell factory worker to find the time to see a doctor, with long working hours and boardinghouse curfews—the doctor never explained why he was treating patients at his office at those hours. Perhaps Maria's claim that it was Graves who asked for the late-night appointments should be believed.

Dr. Graves also might not have been a reliable healer. It was not unusual for male physicians to misdiagnose women's urinary tract or vaginal infections, especially since nearly all the medical literature presumed that the venereal sufferer was male. Although both their stories were vague in details, Graves apparently prepared some medicines, a powder or pills of calomel (mercurous chloride) or injected a compound of zinc sulfate into Cornell's urethra. But both Cornell and Graves agreed that she was not cured after six visits. Dr. Noah Martin, who treated Maria after she had moved to Somersworth, New Hampshire, testified immediately after the Lowell doctor, stating that Cornell was familiar with the "instruments" used in treating this disease from her treatment by Graves (suggesting that both doctors used the same procedure, if not the same medicines). Dr. Martin reported confidently that, although Cornell's infection appeared to have been "long standing," he nonetheless believed that he cured her.[9]

If physicians liked to demonstrate their professional skills and superior morality by expressing skepticism about patients' stories and observing the outward signs of disease on the patient's body, making themselves out to be something akin to detectives, Graves was not very adept at this. He couldn't even recognize the obvious signs of physical discomfort that Cornell displayed. "She kept getting up and sitting down," and walking about the room, he observed, but not once did he attribute this to the itching and pain in her genitals that she must have been suffering from gonorrhea. Instead, the doctor attributed those bodily clues to strange behavior and possible insanity. Graves was no more perceptive than the class meeting leader at Lowell's Methodist church, who also recalled from the witness stand that he had observed Cornell as she came and went from the meeting house. "She appeared as though she could not walk regular nor stand still," he said. Like Graves he questioned her sanity. "She appeared as though she was not rational," he concluded.[10]

At Avery's trial, Graves spoke with the confidence of a self-made professional man. He expected that his word and opinion would be trusted over the claims of any "factory girls." Graves saw himself as an essential part of the "moral police" that guaranteed the economic success of America's largest industrial city. His story focused on sexual promiscuity, on the fear that women's economic freedom would lead to their sexual freedom, and on the blurred lines between religious and sexual passions. Three Lowell men—Maria's overseer at the mill, Dr. Graves, and Ephraim Avery—conjoined their tales of Maria's misconduct to remove the threat of an independent and sexually promiscuous single woman and to shore up their own status. Their tales reveal manly ambition, and those ambitions concealed the fact that rumors and gossip guided their public actions. Stripped of his professional status, Graves seems like a village gossip, tattling to one man after another, starting with the man that Cornell accused, then the doctor's students, then Avery, and eventually the defense attorneys, about the reputation of a sexually promiscuous woman.[11]

Maria Cornell implored Dr. Graves to keep her condition a secret, and she complained afterwards to her co-worker that Graves had "violated his professional confidence" and "done wrong by disclosing her case." Even

Graves admitted that his conduct was, at the least, suspect, that he had willfully disregarded "our rules of secrecy" when he communicated what he knew to Rev. Avery.[12]

With doctor-patient confidentiality yet to be fully established, physicians like William Graves prized professional conduct that maintained harmonious relationships with other men more than protecting patients' rights to privacy. The codes of ethics adopted by the Boston Medical Association in 1808, for example, prescribed privacy only in physicians' obligations to one another, declaring that disagreements in consultation with other doctors should be "held secret and confidential." Venereal specialists had for more than a century employed secrecy to protect first and foremost their practices and their male patients (it was common, for example, to keep a married man's diagnosis secret from his wife).[13]

Maria Cornell's version of her visits to William Graves's office, as told by Caroline Tibbitts, bore little resemblance to the doctor's tale. Indeed, her story sounded more like an account of attempted sexual assault than a medical appointment. She eluded the grasp of the doctor, who was elsewhere described as "an exceedingly corpulent man," topping the scales at over three hundred pounds.[14]

Women's stories of rape in early America often carried these elements of unequal status and authority that men exploited to conceal their unwanted advances or to invent fictions of consent. Cornell's story highlights the perils facing an independent working woman and the fragility of a woman's new assertions of freedom in industrial cities. Her story emphasized the vulnerability of women workers clinging to any degree of control over their own bodies and reputations. The men in her tale were no better than unreliable rakes and dishonest gossips, and the doctor was a disreputable man who could ruin a woman's reputation.[15]

It was Maria Cornell's reputation, not William Graves's, that was on trial in Newport, but in time, Graves became embroiled in a scandal of his own. Neither Avery nor Graves could have fathomed when they met in 1830 to talk about Cornell's sexual sins that both would one day face trials for capital crimes. Yet within a few years, Graves was indicted and tried for murder after a woman died from an abortion he performed. In 1837, Mrs. Mary Ann Wilson, a widow with two young children who had been impregnated by an irresponsible younger man, traveled forty miles from rural New Hampshire to Lowell to solicit Graves's services. She died from complications after a three-week stay. Folks throughout the region were clearly aware of Graves's services in treating the consequences of illicit sex. Wilson told her hometown doctor that she planned to go to Lowell because she had heard "there was a physician there who would perform this operation with safety."[16]

Americans in the early nineteenth century believed that it was neither morally wrong nor a crime to end a pregnancy before the onset of quickening, which usually occurred midway through. They did not use the term abortion (speaking instead of the return of a woman's menstrual cycle) for folk or medical procedures employed before quickening. But because Wilson was thought to have passed the onset of quickening, Graves was charged with Wilson's murder.[17]

Graves's murder trial reprised some the features of Cornell and Avery's trial, with its autopsies and disputes over the suspected age of a fetus. Ironically, a jury acquitted Graves after his defense attorney argued that it was Graves's principled commitment to privacy and protecting his patients from shame, rather than a desire to hide his criminal conduct, that explained why he had falsified the details of Wilson's death. What would Maria Cornell have thought when William Graves was lauded for his benevolent commitment to confidentiality?[18]

"We have been enveloped in fog here" for days on end, Benjamin Hallett reported from Newport at the end of the Avery trial's long second week. The conditions outside, he wrote, seemed "to sympathize with the mistiness of the testimony" inside the courtroom. "We see as it were, through a glass darkly," he mused. Although barred from reading any newspapers, the jurors must have surely felt the same way as they tried to make sense of the two conflicting accounts they heard of a young woman's doctor visits. At the same time, they sensed the visits' importance.[19]

Maria Cornell's encounter with Dr. William Graves marked a pivotal moment in an unfolding personal crisis. Without this visit to Dr. Graves, the spiral of successive events that led Maria to an ill-fated camp meeting in the Connecticut woods, and eventually to a haystack outside a factory village, might well have turned out differently. For jurors in Newport, these events materialized through the voices of a wide array of gossips, starting with Dr. Graves.

18

Sex Talk

ELIZABETH SHUMWAY KNEW MARIA CORNELL before Maria moved to Lowell, when they had worked side by side as weavers in the Slatersville factory. Seven years later, Avery's defense attorneys summoned the twenty-four-year-old Elizabeth, married and a new mother, to take the stand as they tacked toward a bold new strategy.[1]

Nearing the end of its second week, the trial had already extended longer by far than any case in memory. "The trial of Mr. Avery 'drags its slow length along,'" a reporter noted, "and we cannot yet even begin to look at the end." That didn't stop the Newport courthouse from being packed with spectators every day.[2]

For the next two and a half days, Avery's attorneys called thirty-three witnesses to tell tales of every odd or morally questionable interaction they had ever had with Maria Cornell, including every promiscuous conversation overheard during the past decade. A darker biography of Cornell began to take shape in the alternating hands of Avery's counselors, Richard Randolph and Jeremiah Mason, as they questioned a band of memorable characters—doctors, clergymen, tavernkeepers, boardinghouse matrons, and a score of "factory girls"— summoned to attest to their intimate knowledge of Cornell's disreputable character.

Rather than punching holes in the prosecution's evidence about the young factory worker's violent death, the defense shifted direction to put Maria Cornell's moral character on trial. Courtroom observers perceived the trial's dramatic new turn, with one reporter headlining his account,

"TESTIMONY AS TO THE CHARACTER AND INSANITY OF THE DECEASED." Catharine Williams, in her true-crime narrative of the scandal, would refer to the proceedings as "the famous trial of S. M. Cornell, denominated on the title page, 'Trial of E.K. Avery.'"[3]

Elizabeth Shumway's testimony began with a distinct memory of Maria sitting at the window of their boardinghouse, looking out upon the water. Shumway then startled her listeners. "It was pleasant to see it," Maria had said then. "I asked why. She said she wanted to be at the bottom of it."

"Why?" Shumway asked again.

"Because I have been disappointed in marriage," Maria answered.

Shumway then dropped a gossip's bombshell. During their conversations, Maria had admitted to Elizabeth that Grindal Rawson, her sister's husband, "had courted her," adding that "her sister got him away from her by her cunning." But, Maria said, "I have one thing to comfort me. He likes me best now. For he told me himself, and my sister is jealous."

"Why?" Shumway asked a third time.

"Because Grindal and I have been as intimate as husband and wife."[4]

Shumway's story was a veritable godsend for Avery's defense, whose strategy would be adopted by attorneys and accepted by courts for the next century and a half: redirect the attention of a sex crime trial onto the sexual behavior and morality of the female victim, making the character of the woman, not the actions of the man, the key to a verdict. In her brief moment on the stand in Newport, Shumway's tale left the jury with the impression that Maria was suicidal, promiscuous, and a home-wrecker all at once. Although the Rawsons cooperated with the prosecution and testified on consecutive days during the trial's second week, it's unlikely that Maria's family was in the courtroom when Shumway gave her testimony.[5]

New factory towns were bound together by gossip, rumors, and other kinds of storytelling that always involved assessments of character, especially the character of women who worked in those factories. The long queue of defense witnesses at Avery's trial retold boardinghouse tales they had heard and repeated for years. Trial reporter Benjamin Hallett quipped that tales from "half the factory villages in New England" were recited "with exceeding minuteness of detail, and great vivacity of imagination," unveiling sagas of love, devotion, and profanity for curious courtroom audiences.[6]

The court itself was certainly aware that the tenor of the trial had changed. By the third day of this testimony, when Abby Hathaway, a mill worker who briefly knew Cornell after she had fled Providence, began describing what she knew about Cornell's mother, sister, wardrobe, and name changes, the chief justice blurted out that Hathaway's account was "all hear-say." Justice Eddy may have been thinking of the technical legal meaning of the term—that the witness was repeating words she had heard secondhand—but he also meant that the testimony derived from gossip and rumors rather than firsthand observation. Avery's attorneys nonetheless continued to press:

"What was her general character?" Randolph asked.

"Her conduct and conversation was very unbecoming a person of respectability," Hathaway said.

"O! that won't do," the attorney general interrupted. "Do you, of your own knowledge, know anything of her conduct?"

"I do; her conduct was very improper."

"As what?"

"She had very improper conduct with young men who came to the house."

"Do you mean to say you know of any criminal act of hers?"

"No, I do not."

"Did you hear her admit she had been guilty of improper conduct with any young man?"

"I never did."

"Did you see her, on any occasion, guilty of improper conduct at your house?" Randolph asked, knowing that Cornell had boarded with Hathaway.

"Yes, sir."

"What was it?"

"She appeared very intimate with a young gentleman who called one day, and put her arm round his neck."

Such an observation was hardly damning; it was not even revealing as to Cornell's sex life, especially after the witness admitted that the young man was a respectable resident of the same boardinghouse, and that she'd never witnessed Cornell with any other men. But it was enough for the defense's purposes.[7]

Testimony based on impressions and imaginings from gossips-turned-witnesses make it difficult to discern Maria's actual choices regarding love and sex. Maria wrote nothing about her romantic relationships in her letters to her family, nothing about her hopes or her disappointments within the marketplace of love, sex, and marriage. Her letters chronicle only a story of God's love and Maria's affection for her savior and her spiritual family. Yet there's no doubt that Maria was a sexually active woman in a society that frowned on women's premarital sexual activity.

Even if witnesses clouded jurors' minds with vague imaginings of Maria's illicit affairs, they still left behind hints about what was at stake in the sex life and reputation of America's most notorious "factory girl." The stories of love and lust that these witnesses told one another in their mill town gossip networks were all part of the changing world of romance and sex during Maria's lifetime.

As sex talk moved from the boardinghouse into the courtroom, as it passed from private to public, prevailing customs of taste and manners cloaked it in modesty, ignorance, and prudery. Numerous women, and some men too, became noticeably uncomfortable in court. Avery's attorneys called Patty Bacon, a forty-five-year-old mother of nine, expecting her to testify that she'd seen Maria Cornell undress at the Thompson camp meeting and that Maria's breasts suggested she might already be pregnant (if true, Avery had not fathered her child there). At the camp meeting Bacon had apparently said of Cornell that "she was a married woman or ought to be." But on the stand, Bacon refused to describe anything more than the appearance of Maria's face, no matter how hard the attorneys pressed.

"I only want you to describe what you saw," Randolph prodded.

"I can't tell you any more," Bacon replied.

"Is it worthwhile to press her any further?" asked the chief justice.

"Was there any unusual prominence?" Randolph blurted out.

"Oh! Mr. Randolph, don't!" the attorney general pleaded.

"I wish you to describe just how she appeared to you," Randolph tried again.

"I have told you, I think, two or three times. Her countenance was sickly and pale."

Attorney General Greene pressed his advantage. Did the witness "feel authorized" to conclude that Cornell was pregnant "from a pale countenance and dull eyes, and not seeming well?"

Bacon finally gave in, admitting, "Her bosoms appeared rather full."

"Do you know at what time that appearance takes place in a female in that situation?" Greene continued.

"I have said all I have got to say. I don't know that her bosoms were fuller than usual."

"Then her bosoms were not full."

"I have said all I have got to say."[8]

Stories about Maria's promiscuity could also be contradictory, even misleading. Zilpha Bruce, who knew Maria during her earliest years as a factory worker, couldn't even decipher the import of the attorneys' questions.

"What was her character for chastity?" Richard Randolph asked.

"Her character was not good, she was tattling," Bruce replied.

"But what was her character for chastity?"

"She was a young woman unstable in her ways."

"Don't you know what chastity means?" asked the chief justice.

"I don't know what you mean."

Randolph finally restated his question. "Was her reputation that of keeping company with loose young men?"

"Yes, it was."[9]

Sex talk at the trial also slipped into the realm of the fantastic. The most outlandish tale came from the testimonies of Ezra and Ruhanah Parker, tavernkeepers from Connecticut. Trial reporter Benjamin Hallett described Ezra Parker as "a queer tall old man" who spoke in a rustic vernacular with dry humor and "devout self-satisfaction." According to the Parkers, one afternoon about eight years earlier (about the time Cornell worked in Slatersville), Maria had entered their tavern looking eight or nine months pregnant. When William Taylor and his brother Charles arrived that evening, William saw Maria sitting near the fire:

"The devil, Maria, be you here?" William exclaimed.

"Yes, and you can't help yourself, William Taylor!" Maria replied.

Maria then accused William of fathering her child, which he denied, but Maria proclaimed that she intended to swear to it nonetheless. The two talked until eleven o'clock that night, when William's brother finally advised him to settle with her. According to Ezra Parker, they drafted a written bond clearing William of the charge, which Parker signed as a witness the next morning. The Parkers also claimed they had witnessed William hand money to Maria, who supposedly said, "William Taylor, you must get up earlier than ever you did yet, to make a garden of me to bear seed to you." The story got even stranger when Ruhanah Parker testified that she had witnessed Maria undress that night, and that she had a blanket doubled up and wrapped around her body, which when she removed it, revealed that she "looked nothing like having a child." When Maria came downstairs the next morning to settle with Taylor, she looked very trim and "as spare as any woman."

Prosecutors recognized that this tale of an elaborate ruse to extort money from the naïve William Taylor possessed hardly a modicum of consistency or common sense. Why would Taylor have paid money to Maria if the pregnancy was obviously a fake? Why would Maria have staged the hoax if she was going to break off the masquerade before the deal had been settled?

Why would she tell William Taylor before he left the tavern that "she was not with child by him or anybody else"?

For Avery's attorneys, though, none of the inconsistencies mattered. The Parkers had accomplished the objective for which they had been brought to court: to leave jurors with the impression that Maria was wildly promiscuous and that she was as capable of feigning the role of a deeply pious Methodist as she was of faking a pregnancy. Since William had died and his brother had gone off to the West, neither could be called to confirm the account. What made the story so shocking was what it suggested about the severe threat posed by an independent and aggressive woman pursuing her own sexual desires and exerting power over men within the everyday interactions of courtship and sex.[10]

The sex tales that witnesses divulged for the sake of Avery's defense offer a rare glimpse into the intimate lives and romantic choices available to young women in America's new industrial cities. With all the salacious stories trotted out to defame Maria Cornell, some people began to wonder what impact this would have on the reputation of all "factory girls." When Maria's housemate from Fall River, as a prosecution witness, calmly answered all the indiscreet questions raised about Maria's menstrual periods and pregnant body, Hallett was beside himself with praise for "the delicate, unaffected and lady-like manner" evidenced by this "factory girl," whose modesty was sure to "repel the slander" directed at that class of women. To the delight of mill town residents, Hallett's opinion was subsequently reprinted in dozens of New England newspapers.[11]

The most important sex stories at Avery's trial, then, centered on the heart of the matter in the whole scandal: Maria's relationships with men while a factory worker in Lowell, which led Avery and the Methodists to expel her from their church. Maria's reputation for sexual promiscuity might make listeners both inside and outside the courtroom willing to believe in Avery's innocence by envisioning Cornell as the agent of her own demise.

New versions of stories about Maria's Lowell liaisons surfaced during this stage of the trial. Recall that, according to Dr. William Graves, when Maria first visited his office, she asked if a certain young man was his patient, since that man had "treated her improperly and deserted her." Another doctor, who also treated Maria for venereal disease, testified that Maria told him she'd "received the attentions of a young gentleman in Lowell, that she rode out on a Sunday afternoon with him, and at a tavern they passed for man and wife, and slept together, and the consequence was this disease."[12]

Mary Anne Barnes, a young unmarried factory worker and fellow Methodist, disclosed that Maria confessed that she had "behaved improperly with men," as many as three or four of them. Barnes also testified that Maria had told her about riding out to a nearby tavern, adding that Maria "drank so much wine she did not know what she was about." Mrs. Lucy Howe, a middle-aged boardinghouse keeper, added a sordid twist: she'd heard that Maria met the young man at the tavern "once a week."[13]

Whatever the particulars of their narratives, all the storytellers agreed that, in order to be intimate with men, Maria needed to get away from the watchful eye of dormitory matrons and Methodist sisters. Neither factories nor boardinghouses in Lowell offered sufficient privacy for a tryst, so not surprisingly Maria traveled with her beau to a tavern in a nearby town. But once a "factory girl" left the bounds of the factory town, what took place existed only in the realm of rumors and gossip.

Another of Maria's confidantes, Caroline Tibbitts, described by Hallett as "quite a young woman," offered the court a different take on Maria's relationship with this young man. Maria spoke of her tavern visits "as a courtship," Tibbitts recalled, "which she expected would lead to marriage." In Maria's own letters of confession sent to Avery, she admitted that she had received the attentions of a young man, but when they ended the relationship (some accounts say he left her, others that she broke it off), he proceeded to spread rumors in order to smear her reputation.[14]

Stories of failed love and courtship were part of a new dynamic emerging when young people's courtship and sexual intimacy could no longer be as effectively policed by families and small farming villages. White and middle-class Americans began to insist that sexual restraint—what they called purity and virtue—could be ensured only if women kept their own sexual desire in check. Popular representations of the "factory girl" imagined an ending that merged work and love: the best way to escape a lifetime of toiling in the mills was to get married. Elizabeth Shumway, who began working in the mills as a teenager, had married and started a family in her early twenties. But the lives of Maria and some of her co-workers never aligned with these popular conventions. If, as Tibbitts testified, Maria understood her various liaisons with Lowell men as part of this story line that would "lead to marriage," she was sadly disappointed. Maria had been fooled by popular myth, male profligacy, and the changing world around her.[15]

None of this was entirely new. Parents had been losing control over the conduct of young people's courtship and marriage for at least a half century. Yet women like Maria—independent, mobile, wage-earning—hastened women's sexual autonomy, along with all of its vulnerabilities and possibilities. Manufacturing towns like Lowell, Slatersville, and Fall River were designed to create the last bastions of close, watchful communities at the very moment when the movement and rootlessness of wage-laboring men and women made that watchfulness nearly impossible. Mill towns could employ shame and ostracism, but they couldn't successfully exert the power that families and small villages had once invoked to transform illicit sex into marriages and families.

Maria Cornell, then, encountered another of the era's deep transformations—a changing marriage market that could be as revolutionary as the industrial revolution. The mobility of laboring men encouraged male sexual irresponsibility, freeing them from facing any consequences when they falsely promised marriage to a young woman in exchange for sex. When men in Maria's life were named or mentioned in the courtroom, witnesses usually described them as having recently gone West or set out to places unknown. This blatant flouting of accountability increased the vulnerability of young women. As a factory worker, Maria would have encountered this new aggressive and irresponsible male sexuality in relationships with men who passed through mill towns on their way toward better opportunities with more lucrative wages. How risky it was for any young woman to trust a wage-laboring man who promised that he intended to marry her![16]

But what if the tales that Avery's witnesses told about Maria's character reveal instead a young woman's genuine sexual pleasures and desires. Maria's confidantes had noticed a tone of defiance in Maria's confessions, her words of contrition evoking regret and longing alike. Perhaps she pursued these relationships because they provided sexual autonomy similar to the independence that mill wages and Methodist spirituality offered, the type of autonomy enjoyed by young working men. What if another contemporary mill girl had spoken about love and sex, rather than a new dress, when she declared: "I am now almost 19 years old I must of course have something of my own before many more years have passed over my head. . . . I have but one life to live and I want to enjoy myself as well as I can while I live."[17]

Very few of Maria's contemporaries were willing to see her behavior this way, even though their anxieties about "factory girls," independence, and passion hinted at these possibilities. Those willing to admit to Maria's sexual independence could frame that erotic freedom only as a form of prostitution or mental instability.[18]

Women were not alone in engaging in sex talk. Two ambitious men, both non-Methodists—Maria's overseer at the factory and her doctor, William

Graves—felt it their "duty" to volunteer to Avery what they knew about Maria's sexual behavior. Her overseer, as well as the clerk of the Appleton Corporation, became aware of her sexual reputation from talking with other men. Men's gossip about sex could serve many different purposes, but when entwined with their power, it could do more than just expose a woman; men could fire her, expel her from the church, or sue her for unpaid medical bills. If, as Graves testified, Maria had an affair with a clerk in the counting rooms of the Appleton mill, there couldn't have been a riskier choice of a man to fall for, since those counting rooms kept and distributed the records of all the women blacklisted from the mills for bad conduct.[19]

Maria understood the power men exerted in her sexual encounters. She also understood that men protected one another through manipulation of gossip and rumors. Her experiences in Dr. Graves's office—his groping, his willingness to discuss her sex life with other men—reveal the ever-present risks she faced. It was men's sex talk, not women's, that ultimately led to her downfall in Lowell.[20]

Nevertheless, Maria's co-workers and boardinghouse keepers—almost all Methodists no less—befriended her, became her confidantes, listened to her stories, and listened again to one another's re-telling of those tales. After the trial, skeptics wondered how this string of Methodist factory girls could have heard and repeated Maria Cornell's stories without themselves being implicated in illicit sex. As one of Avery's foes remarked, if all this sex talk by and about Maria were true, it only proved that Cornell "however bad herself, considered them of the same stamp, for whoever heard of a loose woman pouring into the ears of a modest one the history of her intrigues?" If "the character of this unfortunate girl was so reprehensible," one reporter puzzled, what did it say that the persons who testified against her "were her intimate associates—ay, members of the same church"?[21]

19

Bad Stories

AS THE TRIAL REACHED ITS twelfth day, Miriam Libby, a young, unmarried woman in her twenties, approached the witness stand. Having known Maria Cornell for only a few months at Great Falls, after her expulsion from Lowell and hasty departure from Dover, Miriam was among the dozens of "factory girls" and Methodist women called by the defense to convince the jury of Maria's disreputable character. As Avery's attorneys redirected his defense toward blaming the female victim in a sex crime, Miriam's testimony exposed how Maria's fate teetered between the snares laid by the gossip's tongue and the practices of her faith.

Miriam Libby related that Maria had told her one day that she had "sent to Mr. Avery at Lowell, to get a certificate to join the Church," but he had refused to comply. Miriam knew from experience that this certificate was an enormously valuable possession. Like a letter of recommendation, it attested to good standing in the church, granting access to boardinghouses where she might otherwise meet a closed door, ensuring a position in the mill, and introducing her into the company of respectable women.

Then, Miriam recounted, Maria grew angry and exclaimed, "Never mind it—I'll be revenged on him, if it costs me my life." What's more, Maria said that she could "get along well enough" without Avery's help, as long as no one who knew her from Lowell showed up at Great Falls, for she could "write a certificate" herself and had done so before. She knew "Mr. Avery's handwriting and could imitate it so that no one could tell the difference." Miriam remained standing as Attorney General Greene cross-examined her.[1]

"To whom did you first tell this conversation?"

"I communicated it to Belinda and Caroline—the girls who worked with me—about the time she told it."

"Have you witnessed any bad conduct by Miss Cornell?"

"Never saw anything very bad in her conduct."

"Did you see anything?"

"Why nothing, she told me some bad stories. I knew nothing bad in her conduct while she was there, except lying."

"What stories did she tell?"

"She said she had a recommendation, and then she said she had not."

"Was there any other story she told you?"

"Not any other."[2]

"Bad stories." What could that mean? Perhaps Miriam meant telling falsehoods. After all, Maria had been excommunicated from Lowell's Methodist church for "fornication and lying." Just as likely, "bad stories" implied tales of illicit behavior: stories that might be too naughty to repeat in the wrong context or company, and certainly stories too shocking or embarrassing for young, unmarried women to describe in a public courtroom.

Bad stories certainly did not mean tales that lacked dramatic intrigue. In fact, these stories were simply too good not to repeat. Indeed, numerous women testified, with an exceptional degree of recall, about every detail of the sexual behavior of their co-worker and Methodist sister. They had listened with keen interest to her stories, then repeated those stories with passionate interest to other women and to Methodist ministers. This was gossip at work, to be sure, but it also overlapped with everyday religious occasions for storytelling.

Another witness, Sarah Worthing, ended her testimony under cross-examination this way:

"From 1828 up to 1830, when you knew Maria, what was her character?"

"Well I knew nothing against her, only she would tell some stories."

"Was she in good standing in the Church?"

"Yes Sir."[3]

Why, with the possibility of excommunication and unemployment, would Maria so freely tell stories about her own questionable behavior, and why did her co-workers and fellow Methodists listen so intently? Even her contemporaries puzzled over the easily blurred lines between what constituted good or bad in stories exchanged between confidantes and betrayers. As Avery's harshest critic asked after the murder trial was all over, whoever heard of a modest, respectable woman "degrading herself by being in the confidence of a wanton?"[4]

Sarah Worthing's testimony offers a clue.

Maria was in desperate straits. Wherever she tried to rebuild her life after Lowell, doors slammed shut at factories, boardinghouses, and Methodist meetings. In June 1831, a year after her expulsion, she made a return trip to Lowell. Taking a stagecoach at her own expense, she confronted Rev. Avery in person, making one more appeal for his forgiveness of her sexual sins and requesting a new certificate. While Avery didn't "treat her with common politeness," leading her to think he was "hard hearted and unfeeling," Maria made the rounds to other Lowell friends and former "sisters" asking their forgiveness as well. She approached Worthing because her co-worker had once lived and worked at the new mill town where Maria was trying to resettle.

"She said she had a paper she wanted me to sign," Worthing testified.[5]

If Maria couldn't acquire a certificate from Avery himself, she had a plan to persuade a group of reputable Methodists to sign a letter affirming that they had forgiven her for her sins, possibly gaining her probationary status in another church and starting her on the way back to respectability. In truth, that's what the Methodists had always led her to believe, that she was "a great sinner" who "found a great Saviour," and that she possessed a free will to work out her own salvation. Maria's plan, however, was the proverbial double-edged sword. To attain their forgiveness and get the signatures, she had to confess her sins. She would have to reveal her dalliances, and if she was to prove her contrition, no detail could be spared. "Bad stories" were exactly what these Methodist women wanted to hear.

This delicate affinity between gossip and confession exposed the uncomfortable intertwining of sex and religion in Methodist practice. In Maria's lifetime, gossip certainly allowed working people to negotiate their reputations in villages or cities, but loose talk and policing also appeared frequently in religious communities. By the early 1830s, with anti-immigrant and anti-Catholic sentiments on the rise, Protestants focused some of their greatest anxieties on Catholic confession, imagining the worst when a young woman spilled out her sins to an unmarried priest in secret. Because confession involved divulging one's deepest desires and longings in the darkness of the confessional, in Protestant minds it was akin to illicit sex. For Protestants, the feared Catholic confessional was sex-talk in religious guise.[6]

This was exactly what Maria Cornell's sister mill girls and Methodists elicited with their habits of confession and surveillance.

"She made the confessions to me," Lucy Davol testified, as she described the occasion when Maria asked her to sign the letter of forgiveness.

Sarah Worthing used the opportunity to ask Maria about the rumors she'd heard. "She said she had been led on strangely," Worthing stated, and then Maria confessed that she had "unlawful intercourse with three men," and that she had been afflicted with the bad disease. Maria also admitted to Worthing that she'd planned to have sex with two other men, but was "deprived of the privilege"—then corrected herself, "she did not say privilege."

Mary Anne Barnes testified that Maria began to tell her these stories for the same purpose, and that hearing them demanded further investigation. "I interrogated her more," Barnes told the court, "and she confessed more, that she had behaved improperly with men." Maria confessed to Barnes exactly how she slipped away from the strict oversight of boardinghouse matrons and posed with a young man as husband and wife at a nearby village tavern. Maria's stories were, in Barnes's words, "as bad as bad could be."[7]

Conversations like these, which teetered between salacious speech and spiritual testimony, were common in Methodist communities, even as they sounded willfully deviant in a public courtroom. More often than not, these women recoiled, but they always listened intently. It might have been easy for Maria to misjudge the way her confidantes heard her admissions, just as her listeners might remember only the facts that were confessed and might misread the context and intention of her "acknowledgments." Still, the key was confession.

Methodist spirituality had taken the Puritan practice of narrating conversions, a once-in-a-lifetime experience, and transformed it into a life of continuous spiritual storytelling. At any time, Methodists were ready to share their hopes and fears, their frailties and shortcomings, as well as their desires and loves. They built their spiritual community around these storytelling practices. They narrated their spiritual experiences every week in what they called class meetings, and every few months in quarterly meetings called "love feasts."[8]

Maria, like all Methodists, attended a weekly class meeting, where her "sisters" told one another the stories of their spiritual journeys, their personal histories of sins and redemption. For all of the closeness of these gatherings ("I never saw such love in all my life," remarked one sister), class meetings also existed to admonish wayward and backsliding Methodists. And they welcomed this inquisitive surveillance, even expressed gratitude for it. Maria, who had been tempted by fashion and consumer desire, found great comfort in it. The two purposes were inseparable—to speak and be heard, and to be carefully watched—proving that you were both loved and disciplined.[9]

Love feasts were larger gatherings, restricted exclusively to Methodists with tickets for admission, but they too revolved around storytelling, with hours devoted to sisters and brothers narrating their personal experiences of saving grace. As one Methodist recalled a New York City love feast, some of the sisters testified that they had been "drawn away from the vain frivolities and fashionable amusements of the world," while brothers spoke of being "snatched from the haunts of dissipation and vice" and transformed from drunkards into sober men. Although Methodists disapproved of reading popular fiction, they offered up their own ample supply of sentimental tales of ruin and redemption at love feasts and class meetings.[10]

Merely the name, "love feasts," along with the doors closed to non-members, sparked plenty of rumors among non-Methodists. "My curiosity was up to the highest pitch," said a man who climbed through a roof to spy on anticipated revelries, only to discover that the love-making was largely spiritual. Still, a liberty of speech reigned once the doors were sealed. Methodists spoke from their hearts and unburdened their souls, with tears flowing from orators and listeners alike. This was also a rare space in public life where women could speak as freely as men, delivering "feeling exhortations and expressions of new-born rapture." Maria's acknowledged talent for "exhorting and praying," or, as Rev. Abraham Merrill recalled, her "power of touching the feelings" must have flourished in this setting.[11]

Perhaps Maria took the invitation to storytelling too far, or perhaps her stories were a little too "bad" to be easily forgotten. One sister testified that Maria once came into her bedroom and offered "a retrospective view of her life," or, as another reporter recorded it, she "began to tell me of her troubles." Here was the Methodist way, an evangelical penchant for self-scrutiny, followed by "witnessing" the great work of salvation in one's life. The sister, in this case, considered it just one of Maria's "many instances of strange conduct."[12]

Nathan Howard from Lowell, the Methodist lay leader who brought formal charges of illicit sex and falsehood against Maria, understood well such confessional storytelling. What Howard recalled most vividly was that he hardly knew Maria when she confessed to him that she had been "charged with theft" and "tempted to destroy herself." The courtroom audience and jurors alike must have wondered: Why would Maria make such an admission to a stranger? Howard, suddenly realizing that others might not comprehend this facet of Methodist spirituality, explained that Maria made her confession "in a religious conversation" about "the trials of mind through which she had passed."[13]

Maria's shoplifting incident occurred more than seven years earlier in one of the dozen other locations where she had lived and worked. But this was her "testimony," the story of the spiritual transformation that God had accomplished in her life. What was more, she was practicing the one-upmanship of Methodist spiritual storytelling. Only a life that had reached rock-bottom could possibly dramatize the heights of grace that God had wrought in the life of a converted sinner.

Severed from the spiritual family that she prized more deeply than her blood relations, and well aware that success as a mill worker demanded it, she longed to be reinstated in their graces. Maria told the story of the theft and her temptations to commit suicide many times to many different people. It didn't matter that the events were nearly a decade old. In the memories of her co-Methodists, and in the courtroom, they were recent history. Dredging deep into her past and confident that she could confess safely without judgment, she had voiced a tale that divulged the nadir of her despair.

Of all the fellow Methodists from Lowell, Slatersville, Dover, and Great Falls called to testify at Avery's trial, not one reported actually seeing Maria do anything illicit or immoral. Miriam Libby, after all, had admitted that "I knew nothing bad in her conduct," and Sarah Worthing that she "knew nothing against her" and Maria was "in good standing in the Church." Rather, all of the bad stories the witnesses repeated in court had been gathered from Cornell's own confessions.

Desperate and alone, Maria entrusted her fate to the combined narrative communities of gossip and religion. She hedged her bets, hoping that the faith community's gossip would be less damaging and more forgiving than that of a wider public. She would, in the end, be sadly disappointed.

Sarah Worthing concluded her testimony: "I considered her a very vile girl, and refused to sign her certificate. She called me a hard-hearted girl; and wept bitterly."[14]

Another of Maria's confessors, boardinghouse matron Lucy Howe, expressed shock as Maria confessed her "lewd" behavior. Howe was quick to admonish Maria, saying, "I can place no reliance on you Maria, until I see a reformation in you, by a well ordered life and a Godly conversation."[15]

Maria Cornell's tales of multiple sexual encounters were undeniably beyond the pale of respectability. But how could she enact a "Godly conversation" if she was required to begin with tales that reputable women would instantly consider "bad stories"?

20

Passion and Self-Murder

SPECTATORS AND JURORS COULDN'T MISS the strategy of Avery's defense. After casting doubt on the medical expertise of Tiverton's women and the Fall River doctors, the defense team turned their courtroom storytelling efforts toward painting a portrait of Sarah Maria Cornell that Jeremiah Mason summarized as "a strange compound truly"—a mixture of sensual indulgence, wild fanaticism, and violent passions. Avery's attorneys certainly intended to shame a dead woman, contrasting her depravity with the seemingly unblemished reputation of a clergyman. Even more, they wanted the jury to believe that Cornell was mentally unstable, capable of suicide, and likely to end her own life. If true, the jurors wouldn't suspect the Methodist preacher of murder. That was the crucial point: to prove that Maria Cornell was suicidal.[1]

The same group of witnesses was used to serve both purposes. Avery's defense deliberately turned first to William Graves, who they thought would offer salacious details about a sexually promiscuous woman with a medical diagnosis of her mental maladies. The court, though, seemed reticent to sanction this new defense tactic, reprimanding Graves as he shifted his analysis to Cornell's mental state.

"She made a number of *strange* remarks, which led me to suspect . . ." Graves began, but the justices stopped him cold, instructing him simply to restate what Cornell had said.

He recounted how she claimed the Methodists considered her a bright Christian and that she could pray and preach as well as any of them.

"She remarked in a way and manner which led me to suspect . . . ," he continued.

Once again, he was interrupted and told just to state the facts, not his impressions.[2]

But Graves's impressions were exactly why Avery's counsel had brought him to Newport. When Randolph eventually asked the doctor directly about his impressions of Cornell's sanity, it set off a sidebar conference over his qualifications to give an expert opinion. Once they had confirmed that he was a physician not a druggist, had practiced and instructed students for many years, and owned enough horses to drive a chaise like a gentleman, the justices permitted Dr. Graves to give his medical opinion regarding Cornell's mental health. Nothing in his answer, though, relied on science or medicine.

"The truth is my mind was not made up," he said. "I was almost inclined to think she was insane. Her language was so different from what I ever heard from a female. I hardly know what to think."

Because this didn't sound like a medical diagnosis, the chief justice asked: "From all you saw and heard, what was your opinion?"

Before Graves could answer, Mason interjected to keep the doctor focused: "How far did your opinion go as to her insanity?"

"When she first came in she appeared very modest and appeared well," Graves explained. "All at once she began to talk in a strange way," leading him to "suspect she was partially insane." Although she seemed well at later visits, the last time he saw her, she "appeared to talk wild, and seemed in a great passion." He added: "Whether it was passion or insanity, I cannot say."

When the attorney general rose to cross-examine Graves, he tried to emphasize the absurdity of this kind of medical diagnosis: Did the doctor think she was insane merely because she had venereal disease and belonged to the Methodist church? Graves returned to Cornell's appearance and manner of talking, resorting once more to the decidedly non-medical term "strange."[3]

Avery's attorneys then summoned witnesses from the dozen factory towns where Maria Cornell resided over the previous decade, beginning with those whose tales might prove most shocking and memorable.

Asaneth Bowen, who had worked with Cornell in Waltham when Maria was trying to regain her reputation and Methodist membership, turned directly to her co-worker's "strange appearance" in the weavers' room. She would start suddenly as if frightened and look around cautiously as if someone were pursuing her, Bowen explained. Then one day, Maria left her looms to go into another room carrying a small string, and Bowen followed her, forcing open the door that Maria had closed behind her. "I thought she went there to commit suicide because she looked around and appeared strange, and had a string in her hand," Bowen said. In her telling, Maria stood, cord in hand, looking upward in search of a beam, and when Bowen entered, she "started back as if alarmed at seeing me," then departed without saying a word. The defense called Bowen as their first witness among Maria's co-workers and Methodists because she allegedly had seen Cornell attempt suicide.

Under cross-examination, the plausibility of Bowen's story began to crumble. She worked halfway across a crowded room from Maria, so she couldn't have observed her behavior that carefully. The cord was little more than a light string some two feet long, and the room where she intruded on Maria was the bathroom. No wonder, then, Maria reacted as if someone were stalking her.[4]

Bowen's story ushered in an onslaught of tales of Maria Cornell's "strange" behavior—the word invoked by nearly all the witnesses.

Mary Ann Lary recounted how one evening Maria returned in tears to their boardinghouse at the Great Falls factory village, saying she had gone out to "make way with herself," but her courage had failed. Lary alleged too that she'd heard Maria frequently speak of being tempted to commit suicide.

Nathan Howard testified that Maria had confessed to him her "powerful temptations to kill herself." She couldn't stand still or walk regular that day, he said, and she "appeared as though she was not rational." When asked to explain, Howard replied, "Her eyes appeared fiery, and looked red."

"Was there any appearance of wildness?" Mason followed up.

"Yes, sir," Howard answered.

The next witness, Mary Anne Barnes, who saw Maria the same day, also testified that she couldn't sit still, her face looking "agitated and her eyes wild."[5]

From across the broad landscape of New England's factory towns, Cornell's co-workers were summoned to recount Maria's confessions of how she had been tempted to commit suicide. "Tempted" was always how Maria framed her confession. This was her version of Methodist piety, her testimony of a life redeemed. For Maria, it wasn't a story of gloom and despair, but she nearly always told it when she was desperate for forgiveness and reinstatement. Usually, she was telling the tale of her downfall in Providence—caught shoplifting, losing out in a sisters' rivalry for Grindal Rawson, and ostracized from her own family.

Maria told this story to Lucy Davol and Mary Hunt in Dorchester, to Elizabeth Shumway and Philena Holmes in Slatersville, to Sarah Worthing in Lowell, and to Miriam Libby in Dover. Because each of these confidantes remembered the story differently, the number of Cornell's suicide attempts grew in the minds of jurors. In some accounts, she took a rope and fastened it to an apple tree; in others she thought about drowning herself in a pond or nearly jumped into a mill town's canal. Sometimes her courage failed, or thoughts of eternity changed her mind; other times friends or strangers stopped her before the act. And yet, the witnesses were all recalling the story of a single incident.[6]

There's no denying that Maria thought about suicide. She had spoken of it to dozens of different people. Even more, she had been an eyewitness to suicides and self-destroyed bodies during her young life. While in Dorchester in 1828, otherwise happy with her work and Methodist faith, Maria recounted for her mother "several shocking cases of suicide." A drunken thirty-year-old man slit his throat only fifty feet away from her. A co-worker drowned herself in the river, her body dredged up for public view. Another day Maria watched out her window as a young man tied himself to a tree, then shot himself through the chest before anyone could stop him. These self-killings brought freshly to mind the trauma of the murder-suicide during her last months at Slatersville. "How short and uncertain life is," she told her mother, "it vanishes like the early cloud and the morning dew." Signing off, she headed directly to her beloved Methodist meeting.[7]

Attorney General Greene knew nothing about Maria's personal encounters with suicide or her letters (they came out after the trial), but he understood that her suicidal talk was woven into the fabric of her Methodist faith. Reframing these stories near the end of the trial, he would remind jurors to consider the occasions when Cornell told this story. Nearly every witness who recalled confessions of suicidal thoughts, after all, placed the episode in the summer of 1831, when Maria was soliciting signatures of forgiveness in order to return to the Methodist fold. "She was confessing her misconduct," Greene explained, and was anxious to impress her hearers with "the extent and force of her remorse." She wasn't saying that that she was going to kill herself, only that she had been tempted to do so. It was merely the idle talk of a woman trying to show how deeply remorseful she was.[8]

Greene was correct: suicide regularly surfaced in conversion stories. Evangelical women commonly mentioned suicidal thoughts when narrating their life histories, illustrating the sinner's lowest state just prior to her dramatic new birth. Since defense witnesses reported that Maria claimed she was "tempted," that she thought she "should" end her life, it seems Maria conceived this as a part of her redemption story, a recap of the sins and temptations she'd endured before seeking forgiving grace. But even if she intended only to convey the depth of her sinfulness and the magnitude of her contrition, in the courtroom, under the direction of the defense attorneys, these confessions were made to sound like Cornell definitely intended to take her own life.[9]

It seemed not to matter that Maria never talked to anyone about suicide during her last three months in Fall River. In fact, when Dr. Wilbur warned Cornell that she might die if she ingested an abortifacient suggested by Avery, she said she would rather bear the child than "do anything to endanger her life." The prosecution had tried desperately to get this testimony into the record. Had Maria wanted to end her life, she didn't need to stage an elaborate public display of hanging herself.[10]

But the jurors didn't hear the prosecutor's final appeal until after Avery's defense mustered a seemingly endless parade of witnesses impugning Cornell's moral character and describing her "strange" appearance and behavior.

When Lydia Pervere, a young factory worker and fellow Methodist, took the stand, she repeated the sort of "bad stories" that Maria confessed of her sexual sins in Lowell. But Avery's attorneys wanted Lydia to say more about Cornell's state of mind. In one instance, Lydia conjured an unforgettable image of Maria's behavior. "She came into the Factory one day dressed in white, and screamed and cried," she said. Lydia had never before seen a factory worker in a white dress, and when she asked Cornell about it, Maria screamed, cried, and threw her arms around Lydia's neck. "I thought her mind was disordered," Lydia said, "and I was disgusted with her!"[11]

Defense witnesses recounted Cornell's "strange" behavior and talk just when attitudes toward mental illness were changing dramatically. Puritans, with their Calvinist outlook, had considered madness a supernatural phenomenon, an act of Providence (a test from God, say, or the work of Satan) rather than a disease. "Distracted" was their most commonly used term for the insane—a benign expression lacking contempt—and accordingly, they tended to tolerate a wide range of "mad" behaviors. A Maine minister, for instance, began covering his face with a handkerchief, turning his back on his congregation while speaking, and insisting on dining at a separate table facing the wall. The church waited three years before hiring a replacement, and even then they let this minister remain in the parsonage and preach occasionally for the next decade. Parishioners at Old South Church in Boston tolerated similar behavior and didn't replace their minister when he began delivering his sermons in gibberish. The "distracted" were part of the community, cared for within households, and rarely confined or hospitalized.[12]

After the Revolution, attitudes toward insanity began to change. Americans became more fearful, more likely to blame the insane for their condition, and more willing to confine or remove them from society. Language became harsher, with people more likely to use terms like "deranged" and "disordered," accompanied by pejorative adjectives like "loathsome" or "disgusting."

Just as some began to see individuals as responsible for their own salvation, the public began to understand insanity as the responsibility or fault of the insane. Dr. Benjamin Rush, physician and signer of the Declaration of Independence, was among the first to characterize madness as a moral disease, a failure of human will. The mentally ill found themselves increasingly confined within hospitals and poor-houses rather than treated at home. In turn, a new reform movement sought to establish asylums for the "moral treatment" of the mentally ill, placed in idyllic locations outside of cities. McLean Asylum for the Insane, an early example of this movement, opened outside Boston in 1818.

In Newport, the defense relied on the cumulative effect of witnesses recalling Cornell's eagerness to talk about suicide, alongside far-fetched stories like Maria faking a pregnancy, to portray her as insane. Richard Randolph called her "deranged," other witnesses described her as perturbed or irrational, while Lydia Pervere concluded that she was "quite disgusted with her!" Words like "strange" and "wild," repeated incessantly, point to an attitude of hostility and fear far more than toleration.[13]

Avery's defense rested on a portrait of Maria Cornell as both irrational and morally depraved. She was out of her mind, yet cunning enough to mastermind a plot to frame the preacher for her death. Avery's defenders formulated an elaborate theory in which Cornell conspired (either alone or with the help of another), using a string of suspicious circumstances— her penciled note, the letters, her conversations in Fall River, and her own suicide—to exact revenge on Avery for his mistreatment of her. The defense then merged this revenge theory with Cornell's supposed insanity. As Randolph had told the jury in his opening remarks, Cornell's conduct illustrated "a desire of revenge, joined with something like insanity."[14]

Methodists contributed the most important evidence for this theory. Witness after witness came forward to recall the threat they heard Maria Cornell make against Avery. Lucy Davol first testified to hearing Maria say,

"I will be revenged on him, if it costs me my life." Ellen Griggs, Lucy Howe, Miriam Libby, and Mary Warren followed, each recounting from different factory towns a nearly identical statement. Sometimes Maria threatened both Avery and the entire Methodist Church, but the phrasing was always the same—"if it costs me my life."[15]

To observers, the testimony of these young women seemed eerily mechanical, even rehearsed. Prosecutors took to asking: Who approached you about testifying? Had you written down or discussed your testimony with anyone else? Replies to these questions revealed the collective labors of the Methodists to defend Avery. Seventeen of these witnesses identified a dozen different Methodist clergymen who had reached out to them, though the most active in tracking down witnesses was a young preacher named Samuel Palmer.[16]

"Did you tell these threats to Mr. Avery, or anyone else?" prosecutors asked Mary Warren from Dover.

"No," she answered.

"Why didn't you warn him?"

"I don't know, unless I thought she would not do it."

"Did it make no impression on your mind? Did she say it lightly?"

"Yes."[17]

Still, the recollections of defense witnesses, told repetitively, reinforced the notion that Maria Cornell was "a strange, unaccountable creature," a wild woman who incited fear. After repeating Maria's threat, "I will be revenged upon him, if it costs my life," Lucy Howe added that "she said it with a look that frightened me," prompting her to think "she must be deranged."[18]

This was a brilliant maneuver by Mason and Randolph. The full breadth of these stories painted a picture of a woman whose behavior could be neither predicted nor logically explained. "Such was her strangeness," Randolph declared, "there is no accounting for her conduct, by any rules of action ordinarily applied to human beings." He had given the jury an out. They didn't need to find logic behind Cornell's scheme for revenge, nor any explanation for her decision to commit suicide. Prosecutors could point out the absurdity of her plan or suggest that the witnesses never took her talk of suicide seriously, but jurors could always fall back on the defense's claim that no one should believe her assertions or rule out the possibility of what this "strange, unaccountable creature" might do.[19]

After nearly thirty witnesses had traced Maria Cornell across New England, relating stories of her promiscuity, odd behavior, threats of revenge, and suicidal thoughts, the attorney general objected when the defense called shopkeepers from Providence to testify about Maria's shoplifting. This was going too far, Greene protested. What relevance did a theft ten years earlier have to whether she had been murdered?

Mason countered that moral character was directly related to suicide. "One very wicked, very profligate, and very much distressed, would be more likely to commit suicide" than a person of sound morals.

That's doubtful, Greene contradicted, since an honest person was more likely than a hardened thief to consider suicide from feelings of disgrace. Investigating the conduct and history of the deceased had to stop somewhere, he concluded, and when the court agreed, asking Mason to cite a precedent for admission of such evidence, he had none to supply. The defense accordingly changed course, arguing that Cornell's wicked character showed her capacity to enact a perverse plot of revenge. This time the justices agreed that the testimony was admissible, in order to show "a depraved and abandoned disposition."[20]

It didn't take much effort for the defense to make insanity a moral issue. Defiance of the accepted notions of respectable behavior became in the 1830s enveloped in a new concept of "moral insanity." Causes of melancholy and madness listed in a popular folk medicine guide—"violent passions" like love, fear, anger, disappointment in love, too much sex, and "gloomy and mistaken notions of religion"—sounded like the litany of defense assertions about Maria Cornell.[21]

Moreover, people associated madness with women's disorderly behavior in particular. On both sides of the Atlantic, by the end of the eighteenth century, cultural images coupled madness and suicide with female emotions, sexuality, and deviance. The theatrical popularity of Ophelia from Shakespeare's *Hamlet*, for one, furnished a ubiquitous literary and artistic depiction of insanity. The suicidal Ophelia was usually dressed in white, her hair disheveled or enlaced with wildflowers, speaking in "extravagant metaphors, lyrical free associations, and explicit sexual reference."[22] Romantic writers in the early nineteenth century added another icon in the sentimental character of Crazy Jane, adorned in similar dress and hair, and driven to madness by disappointment in love or seduction. If not all women diagnosed with mental illness defied conventional behavior, certainly those who tried to escape such constraints found themselves labeled "strange" or "wild" or "deranged."[23]

The two doctors who treated Maria Cornell for venereal disease, therefore, proved valuable for the defense. Dr. Graves suggested that he thought

"Crazy Kate" was among the many literary and artistic representations of female insanity in the early nineteenth century. Johann Heinrich Füssli, *Die wahnsinnige Kate* (1806/07). Courtesy of Freies Deutsches Hochstift/Frankfurter Goethe-Museum, Frankfurt am Main, Germany.

Cornell was insane because her language strayed from what he expected from a woman, but the only example he offered was Cornell bragging that she could out-pray and out-preach any of the Methodists.

Dr. Noah Martin, who treated Maria successfully after she resettled at the Great Falls factory, seemed less shady than Dr. Graves, but he was no less inclined to consider questions of sanity as an invitation to talk about womanhood. Quick to note that he didn't think she was "laboring under mental alienation," Dr. Martin still pointed to Maria's manner of speaking. She was loquacious, he said, and her mode of conversation was irregular, even if coherent. "Her gesticulations were different from what we ordinarily find in females," he added. She would begin talking about her ailment, dissolve into a flood of tears, and then five minutes later burst into laughter.[24]

These crude assessments of Maria Cornell's sanity echoed fears about women workers and new cities, about the unleashing of women's sexual desires, and about the chaotic and emotional spirituality of Methodists and their camp meetings. They worked because of powerful associations with the human passions—a term that could at once connote emotions and vices, spiritual and sexual desires, irrational melancholy, anger and revenge. A catch-all descriptor, "passion" allowed the defense to tie together popular conceits about sexual lust, religious frenzy, and unruly women.[25]

Ironically, doctors who treated venereal disease, whose own practice signaled suspicions about morality, anchored the defense's portrait of Maria Cornell as a mixture of two qualities considered dangerous in females: religious excess and sexual excess. Dr. Graves's reference to either passion or insanity conjured up images of wild camp meetings, love feasts, unbounded sexual desire, and the bold defiance of mobile, independent women. Dr. Martin proved just as adroit at coupling Cornell's "mental anxiety" with "passion."

Jeremiah Mason had turned Avery's defense into the trial of Maria Cornell. In the latter stages of the trial he hammered home how unstable was Cornell's nature. Her life, he insisted, was at once full of piety and shameless immorality, displaying "hypocrisy and religious enthusiasm mingled with a predisposition to insanity." Rising to a crescendo, Mason unleashed a sketch of Cornell's reckless character: "habitual sensual indulgences, with strong fanaticism—a wild enthusiasm, with morbid sensibility, and strange abstractions of mind." Calling her "a creature of passion to which she gave unbridled license" evoked all the associations of passion with sexual licentiousness, women's excessive emotionalism, and religious fanaticism. Cornell's religious enthusiasm made it easy to presume her suicide, or at least to explain away uncomfortable evidence of a violent homicide.[26]

Stories of Maria Cornell's sexual immorality and her wild spirituality were equally crucial when it came to proving her mental instability. Mason focused on Cornell's decades of promiscuous behavior as well as her cunning and fanatical piety. Indeed, he aimed to exploit another popular notion from fiction and reform literature: Americans expected that a seduced woman or a prostitute would inevitably end her own life. No group in society was more likely to commit suicide, Mason argued, than the "miserable class" to which Cornell belonged—meaning prostitutes—who, everyone was told, took their lives so frequently that it was considered a natural death. "Excited by violent and unrestrained passions, driven to extreme distress

and often desperation," he asserted, an unchaste woman would readily resort to self-destruction.[27]

The remarkable courtroom strategy of Avery's attorneys tapped into an
American fascination with insanity and suicide. By the 1830s, people across
all walks of life thought that Americans were especially prone to mental
illness, that suicide and insanity were on the rise.[28] On a near daily basis,
newspapers nationwide printed reports of suicide. During Avery's month-
long trial alone, some two dozen suicide stories appeared. The *Fall River
Weekly Recorder* printed two stories about suicides the day the trial opened.
Benjamin Hallett couldn't help but notice that the proceedings in Newport
aligned with this obsession when a young woman in Providence poisoned
herself midway through the trial ("Suicides are becoming alarmingly frequent," Hallett wrote). Many others agreed that popular writings and daily
news reports had the effect of increasing suicide's prevalence.[29]

Suicide stories, including those told about Maria Cornell, captivated
Americans because they were convinced that they lived in a society that
fostered insanity and suicide. When physicians and asylum directors listed
the most common causes of mental illness, they frequently turned to
descriptors of the world around them. Among the causes they recited were
"religious anxiety," "political excitement," unfulfilled ambition, "disappointment in love," and the vague "present condition of the country." They were
convinced that all the transformations that marked the age of democracy—
economic, religious, and political—were responsible for this perceived per-
vasiveness of mental disturbance. At the same time, the more they embraced
racial theories of white "civilization" and "progress," the more they feared
that white people were especially susceptible to insanity.[30]

More than anything else, it was the "excitement" generated in the culture of a new democracy that provoked concern. Excitement was how
they characterized popular religious revivals, the tumult of electoral politics, urban living, new entertainment, as well as the hubbub surrounding
Avery's arrest and murder trial. The same year, a leading mental health expert, Dr. Amariah Brigham, attributed widespread insanity to "the excited
state of mind which everywhere prevails throughout this republic," as well
as to the "diseases of the heart" occasioned by "anger, fear, love, joy, ava-
rice, ambition, envy, revenge, and all those passions and feelings that agitate
civilized society." Brigham insisted as well that encouraging women to think
themselves "as capable as men" produced the same excitement of feelings
that led to insanity.[31]

Witnesses, jurors, and courtroom audiences in Newport readily accepted these cultural references to women and madness, so that Maria Cornell, in a white dress, hair disheveled, and speaking boldly about her ambitions or remorsefully about suicide, was a familiar tale, one that offered a warning to Americans in this ever changing and volatile new democracy.

21

"Most Extraordinary of All Extraordinary Cases"

THREE WEEKS INTO THE TRIAL, Benjamin Hallett couldn't restrain his astonishment. This seemingly never-ending case probed so many different topics. Prohibited from publishing verbatim testimony or courtroom arguments while the trial continued, Hallett nevertheless sent dispatches to the *Boston Daily Advocate* every day or two with his reflections on the trial's progress. His correspondence then resurfaced in papers up and down the eastern seaboard.

Gobsmacked by the range of human enterprises touched by the trial, Hallett felt it illustrated the maxim that a good lawyer ought to know a little about everything. Here was law for the lawyer, anatomy for the doctor, theology for the minister, knots and navigation for the sailor, storerooms and customers for the trader, the types of cords in a cotton mill for the manufacturer, coal mines and fossils for the geologist, explosions for the engineer, mail regulations for the postmaster, combs and paper for the comb- and paper-maker, weather for the astronomer, the measuring of distances for the surveyor, and "the nature of grounds, stack yards, *husducks*, *fog grass*, &c. for the farmer." Printers had weighed in, and even poetry was not wanting. There was little, it seemed, that had not been explored in "this most extraordinary of all extraordinary cases." A person who wanted to "learn more of human nature in the observation of a day than he can gather in the reading of a year," Hallett concluded, "should come to Newport."[1]

Because both the prosecution and the defense relied so heavily on circumstantial evidence in their respective aims to convict or absolve Ephraim

Avery of murder charges, the testimony took jurors and spectators on a journey across farms and fields, country roads, city streets, ferry wharves, mill town restaurants and bars, and revival meetings in churches and forest groves.

Avery's trial, in short, offered Americans an opportunity to see themselves and their rapidly changing society in new and unexpected ways. As the drama of a murder investigation took center stage, multiple subplots emerged from the disputes over evidence of a crime. Thinking they were simply answering the questions of who-what-when-and-where, witnesses unintentionally disclosed dimensions of their everyday lives and the shifting world around them.

Aside from competing arguments about human anatomy, ropes and knots, medical expertise, insanity, suicide, and morality, the Methodist preacher's guilt or innocence hinged on his whereabouts on certain crucial days. Where had Ephraim Avery been on the afternoon and evening of December 20 when Maria Cornell took her last breath at a Tiverton haystack? Could witnesses account for all of Ephraim's time at the fateful Thompson camp meeting, where Cornell alleged he coerced her into sex and impregnated her? What about the morning in Providence a month before Cornell's death when a tall man resembling Avery handed a pink letter to the steamboat engineer John Orswell? Had Avery been out of sight long enough to deliver that letter when he was in the city for a church meeting?

During the trial's first week, the prosecution called dozens of Tiverton and Fall River residents to testify that they had seen a male stranger on December 20 between the Bristol ferry in Portsmouth (on "the Island" as locals called Rhode Island) and the vicinity of the Durfee farm in Tiverton. Indeed, more than half of the prosecution's witnesses testified about who and what they had seen on December 20. All remembered the man as tall. Nearly all remembered, with some variation, a man wearing dark clothes and a dark, broad-brimmed hat.

A middle-aged farmer named William Anthony was the first to see the stranger. Anthony witnessed a man walking past his house near the Bristol ferry, then veering eastward where the road forked toward the Stone Bridge, but he couldn't discern much more as the stranger passed out of sight. Two brothers, farmers William and Charles Carr, were driving their wagon south over the bridge at about three o'clock, when they passed a stranger wearing dark clothes and a broad-brimmed hat walking fast toward Tiverton. "A tall man," William recalled, but he "did not turn his head so that I could see the features of his face."[2]

A pattern began to emerge. Innkeeper George Lawton, on the Tiverton side of the bridge, observed "a tall man about six feet, dressed in a dark surtout and broad-brimmed hat, walking very fast." "I did not have a front view of the man's face," Lawton admitted, "he did not face me at any time."[3] Benjamin Manchester and Abner Davis were blasting stones on farm property adjacent to John Durfee's stack yard when they noticed a stranger sitting on a stone wall looking out over the town of Fall River. They shouted "look out" just as a boulder exploded. From the other direction, John Durfee was retrieving his cattle for the night when he heard the explosion, turned, and saw the stranger. All three men observed the same figure—a tall man in a dark-colored surtout with a broad-brimmed hat—but as Durfee testified, "His back was towards me. I did not see his face." Manchester recalled that "I was not near enough to see his face." Like silhouette portraits of the era, these witnesses' depictions offered nothing more than the dark outlines of the figure of a man whose dress evoked associations with a circuit-riding preacher. In their stories the stranger became a tall and faceless man.[4]

Later that night, the Island ferryman Jeremiah Gifford woke up to the sound of someone knocking. By the time he roused himself and lit a candle, no one was there. Hearing a sound elsewhere, he made his way to the back door only to discover that Avery had already let himself in. The preacher said he wanted to cross over to Bristol that night.

"It's too late," Gifford told him.

"Not so late as you think," the preacher said. "My family is unwell, and they will expect me home."

"There are physicians in Bristol, if needed," said Gifford. "It's not convenient to cross tonight. The wind is blowing hard and it's very cold. Where have you been at so late an hour?"

"I've been up on the Island on business. Brother Warren told me I could cross at any hour. If I'd known I couldn't get across, I'd have gone to Brother Cook's and spent the night."

Gifford wouldn't change his mind. He fetched Avery a glass of water and walked him to a bedroom. When they passed the clock, Gifford looked over and said (overheard by his daughter Jane nearby) that it was a quarter to ten o'clock. Like the witnesses who had seen the stranger in Tiverton and Fall River that day, Gifford recalled that Avery wore a brown colored surtout with a black, broad-brimmed hat. The next morning Gifford's son ferried the preacher over to Bristol.[5]

A timeline emerged for Avery's possible whereabouts: he boarded the ferry in Bristol at two o'clock, returning that night to the ferryman's house on the Portsmouth side around a quarter to ten. Meanwhile, Maria Cornell left the factory at five-thirty and exited her boardinghouse less than a half-hour later for the six o'clock meeting. Since witnesses heard what sounded like a woman in distress (screeches and groans) near the Durfee farm between seven-thirty and eight-thirty, the prosecution needed to establish that Avery could be seen making his way to Fall River that afternoon, and that he realistically could return from the haystack to the Bristol ferry between those screams and when the ferryman was awakened by the preacher's late-night arrival.

Philip Bennett, another Fall River constable, along with another mill town man, conducted a time experiment one week before the trial, walking as quickly as they could from the Durfee's stackyard to the Bristol ferry, trotting down hills and cutting across fields, completing the trip in an hour and twenty-nine minutes. Prominent Fall River men had collected a purse of $3 to pay them to complete their journey in the shortest time possible.[6]

Prosecutors also needed to disprove Avery's own alibi for December 20. As in most murder trials, Avery's attorneys had no intention of subjecting the preacher to cross-examination. Since the pre-trial hearing, the defense had relied instead on secondhand accounts from Methodists whom Avery had told about his journey on the Island.

Avery's alibi diverged dramatically from the accounts of Tiverton and Fall River residents. In Avery's story, he took a day-long excursion to inquire about purchasing coal and out of "curiosity to view the Island." As he headed south toward the coal mines, he spoke briefly with a man holding a gun, who told him that the mines were closed. Passing through a white-painted gate, he journeyed farther south toward a Methodist's (Asa Freeborn's) house, before speaking to a boy driving sheep who informed him the Freeborns were not at home. Changing plans, he decided to visit another Methodist sister, widow Wilcox, who lived on the other side of the Island. But by the time he arrived at the Union Meeting house on the Island's eastern road, it was well after dark, so he then walked back along the main road until he returned to the ferry. All told, witnesses thought this involved about fifteen miles of walking. At no time that day or night, did Avery meet or talk with anyone he knew personally.[7]

When it was the defense's turn, they called Portsmouth Methodists who recalled that they had seen a similar tall, slender man in dark clothes near the coal mines. All eagerly suggested that it might have been around three o'clock on December 20, but when cross-examined they admitted their uncertainty about the date, the time, and the man's description. "I can neither tell what time or what day it was," said Oliver Brownell, nor "tell what day of the week I saw the man." His wife also confessed, "I cannot tell the time of day, the day of the week, or of the month, when I saw him."[8]

This became the pattern for Avery's defense. Absent anyone who could testify that they had met Avery on his jaunt around the Island, the attorneys instead marshaled a host of witnesses to contradict the prosecution's witnesses or to avow that they were untrustworthy. Defense witnesses were called to raise doubts about the testimony of the Stone Bridge tollkeeper and the young woman who saw a tall man hurrying off the bridge in the direction of Fall River. They arose to explain that they had heard key prosecution witnesses tell their stories differently or to declare that they considered that witness "a poor miserable creature" who should not be believed.[9]

No one experienced the onslaught of the defense's character assassins more than Jane Gifford, the teenage daughter of Portsmouth's ferryman. Eight of the town's Methodists had shown up at the Bristol pre-trial hearing, and five returned at the Newport trial to insist that Jane's testimony should not be believed. Testifying with suspiciously identical phrasing, each one declared: "The character of Jane Gifford for truth and veracity was not considered good."[10]

A year earlier, Portsmouth's Methodist church had expelled fifteen-year-old Jane for reasons the witnesses didn't disclose, but their familiar language resembled the charges leveled against Maria Cornell at Slatersville and Lowell. To counter, the prosecution summoned ten of Jane's non-Methodist neighbors, all of whom attested that they had never heard anything that stained Jane's good reputation.[11]

Jane Gifford's truthfulness mattered for one crucial fact: what time was it when Avery arrived at the ferryman's house that December night? When Jane's father glanced at his home clock, what did he say?[12]

The prosecution's chain of circumstantial evidence, the defense's dispute of that testimony, and Avery's alibi all rested on witnesses' recollections of time. Proof of a murder hung on what witnesses said about a specific day and hour. As they testified, the varied storytellers disclosed how they measured and understood the passage of time.

Trial spectators, whether in person or reading trial reports, faced once again the startling discovery that they were living through a profound transformation. Here the proceedings revealed ongoing conflicts over people's relationship to time consciousness, and as with any moment of deep change, old habits endured alongside new ideas and routines. With witnesses alternating between farm folks and residents of a booming factory town, Avery's trial made clear that a new industrial economy—with consumers who increasingly owned clocks and who organized their lives in conformity to new schedules—incited clashes over who possessed authority over time.[13]

Witnesses from Fall River showed most plainly the disparities arising from different people's control over time. William Hamilton left the factory on December 20 when the mill's evening bells sounded the end of his workday at seven-thirty, stopping first for a drink at a bar. He stayed long enough to hear someone read aloud the South Carolina governor's speech on nullification. Ready to leave, he asked for the time. The bar owner looked at his watch, saying "it wanted seventeen minutes of nine." Three other men in the bar instinctively took out their watches to compare. Their consensus had it to be fifteen or sixteen minutes before the hour. Hamilton would use these declarations to gauge what time he heard a woman screeching in distress near Durfee's stackyard three or four minutes later.

Benjamin Hambly, the bar's owner, remembered from the witness stand that he had taken out his watch that night to tell Hamilton the time. His watch, he explained, was fifteen minutes faster than Fall River time, which ran on the schedule of factory bells. (For the prosecution, this evidence added more potential time for Avery to have walked from the haystack to Gifford's ferry house that night.) The time difference didn't arise from the barman's imprecise timepiece. Every day Hambly could hear the factory bells, yet he deliberately kept his watch regulated by a local jeweler, set for a time faster than factory time.[14]

With each passing decade, cotton mills became more rigidly regulated by time schedules. No one experienced the new time discipline of factory work more than women. A Lowell worker described her workday in 1844 like this: "We go in at five o'clock; at seven we come out for breakfast; at half-past seven we return to our work, and stay till half-past twelve." At one, she continued, "we return to our work, and stay until seven at night." She knew those exact times because mill owners rang bells throughout the workday, notifying factory workers when and where they should be. By the 1840s and 1850s, the schedule of bells had become so complicated that manufacturers began publishing them.[15]

Maria Cornell and her co-workers knew that time was controlled by their employers. They couldn't escape it even in their sleep. The bells of Fall River's factory, a witness recounted, started at nine o'clock in the evening and rang all through the night. But people also well knew that manufacturers could manipulate their employees' working hours by altering factory bells. Striking morning bells earlier and closing bells later increased a day's production of

TIME TABLE OF THE LOWELL MILLS,

To take effect on and after Oct. 21st, 1851.

The Standard time being that of the meridian of Lowell, as shown by the regulator clock of JOSEPH RAYNES, 43 Central Street.

	From 1st to 10th inclusive.				From 11th to 20th inclusive.				From 21st to last day of month.			
	1stBell	2dBell	3dBell	Eve.Bell	1stBell	2d Bell	3d Bell	Eve.Bell	1stBell	2dBell	3dBell	Eve.Bell
January,	5.00	6.00	6.50	*7.30	5.00	6 00	6.50	*7.30	5.00	6.00	6.50	*7.30
February,	4.30	5.30	6.40	*7.30	4.30	5.30	6.25	*7.30	4.30	5.30	6.15	*7.30
March, '	5.40	6.00		*7.30	5.20	5.40		*7.30	5.05	5.25		6.35
April,	4.45	5.05		6.45	4.30	4.50		6.55	4.30	4.50		7.00
May,	4 30	4.50		7·00	4.30	4.50		7.00	4.30	4.50		7 00
June,	"	"		"	"	"		"	"	"		"
July,	"	"		"	"	"		"	"	"		"
August,	"	"		"	"	"		"	"	"		"
September,	4.40	5.00		6.45	4.50	5.10		6.30	5.00	5.20		*7.30
October,	5.10	5.30		*7.30	5.20	5.40		*7.30	5.35	5.55		*7.30
November,	4.30	5.30	6.10	*7.30	4.30	5.30	6.20	*7.30	5.00	6.00	6.35	*7.30
December,	5.00	6.00	6.45	*7.30	5.00	6.00	6.50	*7.30	5.00	6·00	6.50	*7.30

* Excepting on Saturdays from Sept. 21st to March 20th inclusive, when it is rung at 20 minutes after sunset.

YARD GATES,

Will be opened at ringing of last morning bell, of meal bells, and of evening bells; and kept open Ten minutes.

MILL GATES.

Commence hoisting Mill Gates, Two minutes before commencing work.

WORK COMMENCES,

At Ten minutes after last morning bell, and at Ten minutes after bell which "rings in" from Meals.

BREAKFAST BELLS.

During March "Ring out".........at....7.30 a. m..........."Ring in" at 8.05 a. m.
April 1st to Sept. 20th inclusive.....at....7 00 " " .... " " at 7.35 " "
Sept. 21st to Oct. 31st inclusive.....at....7.30 " " .... " " at 8.05 " "
Remainder of year work commences after Breakfast.

DINNER BELLS.

"Ring out".......... ....12.30 p. m.........."Ring in".... 1.05 p. m.

In all cases, the *first* stroke of the bell is considered as marking the time.

B. H. Penhallow, Printer, 28 Merrimack Street.

Mill owners rigidly regulated the workday schedule for their women employees by ringing factory bells at regular intervals. *Time Table of the Lowell Mills* (Lowell, 1851). Courtesy of the American Textile History Museum Collection, Kheel Center for Labor-Management Documentation and Archives, Cornell University.

cloth. Even a mill town booster testified that Fall River's mill clocks varied every day, sometimes by as much as ten minutes.[16]

Labor protests and newspapers alike denounced these practices as "unprincipled conduct." Five years earlier, workers in Pawtucket raised money to build a town clock so they could check the honesty of the factory's bells. This explains why the bartender, jeweler, and non-factory men in the Fall River bar that night all had their timepieces set by other clocks rather than by factory bells. Although they lived in a factory town, self-employed men wanted to demonstrate that they weren't subordinate to "Fall River time" like the mostly female mill workers.[17]

Clock time, of course, had been around for more than four centuries when Maria Cornell began laboring in textile mill towns. The few clocks that most people encountered were public timepieces in church towers or a town's central square, and ordinary folk more often heard rather than read the time. Before the nineteenth century, only the wealthy could afford to own a clock or a watch. A tall case clock was made to order for a gentleman like Maria's grandfather. Farmers and laborers couldn't imagine such an extravagant purchase.[18]

People in farming communities understood time based on nature—the sun's rising and setting, the cock's crowing, the tides, and the seasons—and based on the tasks they needed to complete: there was milking time, lambing time, and laundry day. Many witnesses at Avery's trial still spoke of time in this old-fashioned manner. John Durfee saw the tall stranger "five minutes before the sun went down," while an elderly Portsmouth farmer left home when the sun was "an hour and a half high." A ferryman judged the time based on the position of the midday sun. Ruth Cook recalled that the women finished preparing Maria Cornell's body for burial when the sun was "not half an hour high."[19]

By the early nineteenth century, though, clocks had quite suddenly become an everyday feature of rural life, largely because a clock industry with aggressive marketing made affordable home clocks a consumer desire. A Connecticut entrepreneur, Eli Terry, pioneered the mass production of cheap clocks made with wooden gears and painted faces, patenting his pillar and scroll shelf clock in 1816. By the 1820s, with a water-powered mill and a system of interchangeable parts, Terry's factory was churning out 2,500 clocks a year, with his former apprentices and competitors manufacturing thousands more. At a sticker price under $10, clocks had become an affordable luxury. An army of Yankee peddlers took these clocks into nearly every hamlet in the country. It was hardly a coincidence that the only other man dining at the Fall River tavern on December 20, besides the tall man who resembled Avery, was a clock peddler.[20]

Yankee peddlers succeeded, according to another English observer, in making country people as proficient as city residents "in the matter of knowing time." By the 1840s, an Englishman traveling from Kentucky to Missouri noted that "in cabins where there was not a chair to sit on, there was sure to be a Connecticut clock." Rural folks developed an awareness of clocks and clock-speak even if they didn't live under the regime of factory time. Absent that knowledge, one might appear to be a country bumpkin. When elderly Portsmouth farmer George Brownell testified that neither Avery nor anyone else passed through the white gate near his house that day, his country ways and old-fashioned sense of time became the target of Jeremiah Mason's sarcastic scorn. Having hauled driftwood from the beach, Brownell spent the afternoon stacking it along all four sides of his house, a task that took two hours. "I began banking up the house, about 3 o'clock," he noted, "and worked till sun half an hour high."

"Do you mean to state to the jury that you were two hours banking up four sides of your house?" Mason asked.

"I don't know. I mought not have been two hours, it strikes me it was. I mought have been watering my cattle," Brownell replied.

"Oh! yes, you *mought* have done a good many things, but what did you do?"

"I did not say it was fifteen minutes, exactly," answered Brownell.[21]

Mason thought he could exploit the prejudices that Newport jurors might hold against people lacking a new time consciousness. Urban residents, merchants, and transportation workers, like stagecoach drivers and ferrymen, were the witnesses most likely to testify that they had looked at a clock or watch when assessing Avery's whereabouts.

But even with city markets and stage coaches governing the everyday lives of rural folks, communities still maintained a sense of—almost a pride in—their local time. Witnesses talked about Newport time, Bristol time, and Fall River time as if it belonged to residents. Fall River Committee member Harvey Harnden decided to keep a log of these local times, clocks, and timekeepers as evidence for Avery's prosecution. During the two weeks of the Bristol pre-trial hearing, Harnden acquired a silver lever watch and recorded daily comparisons as he journeyed from Fall River to Bristol to attend. On January 1, the Fall River bar owner's watch was nine minutes fast, Borden's factory clock twelve minutes fast, the hotel clock in Bristol fourteen minutes fast, Bristol's town clock nineteen minutes slow. The next day Harnden checked the ferryman's clock on the Bristol side (fourteen minutes slow), Jeremiah Gifford's clock on the other side (twenty minutes slow), the Stone Bridge tollkeeper's (ten minutes slow). On January 3, the Bristol town clock had become eighteen minutes slow, but David Anthony's Fall River factory was seventeen minutes fast.

"We don't consider this evidence," Richard Randolph objected.[22]

But the justices allowed Harnden to continue. Prosecutors must have known that this litany of time variations was more confusing than confirming of any truth about Avery's alibi. The only important evidence was whether Gifford's clock ran slow on December 20, because that would mean Avery had more time to get from the stackyard to the ferryman's house, but no one could go back in time to check that. Instead, "local time" varied by as much as thirty to forty minutes in towns within a five-mile radius of one another, even within the same town. Eventually, telegraphs and railroads—just beginning production at the time of Avery's trial—would demand a uniform standard of time across the country, occasioning the creation of time zones.

Markets, commerce, and transportation innovations were not the only factors shaping a new sense of time. Avery's trial highlighted how another group, the Methodists, possessed an equally distinctive and keen time consciousness. Two weeks in, the defense called a group of Methodists to testify to Ephraim Avery's whereabouts at the Thompson camp meeting in August, where Cornell alleged he had fathered her expected child.

These Methodists focused on where and when they had seen Brother Avery during the week. Ephraim had driven the forty-five miles from Bristol to Thompson, Connecticut, in his own horse-drawn chaise, picking up two fellow preachers in Providence along the way. Arriving on Tuesday night, he lodged at the Elliot family home nearby rather than in tents at the campground, sharing a bed with different preachers for three consecutive nights, then departed early on Friday morning.

When cross-examining the prosecution's witnesses a week before, Avery's attorneys had anticipated their defense of the preacher's alibi. Grindal Rawson had taken the stand and testified that Maria had told her sister and Grindal after the camp meeting "her fears of what her situation might be."

"What did she say concerning Mr. Avery, at the camp meeting?" Richard Randolph asked.

This unexpected turn in the cross-examination surprised Grindal as well as the prosecutors. Having fought to keep Dr. Wilbur from revealing in court what Maria Cornell had said, suddenly Avery's attorney was offering an open invitation to repeat Maria's account of that camp meeting.

Grindal complied. One day at the campground, Maria told her sister and brother-in-law, Avery approached her. "I should like to see you, Maria, and talk with you," he said. "I will meet you tonight at the house, when the horn blows for preaching." They subsequently met at the Elliotts' house, where it was too crowded to talk, so Avery told her to walk ahead into the woods where he would catch up with her. There they discussed her confession letters; Avery said he hadn't burned them yet, but he would do so on one condition. Suddenly he grabbed her hands, and "put one of his into her bosom."

"She tried to get away from him," Grindal continued, "but could not." Then, Maria told them, he "had intercourse with her, and they returned to the camp." Avery promised to destroy the letters after returning to Bristol. "This is what Maria told me and my wife," Grindal concluded. "She said it took place on Thursday."[23]

Why Avery's attorneys were willing to let Grindal Rawson repeat Cornell's accusation against the defendant became clear once the defense called their own witnesses from the Thompson camp meeting. They accepted Rawson's damaging story in exchange for his pinpointing the day that everything supposedly happened. Since Avery was at the camp meeting for only two days and evenings—Wednesday and Thursday—they knew they could account for his movement and location on that Thursday.

Though they had attended the trial since its first day, Ephraim's colleagues in the Methodist ministry now had their first opportunity to testify. Nine Methodist clergymen took the stand over two days. Rarely speaking as Avery's friends, they disclosed instead the routines of Methodist preachers and spoke of when and where they had seen Brother Avery at the camp meeting.

Rev. Henry Mayo, about the same age as Avery and recently married to a Lowell "factory girl," anchored Ephraim's camp meeting alibi, vouching they had spent most of the day together. Most important, he could account for Avery during the Thursday evening preaching when, as Cornell alleged, Maria and Ephraim supposedly met and walked alone into the woods. "I was with him from rather before sunset," Mayo testified, until "half past eight or a little before nine." They remained together until Avery walked off the campground with another preacher with whom he shared a room. Avery would depart the camp meeting the next morning. "He could not have been out of my sight more than three minutes at a time, in all that time." The attorney general couldn't get Mayo to waver under cross-examination.[24]

Tracing their encounters with Avery at the camp meeting, Methodist witnesses used the exact same time references. "Saw him, and went into the preachers' tent half past ten, left him about noon," said Henry Mayo, "again saw him at half-past five in the Weston tent." A layman echoed these phrases: saw Avery "Wednesday morning at seven o'clock, again Wednesday noon, and about four o'clock, P.M.," then later took tea with him at half past five. The same times were repeated again and again, none more often than "half past seven" in the evening.

None of the fifteen camp meeting witnesses mentioned taking out a timepiece to check the time, yet they knew precisely the time of day.

As it turned out, each one was reciting the pre-arranged schedule for a camp meeting. They were called Methodists for a reason. Breakfast started at seven, ending at eight. Morning preaching began at half past ten. Lunch came at noon, followed by afternoon preaching at two, and tea at half past five, which lasted exactly half an hour, followed by a prayer meeting. Then the evening's preaching service—always the highlight of the day—commenced precisely at seven-thirty. Methodists were given to organized and disciplined devotions; camp meeting rules, one explained, were "published from the stand, and a committee appointed to enforce them." Everyone was required to attend the scheduled events, and someone blew a trumpet to signal the time. If evening preaching always started at seven-thirty, it was sure to end at half past eight.[25]

By the time the defense called layman Milton Daggett as their last camp meeting witness, he was locked in on Avery sightings at exactly those times.

"How did you ascertain time?" the prosecutors wanted to know. "May not the time have varied fifteen minutes, more or less?"

Daggett was taken aback by even the suggestion. "I should say it was half past five, because that was the hour fixed by the regulations," he countered, "and if it was so one day, I don't see why it should not be another." He knew what time tea was scheduled, so it must have been exactly that time when the horn blew. No one bothered to compare timepieces.[26]

These habits of time discipline must have made Methodists appealing to manufacturers in Lowell, who wanted their mill workers most of all to follow regulations and time schedules with Methodist-like "utmost exactness." Many Methodists aspired as well to join the growing middle classes of the North, for whom punctuality, efficiency, and making the most of precious time were virtues of their domestic arrangements at home and of capitalist practices in the accounting room or retail shop. Methodists promoted a mindset suited to the nation's new economic order.[27]

Camp meetings, though, might not have followed the regimented and disciplined practices that these rules suggested. Realistically, the rules couldn't always be followed with "utmost exactness" when the meetings also witnessed spontaneous outpourings of supernatural encounters with God's spirit. As the week progressed, evening services exhibited extraordinary mass expressions of religious feelings, making even the most steadfast advocates of rules and order relent. Scores of people cried out, fainting and falling to the ground, sometimes entering trances. Preachers and lay leaders flocked to their side, praying and imploring them to give in to the spirit. Hundreds of convicted sinners rushed to the altar to be saved, with more exhortations ringing out over the cacophony of groans, sighs, and prayers.[28]

These kinds of explosive affairs could hardly be contained within a rigid time schedule. One Methodist who stressed the required obedience to time regulations admitted that on the last night of a most memorable meeting, the singing, praises, and preaching "continued more or less until 3 o'clock next morning." Thursday night's service at Thompson could have unfolded as a rousing, even uncontrolled, display of spiritual and emotional revelry. Nevertheless, Avery's defense witnesses projected an impression that they kept their eyes on Avery, and the horns told them the precise time for each occasion.[29]

But what if Grindal Rawson remembered incorrectly the day of the week? If Maria had told Grindal and Lucretia that Avery had forced himself on her on Wednesday night, that would change everything. The Methodist witnesses certainly observed Brother Avery on Wednesday, but not with the same ironclad certainty as Thursday. Fellow preachers could recall seeing Ephraim that afternoon, but not again until the next day. One saw him when the horn blew at seven-thirty but not afterward. Another watched him enter the preachers' tent after the horn but didn't notice him again until seeing him walk off alone at the end of the night.

Once again, Henry Mayo would be the Methodists' most reliable alibi witness. They spent most of Wednesday together until the evening horn blew. When Mayo seemed reluctant to head over for the night's preaching, Ephraim implored him, "Come Henry, come go to meeting." The men both left the preachers' tent at some undetermined time prior to the end of preaching—Mayo thought, "fifteen minutes before the services closed," which was usually at eight-thirty. If true, Ephraim could have walked off to meet Maria before the preaching ended. He didn't return to his lodgings until nearly ten that evening. Or, if the Spirit was in full force that night, he could have slipped away and returned while the emotional religious exercises stretched out much later than the planned schedule.[30]

If the coerced sexual encounter happened on Wednesday night, this would also explain the fixations on Maria Cornell's bodily appearance.

All the witnesses who spoke of her walking in an irregular, uncomfortable manner, or having a sickly look on her face, were describing Maria's appearance on Thursday morning, the night after the possible encounter in the woods. "Her eyes did not look well," and "she said she was out of health," one woman reported, adding "her eyes were dull and heavy. I thought they looked duller than people's usually do." Unwilling to talk publicly about Cornell's breasts, this witness might have unwittingly described the post-traumatic appearance of a woman who had been raped the night before.[31]

One day during her final weeks in Fall River, Maria had discussed this camp meeting with Lucy Hathaway, her co-worker and housemate.

"She asked me one morning if I did not think a girl might innocently be led away by a man she had confidence in and rather looked up to," Lucy testified at the trial. "I told her I didn't know."

"What can a poor weak woman do in the hands of a strong man, and he using all kinds of arguments?" Maria asked.[32]

The same concerns about precise time cropped up in testimony about Ephraim Avery's whereabouts in Providence in November when, as the steamboat engineer recalled, a man resembling Avery asked him to deliver a pink letter to Sarah Maria Cornell in Fall River. John Orswell was certain this happened on a Tuesday morning, when the Methodists were holding a four-day meeting in the city, between eight and nine o'clock, because he'd already begun stoking the fire so the steamboat could depart at ten. That's why the fingerprints he left on the pink letter were sooty.

Avery lodged at a Methodist baker's home, beginning his day at a sunrise prayer meeting. Rev. Jotham Horton had asked Avery to start a nine o'clock service, so Horton could retrieve a package arriving at the port. Fellow preachers, and the Methodist workingmen who lodged them, testified that Avery was at meetings or dining for breakfast or conversing with them at various times between seven-thirty and this nine o'clock service. When Rev. Horton arrived ten minutes past nine, he found to his surprise that Avery was at the church but hadn't yet started the service. Horton took charge.[33]

To deliver a letter to the steamboat engineer, Avery would have needed at least twenty-five or thirty minutes. He could have slipped away before the sunrise service ended and made his way to the steamboat before returning to the baker's house for breakfast; or he could have hurried off after breakfast, thereby becoming late to the service at nine. Yet Methodist witnesses made it appear that Avery was in their presence during that entire morning. But when asked about measuring time, they offered precise details where it could help Avery's alibi and more fuzzy answers when recalling details that could hurt his case.

All told, Avery's defense team called seventy-two witnesses to either corroborate Avery's alibis or contradict prosecution witnesses regarding Avery's movement on December 20, at the camp meeting in Thompson, and on the morning that a pink letter was delivered in November. The vastness of this testimony overwhelmed and exhausted the jury, spectators, and court members alike.

Of all the women who testified for either side regarding days and times relevant to Avery's whereabouts—more than thirty-five in total—not one woman mentioned looking at a time piece and reading the time for herself. Eleanor Owen heard church bells, working women reacted to factory bells, and the Methodist faithful remembered trumpets at the camp meeting. Jane Gifford, along with Nancy Bidwell, heard other people announce the time after glancing at time pieces. Women knew how to tell time, and some displayed their new clocks proudly in their homes, but women's work and women's time was not entirely their own. Farmers' wives, including the women who buried Maria Cornell, still measured time by familiar tasks and labors, even as their daughters went off to workplaces that rang bells to signal the manufacturer's control of time.

Amid all this talk about time, "this everlasting trial," in the words of reporter Benjamin Hallett, ground on interminably. Dozens of additional witnesses came forward—for both the defense and the prosecution. One exhausting day faded into another. The trial, a Newport newspaper declared, "will probably be of longer duration than any criminal trial that has ever taken place in this country."[34]

The press grew impatient. How much longer newsmen wondered, must they keep their pledge and refrain from publishing their trial notes. On the trial's sixteenth day, the *Boston Morning Post* defied the pledge, publishing their account of the first days of trial testimony. Trying to scoop the other papers, the *Post* was guessing when the defense might rest, but Avery's trial was nowhere near its end—there would be three more days of defense witnesses, four more of rebuttal witnesses on both sides, followed by two full days of attorneys' closing arguments, and then the jury had to decide.

The justices responded by removing the *Post's* reporter from the courtroom, but they couldn't stem the tide. Once newspapers from Salem to Philadelphia began reprinting the *Post's* account, the New York papers considered the pledge voided and published their own reports, with each installment appearing in Providence the next day. Richard Hildreth and Benjamin Hallett remained true to the court order, but they now advertised their imminent reports as "full" and "correct," rather than hastily rushed to the public. Newport's newspapers kept the testimony out of the press, and no one ever claimed that the early publication of trial reports tainted the jury. Yet the appetite for information was insatiable.[35]

Attorneys for both sides kept pushing to submit more evidence. The defense's last witness was a factory worker who stunned the courtroom by tying a clove-hitch knot around her neck with a rope, claiming it was regularly used to repair a weaver's harness. Prosecutors rebutted with Cornell's Fall River co-workers, all of whom testified that they had never seen anyone, including Cornell, use a clove-hitch in the factory. The defense witness, when recalled, had to admit that she'd first tried a clove-hitch only a few weeks earlier.)[36]

In the trial's closing skirmishes, prosecutors sought to prove that the letters in Cornell's trunk matched Avery's handwriting. They summoned Fall River's Methodist minister, Ira Bidwell, with Mason and Randolph objecting at every turn. Confirming Avery's signature on a letter he had received, Bidwell identified the same signature on a letter that Avery wrote to another Methodist preacher about Maria Cornell. The attorney general wanted jurors to see the same peculiarities of spelling: words like "haveing," "comeing," "tine" instead of time, and "sens" for sense, along with a similar penchant for dashes and underlining. Most important, the writer misspelled Maria's last name as "Connell" in all the letters.[37]

Tempers were short and frustrations abounded on both sides. Sixty-five-year-old Jeremiah Mason was becoming noticeably fatigued by the trial's fourth week. By May 28, Mason lamented that the trial "had already extended to a length unparalleled" in legal history. "There never was a capital trial in any one of the United States, so long continued, and yet it still seems to grow broader rather than narrow."

Prosecutors shot back. The blame for this protracted trial should be laid at the feet of Avery's defense counsel. "For the last fortnight," Dutee Pearce insisted, "we have not been trying Ephraim K. Avery, but Sarah Maria Cornell." Why was the defense "permitted to trace this girl through every cotton-mill in New England, to collect every syllable she had uttered" as threats against Avery and the Methodists, when prosecutors couldn't repel the notion that Cornell plotted revenge by showing her true feelings prior to her death?[38]

Testimony of witnesses ended twenty-four days after the trial began.

22

Closing Arguments

AS JEREMIAH MASON ROSE TO address the jury on Friday morning, May 31, 1833, the trial's twenty-third day, everyone could see the physical toll on the venerable attorney. Raising his massive frame once again, Avery's star counsel commenced his closing arguments. With his lingering Yankee accent and conversational style, Mason cozied up to the jury, connecting with them over their fatigue, the feat of sitting through the longest capital trial in the country's history, and the enormous work of memory facing them.

Pivoting, he reminded jurors that the defendant had placed his trust in them to rid their minds of the "unparalleled public excitement and prejudice" surrounding this case. Standing at times with one foot firmly on the floor while the other rested on his chair, Mason devoted the next hour to describing the dangers that the public's prejudice presented for fair and impartial justice. He took the jury on a journey through the long history of bigotry and intolerance, especially in matters of religion, from Salem's witch trials to England's Popish Plot, before landing at the neighborhoods of Tiverton and Fall River. A large portion of the witnesses, he reminded the jury, may have been influenced by the frenzy stirred up there. An "active and wealthy community," he said, heard of a supposed murder in its vicinity, got up an excitement—called town meetings, appointed committees, let its suspicions fall on a single individual—while the fever was "raging high." Witnesses had listened to all this talk of guilt until they had no doubt in their minds.[1]

With a sleight of hand, Mason alluded to hatred of clergymen by the irreligious, or jealousy of the Methodists, while also commending jurors as Rhode Island men who would never succumb to such intolerance. Yet it was the pre-trial mischief in Fall River that Mason returned to again and again. The factory town had held large meetings and selected committees not for the purpose of investigating the crime but to search for evidence against Rev. Avery. The press seized on this and flooded the country with publications, all "inflaming the public mind with bold statements of the defendant's guilt." Mason pointed directly to Harvey Harnden, "an active agent and important witness for the prosecution," who himself published 13,000 copies of his narrative of Avery's arrest. Jurors, Mason argued, could demonstrate their unbiased minds by standing against "the almost universal popular opinion" that "has already condemned the defendant without trial."[2]

Proving his high-ticket value as defense counsel, Mason turned next to disputing proof of a homicide, raising time and again the possibilities for doubt. "So long as there is hesitation, a tremor of the mind, a doubting or hanging back," Mason told the jurors, "there is not moral certainty." Repeating the phrase "moral certainty" nearly two dozen times over the next two hours, with equal doses of "probability" and "doubt" sprinkled in, he chipped away at the prosecution's mass of circumstantial evidence. "If there were but one chance in one hundred of his innocence, you cannot find a verdict of guilty upon circumstantial evidence. You have no right to calculate chances. There must be a moral certainty." Mason craftily transformed the legal doctrine of reasonable doubt into the benefit of remote probability.[3]

Nor was Mason averse to stating incorrectly the facts of the prosecution's testimony. In his recollections, witnesses made different claims and Fall River's doctors assisted with the initial coroner jury's suicide verdict, even though they didn't, in fact, examine the body until after the Tiverton farmers' first verdict.

Even more, Mason concocted his own conspiracy theories to explain the evidence. The penciled note ("If I am missing . . . ") incited his imagination: Who exactly took this paper out of Cornell's bandbox? How can one know whether one of the "Factory girls," seized by "Fall River zeal," had secretly manufactured this evidence? How could you say, he pleaded with the jury, what these hundreds of young women might do, "the whole village alarmed, highly excited, suspicion busy against the Defendant"?

No evidence was ever presented to suggest that anyone might be assisting Cornell, nor had she ever been seen with any other man during her three months in Fall River. This hardly slowed the imaginings of Jeremiah Mason.

He wanted to fix these possibilities into the minds of the twelve men of the jury. Someone undoubtedly handed the pink letter to John Orswell, Mason admitted. If Cornell had a partner in her conspiracy—a paramour—then he could have handed the letter to the steamboat engineer. Why had Cornell so willingly displayed different colored letters, exciting the curiosity of her co-workers? Had she hatched this plot from the moment she left Connecticut following the camp meeting? "All this looks like design—like conspiracy," Mason declared.[4]

Eventually Mason presented his conjectures as established fact. "Now if you believe that the deceased was carrying on a plot against the defendant," he continued, then you may easily suppose that "this artful woman" could have planted the torn half sheet of paper, identical to the December 8 white letter in Iram Smith's shop. Or another person might have placed it there— "That this woman had a paramour cannot be doubted," Mason insisted, giving the jurors free rein to conjure up Cornell's illicit lover, someone who would obviously derive "some benefit from charging Avery as the father of the child."[5]

Mason knew that a great defense attorney must argue both ways about trial evidence, and he was a master of his craft. The green stains on Cornell's knees could be explained away: first he argued that there was no green grass at the scene; then he surmised that Cornell knelt to pray before taking her own life. Maria Cornell could at once be characterized as insane and "far gone in wickedness" while also brilliantly artful enough to become close friends with the "most respectable" women in every factory town. Cornell's Methodist spirituality was all sensuality and fanaticism, while Avery's same religious feelings were the model of respectability and decorum.[6]

Nowhere did this two-way arguing become more obvious than in Mason's tactful dance around Cornell's relationship with Grindal Rawson. Disappointment in marriage, Mason observed, was "the disease that had preyed upon" Cornell's mind, but he never pointed a finger of blame at Rawson. Before leaving Connecticut for Fall River, and after consulting with Rawson, Cornell had already plotted her charges against Avery—it looked "like conspiracy," Mason declared, yet he refrained from linking Rawson to the plot.[7]

Hour stretched into hours, and although fatigued, Mason rehearsed and rebutted the evidence, questioning the trustworthiness of the prosecution's witnesses regarding Avery's whereabouts on December 20, at the camp meeting, and on the November day when Orswell received the pink letter, even if observers could tell that the legendary lawyer was least confident when trying to disconnect Avery from the letters found in Cornell's trunk.

Mason's energy reached its peak when he boiled the trial down to a question of character. In his words, Cornell was "subject to violent passions," marked by lewdness, prostitution, fanaticism, and insanity. Avery, on the other hand, was "as chaste, as peaceable and as blameless as any in society"— overlooking Avery's past incidents of slander and his guilt in Norris's lawsuit. Dismissing the prosecution's chain of circumstances pointing toward Avery's guilt, Mason insisted that "character is of itself circumstantial evidence." At one point, facing the jury, he reminded them that they had been asked to believe that a Methodist minister, not insane, but rather in command of his senses, would choose a camp meeting to gratify his lusts, while "this woman, common as the air, abandoned and profligate, was almost ravished, almost violated!" "The defendant was a clergyman," he concluded, and his profession "removes him from many temptations to which others are more exposed," and you, gentlemen of the jury, must "weigh this character of the defendant and these circumstances, and weigh them well."[8]

It was eight o'clock on a Friday evening, and with the exception of a short break, Mason had pleaded with the jury for seven and a half hours. Exhausted, Mason was unable to attend the next day, Saturday, June 1, when Attorney General Albert Greene delivered his closing arguments.

Greene rose to speak, and jurors had to notice that he seemed, compared to Mason, none the worse for wear as this marathon of a trial approached its end. Dignified, nattily dressed, and forever genial, he carefully calibrated his voice for its persuasive effect. Pitching into Mason's remarks, Greene dismissed the accusations that the prosecution was motivated by anti-religious prejudice. "The Government wages no war against Methodist ministers, or the ministers of any sect," he declared. "It is not the ministers of the Methodist Church who are tried, but the defendant himself, and he only, for his individual acts."[9]

Greene turned next to the aspersions cast on the citizens of Fall River, depicted a day ago as feverish witch-hunters, their feelings excited without restraint. What had these good people done? A resident of their industrious community was found dead, suddenly and extraordinarily. Certainly, they held meetings and appointed committees; their only object was to investigate this mysterious death. "This is what any community ought to have done," Greene reminded the jury. "The conduct of this prosecution," he continued, "was put into the hands of the most respectable among the respectable people of that village." He listed the men of the Fall River Committee by name, calling them "sound and capable men of different pursuits and sentiments." They were not carried away "by waywardness, caprice, or excitement," but rather conducted themselves "coolly, deliberately, like prudent men."[10]

The crime of murder, Greene reminded the jurors too, rarely has eyewitnesses—in fact it requires darkness and secrecy. A jury must commonly look to circumstantial proof, which could be every bit as reliable as positive proof. The gentlemen of the jury must combine all the circumstances, for it was "on the strength of the *whole* that you are to come to the result."[11]

Do not confuse reasonable doubt, Greene continued, with the mere possibility of innocence, for there was "no end to possibilities—no end to the suppositions, and conjectures, and caprices of the human mind." As such, "you are not to be led away from your duty by fanciful theories, or by the fear of the consequences." Rest assured that the distinguished (expensive, he could have added) counselors on the other side had ensured that the defendant was given a fair trial.

Greene went on to refute the defense's theory that Cornell carried out a plot to enact revenge, culminating in suicide. Painting Avery's conduct toward Maria Cornell as neither hostile nor persecuting, the skilled prosecutor argued that Cornell had no motive for harboring "feelings of deadly revenge," negating the defense's theory of her "desperate conspiracy" to ruin Avery and leave him charged with murder. Mason's conjecture that some young woman in Fall River forged Cornell's December 20 note and planted it in her bandbox in order to frame Avery was "utterly absurd," Greene insisted. "Gentlemen," he implored the jury, "you do not believe it—you cannot believe it." Indeed, Mr. Mason "could not have been serious in his attempt to excite such suspicion."[12]

For hours the attorney general reminded the jury of the testimony and evidence in the case that "proves, to a moral certainty and beyond all reasonable doubt, that this was a case of homicide." Recollect the condition of Cornell's dead body, he said, calling up images of her cloak, buttoned up all the way, both hands wearing gloves underneath it, and a cord drawn tight in a horizontal circle of equal depth around her neck, tied to a stake with six inches of rope. Could she have hung herself and caused the rope to leave this mark? No, Greene insisted, common sense dictates that if the rope had slipped when her body was suspended, the cord's indentation would be higher on one side and deeper and lower on the other.

Remember too that the knot was a clove-hitch, he continued, the kind of knot that could "only be tightened by both hands being drawn horizontally." No person could draw tight this knot, cutting off all respiration and sensation, and then afterwards tie the rope onto a stake to hang herself. It was a physical impossibility. Why, Cornell could easily have resorted to an ordinary slip-knot to accomplish her objective. What was more, the clove-hitch was "a knot which women are not acquainted with and do not ordinarily tie," and she was found with her gloves on; it would have taken a naked hand to tie that knot and suspend the rope onto the stake—"she could not have put her gloves on *after* she had done it."[13]

What motive did Cornell have for self-murder? It couldn't have derived from fear of the shame if her pregnancy were disclosed, Greene said, for her family already knew and she'd consulted a local doctor. The defense's testimony regarding her character, Greene argued, "utterly destroys their own argument." If the jury believed what the defense suggested, that she was a lewd woman who had been pregnant twice before, could they believe that she would have destroyed herself to escape the shame of exposure?[14]

None of the circumstances surrounding this death, Greene declared, confirmed a suicide. Cornell had refused to take a dose of oil of tansy that Dr. Wilbur told her would be fatal. She was unusually cheerful her last day at the mill and held in her possession a letter from December 8 making an appointment for that same evening. What was more, a woman would naturally shrink from the kind of exposure involved in hanging herself in a public place, thereby revealing her situation to all.[15]

As for the medical testimony about Cornell's dead body, Greene admitted he knew little of the actual science about which the defense's physician witnesses testified, but he would "sooner trust to the EYES of four sensible, experienced women, to ascertain the real state of the facts, than to the theories of a whole college of physicians." Indeed, "the women themselves swear to what they *saw*," while the medical experts testified to "what those women probably *could see*."[16]

If this death was a homicide—and here the attorney general felt he had his strongest evidence—then the jury must consider the question of who was the author of the letters in Cornell's possession. He turned first to the pink letter, dated November from Providence, and noted how its author let slip that he was inviting Cornell to "come to this place, viz. Bristol." In addition, the writer asked Cornell to direct any responding letters to Betsey Hills, a member of Mr. Avery's family.[17]

Greene also directly confronted Mason's revenge conspiracy theory—that Cornell and a paramour had planned the letters to incriminate Avery. How could Cornell and her supposed paramour have known to deliver the letter to John Orswell precisely when Avery was in Providence? Why, if they intended to frame Avery, had they omitted his name or signature? And would Cornell or her paramour have known to misspell her own name ("Connell") in exactly the manner that Avery himself had written her name in his letters? "I repeat," Greene intoned, "no human agency could produce these coincidences."[18]

The attorney general ended his closing remarks by returning to December 20, and the absurdity of Ephraim Avery's alibi. To do so, he brought out a map and outlined for the jury the journey of the tall stranger seen by Tiverton and Fall River witnesses. Moving from the ferry to the stone bridge to the vicinity of John Durfee's farm, he was on his way to meet his appointment with the now-deceased as promised in the December 8 white letter. "He was making his way to Fall River leisurely," Greene narrated, "surveying the ground in the vicinity where the homicide took place."

Greene turned to face the jury. If he had brought the prisoner and the deceased together at the stack yard, and "he was the man who was last with her, and her death was caused by homicide," then he must call upon the preacher to account for this. "She is dead and dead by violence," Greene said, "and I have a right to require her blood at his hands."[19]

Avery's alibi, Greene insisted, was too absurd to believe. "Believe it, if you can, gentlemen, that a fond father, a kind husband, on the shortest day of the year, in extreme cold weather, should have left his sick family, crossed a rough Ferry and wandered upon the Island, no one knows where, from half past two o'clock, until half past nine," all for the purpose of indulging some passing interest in geology. He was apparently so forgetful that he remained unconscious of time's passing, "so unmindful of his friends as not to call upon one of them," so disregarding of his own needs as to not seek any refreshment, and "so devoid of thirst as not to have stopped at a door, even for a glass of water." Indeed, Avery's alibi was "a most strange and lame account."[20]

After nearly six hours, at half past six o'clock on Saturday evening, the attorney general closed his argument, with a final appeal to the jury: "look to your own consciences!"

Many local newspapers would praise Greene's eloquence. A writer for the *Providence Journal* declared his oration "not only the best speech ever made by the Attorney General in his capacity of prosecuting officer, but one of the best arguments on facts that I have ever heard." Greene had "reached the hearts of the jury."[21]

The chief justice took only a few minutes to deliver his charge to the twelve men to proceed with "candor, firmness and impartiality." He reminded them on what grounds to consider the letters from Maria Cornell—not to prove they had been written by Avery but to rebut the assumption that she had committed suicide.

Before seven o'clock on Saturday night, the jury was ushered to a private room to deliberate. With so much to remember from a month-long trial, perhaps Mason's words that "character" must carry a "great weight" still lingered in their minds, or perhaps they focused on the attorney general's final plea to "look to your consciences!"[22]

ACT III

Scandal

23

Mobs and More Murders

A PALPABLE MIX OF ANXIETY and anticipation hung over Newport on the morning of Sunday, June 2, dawning as a pleasant early summer day. Late into the previous night, crowds walked the streets or gathered in the courthouse square, awaiting the tolling bell that signaled a jury's verdict. Though weary, the faithful headed off to worship at one of the city's eleven churches.[1]

Newport's Methodists joined with their out-of-town brothers and sisters at their white meetinghouse across the street from the jail where Ephraim Avery had been confined for four months. Rev. Asa Kent looked out across a sea of concerned faces, worried for both his congregation and his brother in ministry across the street. "Prayer was made to God, without ceasing," he recalled, since "all human help seemed to fail." They had waited and prayed until midnight the night before, then filled the pews again that morning, while "a painful suspense sat brooding over the heart." Kent feared that the jury might never agree, and brother Avery would waste away for many more months in his dark prison cell.[2]

About half past eleven the courthouse bell rang, and the rush was on. Churches instantly emptied of worshippers, and hundreds raced off, crowding against the courthouse doors until they opened, pushing to secure a place to hear for themselves the jury's decision. Hard to imagine, but the crowd, Benjamin Hallett reported, far exceeded even those that had previously packed the courtroom.

The justices entered first, followed by the court clerk, the prosecutors, and the twelve men of the jury. Ephraim Avery was once again led to the courthouse by the jailer, but this time he walked arm-in-arm with Rev. Samuel Palmer, who had worked harder than any of his compatriots on behalf of the defense. Ephraim took his seat at his counsel's table, but it suddenly became apparent that someone was missing. The courtroom waited in pin-drop silence for an entire ten minutes—maybe fifteen—for Avery's attorney, Richard Randolph, one of the few who apparently sat through the entire service before leaving his pew at Trinity Church.[3]

All eyes fixed their attention on the jury, whose faces looked "so haggard, care-worn and severe," Richard Hildreth noted, that spectators concluded that they were certain to return a guilty verdict. The court instructed Avery to stand and look at the jury.

"Gentlemen of the jury, have you agreed upon your verdict?" the clerk cried out.

"We have."

"Who shall speak for you?"

"Our foreman."

"Mr. Foreman, is the prisoner guilty or not guilty?" the clerk asked.

Eleazer Trevett announced the verdict forcefully. The clerk then repeated the verdict, asking each juror if they agreed: "Is that your verdict?" They all replied, "It is." The verdict? "Not guilty."[4]

The chief justice hammered his gavel and discharged Ephraim Avery, announcing that he was free to go. Until that moment, reported Hallett, whose seat allowed him to observe the defendant's every motion, the preacher maintained the same stoic steadiness, his emotional demeanor generally unwavering since the trial's first day. As he heard the clerk repeat the verdict, Avery dropped unsteadily into his chair, his face flushed, a tear starting from his eye. Sliding his right hand under his glasses, he covered the tear, and kept his hand there until he regained his composure. Soon he was enveloped in the boisterous congratulations of his friends.

The preacher was hustled off to Asa Kent's home, where he rested briefly before his attorneys drove him in a carriage to the waterfront to board a boat for his return home.

Bristol residents, meanwhile, had no idea that the jury had reached a verdict. The last news they had heard was a rumor that ten of the twelve jurors were decidedly against Avery's innocence before they entered their deliberations. While men milled around the wharves discussing Avery's possible fate, a sloop sailed in, leading one person to exclaim, "There's brother Avery now!" Word spread, and suddenly the preacher found himself surrounded by a crowd of welcoming Methodists and neighbors who accompanied him to his house. Bursting through the front door to escape the throng, he announced the end of his ordeal. Sophia Avery sank to the floor in a swoon.[5]

"The long agony is over," the *Fall River Weekly Recorder* declared. Expressing faith in justice and the rule of law, the editors accepted the verdict with sober resignation. "We are satisfied," they wrote. They even declared that they "rejoice that he has been discharged" and admitted that the jury were "honorable men—men of character and standing in the community." At the same time though, they felt Fall River deserved something more.

No community could have been more disheartened by Avery's acquittal than Fall River. Having invested months of resources and emotion in assisting the preacher's prosecution, the mill town's citizens had a great deal riding on the trial's outcome. Although initially they expressed no public anger and issued no calls for protest, they must have been enraged.

The *Weekly Recorder* editors hoped that justice might take a different form, and that required patience. Rev. Ephraim Avery must face a less formal but no less important tribunal. The facts of the trial must be laid before the public, who could then "decide whether *their* opinion accords with the verdict."[6]

This posturing arose in part from the drubbing the mill town had taken during the long trial. Accused of stirring up unparalleled excitement and religious persecution comparable to witch hunting in Salem, Fall River's leaders wanted to regain the wider public's confidence. Two weeks later, the *Weekly Recorder* reported its pleasure in seeing "so much calmness and deliberation" and "so little excitement" in the town's response to the verdict. "Let us hear no more, then, of this slanderous charge of excitement and persecution."[7]

After spending just two nights in his own bed in Bristol, Ephraim Avery took to the road again, summoned by his Methodist colleagues to attend the New England Conference's annual meeting in Boston. Having set the date a year before, Methodist leaders couldn't have foreseen holding their gathering only days after the momentous verdict, nor predicted their suspected complicity in Avery's acquittal.

Methodist preachers had faced increasing hostility since the trial began. Newspapers questioned their motives, and crowds of young men and boys shouted insults from street corners in Newport. It was time to control the damage. As the conference opened, Wilbur Fisk, president of Wesleyan University in Connecticut, rose and called for an investigation into Avery's case. Fisk would chair the committee, joined by six other prominent ministers, including Joseph Merrill and Asa Kent.[8]

Meanwhile, throughout Boston, rumors circulated as people began speculating about whether they might set eyes on the notorious preacher. On the second night, "a mob of men and boys" gathered at the Methodist church in Charlestown, hearing reports that Avery might be there to preach. The crowd surrounded the meetinghouse, eventually forcing their way in, bent on provoking a confrontation. Avery didn't ascend the pulpit and soon a justice of the peace ordered the rioters to disperse. No one reported any serious threats to Avery's safety.[9]

Less than a week later, on June 11, the Methodist investigative committee read its report to the conference in the Bennet Street Church. The seven ministers, led by Fisk, concluded that the trial reports fully exonerated Avery of any wrongdoing: "Ephraim K. Avery is innocent, in the opinion of this Conference, of any criminal intercourse with Sarah M. Cornell, and of any other act, connected with this unhappy affair, at all involving his Christian or ministerial character." Repeating the assault on Maria Cornell's character begun during the trial—accusing her once again of "moral depravity," "mental derangement," and a "revengeful spirit"—the committee found no evidence implicating their colleague, except for the testimony of "the wretched woman herself." It was "the respective characters of the parties," they declared, that decided the matter once and for all. Like so many others, Ephraim's brothers saw proof in his demeanor: how he never exhibited any signs of guilt in either prison cell or courtroom.

Faced with a torrent of animosity throughout the trial, the Methodist ministers saw themselves as victims too. "The most flagrant and injurious prejudices" had poisoned the public mind against the Methodist Church, even though they had done nothing more than offer "friendly aid" to ensure that an accused brother received a fair trial.[10]

Ephraim sat silently while the committee's report was read. This time he could listen to arguments in his defense without fear. Asked by the bishop if he would like to speak, Ephraim rose, but said only that "so long as his pulse beat" he would be grateful for the support he had received from his Christian friends and brethren. The committee's report was unanimously approved and ordered to be published immediately. This was a bold, chest-thumping, exoneration of Avery and the Methodists, and it was sure to be noticed.

Ephraim didn't remain silent for long. Invited by his fellow ministers to preach the next afternoon, he accepted. No riot disrupted the

The 1833 annual meeting of the New England Conference of the Methodist Episcopal Church, which cleared Ephraim Avery of all wrongdoing. From James Mudge, *History of the New England Conference of the Methodist Episcopal Church, 1796–1910* (Boston, 1910).

service—although this had more to do with the timing of a Wednesday afternoon service than with the extent of opposition in the city. Taking Psalm 31 as his text—"How great is thy goodness . . . "—Ephraim described the trials the faithful faced and praised "the goodness of the Almighty in preserving him from the persecutions of wicked men." At one point he seemed overwhelmed, near tears, while his supporters noted that many eyes in the audience also welled up. Before adjourning, the conference reappointed Ephraim to Bristol; indeed Methodists there stated that they would "consider themselves unhandsomely treated" had he not been allowed to return.[11]

Methodists released their defense of their persecuted brother just as the public—on street corners and in newspapers—began to weigh in on the jury's verdict. Until then, many newsmen thought it inappropriate to object to a lawful jury's judgment. Those who disagreed, New York's *Evening Post* declared, should "entertain their opinions in silence." The *Providence Journal's* opinion that "the judgment of the community should harmonize with the verdict of the jury" was repeated in papers from Maine to South Carolina.

Not every voice showed the same restraint. Despite Avery's acquittal, the *Pawtucket Chronicle* wrote, suspicion would always haunt the steps of "that foul fiend" and poison his private hours. Newport's *Rhode Island*

Republican insisted that the people no more believe that Cornell put an end to her life than that she fabricated her own existence, and a contributing writer insisted there was "scarcely a man, woman or child in this State" who believed Ephraim Avery was not "a hypocrite and a murderer."[12]

Reactions to the Methodists' report mirrored the divisions that had prevailed since Avery's arrest and trial. An occasional Presbyterian or Episcopal newspaper joined the Methodists in believing in the innocence of a persecuted clergyman, but louder voices declared the Methodists' report a "whitewashing" and a deeply partisan take on the trial. Sentiment was growing that the Methodists had made "common cause with Avery."[13] Acknowledging a jury's rightful authority, a chorus of voices insisted that Avery must face the judgment of a different court: "the tribunal of the people," as Providence's *Republican Herald* put it, "and the verdict of their opinion, he cannot possibly evade."[14]

Before leaving Boston the next day with the full blessing of his fellow Methodists, Ephraim walked down to the shops on Kilby Street—after months in a Newport jail he no doubt needed to replenish his wardrobe. Recognized immediately, he found himself followed by a sizable throng and slipped quickly into one of the stores. As young men and boys hooted from the street in "harsh and menacing language," a crowd amassed. A nearby shop owner, a Methodist, pushed through the crush, offering to escort the Bristol preacher to his own store. Crossing the street, the two men endured an unceasing harangue of epithets and threats of personal violence.

Soon the mob had ballooned to nearly 500. Removed from the intimate embrace of his fellow Methodists, Ephraim Avery met the other face of a divided populace and the first genuine threat of vigilante violence. Indeed, from one newspaper's perspective, the crowd represented the "general sentiment" of the Boston public against Avery and the Methodists. Once again, the acquitted preacher escaped harm when the sheriff arrived, ordering the crowd to disband and clear out.[15]

Boston had long known the politics of street theater. A century earlier, colonial Bostonians had staged a raucous annual Pope's Day festival, when the poorest working folk turned the city upside down, parading, fighting over, and burning giant effigies of the devil and the pope. Bostonians also created their own versions of Europe's long-standing mob actions, called charivaris, rough music, or skimmingtons, wherein town folk shamed the village's transgressors.[16] When aggrieved by new forms of tyranny from the British empire, like the Stamp Act and the Tea Act, they again turned to villain-shaming rituals when fomenting a revolution. These kinds of protests resurfaced whenever ordinary people sought to avenge offenses against local lives and livelihoods.[17]

As news of the Methodist report spread, people across New England turned to these familiar expressions of popular justice. The day after the Methodists declared Avery "entirely innocent," residents of Providence awoke to find a coffin floating down the river. As a large crowd gathered, a boatman retrieved it and displayed its empty contents and a lid with the label "Ephraim K. Avery." Within a week, reports of this mock funeral appeared in newspapers as far away as Alexandria, Virginia. Though dismissed as the playful rebellion of "boys," newspapers cried out "Scandalous!" for such an "insult to the public," but it wasn't clear whether they were referring to the coffin or to Avery's acquittal.[18]

A few days later, three miles from Newport's courthouse in neighboring Middletown, at an oceanside bluff aptly known as "Hanging Rocks," opponents of the verdict erected elaborate *tableaux vivants*. First they burned an effigy of the twelve-man jury, then they constructed another with the Bristol preacher hanging from a mock gallows. On the beach below sat another likeness of Avery in a posture of prayer with a rope around his neck. This scene remained in place for at least a week. Since the people of Middletown were "not apt to be moved at trifles," remarked a Newport newspaper, "they must have felt the indignation deeply to have thus given vent to it."[19]

For weeks, such street-theater spectacles broke out. On the Fourth of July—prompted by popular memories of the mob actions that had inspired Independence—communities that felt the sting of Maria Cornell's death and Avery's acquittal turned to similar rituals of mock justice. By then, Fall River's residents refused any longer to silence their anger. They first hung an effigy of Avery from a tree near Durfee's stackyard, where boys used it for target practice, then burned it triumphantly in a village square at nightfall. Across the stone bridge in Portsmouth, not far from Gifford's ferry, an effigy hung all day until the desecrated image of the preacher was eventually given to the dogs. Even in Bristol not all town folk shared the Methodists' enthusiasm for Avery's return. The town, known to this day for the oldest continuous celebration of Independence Day, dating back to 1785, burned an effigy of Avery on the Fourth. Rumors began circulating that Avery was too afraid to appear in public in Bristol or that he had once again gone into hiding, although neither was true.[20]

All summer the protests persisted. Providence's town folk, on several occasions, suspended effigies from poles or trees, selecting high elevations that could be seen by all. After displaying them all day, people cut down the effigies and paraded through the city, with a makeshift float dragged through the streets by a team of dogs for the entertainment of crowds of spectators. Avery's image was also hung near cotton factories in nearby mill towns, accompanied in one instance by the tragic suicide of a young man who mistakenly thought the effigies were taunting him. Effigies were also exhibited repeatedly throughout the summer in Bristol and Newport. Avery's supporters were aghast, but most respectable citizens silently gave a wink of approval to "these monuments of the 'prince of crime,'" as one newspaper called them.[21]

It was no coincidence that these mock hangings became associated with liberty trees, the gathering sites for popular resistance by "true-born sons of liberty" during the Revolution. Back then, it was loyalists and British officials who found themselves hung in effigy or even tarred and feathered under the trees' branches. British forces, understanding their significance, destroyed liberty trees when they occupied cities like Newport during the war. Once independence was achieved, Newport residents replanted their Liberty Tree at the corner of Thames and Farewell Streets. It did not again serve as a site for popular protest until the summer of 1833 when residents gathered under its boughs to hang Ephraim Avery in effigy.[22]

Effigy pageantry reminded elites that a politics of the people had not disappeared after the American Revolution. Within a few years, though, rioting in America would become more dangerous than mere street theater. Whenever a riot broke out, it was more likely to turn violent, spurred by hostilities that grew from a divided populace—riven by the new economic and political order and the growing intensity of racial, class, and ethnic conflicts.[23]

Avery-inspired mobs provoked an unsettling question: How would criminal justice work in a participatory democracy? Could justice be achieved when the people themselves were glorified as judge and jury? At a moment when public opinion was being canonized as the principal force in an emerging democracy, the engines of public opinion—news media and popular demonstrations in the streets—posed the gravest threats to the execution of criminal justice within the rule of law. These were existential questions for the young republic.[24]

Thoughtful observers pondered whose judgment represented the true voice of the residents of Newport: the jury or the people? Despite playing host to the nation's longest trial, with ten of the twelve jurymen hailing from the city, the press insisted that most Newport residents sided with the effigy-burners who believed Avery guilty of Cornell's death.

While some raised a cry of disorder and indelicacy, others asked how anyone could suppress the people's anger when cheated out of true justice. "The fire of popular excitement cannot and will not be abated," declared the *Providence City Gazette*; a "war of passion—the war of just and honest indignation" has commenced, and those standing in its way are liable to face "the violence of popular anathema." These mock funeral rites represented their own "kind of justice," displaying a "spontaneous and general expression of public opinion."[25]

The bold exoneration of Avery by the Methodist conference brought more than protests in its wake; it incited denunciations too, even from fellow Methodists. Newspapers across the country warned New England's Methodists against imprudently forcing Avery back into the public sphere while "doubts and suspicions" still prevailed. In their critics' eyes, Methodists defied the public by declaring Avery's innocence "with a triumphant flourish."[26]

In response, the Methodists began conflating the church's media foes with disorderly, vice-ridden mobs. Tired of the repeated cries that only public opinion could determine Avery's (and thereby the Methodists') true innocence, Boston's Methodist newspaper fought back, asking: What is "Public Opinion"? Was it the obscene rantings heard on street corners or in rum cellars? Was it "to impugn the motives of the Court" and an impartial jury, "to threaten these men with personal abuse for deciding the case contrary to the savage wishes of an unprincipled MOB?" Was it to insult and persecute "a whole Christian community," and "treat them as though they had no rights and privileges with other citizens?"[27]

Conservatives and defenders of religion, perceiving an all-out assault on clergymen and Christianity, joined in condemning any popular reactions outside the bounds of established civil and political institutions. From their perspective, new raucous partisan politics in Jacksonian America offered ordinary white men a public voice as voters, and anything beyond that, traditionalists argued, constituted the misrule of the mob. By the time the jury acquitted Ephraim Avery, conservative New Englanders, facing discontented workers and bitter divisions over abolitionism, deliberately erased the memory of unruly lower-class crowds during the American Revolution, refashioning it into a genteel ritual or child's play called Boston's "tea party." Despite such purposeful forgetting, ordinary citizens had never left behind the tradition of street protest.

The Methodists' most vocal critics exploded over denials of the public's right to judge. How dare these "most Reverend divines" pretend to believe there was "not even the remotest chance" of Avery's guilt. "'Mob!' to be sure—Ha—Ha—Ha," retorted the Providence *Republican Herald*. "All that do not subscribe" to the "pretended belief in the spotless innocence of E.K. Avery, are the 'mob.' . . . And who are you, that talk about a 'mob,' and class together a vast body of citizens, ten thousand times more respectable than yourselves, under that degrading appellation?"[28]

By late summer, crowd demonstrations began to wane but not the public's white-hot fascination with Avery, Cornell, and the Methodists. The scandal continued to play out as intense battles in print media and inside theaters. Yet street-theater expressions of justice didn't go away entirely. In Bristol, where Avery had been reassigned along with a young and respected Methodist minister, demonstrations and effigy burnings never ceased, forcing Ephraim to withdraw from regular preaching. News of his invitation to a pulpit anywhere else immediately raised the specter of rioting.

Near year's end, Ephraim tried to return to towns where he had formerly gained his reputation, hoping to find a receptive audience. On Sunday, December 15, he preached in Saugus—where three years before he had slandered the rival preacher Thomas Norris—and Methodist papers reported that a respectable audience welcomed him with decorum and solemnity. News of his preaching, and rumors that he would appear at another meeting in Lynn the same day, however, set off further demonstrations. Lynn residents erected a gallows at High Rock overlooking the town center, where they hung a likeness of the hated preacher, attracting a large crowd that spent all afternoon "shouting, hurrahing, and firing guns at the effigy" before torching it at nightfall. Two other effigies were hung in town that day, including one raised on the Liberty Pole at Liberty Square.[29]

Avery arrived in Lowell a few days later, but his reception there was no more welcoming. When word spread that he might preach on Sunday, Lowell rioters devoted an entire weekend to a saturnalia of justice by public opinion. Avery was hung and burned in effigy on both Friday and Saturday evenings. By Saturday night, rioters had constructed a replica of a haystack along with an effigy of Avery running away from the stackyard, with a rope dangling from one pocket and a woman's handkerchief visible from the other. The tableau remained in a public square until town officials ordered it removed the next day. Crowds broke into homes all day Saturday, looking unsuccessfully for the Bristol preacher, and by Sunday morning the Methodist meetinghouse was jammed with people intent on preventing

Avery from preaching. The *Lowell Mercury* voiced its astonishment at the audacity of this attempt to "browbeat public opinion," while the *Boston Transcript* marveled that Avery's supporters still insisted on bringing him to a pulpit, when he was sure to face "a whirlwind of popular indignation," inciting "the brute passions of the mob." Avery fled town, narrowly escaping personal injury.[30]

While the crowds protesting Avery's acquittal remained largely peaceful, in ensuing months his trial began to incite deadly violence. The not-guilty verdict inflamed disputes in bars, workplaces, and church grounds. A crucial impetus was the rapid publication of accounts of the trial, causing angry words to incite physical violence.

With a reading public clamoring for news, and newsmen eager to publish their transcripts, newspapers all over New England, in upstate New York, and as far south as Virginia gave over nearly every column to these transcribed reports. Like sideshow barkers, editors encouraged the public to read the whole trial before making up their own minds. It was good for newspaper sales, but so too were decisions by some editors to cast their papers as moral alternatives to publications eager to exhibit the "indecent and disgusting" details from the trial's testimony.[31]

Meanwhile, all through the summer, booksellers from Maine to South Carolina advertised the lengthy trial reports from lawyers-turned-journalists like Richard Hildreth, George Rivers, and Benjamin Hallett. Hildreth's report stretched to 143 pages; Rivers's ran 178 pages, and Hallett's, the most comprehensive of all, topped 340 pages. Turning the pages, readers felt almost as if they were present in the courtroom. All told, Avery's prosecution generated eight different trial reports, which were part of more than twenty published books and pamphlets about the case, more than for any comparable crime.[32]

Trial reports, among the most important new in-print genres, became popular entertainment for Americans, both satisfying morbid curiosities and contributing to new ways of understanding murders and murderers. Through the trial report, courtroom storytelling translated into a new style of popular literature, enthralling readers with evidence and adversarial narratives, fostering an insatiable Gothic obsession with the horror and mystery of violent crime, and displacing older colonial-era notions of the murderer as a common sinner. The killer was transformed into a moral monster, an alien creature both different and isolated from the community. Avery's trial elevated the popularity of trial reports, eventually spawning a reading audience eager to consume murder mysteries and detective fiction.

From the start, trial reports contributed their own drama to the murder of Sarah Maria Cornell.[33]

Ten days after the verdict, two men living 300 miles from the site of Maria Cornell's death, succumbed to the red-hot emotions already raging in the vicinity of Fall River. James Tilly and Clark Babcock, both in their mid-twenties, were partners in a barrel-making shop in the upstate New York town of Verona. Babcock began reading aloud a newspaper account of the Avery trial testimony at their shop and railing against the jury's decision. An angry argument ensued, with Babcock excoriating the Methodists for helping Avery escape justice, and Tilly taking the opposite side. As a Methodist, Tilly could bear it no longer and stormed out, but Babcock followed, his furious criticism of the Methodists unceasing. A brawl began. Tilly grabbed hold of his partner, threw him to the ground and pinned him for several minutes, before asking Babcock whether he would "behave himself." Witnesses weren't sure of Babcock's answer, but as Tilly relaxed his hold, Babcock drew a large knife and thrust it into his combatant's belly, opening a four-inch gash from which Tilly's bowels began to extrude. Local physicians couldn't repair the damage, and Tilly died the next morning.[34]

Nine days after Tilly's death, Avery's trial again became entangled in murderous violence, once more with the trial reports gravely implicated. On a pleasant summer Sunday morning at a farm near Concord, New Hampshire, a young laborer named Abraham Prescott invited Sally Cochran, the farmer's wife, to join him picking strawberries in a nearby field. He also invited Sally's husband, Chauncey, to join them. Chauncey declined curtly, saying that he was absorbed in reading Avery's trial report. An hour and a half later, when folks in the farmhouse heard strange noises outside, Chauncey put down the trial report to investigate, finding Prescott sitting at the barn door, his pants and shirt covered in blood. To Chauncey's inquiry, he replied, "I struck Sally with a stake and killed her."[35]

Prescott's subsequent murder trial hinged on the tangled arguments of his defense attorneys. For the first time in the United States, sleepwalking—somnambulism—was offered as a defense for murder, because the eighteen-year-old Prescott had assaulted the Cochrans once before. He had struck both of them with an axe while asleep in their bed, yet they believed Prescott's story that he too was asleep, since he'd otherwise been a "very good" and "obedient" boy. Prescott again claimed that he had fallen asleep only to awaken and discover Sally's death scene. His attorneys recited a slew of anecdotal medical evidence regarding somnambulism, while also arguing that his family had a history of insanity. Even Dr. William Graves showed up again as a medical witness; Graves had been the Prescott family physician before relocating to Lowell, and the defense claimed that Graves had earlier predicted that the boy "might be crazy" later in life.[36]

Abraham Prescott's attorneys also blamed the Avery trial for Sally Cochran's murder. Prescott teetered on the precipice between sanity and insanity, they told the jury, asking, "What was that mental irritant, that excitement of the imagination, which helped to throw him off his balance?" and answering, "Why, it was the Avery trial, which Cochran was reading at the time they left the house." With Avery's trial captivating the thoughts of this family and the whole community, and Abraham and Sally talking about it as they strolled toward the strawberry field, an astounding thought echoed in his brain: "that a minister of a holy religion should have been on trial for so monstrous a crime." "By means of the Avery trial," a specific act of violence—killing a woman—grabbed hold and "helped unman his diseased intellect."[37]

New Hampshire's attorney general, George Sullivan, countered this claim, arguing that the defense needed to show that Prescott had actually read the trial report himself rather than being brushed aside by Chauncey Cochran's reading. Did the mere mention of Avery cause Prescott's derangement? Why didn't it produce that effect when the story of Cornell's murder was first told, or during the past month when the trial's outcome was so much the conversation of the day? Sullivan didn't discount the region's obsession with Avery but suggested instead that Prescott exploited it to carry out his "diabolical purpose."[38]

The jury didn't buy the somnambulism defense, let alone the argument of temporary insanity caused by Avery's trial, and they found Prescott guilty.

All the features of Avery's scandalous trial got rehearsed in Abraham Prescott's case: sexual violence against a woman, doctors and lawyers asserting insanity, mobs and spectacles of public justice, and most important, the sway of publicity and popular reading about violent crime and criminal justice. Some Americans asked—in a refrain that would echo for generations— whether popular media's obsession with a crime only caused more violence, either in the form of copy-cats or vigilantes. "Does not the publicity given to crimes," one newspaper asked that summer, induce "the vicious to do the same?" Avery's trial incited that conundrum. And the public's fascination with the Methodist preacher showed no signs of waning.[39]

24

Conspiracies

ALL THROUGH THE UPROAR OVER Cornell's death and Avery's trial, another murder occupied the minds of Americans. Six years earlier, in 1826, a disgruntled, down-and-out stone mason named William Morgan ignited a firestorm. A Virginian by birth, and nearing fifty, Morgan sought a fresh start in the booming Erie Canal towns of upstate New York. Quarrelsome and hard-drinking, he found no fortune there. Yet somewhere along the way, he gained membership in the Fraternal Order of Freemasons.

When local Masons in Batavia, New York, denied Morgan membership in their new lodge, he teamed up with a local newspaper publisher to write a tell-all book, *Illustrations of Masonry*, disclosing the fraternity's secret rituals, oaths, signals, and hand-grips. Masons immediately began harassing Morgan and his publisher, ransacking their homes and shops in search of the manuscript, and drumming up false charges against Morgan. By autumn, Morgan found himself confined to jail for failure to pay a $2.67 debt. The next night, while the jailer was away, several Masons paid the debt and coaxed him from his cell. Once he was outside, the jailer's wife heard a shrill whistle and rushed to the window to witness Morgan crying, "Murder! Murder!" as he struggled against men forcing him into a carriage. Morgan was never seen again.[1]

Rumors spread and excitement mounted. A news editor remarked that he'd heard "nothing talked of, in the stages and bar-rooms, but Morgan." As local officials dragged their feet in prosecuting the crime, suspicions galvanized a movement in opposition to Freemasonry. For five years, across five counties, more than twenty grand juries held investigations and indicted dozens of Masons. Ultimately only four men were convicted for involvement in Morgan's kidnapping; they received light sentences, and none faced murder charges. Many believed that if the Masons could shield their members from prosecution—if they swore secret oaths to defend a lodge brother even to the point of perjury—then the fraternity could subvert the entire criminal justice system. After all, weren't many county judges, prosecutors, sheriffs, and jurors Masons? To a growing group of Antimasons, the "cry of Morgan" came to symbolize a massive conspiracy against the republic and against equality before the law.[2]

When Ephraim Avery walked free from Bristol and went into hiding, rumors spread that he must be a Mason. This had to be the reason, they surmised, why two Bristol magistrates blatantly ignored the overwhelming evidence pointing to the preacher. In this view, justices Howe and Haile were part of a Masonic plot to shield Avery from prosecution for his crimes.[3]

By the time Ephraim Avery was charged with Cornell's murder, Antimasonry, like waves of revivalism, had already spread across the Northeast. Local outrage grew into a social movement, with its own newspapers, books and pamphlets, local committees, and traveling lecturers, all spreading a message of conspiracy. The mass movement in turn became a political party—the nation's first third party.[4]

A suspicious death was sure to excite the collective fears of the Masons' critics. When Masons in Boston carried a dead man's body from their lodge in 1829, and a year later another Mason's corpse floated to the surface of a river, Antimasons raised the alarm of foul play. Broadsides were plastered all over Boston, crying out, "ANOTHER MASONIC MURDER" and "Masonry Is the Same All Over the World."[5]

An Antimasonic broadside that circulated throughout Boston in 1830, accusing a lodge of Freemasons with murder and subversion of justice. *Masonry Is the Same All Over the World:* ANOTHER MASONIC MURDER ([Boston], 1830), broadside. Courtesy of the American Antiquarian Society.

Scores of men had flocked to Masonic lodges after the nation's founding. With men and women constantly on the move—to cities, factory towns, or the western frontier—Freemasonry offered men a familiar retreat where friendships and connections helped them conduct business amid a world of strangers. Even before Morgan's disappearance, Antimasons feared that these ties gave Masons unfair advantages. By their secret signals and sworn oaths, Masonry seemed intent on destroying "all principles of equality" by bestowing favors on members while excluding the "equally meritorious and deserving." With their highfalutin titles like "high priest" and "knights," they encouraged a spirit of aristocracy, antithetical to the nation's democratic culture. Masons also enjoyed the conviviality of an all-male society, often lubricated by prodigious drinking, as an alternative to the feminized church, home, or revival meeting, prompting women and moral reformers to find common cause with the Antimasonic crusade.[6]

After William Morgan's disappearance, Antimasonry devolved into a tangled mess of a conspiracy creed. All Antimasons shared the belief, stated by one leader, that Morgan had been murdered by Masons, "the result of a conspiracy" carried out with "peculiar deliberation, malignity and terror." Antimasons obsessed about the corrupting power of the Masons' secrecy; while some monarchical governments might tolerate secrecy, "Ours, never," they declared. That made the Masonic order, with its aristocratic and undemocratic practices, essentially foreign, un-American, and "anti-republican." Masons, they believed, posed a grave threat not just to American equality, but even more so to the fair working of justice. "Are not the principles of Masonry dishonest," asked one foe, if they could command members "to conceal all the crimes and faults" of a brother Mason?[7]

According to Antimasons, ordinary Masons were not the real problem. They were more often than not manipulated by a machine-like organization that exerted "an *all-controlling influence*" over its members, corrupting and entrapping them in their practices, stifling access to truthful information. That's why the charters of Masonic lodges needed to be revoked, their doors padlocked, and their secrets disclosed; why the free press must multiply, and the republic's institutions protected from their wiles—because "public opinion is the true source of power in this country." This was the crux of a political movement founded on a conspiracy theory.[8]

Conspiratorial thinking still burned hot when a Tiverton farmer discovered Maria Cornell's dead body on that cold December morning. Even before Avery's pre-trial hearing ended in Bristol, Boston's Antimasonic newspaper was speculating about the Masonic membership of those who defended the preacher's innocence. Despite his attorneys' declarations that Avery was "*not and never has been a Mason*," rumors persisted. The Antimasonic *Boston Daily Advocate* printed that denial, admitting that most sources confirmed it, yet couldn't resist raising doubts. Boston's *Masonic Mirror* offered an emphatic denial, countering that the crime Avery was charged with was itself "altogether *antimasonic*." Three Freemasons in Boston were so confident that they offered a hefty reward to anyone who could prove that Avery had been a Mason. Meanwhile, many writers lamented how conspiracy politics surfaced so easily, how the "envenomed question of Masonry and Anti-Masonry" had become entangled in this case.[9]

Conspiracy politics surfaced in Newport as early as the first day of trial testimony. Richard Randolph didn't wait long when cross-examining Dr. Foster Hooper before steering the witness away from medical inquiries about autopsies and bruises.

"Did you not deliver an antimasonic lecture in Swansea, in which you introduced the name of Mr. Avery?" Randolph asked.

Yes, Hooper answered, but he insisted he'd spoken on a different subject.

"Mr. Randolph, I do not perceive what that has to do with this trial," interjected the chief justice. The prosecutor agreed.

"I have understood that the witness delivered a lecture in Swansea, in which he stated that Avery was a Mason, and that Howe and Haile, the examining Justices who discharged him, were Masons," Randolph explained.

"I can see no possible benefit from going into that inquiry in this case," the chief justice asserted. Justice Eddy knew that Rhode Island politics had become bitterly divided by the Antimasonic Party and hoped to keep the trial yet again from heading in an uncontrolled direction. When Randolph said his only intention was to show the witness's attitude toward the defendant, the court allowed him to proceed.

Dr. Hooper admitted that he had in fact lectured on Freemasonry but defended his right to his political opinions. He insisted that he hadn't mentioned Avery until a private conversation afterward. All he'd said was that he'd "heard" that Avery, Howe, and Haile were all Masons. Asked if he had also declared that prominent Bristol men had protected Avery "on account of his Masonry," Hooper answered, "I might have said there were fears on that subject."

"Go on, sir, and show your prejudices against Mr. Avery!" Randolph shouted.

"I have none to show," Dr. Hooper declared.

"The gentleman has no right to tell a witness to show his prejudices," the attorney general retorted. At that, the court cut off the questioning, but not before the prosecution asked Dr. Hooper if he had any prejudices against Avery. "None at all," he repeated.[10]

Randolph didn't give up. When Hooper was recalled as a rebuttal witness three weeks later, Randolph returned to the doctor's Antimasonic lecture, asking who had been present that night. The doctor named three prominent Antimasons from Fall River.

"How many belong to the Fall River Committee?" Randolph asked.

Only Nathaniel Borden, Hooper answered.

The mill town was a hotbed of Antimasonry, having established one of the nation's first Antimasonic Reading Rooms, and two-thirds of Fall River voters cast their ballots for the Antimasonic ticket in the 1832 presidential election. Randolph knew this and hoped to smear the Fall River community's response to Cornell's death, suggesting that it was a hysterical conspiracy directed against Avery and the Methodists. This wasn't entirely a stretch: Borden was chair and principal financier of the Fall River Committee, and he was also the county chair of the Antimasonic Party.[11]

But Attorney General Greene wasn't going to let Randolph leave that impression uncontested. "Has your Fall River Committee anything to do with masonry and antimasonry?" he asked Dr. Hooper.

"No, Sir. Not at all," Hooper replied. "There are two masons on the Committee."

"Is that a proper question?" Randolph asked, addressing the bench.

"It is all out of order," Chief Justice Eddy responded. "You introduced it."

After Randolph insisted on his right to show a witness's prejudice, the prosecutor asked Dr. Hooper if he was now satisfied that Avery was not a Mason, and he answered "entirely."[12]

These exchanges only scratched the surface of the conspiratorial rhetoric swirling around the Avery case. Conspiracy thinking permeated the era's political climate. In truth, once it became clear that this was not a Morgan-like Masonic cover-up, the Antimasonic Party was happy to turn its attention away from Avery. Just the same, they supplied many Americans with a handy political language for talking about the subversion of justice in a democracy.[13]

From the start, critics accused Methodists of behaving like Masons, screening Avery from punishment while "knowing his skirts to be dripping in blood!" When crowds outside the Newport courthouse began hooting and jeering at Methodist ministers attending the trial, one Newport newspaper spurned this popular denunciation of "the *whole* Methodist denomination, Anti-masonic-like," unwilling to believe that the Methodists would "screen *any one* of their number, charged with the commission of a capital crime." Not everyone remained so charitable. All the talk about Masonry paled in comparison, another Newport paper declared after Avery's trial, to "the vile, the unholy," the most "dangerous combination of knavery and fanaticism" perpetrated by the Methodists to wrest a "foul and unnatural murderer" from the hands of justice.[14]

For months after the verdict, Avery's case unleashed a flurry of conspiracy talk, the air rife with accusations of nefarious plots and subversive groups. The rhetoric began when news first broke about Cornell's death and continued all through the trial. The verdict only raised it to new heights.

Adopting a pseudonym, Proteus, the editors of Newport's *Rhode Island Republican* leaped in, becoming the first to retry Avery in the post-trial court of public opinion. Week after week for two months, they penned new opinion pieces denouncing Avery and the Methodists. With criticisms assuming different shapes and forms, their avowed aim was truth and justice. Like others, Proteus refused to malign the jurors' integrity. Still, the jury had reached their verdict only, argued Proteus, because they were hesitant to impose a death sentence, no matter their belief in Avery's guilt.

Before long, Proteus pivoted toward his real target: the Methodists. From the moment Avery first faced a murder charge, his church associates had displayed a misguided, even a "criminal zeal," to protect him. The trial merely confirmed their willingness to shield him from justice, "to stoop to means as black as night and false as Hell!" Everyone in the Methodist Church, in this view, from elders to preachers to parishioners, willingly degraded themselves, but none more disarmingly than the women witnesses eager to destroy another woman's reputation in order to protect Avery.[15]

Since the Methodist leadership had absolved Avery entirely, someone, insisted Proteus, had to step forward and expose their grand conspiracy. Avery alone was not responsible for "this wicked act," but rather, on the heads of the Methodist conference "must rest the consequences of this shameless attempt to extinguish the torch of Truth by conniving at, and sanctioning the foulest of murders." Far more dangerous than individual misconduct was a deeper plot the Methodists engineered on a foundation of blind, fanatical support for moneyed religion. Proteus branded such conspiracies as "priestcraft," imagining a collective group of plotters—"E.K. Avery & Co."—who constituted his co-workers, accomplices, or accessories in murder and perjury. Familiar villains like "Popery," priests, and superstitions donned new clothes in populist fears of powerful, secretive, and corrupt aristocracies.[16]

In the mind of Proteus, the collaborators in "the Avery plot" showed their hand most daringly by their "preconcerted" scheme to handpick jurors sure to acquit the Bristol preacher. By now, Benjamin Hallett's trial report had become a favorite with readers, and the Antimasonic newsman—alone among his peers—recorded the peculiarities of the jury's selection. Ephraim Avery's inexplicable choices in the courtroom not to use all of his preemptory challenges or to favor jurors admittedly biased against him while preferring those his attorneys hadn't bothered to question, fed critics' conspiratorial suspicions. At least twice, Hallett noted, Avery smiled before deciding to dismiss or accept a juror. Ephraim Avery's stoic and unflappable demeanor nearly throughout the trial, considered by his supporters to be undeniable proof of his innocence, was turned on its head; his ability to laugh and smile became evidence of his "most hardened villainy" and his assurance in "the power of priestly dominion."[17]

Proteus took these imaginings further, offering readers never-before-seen evidence of conspiracies at work. If Avery should be tried at the "bar of public opinion," it was only right to offer more proof of his guilt, especially new evidence of secret plots that could explain the seemingly inexplicable not-guilty verdict.

Proof of nefarious plotting could be seen in some men's apparent eagerness to be chosen as jurors when most made every effort to avoid being selected. One juror, who at first news of Cornell's death told everyone that he thought Avery guilty, was swayed by Avery's allies and then shadowed the deputy sheriff until he was summoned. In court, of course, he swore that he had neither formed nor expressed an opinion. Another man, who supposedly stated before the trial that he would "starve to death" before bringing in a guilty verdict against Avery, was selected after swearing that he'd never expressed an opinion. It didn't matter that none of the jurors were Methodists; in the minds of their critics, the Methodists had extended their powerful influence to corrupt the sacred process of jury selection. As Proteus concluded, the wire-pullers in this plot were "a thousand times more worthy" of prosecution than any of the suspect jurors.[18]

Who was safe, Proteus asked, "when a powerful combination of hypocrites and fanatics shall thus be able to thwart the ends of justice? Whose life shall be safe if an assassin chance to belong to a powerful religious denomination, which may thus 'pluck" him from the hands of justice?" The only protection rested with the public and the truth-telling press.[19]

Meanwhile, one more writer entered the fray, wielding a pseudonym and amplifying conspiracy-minded combat for even wider audiences. Calling himself *Aristides*, an allusion to the ancient Athenian statesman, "Aristides the Just," his goal was to retry Avery before a new jury of the reading public. Penning twice-a-week essays in the Providence *Republican Herald*, Aristides, even more than Proteus, relied on his readers knowing the details of the case from the widely published trial reports. Akin to a prosecutor's closing argument, only this time lasting for months, the essays by Aristides invited readers into a virtual courtroom on the printed page.

To Aristides, the public had a perfect right to think and judge for themselves, unfettered by a jury's opinion. Avery might have been freed by "technicalities of the law," but that couldn't protect him from "the bar of public opinion." The burden of proof presumed to rest on the prosecution was reversed in this courtroom. The Methodist preacher must prove his own innocence: "Public opinion requires the proof from him, and without that proof, public opinion will not acquit him."[20]

Repeatedly Aristides upended the theory that Cornell conspired to exact revenge on Avery by leaving a note, forging letters, and taking her own life. "What a nonsensical idea," he wrote, that this "artful, designing girl" tried to pin a murder charge on the preacher by hanging herself out in the open when she had no way of knowing where he would be on that day. And how artful could she be to leave a note that read "If I am missing" when she had planned all along to hang herself in a public place—wouldn't she have known that "she would *not* be *missing*"? Only a person bereft of common sense would hatch such an absurd plot, certainly not the cunning Sarah Maria Cornell depicted by Avery's defense.[21]

Sarcasm dripping from every page, Aristides lampooned the magical talents ascribed to Cornell. Of course, Cornell could have more easily exacted her revenge: All she had to do was swear a public complaint against Avery as the father of her child; or, if she had forged the letters, she could just as well have signed Avery's name on the unsigned letters. Wouldn't it have been easier, and more pleasurable, for Cornell to witness the havoc and harm caused by her own revenge plot? Avery and his friends had to explain why she would choose to kill herself for retribution, rather than live "to witness and enjoy the fruits of her vengeance."[22]

Instead of proving the preacher's innocence, Avery's allies put a young woman already in her grave on trial in Newport, ransacking the countryside, as Aristides put it, to unearth musty old maid's gossip tales of Cornell as an "abandoned wretch, with whom an *honest* man and a *Christian Minister* might cohabit without shame, and afterwards murder without guilt." Then they hired a high-priced lawyer to dress up these fabulous tales "with all the flippery of romance" to convince gullible minds that Cornell took three years to deliberate on the best means of revenge, only to conclude "that the most certain way to doing it, would be to forge two or three letters, and then hang herself in a 'stack yard'!"[23]

For nearly two months Aristides re-prosecuted Ephraim Avery in the *Republican Herald*, until his eighteen essays gained such popularity that he published them as a 100-page pamphlet, *Strictures on the Case of Ephraim K. Avery*, selling for twenty-five cents. Newspaper editors across the Northeast praised its able arguments while the *Strictures* sold as far away as Charleston, South Carolina. Boston's Universalist paper, the *Trumpet*, called Aristides's essays "the most fearless exhibition" of Avery's blame for Cornell's death they had ever seen. The Universalists, after all, were one of the Methodists' principal rivals, and as local newsmen were aware, the author of Aristides's *Strictures* was himself a Universalist minister named Jacob Frieze. An accomplished mudslinger in politics, labor conflicts, and religion, Frieze attacked the Methodists for fostering an antidemocratic union of church and state that he believed was growing among moneyed evangelical denominations.[24]

Aristides had no qualms about introducing new evidence, as standards of proof began to slip. Rumors and hearsay from unseen witnesses were presented to a public invited to reach its own verdict. A new witness had seen Avery walking toward John Orswell's steamboat to deliver the pink letter, and another man had crossed the Stone Bridge with Avery (coming from the direction of Fall River) around ten o'clock on December 20. Aristides vouched for the veracity of these new witnesses, especially a gentleman he insisted could swear that he had seen Avery and Cornell together in the woods near the Thompson camp meeting.[25]

Aristides proceeded also to turn upside-down the character issue so vital to Avery's trial defense. A respected man of the cloth, his defenders insisted, should be trusted more than a woman of questionable morals. Yet for Aristides, the more others tried to blacken Cornell's character, the more they degraded Avery. After all, if Cornell's character was as immoral as they claimed, what did that say about Avery's secret meetings and conversations with her, and why did he make no effort to denounce her either at Fall River or the Thompson camp meeting? "I only say, bad as she may have been," wrote Aristides, Ephraim Avery was "at least no better than she, and deserved to be detested by every member of the community."[26]

Why shouldn't Sarah Maria Cornell be believed as much as Avery? The preacher, Aristides insisted, was a proven liar, telling a false tale to Jane Gifford about his business on December 20 and found guilty of speaking slanderous lies about rival clergyman Thomas Norris. "Does the fact of her having had intercourse with a man, prove her a liar?" Aristides asked. After all, "who has said she was a liar? *Avery*, with his sanctimonious Alas! Alas!! Alas!!! And who believes him?"[27]

It didn't take much effort for Aristides to pivot from reasoned argument to full-blown conspiracy theories. Never once, though, did he point to the Masons. Jacob Frieze was himself a loyal Mason and one of the fraternity's most vocal defenders against the Antimasonic onslaught. Nonetheless, conspiracy thinking was so pervasive at that time that even Frieze sounded remarkably like an Antimason.

His target, instead, was the Methodist Church. The secretive workings of a fraternity of circuit riders had conspired from the start to shield their brother from facing justice for his lustful and murderous crimes. The Methodists would stop at nothing, Aristides insisted, to elevate their organization over the people's right to justice. Like a foreign invader, corrupting the legal system and abusing their power, Methodists strong-armed witnesses and tainted the legitimacy of the trial. "The whole machinery of the Methodist Institution has been brought into operation, and its artillery made to bear on the battlements of the hall of justice," Aristides declared. "Perjury base and foul has been committed on the stand, under the sanction of a religious garb, to protect a wretch from punishment," while his brethren "sat and smiled."[28]

Recalling how defense witnesses from church and factory used the exact same phrasing when recounting Maria Cornell's promise to avenge Avery even "if it costs me my life," Aristides saw underneath it all a Methodist plot. Prior to the trial, Methodist clergymen met with witnesses, doubtless drilling them in preparation for their court appearances. "Their stories, true or false, bear marks of previous study," he charged. The Methodists could also have paid witnesses to commit perjury or concoct stories. Such machinations explain why Avery's defense cost the Methodist Church $6,000 and why they were feverishly fundraising to cover the expense.[29]

Aristides knew how to spin a suspenseful conspiracy yarn. Across pages and pages, readers learned how a Newport deputy sheriff, ordered to summon a Portsmouth woman to testify for the prosecution, unknowingly raced with a Methodist clergyman to reach her residence. Though the sheriff had the swifter horse, his decision to stop and enlist an assistant meant that the Methodist arrived first. The clergyman then proceeded to tamper with the witness and "put a lie into her mouth"—making her feign an illness and declare herself unable to attend the trial—all to shield "a guilty wretch from the grasp of human justice!" Never was there a criminal trial, Aristides concluded, "in which so much baseness was manifest, so much chicanery practiced, the public, the government, court, and the jury, so deeply insulted."[30]

But there was an even bigger crime, Aristides protested, than Cornell's murder or Avery's acquittal, and that was the plot to subvert a democratic society. Jacob Frieze brought Aristides's *Strictures* to a close and followed it with five more newspaper editorials that autumn and winter, all depicting the Methodist Church as a subversive organization that exerted unchecked power. Frieze tapped into a vein of American conspiratorial politics that portrayed its enemies as foreign, invading, despotic, and antidemocratic, whose sinister objectives always exercised an "all-controlling influence" over ordinary people's thoughts and actions.

"You, Gentlemen," he addressed the New England Methodist Conference, must share responsibility with Ephraim Avery and face the public consequences for this flagrant outrage. Abuses of justice, from silencing or tampering with witnesses to packing the jury, all derived from the church's despotic impulses. In contrast to churches with democratic or republican styles of governance, the Methodist Church was an autocracy where "a few men"—the band of circuit riders and a couple of bishops—exercised "supreme control" over their parishioners. Ordinary Methodist churchgoers were "under the necessity of submitting to all your decrees in silence, of believing what you believe, of advocating what you advocate, of condemning what you condemn, and of doing what you command." That was why witnesses succumbed to the coercions of clergymen and why none dared raise their voices to challenge the unified front in defending Avery at any cost.[31]

Like the menace of all subversive groups, the Methodists' threat derived from shutting down the free thinking, independent action, and popular participation so central to American democracy. Religion itself was not the problem—it was instead "the foreign garb in which fanaticism has arrayed her" and corrupted her. That was why Aristides and other critics threw around the epithet "anti-republican" so frequently. Any organization that constrained the people's right to think for themselves and decide who should govern them was despotic. Clergymen in the nation's largest and fastest growing religious group "wield the entire power of the church, without accountability to anybody on earth, but *themselves.*"

But it was too late, insisted Aristides, to fool the public. Ultimately, they would reject any "antirepublican, anti-christian form of church government."[32]

Frieze joined writers and activists deeply concerned about the growing power of evangelical groups in America. Liberal clergymen, labor activists, and free thinkers—sometimes separately, though Frieze was all three—viewed the rapid increase in evangelical sects like the Methodists and the benevolent enterprises of missionary and Bible societies as threats to the separation of church and state. They saw all these as antidemocratic usurpers of the people's authority to think for themselves. The grave threat to the republic, Frieze and his fellow critics insisted, extended beyond the church's corrupt defense of a guilty brother and resided instead in "the power and controlling influence of the Methodist Church," a despotic power that was antithetical to democracy.[33]

25

Vindication

NO ONE WAS SURPRISED WHEN the Methodists lobbed conspiracy accusations right back at their critics.

It wasn't easy for Ephraim Avery to find people willing to listen to him after he was acquitted by a jury and cleared by the New England Conference. Even at his home pulpit in Bristol, the Methodists had assigned another preacher to assume his weekly preaching responsibilities. And when Avery kept trying all summer and fall to speak at Methodist gatherings where he'd previously ministered, his presence only provoked riots and effigies and mock executions. Coming from a people who freely talked about their tribulations and faith journeys, Ephraim Avery surely wanted to tell his tale of a different kind of redemption.

Avery knew that many Methodist congregations were bitterly divided over his case and over the hostility they faced from neighbors certain about his guilt. While conference leadership silenced internal dissent, scores of churchgoers abandoned the Methodists after the verdict, unable or un-willing to be associated with the church and its infamous preacher. Local histories later revealed that those congregations implicated in Avery's case—Newport, Portsmouth, Fall River, even Bristol—faced existential crises. Methodist churches in Newport and Fall River were reported "greatly crip-pled" by the scandal, while a Portsmouth preacher wrote in that church's records: "The Avery Case. 1833. Church in great depression." For years, one chronicler noted, Methodist ministers in those towns were "looked upon with suspicion, and any slander however absurd or vile was eagerly received and as eagerly circulated."[1]

Methodist leaders surely were keen to respond to the torrent of vitriol they faced following their complete exoneration of Avery. Still they waited. All summer and fall they kept an observant eye on effigy burnings, newspaper screeds, essays by Proteus and Aristides, and popular songs, plays, and artistic renderings of the case. They watched and read while audiences feasted on a steady diet of the factory girl's murder and the villainy of church and clergy alike.

Finally, just as Aristides was concluding his series of essays, prominent Methodists announced their intention to respond with a defense of both Avery and the church. They promised proof of Avery's "entire innocence" with a mass of new evidence, including a statement from Avery himself. Three leading Methodists—Timothy Merritt, Joseph Merrill, and Wilbur Fisk—published *A Vindication of the Result of the Trial of Rev. Ephraim K. Avery* in February 1834.[2]

The three authors had been the Methodist Church's leading intellectuals and stalwart defenders for decades. Joseph Merrill, a New England Conference leader, was Avery's supervising Elder and played an active role in his defense from the start. Wilbur Fisk, president of Wesleyan University, had chaired and written the previous report clearing Avery. The *Vindication*'s principal author was Timothy Merritt, an old-school circuit rider and accomplished apologist in disputes with Calvinists, Unitarians, and Universalists, and in defense of the scandalous John N. Maffitt. He had been editor of Boston's *Zion's Herald*, and when Avery's trial began, he was in New York assisting with the city's Methodist newspaper.[3]

In recent years all three men had spearheaded a growing movement to enhance the church's reputation for respectability. At this point in their history, with more wealthy members, Methodists were trying to shed some of their wild, countercultural, and plebian features and to cultivate instead more middle-class characteristics of decorum and social prestige. They did so by playing down the excesses of camp meetings, emphasizing higher education at newly founded colleges, and making an effort to situate evangelical revivalism at the center of the nation's civic life.[4]

Ephraim Avery and the authors of the *Vindication* yearned to state their side of the story, to declare before the public a convincing tale of innocence and persecution. The Bristol preacher spoke first, and his version of events, in his very own words, was exactly what the public had longed for since his arrest.

Ephraim's "Statement," near the beginning of the *Vindication,* merged the text from his pre-trial explanation (published in Luke Drury's report) with a new narrative written in January 1834. Offering little in the way of new facts, he hoped to refute the ever-present suspicions about his behavior. Why had he been out so late talking with Maria Cornell in Fall River when (as she claimed) she first informed him of her suspected pregnancy? In a meandering explanation he insisted that he'd merely read Cornell a chapter from the gospel of St. Matthew, "after which we had prayers and exhortations." Why had he gone into hiding? He stressed that it wasn't his idea. Why had be grown a beard? He'd only skipped shaving for a few days, never intentionally to disguise himself.[5]

Ephraim doubled down on his alibi for December 20, repeating the same story about an island excursion that supporters had circulated since his arrest. He tried to align his story with those who testified for the defense that they had seen a tall stranger in Portsmouth that afternoon and night. All in all, neither the undecided nor Avery's staunchest defenders would find much in his account to bolster a factual argument for his defense.

What Ephraim wanted most of all was to convey his faith and feelings throughout the entire ordeal. When Rev. Bidwell arrived to tell him that Fall River residents were accusing him of murder and adultery, "I felt at this time," he stated, "such a perfect consciousness of innocency" that he expected absolutely nothing to come of it. Even after conveying "the heart-rending and soul chilling" news to his wife, he told his readers, he found "ready access to God" and trust in Him, so much that "I should lie against God if I were to deny that he comforted my soul." All through his imprisonment and trial, Ephraim added, he experienced "seasons of refreshing from the presence of the Lord."[6]

He laced his version of events with further expressions of "feelings," "emotions," and that brand of first person spirituality that attracted Maria Cornell and thousands of others to the Methodist faith. On one page he wrote, "My heart bled," and on another, "God only knows my emotions, and the anguish I felt." But always, Ephraim reminded readers, he "felt more for the church than for myself," even to the point of caring more about the harm his scandal might inflict on God's cause than on his family's reputation.[7]

It was as a man of God, then, that Ephraim repeatedly swore his innocence. Indeed, he swore he had never set foot on Orswell's steamboat in Providence, never penned any of the alleged letters nor seen them before his trial, never set foot in Fall River on December 20, nor crossed the stone

bridge, nor had a meeting with Maria Cornell, nor saw her at all that evening. It was not that he denied all the charges but rather how he denied
them that mattered most for Ephraim and the Methodists; he swore before
"that Being" who will judge all and appealed to "Him whose all-seeing eye
marks every thought, every word, and every action." Restating a denial he
had spoken when first charged, he declared: "Heaven is my witness, that
I never desired to touch, and I never did, that woman, in any unlawful way,
since I had my being." He closed by asking for readers to pray for him and
his family.[8]

"I have only to repeat, in the close, that I am innocent of the great crimes
laid to my charge," he concluded, "and that I entertain no enmity towards
my *bitterest foes* and most *persevering persecutors*."[9]

New England's Methodist leaders were not so openly forgiving of those
"persecutors." Following Avery's statement, they devoted the remainder of
the *Vindication* to defending the Bristol preacher's innocence in an effort
to clear the Methodist Church, tarred by the alleged criminality of their
brother.

Redirecting attention to those who had drummed up a "great excitement," Timothy Merritt and his co-authors began by accusing specific interest groups of stirring up prejudice among the local populace, never giving
Avery the "usual mercy" of the presumption of innocence. The village of
Fall River became their first target. Describing the plotters against Avery
as "managers" and "movers of the excitement," they conjured images of
manufacturers and businessmen exerting control over ordinary individuals'
lives. Through fundraising and town meetings, Fall River's citizens were
"brought to feel a *personal interest*" in Avery's conviction and a duty "to
pursue him to the extremity." Meanwhile, the print media, with similar
enmity, joined in this attack, hawking pamphlets, placards, caricatures, and
songs that flew off the presses. For Merritt, even the difficulties in selecting
a jury bespoke a prejudice inflamed by the press and the mill town.[10]

Merritt quickly turned to what the Methodists considered a scheme by
"those secret persecutors of Mr. Avery" who harbored an "implacable hatred of religion and clergymen." Here lay both a deeply held Methodist
belief as well as a smart strategy for eliciting sympathy from other Christian
denominations: the charge that "haters" wished to bring down evangelical
religion at the height of its popularity. With a long history of imagining
themselves as embattled martyrs facing a hostile world, Methodists found
it wasn't a big step to believe that Avery's case originated from godless foes.
These enemies of religion, wrote Merritt, plotted against the preacher,

carrying out a "systematic persecution" designed to destroy the "character and standing" of both Avery and "his brethren in the ministry."[11]

For the most part, Merritt's *Vindication* echoed the defense's case in Newport, reminding readers yet again of how trustworthy Methodists could account for Avery's precise location at any time in Thompson and Providence. Now and again, Merritt sounded like a skilled defense attorney, able to argue both ways about all the evidence to maintain Avery's innocence. As needed, the Methodists also amassed depositions and affidavits from witnesses to refute prosecutors' charges or Aristides's post-trial theories.

One thing was certain: Methodist leaders were eager to sustain, even escalate, the character assaults begun at Avery's trial. Nothing mattered more to these churchmen than the stark contrast between the reputations of Cornell and Avery. Hurling invective that readers recognized from the trial reports—vicious, ruined, strange, deranged—they tapped a seemingly bottomless reservoir of moral epithets. "There was scarcely a vice," Merritt intoned, that "she was not in the habit of committing." "The history of abandoned females will hardly produce an instance" of one "so adroit in all kinds of wickedness and obscenity—in lying, stealing, deceiving, both with her tongue and pen; in fornication and hypocrisy"—than Sarah Maria Cornell. With no qualms about demeaning a dead woman, they even blamed Cornell's character for the fact that she died friendless and without family.[12]

Cornell's immoral character, in Merritt's mind, spilled over onto an enemy of Avery and the Methodists—"the powerful Aristides." Could a man who stood as friend, advocate, and champion of a wanton woman be trusted by his fellow citizens? Merritt asked. "Can he have a fair mind" or "any honorable motive?" The *Vindication*'s aim was to counter Aristides's conspiracy theories; and to do so, its authors leveled the same kind of character assassination at Aristides that they had perfected with Cornell, slamming him as a liar, a slanderer, a villain with "no sense of moral right or wrong," a man devoid of authority, reputation, or character. "But who is Aristides?" Merritt exclaimed at one point. "He is nobody."[13]

It was to be expected that Merritt and his fellow Methodists turned to conspiracy theories to counter Aristides and to explain how their brother clergyman became ensnared in a murder accusation. Deploying the familiar American language of political quarrels, Methodists stepped forward as experienced operatives. "We believe there was a *conspiracy* to ruin Mr. Avery," they declared. Resorting to variations on a theme—a "deep-laid plot," "systematic persecution," "unlawful design," a "scheme"—they lobbed charges of conspiracy more than two dozen times in the *Vindication*. And, much as they had entwined the characters of Cornell and Aristides, they accused both of designing a conspiracy to carry out their hatred of clergymen.[14]

It began with Maria Cornell. With a vengeful spirit "long harbored in her breast," Cornell had pursued her objective of ruining Rev. Avery with unflinching resolve. All incriminating evidence, Merritt insisted—conversations with the Rawsons, the letters and note, visits to Dr. Wilbur, talk of abortifacient drugs, even her body hanging from a stackyard—proved that "she had laid a scheme to ruin him." Why shouldn't the Methodists believe that Cornell concocted a conspiracy against Avery? Hadn't she threatened revenge on him? Several times Avery's vindicators suggested that Cornell had been assisted by another lover, who worked alongside her to entrap Avery, a theory his defense attorneys had introduced at the trial. Avery's vindicators were also the first to suggest that Grindal and Lucretia Rawson had been in on the plot from the start.[15]

After Avery's acquittal, Merritt continued, Cornell's conspiracy merged with the witch hunt perpetrated by people like Aristides, the "haters of all clergymen." Nothing seemed to illustrate this more than the secrecy behind the use of a pseudonym. Why, Methodists wondered, did such "secret persecutors" need to conceal their true identities? Speculating that Aristides could be a lawyer, a Universalist preacher, or even part of a secret cabal that had persecuted Maffitt a few years earlier, they insisted he couldn't be trusted precisely because he concealed his name, operating like "the thief and the assassin" who "choose the cover of night for the perpetration of their deeds."[16]

Countering Aristides's theories about Methodists tampering with and silencing witnesses, the vindicators marshaled pages of signed affidavits from witnesses who told different accounts of, say, the man who saw Avery and Cornell at the Thompson camp meeting, the one who allegedly crossed the stone bridge with Avery, or those who spoke of the reputation of Jane Gifford. They assembled plenty to comfort the Methodists' supporters. Still, the principal contention of Avery's vindicators was that all of the mysteries of the case could be accounted for by the "machinery" of a deep-laid plot carried out by the secret haters of religion and clergymen.

Like most conspiracy thinkers, Merritt and company also reached into their imaginations. They conjured a conspirator "hanging about the Methodist church" in Providence waiting to see Avery before he delivered the pink letter into the steamboat engineer's hands, and they dreamed up unspecified persons intent to swear that they had seen Avery entering Fall River on December 20. Add to that an unnamed physician offering to sell clues to Avery's defense team, and overeager potential witnesses boasting of new evidence while riding the stagecoach with Justice Howe. "Is there no appearance of conspiracy in all this?" they asked.[17]

If nothing else, the *Vindication* proved a profitable endeavor for New England's Methodists. Clearly the public hadn't yet exhausted their appetite for the scandal. Six weeks after the *Vindication*'s release, Boston's Methodist newspaper reported that as many as 7,000 copies of the partisan text had been sold, likely netting the church nearly $2,000—much needed revenue, since it was widely reported that Avery's defense had cost the Methodists upwards of three times that much.[18]

It surprised no one when Aristides fought back. Though hoping the pamphlet might show the Methodists' willingness to heed public opinion, he ultimately thought it amounted to a whole lot of nothing—like the ancient proverb, "the mountain labored, and brought forth a mouse." The only new information he considered worth acknowledging was Avery's now "thrice-told tale" about Cornell and December 20, yet even that was regrettably enveloped in Avery's "pious cant" about his spiritual feelings. As for Avery's defenders, Aristides refused to accept the notion that questioning the preacher's innocence was an attack on religion itself or that it was the work of a secret cabal of anticlerics. Who, then, was the true friend of religion? Aristides asked. The person willing to wrap an embrace around a villain to prevent his exposure, or the one who would "uncloak the villain" dressed in the robes of a feigned spirituality?[19]

An echo chamber of conspiratorial thinking and rhetoric emerged from the ongoing scandal, as people scrambled for explanations, searching for ways to adapt to, and find comfort in, the uncertain feeling of not knowing the truth. Yet the imagined enemy in American conspiratorial politics shared similar characteristics—secretive, deceitful, corrupting a gullible public—no matter which conspiracy one believed, and the danger remained the same: the disruption of the fair and honest workings of justice in a democracy. Conspiracy-minded groups in America, determined to ferret out subversives, always came to resemble the style and features of the foes they imagined.[20]

Aristides and the Methodists were both correct when they looked for a resolution in the concept of belief. An era that witnessed the explosion of religious revivals and new religions left countless Americans wondering: Who could anyone trust?

26

Fake News

WHEN THE METHODISTS ANNOUNCED EARLY in 1834 that they would soon release a publication that would vindicate their actions and prove Avery's innocence, they added an irresistible teaser: a promise to include Avery's own account of his acquaintance with Sarah Maria Cornell. Anticipation grew for weeks. After all, Avery had by this time become something of a phantom. Rumors spread of sightings of the preacher in one town after another, sometimes hundreds of miles apart, and the public clamored for the preacher's story from his own perspective and in his own voice.

Before the Methodists could release their *Vindication*, though, another pamphlet beat them to the punch. It bore the title *Explanation of the Circumstances Connected with the Death of Sarah Maria Cornell*. The title page was unequivocal about the author: "by Ephraim K. Avery."

"I have stood before a solemn tribunal of my country," the pamphlet began, charged with "the greatest crime known to its laws." The writer lamented that, although he was "declared innocent" by a jury, the goodwill one should expect from that verdict had been "wrested from me by the fangs of a rapacious, ruthless, public prejudice." Familiar refrains, indeed: this was what readers expected to hear. Over the first few pages, the author declared twice in boldface: "YET MY CONSCIENCE IS GUILTLESS OF THE WILFUL MURDER OF THAT WOMAN!"[1]

In truth, this wasn't the much-anticipated explanation from Ephraim Avery. Neither a vindication nor a full confession, the pamphlet was soon discovered to be a fake. It hadn't been penned by the Bristol preacher. It was instead the slapdash production of a pretender.

Written for readers who had avidly consumed the trial reports and Aristides's *Strictures*, the fake narrative carefully connected every detail of the preacher's explanation with witnesses and evidence that raised suspicions about Avery's whereabouts and behavior. Speaking exclusively in the passive voice, the fictitious Avery spun a tale of an illicit sexual relationship that reconciled rumor, court testimony, and post-trial speculations.

"She possessed considerable personal attractions," the author wrote of Sarah Maria Cornell when describing their first meeting in Lowell. Hearing rumors and accusations of her immoral conduct with other men only amplified opportunities for private interviews with Cornell, including secret "visits to her lodgings" until their relationship became what he described as "our guilty connection." Throughout their interactions—excommunication, confessional letters, mutual accusations and threats—a merging of revulsion and attraction remained. The author repeatedly called Cornell "that woman," "that hapless woman," or "the unfortunate woman." Still, the "air and intonation of her address were peculiarly insinuating," he admitted, "alas! even fascinating and seductive." From the beginning of his tale, fictitious Avery had carefully positioned himself within a seduction story. But in this drama he was the seduced, not the seducer.[2]

The fateful event at the Thompson camp meeting he explained in the most matter-of-fact manner, writing merely, "That conversation and that guilty act occurred" just as Dr. Wilbur and Grindal Rawson had testified. When the writer came to the night of Cornell's death (calling it "the last gloomy scene of this appalling drama of guilt and shame and death"), he narrated his emotional appeals for her to submit to a makeshift attempt at abortion. After his unskilled efforts and her cries and groans, "she fell to the ground *a corpse!*" She died from shock. The preacher then clumsily hung her body at the haystack with no attention to the details that would make a suicide appear believable.[3]

Only the most gullible readers would have been fooled into thinking this an authentic confession by Ephraim Avery. Those who desired a heart-felt confession of guilt would put down the *Explanation* sadly disappointed. Like the faux apologies of so many other men for sexual indiscretions, this imaginary Avery didn't admit culpability in anything criminal.

The Methodists and Avery's defenders were quick to denounce the author as an imposter, declaring the pamphlet "A GROSS FORGERY." Avery published a note in New England newspapers branding the publication "a barefaced imposition," assuring readers that his only authentic statement would appear in the Methodists' *Vindication*.[4]

This episode marked just the proverbial tip of the iceberg of false stories and fakes that erupted around the case during the months following the jury's verdict. New witnesses popped up with new tall tales; trial witnesses were alleged to have been common thieves paid to impersonate people who knew Cornell; and, most curious, a whole slew of stories spread that there was another woman, still alive, also named Maria Cornell.

The *Fall River Monitor* broke that story only twenty days after Avery's not-guilty verdict, with the headline "WHAT NEXT!" Another woman by the name of Maria Snow Cornell was supposedly living in Providence. Speculating that this must have been "the identical girl" whom trial witnesses demeaned for all her vices, the paper insisted that some party ("a fiend," a "devil in human form") was responsible for imputing her bad reputation onto the dead woman. The story circulated throughout the Northeast, kept alive for weeks by newspapers, leading one New York paper to claim that if true, the whole affair was "revolting to every feeling of justice."

Of course, the story was nothing but a rumor. As a Massachusetts paper reminded readers, the *Fall River Monitor*'s lede began, "We have been informed on good authority," the oft-used dubious source for unsubstantiated gossip. Another paper declared outright that the story was "a mere humbug," then pointed to a similar tall tale: a Rhode Island man had come forward to claim that he (not Avery) had delivered the pink letter addressed to Maria Cornell to the Fall River steamboat engineer.[5]

One person's rumors could be another person's facts. A month after Avery's trial ended, as the trial reports sparked conversations throughout southern New England, Nathan Spencer, a western Rhode Island shoemaker, came forward with a tale: he had driven his wagon into Providence back in November and passed a gentleman along the road who asked him to deliver a pink letter to the steamboat bound for Fall River. Spencer swore he was the man who handed that letter to John Orswell. Avery's supporters spent months spreading the multiple sworn depositions from Spencer and family as proof that vindicated Ephraim Avery, while Aristides devoted equal energy to undermining the new evidence. "Can such a loose tale, told, for the first time, *seven months* after the transaction," Aristides bellowed, "be allowed to invalidate such testimony as that given by Orswell? The very thought is preposterous." In the end, it came down to whom one chose to believe, a matter of faith and presumptions that might never be settled.[6]

Conflicts between belief and facts surfaced again when a Newport bookseller decided to give readers an opportunity to judge for themselves whether Avery's handwriting proved him author of the letters. David Melvill traced the letters on file in the court clerk's office, then contracted a Boston lithographer to reproduce those "facsimile" letters to be sold and distributed throughout the country. The packet included the letters found in Cornell's trunk and bandbox and three letters from Avery to fellow Methodist preachers to allow comparison of Avery's handwriting. Melvill also appended sworn statements from prosecutor Dutee Pearce, the court clerk, and two Newport bank cashiers (apparently experienced in comparing forged signatures), certifying that the facsimiles were accurate copies.[7]

For all this, no greater clarity emerged about the letters or about Avery's guilt. Since readers had no more expertise in evaluating handwriting than anyone else, conclusions tended to fall into predictable camps. The Methodist authors of the *Vindication* first discredited the facsimile letters as a ruse to excite a popular persecution of Avery, then dismissed them as inaccurate forgeries, and finally relied on the facsimiles to prove that Avery's own handwriting didn't match the letters in Cornell's trunk. One zealous Avery supporter even boldly claimed that the facsimiles proved Cornell hadn't even penned her infamous December 20 note. Boston's Universalists, on the other hand, countered that the letters firmly proved the fact of Avery's authorship of the anonymous letters written to Cornell.[8]

Regardless of their authenticity, the packet of facsimile letters resembled the kinds of relics and mementos that notorious crimes often generate for collecting consumers. Melvill ensured that the letters from Cornell's trunk were printed on yellow, pink, and white colored paper, just like the originals, and handsewn together along the edges to resemble a scrapbook. Copies sold as far away as Virginia.

The Avery murder scandal was filled with instances of what today would be called "fake news," fictional or deliberately false news stories, which weren't even entirely new in the 1830s. Rumor, gossip, and other forms of hearsay and false reports have been around for a long time. What made Maria Cornell's death and Avery's trial a nationwide scandal was the massive expansion in popular print media available to ordinary American readers, an explosion that coincided with the Avery case.[9]

Two widely democratic forms of media—the trial report and the penny press—converged to prompt the proliferation of fake news. Unlike the street ballads and execution sermons on which early modern Europeans and Americans had relied, the trial report was a virtual courtroom on the printed page. Reaching unparalleled popularity during this scandal, the Avery trial reports generated a nationwide readership that picked up the printed word to satisfy their insatiable desire for novel and sensational news.

Meanwhile, just months after Avery's trial ended, the nation's first successful penny press newspaper, the *New York Sun*, began publishing a new style of reportage. Characterized by sensationalist content, penny dailies focused on local crime stories, manufacturing news when necessary, to attract tens of thousands of working-class and middle-class readers. Within a few years, all the major northeastern cities had profitable penny papers in circulation. Advances in print technology quickly extended their reach to thousands of readers previously untouched by more costly newspapers. By the summer of 1835, New York City boasted three penny dailies with a combined circulation approaching 50,000 consumers.[10]

Ephraim Avery made his way onto the page at the birth of American tabloid journalism. In its first issue in September 1833, the *Sun* ran a story that tapped the continued fascination with Avery's travels and preaching after his acquittal, noting that mobs formed at even the rumor that he was on a steamboat or arriving in a town. Penny papers loved attention-grabbing headlines, like "A Most Horrible Murder," but for this first article, the headline "E. K. Avery" sufficed. For audiences who had been hearing about this case for the previous nine months, the preacher's name was sensational enough on its own.[11]

What's more, in the years following the trial, Richard Adams Locke and Richard Hildreth, both of whom produced trial reports for the Avery case, became known for producing the most famous literary fakes of their time.

Two years after reporting at Avery's trial, Locke penned a series of articles for the *New York Sun* that was a deliberate hoax. He crafted a tale about a British astronomer who invented a telescope so powerful he discovered life on the moon—rational, winged, bat-like men, "engaged in conversation," gesticulating in an "impassioned and empathic" manner. The moon story was a smash hit. The *Sun* couldn't print enough copies. When rival papers called it a hoax, that only further boosted readership for all the penny papers. Locke and the *Sun* kept the stories (and the denials that they were perpetuating a hoax) coming for months, until the reporter claimed to have hired one of those man-bats as a correspondent, and the story ran its course. Readers knew all along that the story was a humbug, but they didn't care. Here was news as entertainment, and readers were delighted to be hoaxed just for the pleasure of it.[12]

A year later, Richard Hildreth published a different fake, just as the new abolitionist movement was garnering increased attention and readership. Presented as the authentic tale of an enslaved man's experience, Hildreth's *The Slave: or Memoirs of Archy Moore* was entirely the fictional imaginings of its white author. Even when *The Slave* was exposed as Hildreth's creation (trial reporter Benjamin Hallett's newspaper was one of the first to declare it "fiction woven apparently out of terrible truths"), that still didn't diminish readers' interest. The faux slave narrative went through as many as eight editions over the next twenty years. A tale rooted in a melodramatic love plot, seeking to unveil the painful feelings of Black slaves, was exactly what white northern audiences, whether abolitionist, evangelical, or sentimental, longed to read.[13]

Clearly, neither technological breakthroughs nor enterprising hucksters were solely responsible for the new sensationalized approach to crime, murder, and news. The American public, as the Avery murder case reveals, had already begun to embrace a popular culture of rumors, gossip, hoaxes, and printed falsities—fake news—even before the birth of the penny press. It was the ready and willing audience, eager for widely democratic forms of communication, who drove the desire for sensational news that far too often crossed the line between fact and fiction. In turn, new media made it hard for readers to tell what was real and what wasn't. This was what readers wanted. They weren't gullible consumers. They longed for mysteries as much as certainties, and they found hoaxes and fakes to be the pleasurable entertainment that helped them navigate a sometimes overwhelming new world.

27

Stage and Song

THREE MONTHS AFTER AVERY WAS set free by a jury's verdict, just as the summer's mob violence and bitter media battles began to subside, Maria Cornell and Ephraim Avery returned to Newport, this time as characters on stage in a theatrical entertainment rather than in their own real-life social drama.

Newport's Theatre stood directly across the square from the courthouse where Avery had been tried. While America's theater universe rarely tilted toward Newport, a small city just starting to realize its potential as a playground for the wealthy, theater had become one of the country's most widely popular forms of entertainment. Star actors and small companies took theater productions into all regions and communities, small and large, across the continent, offering a potpourri of entertainment appealing to all groups and classes of white Americans.[1]

As it happened, in the spring and summer of 1833, an eccentric New York City poet had resettled in Newport, while a company of traveling celebrity actors took over management of the town's theater. Together they debuted the unexpected drama, announced at first with the provocative title of *Unnatural Murder! Or, Retribution!!!* It opened on September 2 as *Factory Girl; or, the Fall-River Tragedy!!*[2]

Factory Girl came from the imagination of the darkly romantic poet McDonald Clarke. With Medusa-like waves of hair, dressed in an enormous military-style cloak, he drifted along Broadway muttering in verse, the victim of ridicule and violence on the streets. Along with his melancholy temperament, this earned him the nickname "the Mad Poet."[3]

For unexplained reasons, Clarke returned to his native New England just in time for Avery's trial. Spending many days listening in the courtroom, he passed some nights dining with reporter Richard Adams Locke, a writing crony and drinking companion from Broadway saloons. Clarke was nearly the same age as Avery, and the story of Cornell's life and death must have appealed to his melancholic but romantic sensibilities: Maria's unrequited longings for love and acceptance, the bitter gossip and invectives directed at an outcast, the accusations of madness as well as her unrewarded ambitions and encounters with professional hypocrisies.

His contemporaries knew that Clarke's writings "breathed from the impulse of the moment." Though Clarke had never written a play, he dashed off *Factory Girl*, and the actors didn't wait long to bring it to the stage. Clarke gave his manuscript to the theater company on a Friday, and they printed playbills and advertisements and staged its first performance on Monday evening.[4]

Confused and conflicted, *Factory Girl* leaned toward a tragic love story, a melodramatic tale of seduction, and a murder unpunished, all at the same time. This seemed to be what local audiences wanted. New Englanders came back to witness one more time and relive the same feelings they had experienced when first hearing of the young factory girl's death. The earliest reviews of the first nights' performances declared that the play was "rapturously received" and the audience "highly gratified," with a house that was "full to overflowing."[5]

John and Mary Greenhill Barnes managed and headlined the acting company that took up residence at Newport's Theatre that summer. Among the first English actors to tour the United States following the War of 1812, Mr. and Mrs. Barnes, as they were usually listed in playbills, joined a wave of Brits crossing the Atlantic to establish the star system of celebrity actors who dominated the American stage for decades.

The poet-playwright changed the names of the principal characters, so Mary Barnes's character, Susan Collins, resembled Sarah Maria Cornell in playbills only by her initials, while the Rev. Avery became Brother Wolfton. By choosing a popular term for a sexual predator—wolf—Clarke offered his audience the libertine villain they had come to expect. Given the play's preliminary title—*Unnatural Murder!*—and newspaper reports that "the character implicated, and the events of the murder, were very strongly delineated," the new playwright must have shared the prevailing public opinion about Avery's guilt.[6]

Nonetheless, Clarke filtered this story of violent crime through his own romantic inclinations, combined with his era's conventions for fictionalizing a woman's amorous desires. No copy of Clarke's three-act play has survived, but one text remains from these Newport performances. The company set aside the third night of the play's run as a benefit for McDonald Clarke. Benefits constituted the real paycheck for actors, playwrights, and theater managers, with an individual taking home the proceeds from a given night's performance, and Clarke certainly needed the income. For that night, the "Mad Poet" composed an original "Epilogue" that Mary Barnes recited at the play's end. This epilogue was most likely the same poem that Clarke entitled "Seduction," and it reveals how the playwright crafted the arc of his longer drama.[7]

Clarke situates Cornell and Avery's relationship as a seduction, the temptation of a beautiful and passion-filled woman, not a powerful man's act of sexual violence. The poem opens with a wild sigh that could be heard "where the lonely stack-yard stood," saying "more than a modest maiden should," telling a tale of "flushed feelings, uncontrolled—/Hot passions that the heart consume" and desires that could "wither a girl, in her virgin bloom." When audiences heard that the young maiden "met a scoundrel, with a saintly shape," they knew exactly who the villain was.

McDonald Clarke's imaginings of Cornell and Avery's tragic encounter didn't stray far from the first thoughts of the coroner's jurymen on the morning that Maria's frozen body was found. Her desires and passions were what determined the deadly outcome. When she met a saintly-shaped scoundrel, "she felt that passion's power," "her heart beat quick, and her cheek turned pale,/ While she heard his voice with its dizzying charm," she was the one who must resist the temptation.

Clarke and the Barnes's company performed the *Factory Girl* nearly every night for two weeks. This was a long run for American theater at the time; even top stars performed their repertory for only a week or so. The popularity of the Newport performances reminded many of the "excitement" that seemed to follow this case from its beginning. Indeed, the strongest criticism of the play was directed at the crassness of the crowds who flocked night after night to the theater. Other critics thought it obscene to recount in any manner the lurid tales already circulating in the trial reports. One New England paper called Clarke "a crackbrained poetaster" and his play "a crude dramatic sketch."[8]

Popular demand for dramatic presentations of Cornell's story made it easy for other aspiring writers and performers to find eager audiences. Two days after *Factory Girl* opened in Newport, a different play called *Sarah Maria Cornell, or The Fall River Murder* debuted at the Richmond Hill Theatre in New York City, the nation's theatrical capital. The proximity of the opening dates was just one of the many reasons Americans understandably mistook it for the same play in two separate locales. Both playwrights had the same last name (Clarke), the Barnes troupe had managed their company at the Richmond Hill until they departed for Newport, and both plays were three-act dramas with Fall River in their titles. Contrary to Oscar Wilde's remark that "life imitates art far more than art imitates life," the Richmond Hill production of *Sarah Maria Cornell* relived the main themes of a scandal that had been playing out all summer in the press and on the streets.[9]

Theatergoing at this time was not so much a spectator event as a participatory activity. Audiences and performers interacted in vocal and physical ways, with playgoers calling out for favorite ballads or repeated soliloquys, and actors commonly speaking in asides to encourage dialogue with spectators. If theatergoers wanted, as Melville remarked, "more reality than real life itself," they also wanted to experience the reality they had begun to believe in, the familiar ways they had come to think about the factory girl and the Methodist preacher. So, a playwright gave them a drama set in three familiar locations—a factory, a farmer's haystack, and a camp meeting—echoing refrains of conspiracy, hypocrisy, sensual spirituality, and true justice subverted by the courts.

As the play opens in a Fall River factory, the mythical qualities of Cornell unite with the stock character of melodrama's virginal heroine. Her fellow "factory girls" sing Cornell's praises for her generosity in helping them with their mill work and lending money to their poor mothers. She is later described as "the boast of the country; well-born and properly educated; very smart, intelligent, and industrious." Yet despite her worldly savvy and confident success as a working woman, she is hopelessly naïve in the presence of her seducer. Wary of all other Methodist clergymen, she follows Avery (named Averio in the play) willingly into the dark spaces of the camp meeting and haystack to be raped and murdered. Only her Fall River housemate (modeled on Lucy Hathaway) is the kind of "true-born New England girl" capable of fending off sexual advances from the camp meeting's ravenous sexual predators.[10]

If this were a typical melodrama, Cornell's hopes for a happy ending might have resided in marriage to the honest Yankee farmer, Jonathan, who early expresses his longings for her. But audiences were not shocked by Cornell's tragic fate; they had been prepared by newspapers and trial reports all summer. The play's dramatic arc both exposes the dangers of the public woman and lauds the virtuous "factory girl."

Given the playwright's story, it's no surprise that this era's unresolved anxieties regarding independent working women surfaced again. *Sarah Maria Cornell* was the brainchild of a woman writer who had previously associated with and penned adventures of infamous women. Mary Carr Clarke was among a growing number of self-supporting women writers in the 1830s. In 1814, she became the first woman to own and edit a weekly women's magazine, filling it with her own poetry and serialized plays and novels in the style of contemporary seduction fiction.[11]

Over the next two decades, Carr Clarke struggled to make ends meet or achieve a breakthrough in the theater world by her pen. She anonymously published the trial report of a Catholic priest accused of sexually assaulting a young servant woman (ironically, she defended him). While in Philadelphia during the 1820s, she spent a few years ghostwriting the memoir of one of the early republic's most notorious women, Ann Carson, who drifted from rebellious wife to outlaw. Separating from her ne'er-do-well sea captain husband, Carson became an independent proprietor and breadwinner, courted sexual relationships with men, faced bigamy charges, and then tried to set free her second husband (who'd murdered her first) by plotting to blow up the prison and kidnap Pennsylvania's governor, before she eventually joined a criminal gang of counterfeiters.[12]

Two interrelated story lines coursed through all of Carr Clarke's writing—independent laboring women and scandals of sex and crime—and both aligned perfectly with the dramatic undercurrents beneath Maria Cornell's and Ephraim Avery's lives.[13]

Unlike the play in Newport, Carr Clarke's drama gave audiences well-versed in Avery's trial reports a full dose of familiar characters and details. Dr. Wilbur reappears as Dr. Neverflinch, a leading threat to Avery. A benevolent factory owner, Mr. Thornhill, was a nod to Fall River's David Anthony or Nathaniel Borden. Previously unknown Tiverton and Bristol residents like the coroner, the Durfees, Meribah Borden, Jeremiah Gifford, and Betsey Hills all make appearances when the drama turns to Cornell's death and burial and Avery's arrest. Spectators couldn't miss the references to a pink letter, a clove-hitch knot, screams in the night, a tall stranger wandering near the mill town and haystack, and gibes directed at Avery's dubious alibi, including a ballad about a dog and a gun.

Like that summer's battles in the press, the Richmond Hill play sought to retry "the trial of S.M. Cornell," the assault on Cornell's character in the courtroom, by presenting this character assassination as the Methodists' plan all along. Once Averio realizes that Cornell could expose his deeds to public attention, he muses, "Who will credit her assertions? A poor and unknown girl, in opposition to a wealthy popular man, will stand a small chance to injure me—and I can easily ruin her character." The other clergymen then plot how to "employ" witnesses who will declare that Cornell was insane "and a vile girl" so that no one will believe her account.[14]

All the Methodist preachers in the play are lecherous wolves, which Carr Clarke underscores by adding John N. Maffitt (renamed Muffitt) to the cast of characters. When the clergymen first gather, they discuss their sexual escapades and insatiable lust for young girls, older single maidens, and married wives, all objects of their "Christian love." Their licentiousness is portrayed as the unique practices of Methodism itself—referred to as "the secret acts of our society"—alongside their love-feasts and prayer meetings. Even "conversion" becomes a euphemism for sexual conquest. Carr Clarke further taps into the anticlerical criticisms of evangelical clergymen by depicting them as money-grubbing cheats.[15]

Through it all, the camp meeting provides the main source of tension in this drama. It's at once a place to fear and to desire, a dark space where the threat of sexual crimes is realized. And when the final act begins with a trumpet blowing to start a camp meeting, it soon devolves to the point where "all is a scene of confusion." Girls cry and men shout, jewelry is seized, as is the prized jewel of virginity, until "this scene of fanaticism and hypocrisy" is broken up by factory owner, constable, and farmers.[16]

Characters in this play would occasionally break into song—brief ditties as comic asides. All through the summer, audiences had longed for songs about Cornell and Avery, and verse writers obliged. At least five ballads arrived for lovers of song to purchase in the months after Avery's trial, sung to tunes like the "Star Spangled Banner" and "Auld Lang Syne." "In times like these, when murderers roam/ And search around for prey,/ 'Tis a fearful step to leave our home, / Lest dangerous men betray." So began one song, forewarning readers that violence and fear, deceit and betrayal, and calls for the villain's punishment, were the songsmiths' oft-repeated themes.[17] The song "The Clove-Hitch Knot," featured the lyric "He killed the mother and the child,/ A wicked wretch was he," and went on to describe graphically how she was hanged to a stake, before ending with a call, "Oh, hang him, hang him on a tree,/ Tie round the clove-hitch knot;/ And there forever let him be,/ And never be forgot."[18]

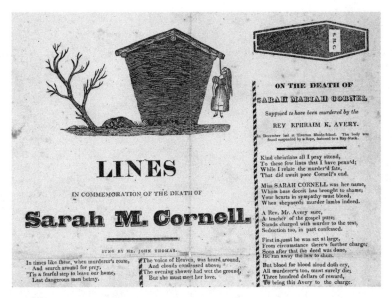

Songs and poems allowed Americans to experience the scandal surrounding Maria Cornell's death and Ephraim Avery's trial through popular culture. *Lines in Commemoration of the Death of Sarah M. Cornell* (Philadelphia, 1833). Library of Congress, Rare Book and Special Collections Division.

The song "The Factory Maid," composed by a blind poet named John Graham, had a weeks-long run in New York theaters, often at the audience's request. Theatergoers could sing along when the chorus repeated, "Oh! weep for Maria, the poor factory maid,/ So charming, so fair, and so basely betrayed." Without exception, popular ballads sang about a seducer and false lover, and the graphic violence was always about her murder and never about a coerced abortion or sexual assault. Not surprisingly, popular songs about Avery and Cornell tilted away from comedy and toward tragedy.[19]

Meanwhile, moral-minded theater critics became incensed by the New York play's depiction of lust-filled, money-hungry Methodists, its open and graphic talk of sex, rape, and abortion, along with how it subverted the conventions of melodrama (the virtuous do not triumph in the end). "We were never more disgusted," wrote *The Truth Teller*. After its first three performances, the *New York Commercial Advertiser* called it "a flagrant outrage" to "public decency and morals" and demanded that the theater's license be revoked and its actors indicted. Two weeks later, when the play

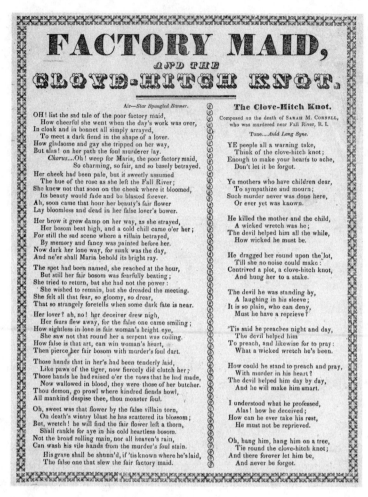

Some songs became a part of Broadway revues for months after the Avery trial verdict. One of the most requested was "The Factory Maid," with its chorus: "Oh! weep for Maria, the poor factory maid,/ So charming, so fair, and so basely betrayed." *Factory Maid, and the Clove-Hitch Knot* ([Boston?], 1833). Courtesy of the American Antiquarian Society.

showed no signs of closing, the *New York Mirror* considered it "so gross a violation of propriety and public decency" that they too called for the playwright and actors to be indicted.[20]

Whether or not critics had actually seen the play—the *New York Mirror*'s critic hadn't bothered to attend a performance by the third week of its successful run—the title character alone was enough to provoke a moral panic.

The taste of New York audiences inclined toward vice, opined Philadelphia's *Atkinson's Saturday Evening Post*, if they were willing to tolerate a play named after Sarah Maria Cornell. "To bring a prostitute upon the stage, for the purposes of engaging public sympathy to embalm and purify her memory," the *Commercial Advertiser* declared, "is the greatest insult to the moral sense of the community." Was this the type of story or character to be represented for young men and women's moral edification? critics asked. Moralists were convinced that when religious papers stooped to puffing these obscene plays, it marked the "gross licentiousness" of the age.[21]

This was at once an old and a new struggle between religion and the theater. There was something more here than the familiar criticism leveled at the temptation of the theater by churches and their clergy. Theatrical entertainments gained predominance among the nation's amusements at exactly the same time that evangelical religion flourished. They were competitors and rivals in a democratic popular culture. They offered similar styles and competing paradigms for expressions of self, class, or gender, and they vied with each other to offer moral instruction. The theatricality of Methodism, from its circuit riders to camp meetings, further provoked that rivalry. Both actors and preachers were itinerants struggling for self-made success and attention.

Critics were equally incensed by how the play reached out beyond the theater and onto the streets of New York. Graphic art depicting Rev. Avery strangling and hanging Maria Cornell to a stake at the haystack was exhibited as an "enormous" mural at the front of the Richmond Hill Theatre, then displayed on handbills and posters affixed to fire pumps and fences at street corners all over the city. The posters were reproductions of two lithographs created and sold by printmaker Henry R. Robinson, who would eventually become one of New York City's most notorious pornographers of the nineteenth century. The prints combined old-fashioned caricatures of the devil and his imps, and a pun that the murderer was "AVery Bad Man," along with the specific details of Cornell's death, such as her shoes and handkerchief arranged near her body and a pencil and handwritten note left behind.[22]

Sarah Maria Cornell became a blockbuster hit. Theater company playbills tended to "puff" a production to boost its box office, insisting that "a full and crowded audience" on the play's opening nights responded "with the most thrilling and wonderful applause." But that seemed unnecessary, as critics and reporters alike observed the overflowing houses night after night. After two weeks, then three, newspapers were still reporting large audiences of city residents and out-of-town tourists flocking to see the spectacle. "Country

One of two lithograph prints of the death of Maria Cornell, in the style of the era's political cartoons, produced by Henry R. Robinson. These prints were also likely used in publicity for drama performed at the Richmond Hill Theatre in New York. *A Very Bad Man* (New York, 1833). Library of Congress, Prints and Photographs Division, LC-USZ62-50464.

people, especially," one paper noted, "are all agog to hear it." The play took top billing and ran successively for nearly two months, showing no signs of diminishing for nearly all of that run. When the production finally ran out of steam in late October, Matilda Flynn left for the Bowery Theatre and the rest of the mediocre cast vanished from memory. By the end, the Fall River play could boast one of the longest successive runs of a theater production in the first half of the nineteenth century.[23]

Because Cornell's death and Avery's trial had already played out in public, there was little mystery to this drama. Even then, in the opening scene Cornell announces her premonition that a minister will murder her. Antebellum Americans, of course, knew the outcome of Shakespeare's tragedies, but still thronged to see his plays. While country visitors revealed the far-reaching appeal of the Cornell-Avery scandal, urban working men and women also found a story of unlimited appeal in a defiant working

A MINISTER EXTRAORDINARY TAKING PASSAGE & BOUND ON A FOREIGN MISSION TO THE COURT OF HIS SATANIC MAJESTY!

Second of two lithograph prints produced by Henry R. Robinson in New York. After killing Maria Cornell, Ephraim Avery is led off by demons (her note saying "If I am missing" is on the ground nearby). Robinson later became one of the city's most notorious sellers of printed pornography. *A Minister Extraordinary Taking Passage & Bound on a Foreign Mission to the Court of His Satanic Majesty!* (New York, 1833). Library of Congress, Prints and Photographs Division, LC-USZ62-1567.

woman's tragic death at the hands of a conspiratorial, secretive, and aristocratic group of clergymen. As has been true for democratic audiences across the long history of popular entertainment, the louder censors rant about indecency and the greater the moral panic they stir, the greater the box office appeal for curious consumers. As P. T. Barnum well knew, any publicity, good or bad, is good for show business.

28

Camp Meetings

CURIOUSLY, FOR ALL THE TALK about moral lessons to be learned from Maria Cornell's death, very few women stepped forward to comment on her murder or on Ephraim Avery's guilt. While the nation's journalists, lawyers, politicians, and church leaders were overwhelmingly white men, there were places in the booming world of print where women could voice their opinions. For decades, white women had filled the ranks as writers of favorite popular genres. They wrote sentimental novels, biographies, and household manuals and made occasional forays into political and moral controversies. Other women edited magazines directed at female readers. The saga of Maria Cornell and Ephraim Avery coincided with the birth of *Godey's Lady's Book*, which became the nation's most widely read magazine before the Civil War. An explosion in new print media stemmed from a surge of women readers and authors.[1]

Just as Proteus and Aristides were intensifying their attacks on the Methodists, Catharine Williams of Providence began her own tireless effort to re-try the Avery case. Allying at times with Avery's persistent critics, Williams published her book near the end of 1833, six months after the not-guilty verdict. *Fall River: An Authentic Narrative* was unlike any other publication in this social drama.

Catharine Williams's personal history explains why she was one of the only women willing to stand up and defend Maria Cornell. The powerful force of respectability was what kept other female authors from commenting on Cornell and Avery. The scandal was simply too saturated with salacious details about shoplifting, premarital sex, adultery, rape, abortion, and lustful passions to fit comfortably with the moral tone assumed by American bourgeois women writers. Moral reformers learned this lesson the hard way, as white and Black women who spoke publicly against "licentiousness"—a term for the male double-standard inherent in prostitution and the sexual exploitation of enslaved women—frequently faced riots by threatening crowds.[2]

A native of Rhode Island, connected by kin to the state's founders and leaders, Williams didn't seem at first glance like a woman who would be willing to associate with the disreputable Maria Cornell. Williams was decidedly middle class and avowed an Episcopal faith that disdained evangelical Methodism's unrestrained spirituality, making her very unlike the nation's most notorious factory girl. Yet for many personal reasons, she identified with Maria Cornell's story. Catharine's mother had died while she was in her teens, and her sea captain father sent her to be raised by two strict aunts. When one aunt died and the other married, Catharine was, in her own words, "launched into the world" at age twenty-three to make her way as best she could.[3]

Sometime later she showed, admittedly, the poorest judgment of her life when she wed Horace Williams, who moved the family west, then fell in with a band of drunken and deceitful men and left Catharine with "no domestic happiness." After two years, she returned to Providence with an infant daughter and a divorce. Catherine became an independent woman, publishing four popular books in the five years before Avery's trial.[4]

For Williams, Cornell's story seemed a sympathetic choice and Avery's villainy a logical conclusion. No book Williams wrote seemed as personal and as committed to truth-telling as *Fall River*. Here she rose to defend independent and vulnerable women from the many incorrigible men who threatened them with dominance, violence, and abandonment.

In part, *Fall River* was a work of investigative journalism. Williams conducted conversations with numerous (though unidentified) mill town residents, key players in the prosecution, town gossips, and Maria Cornell's family. She amassed evidence too from all the occasions when Ephraim Avery clashed with and slandered churchgoers and clergymen. And Williams alone collected and published Maria Cornell's own letters to her mother and sister.

Williams wanted readers to experience *Fall River* as an "authentic narrative." She represented it as a true story—a "fair and candid statement of facts"—even though at times it undeniably drifted toward a work of imagination. Part factual investigation, part impassioned opinion, part fiction,

Williams's narrative was one of the earliest known true crime stories in American popular culture. If it was difficult sometimes for readers to tell fact from fiction in the story, that was the point. Her intent was to make it feel truthful and authentic. Like any true crime story, hers was a tale designed to lead readers to a deeper understanding of the murderer and murder victim: what brought him to his evil deed and her to a calamitous fate.[5]

More than anyone else in this nationwide scandal, Catharine Williams was determined to defend Maria Cornell, to speak on behalf of the "unfortunate girl" denied the opportunity to speak for herself. She was the one who dubbed Avery's trial "the famous trial of S. M. Cornell" owing to the courtroom obsession with the victim's life and character. "Those who wished to make her appear a monster of wickedness" had their say "from a place '*where she cannot answer them back again*.'" It was "no more than fair," Williams contended, that Maria's letters (and Williams) should "speak for her."[6]

In Williams's account, nearly all of the powerful men in Maria Cornell's tale—her father, her beaus, Dr. Graves, Methodist leaders, and especially Ephraim Avery—are depicted as scoundrels, rakes, and violent criminals. As Cornell wandered from one mill town to another, she attracted the attentions of numerous male admirers, since she possessed, in Williams's words, "the curse of beauty." Several young men courted her, but none of them acted honorably. "Many young men make a practice," Williams declared, "of amusing themselves at the expense of young women who are apparently without friends and natural protectors." Although Williams could imagine Maria Cornell settled as a wife and mother, making a "very respectable figure in society," she couldn't picture any of the men worthy of that description.[7]

Echoing a form common to early novels, Williams promised her readers that this story would serve as a warning to young women who might be "in the same situation in life" as Cornell. She intended it to check two phenomena that had gotten out of hand: the "baneful" habit of "moving from place to place" and the "idolatrous" fawning over clergymen who placed "the young and the beautiful" as potential victims of the gossip, the seducer, and the assassin.[8]

By the time Williams's narrative came to Cornell and Avery's days in Lowell, it veered sharply toward rumor and innuendo. Although no one could confirm that there had been a romantic intimacy between them before the fateful camp meeting, Williams assumed that because Cornell never mentioned Avery's name in her family letters she must have been hiding an illicit relationship. Williams turned to gossips, too, who claimed that Avery was "a very polite man to females," frequently inviting some, including Cornell, to ride to an evening meeting in his covered carriage.

Williams repeated their gossip: that Avery often shut the doors of his study "with some young woman or other almost every day"; that Maria Cornell resided in the Avery home for a week, during which time he was known to exit her room late at night; that his young son once blurted out on returning from a carriage ride that "Pa kissed Sarah Maria Cornell on the road." These were the reasons that Sophia Avery insisted "she would not have the girl in the house any longer."[9]

When Williams came to the sexual encounter between Avery and Cornell at the Thompson camp meeting nearly four months prior to Cornell's death, however, she shrank from the kind of explicitness that she directed at the Methodist preacher's other foibles and misdeeds. Ephraim Avery's guilt, of course, hinged on Maria Cornell's claim, reported to her family and to Dr. Wilbur, that he forced her to have sexual intercourse at that August camp meeting.

This was all too much for Catharine Williams's modesty. She knew all these facts from newspapers and trial reports that she had read carefully. She could embellish Dr. Wilbur's recollections to make him declare Avery to be "monstrous!" and she could invoke innuendo and gossip about potential trysts in Lowell, but she simply could not bring herself to depict this encounter in the woods with any more graphic detail than to say that Avery "proceeded to take unwarrantable liberties" and that Cornell "made ineffectual resistance."[10]

Instead, Williams resorted to popular stereotypes about camp meetings to insinuate crimes she couldn't bear to describe. At the end of Fall River, she appended a tale reported to be an "authentic" account of her visit to a camp meeting in rural Rhode Island.

"So many stories had been told me of Camp Meetings," she wrote, "and such various and contradictory ones, that I felt determined to see and hear for myself." This was not, in fact, a journal account as Williams pretended, but rather a semi-fictionalized tale—and a skillfully crafted anti-camp meeting polemic at that.[11]

Opening by evoking the beauty of the sylvan scenery, Williams insisted, "I was never more amazed" than by the loveliness of the pine wood clearing. "The setting sun lent its last bright beams to the scene, while the snowy tents stretched far and wide," complete with "many happy faces peeping from beneath their white curtains." When she remarked to a friend, "It is very quiet here," her less naïve companion informed her, "The meetings have not begun."[12]

Over the course of the weeklong gathering, Williams pieced together a portrait of raucous, tumultuous, and disorderly behavior masquerading as religious experience. All around her, she wrote, in emotional reactions to heated preaching, young people, particularly young women, fell and tumbled to the ground, shaking violently, shrieking and shouting, "struck down" in states of mystical ecstasy that became openly sensual, even sexual.[13]

"Cries for mercy," "groans of distress," and "triumphant exclamations" were repeated in orgasmic mimicry: "I'm full—I'm running over . . . glory! hallelujah!" "God, I'm willing—I will own my Saviour—I will, I will." People urged others to "sink right into Jesus," and "you will be happy in a minute" and "Die in the arms of Jesus." People cried, "Lord, I want to die. . . . Lord, I want to die to-night." Since death and dying were common literary metaphors for orgasm as well as for rebirth or conversion, Williams deliberately conflated revivalist religion with illicit sexuality.[14]

For Williams, the hustle and bustle of a camp meeting was all "discordant noise and unseemly riot," chaotic movement and confusion. As her narrative gained momentum, it became more difficult to distinguish the turbulent behavior of the converts from the "people notorious for dissolute morals and disgraceful conduct," who appeared to be swarming in the woods, the "dissolute and drunken people," "swearing and talking in the most profane and indecent manner," the "hack loads and wagon loads of very bad people," and the gamblers and rum-sellers who followed along.

Her description of participants at a camp meeting reads like a nearly perfect metaphor for the incessant social mobility of the early republic: "There was a continual traveling from place to place—nobody except the immediate actors in the scene seemed stationary for a moment at a time; crowds of people passing and repassing all the time."[15]

For Williams, this was neither a proper nor a decent place for women. Amid endless motion and bodily expressions of religious ecstasy, she repeatedly noted the lustful glances and impudent advances of young men, and the various ways in which women were "grossly insulted." There was, she wrote, "a great deal of joggling, pinching and looking under bonnets." And some of the "young ladies" reported that "they were aroused by some of the men pressing so near, they could almost feel the pulsation of their hearts, and sometimes the press of their arms." Unsurprisingly, Williams concluded that camp meetings were not a safe place for "those whose business is at home—among those whose feet ought to abide in their own house." This was an impassioned plea for the nineteenth-century cult of domesticity.[16]

Methodist camp meetings attracted people from the margins of American society, formerly enslaved persons and female factory workers, further intensifying anxieties about how spiritual ecstasy could led to an unfettering of sexual restraint. As it turned out, Williams's story of camp meetings is the one place in all the writing about the Avery scandal where Black Americans appear, revealing how easily white northerners associated blackness with illicit sex.

For Williams and thousands of others, camp meetings embodied what they feared most about women roving about in public outdoor settings, and the all-too-common descent from religious excess to sexual sins. These emotionally and spiritually frenetic events proved crucial to the dramatic expansion of the Methodist Church, yet camp meetings were also a lightning rod for controversies over the link between the spiritual and the sensual in evangelical religion.

Williams crafted a true crime story with a Victorian flavor—a tale of lecherous men and vulnerable women. No one other than Williams cast Maria Cornell as the epitome of womanliness—docile, good-natured, forgiving—echoing the bourgeois language of true womanhood, even mustering anonymous respondents who recalled Maria as "the kindest and best person to the sick" they had ever seen. Cornell's downfall resulted from being a too-trusting woman who confronted wicked men and hypocrites. "Woman will be woman still," Williams concluded.[17]

The irony, of course, was that Maria Cornell genuinely loved camp meetings. She frequently chose to spend her extra income to attend one rather than return home to the family that disapproved of both her Methodism and her factory work. When Avery's defense attorney wished to associate Cornell's character with sexual promiscuity, emotional excess, irrational piety, even insanity, his description sounded eerily like critics' sexual fears of Methodist camp meetings: she blended "habitual sensual indulgences, with strong fanaticism—a wild enthusiasm, . . . extreme distress and agony of mind, at times, without any apparent cause—screaming, laughing, and crying, all in the same moment, with starting and convulsive motions."[18]

For all her efforts to defend Maria Cornell, Catharine Williams succeeded in depicting Avery as a reckless and violent rake, but only at the cost of insisting that independent women need to remain at home and that their religion should remain indoors.

29

Seduction

THEY KNEW IT WHEN THEY saw it: an incident of passion corrupting and ruining virtue; licentiousness destroying personal happiness; misguided or misused independence; and youthful, impetuous choices leading down the road to betrayal, tragic downfall, and almost always premature death. Indeed, many people were convinced that this sequence resembled Maria Cornell's ill-fated experiences from the moment her body was discovered to the end of this lingering scandal. It all seemed familiar because it was the best-known plot in American popular culture: the story of seduction.

That story was inseparable from the birth of the novel in the previous century, and during Maria Cornell's childhood popular fiction based on the seduction tale still crowded bookshop and library shelves. By then it had devolved into a formula, varying little from its first telling by Samuel Richardson in his 1747 novel, *Clarissa*. America's bestselling novelist, Susanna Rowson, even wondered why readers weren't "tired of reading one story so many times, with only the variation of its being told different ways." The common elements were the young woman's pressing choices between independence and marriage, unwelcome signs of parental power, and (always) the male villain, dishonest about his intentions and status (often having another lover or wife) who never failed to desert and abandon the heroine. There was also, of course, illicit sexuality, loss of virginity, illegitimate pregnancy, and the heroine's premature death, not infrequently from suicide.[1]

Although neither Ephraim Avery nor Maria Cornell ever mentioned any books they might have read, their scandal took place in a nation filled with readers of seduction fiction. Coincidentally, Maria was one of the most common names for heroines in such stories, including in the first American novel, *The Power of Sympathy* (1789), in which a character named Maria, having borne a child out of wedlock and feeling lost to the world and her friends, welcomed her own death, since her life was "no longer a blessing to its possessor, or a joy to those around her."[2]

From the very first news stories to the year-long, post-trial contests in the press, there were those who couldn't let go of this way of understanding the real-life saga of Cornell and Avery. Fall River newspapers defended their community because their residents "do not view with indifference, *seduction* and murder, however humble the unfortunate sufferer." Lowell papers, which ran at least a half dozen news stories about real-life seductions during the years that Maria Cornell lived there, printed tales of seduction alongside their earliest news stories of Avery's murder charge. After the trial, when it should have been apparent how unlikely it was that Maria and Ephraim had had a romantic affair, Avery's critics kept up the references to the preacher as "seducer," even calling him "Reverend-seducer." On the other side, the Methodists who authored *The Vindication* were determined to quash any accusations of seduction voiced by his critics.[3]

It's striking how few voices throughout the whole scandal—whether in newspapers, pamphlets, or popular culture—discussed Avery and Cornell's relationship as sexual assault. In the post-trial court of public opinion, the facts about that sexual event remained more clouded in mystery than an honest appraisal of sexual violence warranted.

Nothing in Maria Cornell's own account of that fateful encounter with Ephraim Avery at a camp meeting months before her death addresses Cornell's pleasure or desire—it speaks only of Avery's coercion or violence. Once the two of them were alone in the woods, away from the Methodist services, Avery made clear his intention to extort sex from her. As Cornell reported, the only condition under which Avery would settle their differences was "that he should enjoy sexual intercourse with me, promising . . . that if I would consent to it, he would do me no mischief." In return for sex, Avery promised to destroy her confessional letters, in which she detailed her sexual sins, and no longer interfere with her attempts to join other Methodist congregations.[4]

Did Ephraim Avery rape Maria Cornell? Secondhand evidence only adds to the uncertainty. He certainly placed her in a situation where he could extort sex while still invoking a language that implied her consent. Lucy Hathaway, Maria's housemate and co-worker in Fall River, testified that

Maria asked her whether she thought "an innocent woman might be led away by a man she had confidence in and rather looked up to." When Lucy said she did not know, Maria then said, 'What can a poor weak woman do in the hands of a strong man, and he using all kinds of arguments.'" Cornell recounted to Dr. Wilbur, "It was dark or dusk, I was in his power, and finally consented." Her phrase, "I was in his power," could have meant that Avery controlled her future as a Methodist, directly affecting her prospects for factory employment, or it could have alluded to Avery physically overpowering her. In the end, the difference mattered little to Cornell. Rape and coerced sex were two sides of sexual assault in early America. The privileges of being a white man allowed men to imbue coercion with the appearance of consent.[5]

Nevertheless, Cornell did describe the camp meeting encounter as forced sex. "I could not quite call it forcing me," she told Wilbur, "but it was very near to it." Grindal Rawson testified that Cornell described how Avery "took hold of her hands, and put one of his into her bosom," then, she said, "she tried to get away from him, but could not."[6]

A sexual assault simply didn't fit the seduction narrative that people wanted to believe about a Methodist preacher and a factory girl. The prosecution never presented their encounter as an unwanted sexual advance, perhaps because they didn't want to face the burden of proving a rape charge, but also because the prosecutors accepted prevailing narratives about sexually promiscuous and religiously passionate women. In the public's mind, Maria's sexual history seemed to make the idea of unwanted sexual advances unimaginable. So too did popular perceptions of Methodists and camp meetings, since it was easy to imagine uncontrollable sexuality among enthusiastic believers at revival meetings and to envision charismatic preachers as seductive. These narratives easily trumped explanations based on sexual violence.

Seduction became the catch-all term in the young republic to explain any form of deceitful or coerced sexual liaisons, including sexual violence. It provided an uncomplicated way to address changing ideas about sexual desire, with men driven by their inability to control their sex drive while women were expected to rein in their pleasure-seeking passions. Seduction lent a familiar narrative to capture the sexual vulnerability of unmarried women and the too often unspoken instances of rape. As opposing caricatures, Ephraim Avery could be portrayed as the seducer and Maria Cornell as the prostitute, although neither label truly fit the details of their lives and their relationship.[7]

At the time of Cornell's death the idea of seduction also touched Americans' deeper anxieties about the changing world around them, especially the problem of how to live a moral life in an economic and political environment in which deceit and hypocrisy prevailed. In most people's minds, Maria Cornell had in fact been seduced, but who the seducer was remained uncertain. Was she ruined by a reckless married man of unquenchable passion? Or had she been seduced instead by the promise of an independent life in which she could support herself, follow her own desires, make her own choices, buy the fashions available in a new commercial marketplace, and arouse the sexual desires of equally mobile young men?

The firestorm from this scandal made the Methodists particularly aware of how their ecstatic religious practices and spiritual intimacies made them vulnerable, as a group, to charges of seduction. That's why they fought so hard against the accusations leveled against their brother clergyman.

Nothing illustrated this better than their reaction to a portrait of Ephraim Avery that circulated after the trial. The image aroused heated reactions from Methodists, especially because the church had silently commissioned attorney George Rivers to prepare the trial report in which the portrait first appeared.[8]

Trial reporters announced that the woodcut image was "drawn by a very celebrated Portrait Painter," and "taken from a first-rate Painting, by an eminent Artist, and may be depended on as AN ACCURATE LIKENESS." They had good reason for thinking it captured the man. After all, reporters had described the preacher who appeared in the Newport courtroom. Richard Adams Locke observed that "the prisoner is a man of very respectable appearance" and "considered handsome," his forehead "high and unfurrowed," while Benjamin Hallett noted that Avery's dark hair was "cut close round his forehead, and his face may be called handsome." More than any other features, the portrait seemed to capture the one aspect of Avery's appearance that all observers positively obsessed about: the preacher's implacable, unmovable, expressionless countenance maintained throughout the trial, no matter how graphic, emotional, or damning the testimony. The portrait's authenticity rested in its record of the firm and unwavering emotionless demeanor that Ephraim Avery displayed during the entirety of the month-long trial.[9]

The Methodist authors of *The Vindication* vehemently disagreed, declaring it not at all a good likeness of their brother. They pronounced the portrait "a caricature, done with the design to impress the beholder that he is a savage and libidinous monster." The publishers never said they were

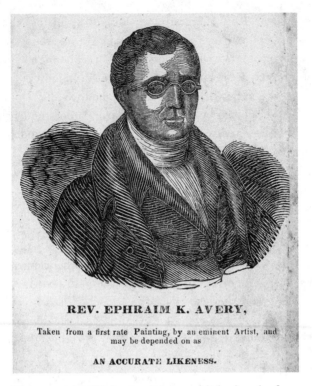

REV. EPHRAIM K. AVERY,

Taken from a first rate Painting, by an eminent Artist, and
may be depended on as

AN ACCURATE LIKENESS.

This portrait of Ephraim Avery, published as the frontispiece of at least two different trial reports, provoked
recriminations from the Methodists, who denounced
it as "a caricature, done with the design to impress the
beholder that he is a savage and libidinous monster."
*The Trial of the Rev. Ephraim K. Avery, for the Murder
of Sarah Maria Cornell* (New York, 1833). Courtesy of
the American Antiquarian Society.

offering an accurate likeness of a seducer, but the Methodists assumed that
this was exactly what they intended. In this image they saw the telltale signs
of a hypersexual man.[10]

For one thing, Avery was portrayed with fuller lips than would be typical of clergymen's portraits of the era, heightening his sensuality. Likely
the Methodists were equally galled by Avery's attire, with its new-style coat
and high fashion, which—while signaling efforts to embrace middle-class
respectability—clashed with their disdain for luxury and fashion. All in all,
Avery appeared in this portrait more like a dandy than a spiritual leader

or a "man of the cloth," his clothes bearing no resemblance to the well-known rustic uniform of a circuit rider's shabby black cloak and broad-brimmed hat.

Yet there was more in this facial portrait that sparked the Methodists' ire. Avery's tinted spectacles (trial reporters described them as having a purple hue) masked his eyes, implying a man who had something to hide. In an era fixated on people's faces as guides to ascertain their honesty and trustworthiness, any effort to disguise one's face through makeup or tinted glasses raised the specter of hypocrisy. And nothing was as touchy an issue for clergymen than the accusation of being a hypocrite. Methodist leaders were especially keen to distance themselves from the imagery of preachers as confidence men and churches as the nurseries of hypocrisy.

Most threatening of all, the woodcut's dark shading across the preacher's face made his complexion appear intentionally dark, hinting at black skin. Indeed, the sensuality of the image, to which Methodists so strenuously objected, relied on racial fears and stereotypes of Black male hypersexuality that had begun to take hold of the white American imagination in the nineteenth century. The Methodists' choice of words to denounce the image— "savage" and "libidinous"— equally tapped into white racialist thinking. The Methodists perceived racial classification as well as sexual depravity in the portrait of Ephraim Avery precisely because they couldn't help thinking about the accusation of a seduction.

Epilogue

After the Curtain Falls

CATHARINE WILLIAMS HEARD THE SENTIMENTS of her neighbors. They were saying to her that she should just let go of the whole scandal of Maria Cornell and Ephraim Avery, that there was no point in rehearsing the past when it wouldn't alter the outcome. As Williams brought her true-crime book to a close, she took a jab at her critics, defending the mill town that had tried so valiantly to attain justice for a crime that outraged their community.

"It is in vain," Williams wrote, "to say 'it is time this subject was dropped—this excitement ceased.'" To escape it now, she declared, one would have to go "where a *hay stack* was never heard of." It was unimaginable to Catharine Williams that there would ever be a time when people didn't remember the terrible haystack murder.[1]

For all the seemingly endless passion about the scandal, interest did inevitably subside, just as it would for nearly every other "crime of the century" that followed. Personal memory is fleeting, but a social drama, and a culture's immersion in it, also depends on how long a disturbing episode—a crime or a breach of a community's norms—continues to touch deeply the politics of people's everyday lives. Whether it was moral outrage, insatiable curiosity, or conspiratorial dreaming, the public frenzy over the factory girl and the Methodist preacher lasted far longer than anyone at the time expected.

The red-hot, sharp-tongued disputes in newspapers and pamphlets came to an end with Aristides's last newspaper column as springtime neared in 1834. Ephraim Avery still remained a minor curiosity, an object of occasional rumors, and the butt of sporadic jokes for a few more years after Maria Cornell had been laid to rest.

Crowds of visitors who trekked to the Durfee farm to see Maria Cornell's grave, a busy tourist attraction during the heyday of the scandal, also tapered off. The family kept up the cemetery and treated her grave as they would the burial site of any of their kin. After the trial, Fall River residents offered to erect a monument to Maria, but her mother, sister, and brother-in-law opted instead for a simple headstone engraved with the words: "In Memory of Sarah M. Cornell, daughter of James & Lucretia Cornell. Who died Dec. 20, 1832, in the 31st year of her age."

The mill town of Fall River witnessed continuing boom times over the next eighty years, with more and more mills producing more cotton print cloth than anywhere else in the United States, until New England's textile production bottomed out and shifted to states in the Jim Crow South. And six decades after Cornell's death, Fall River became the locale of another famous crime, the notorious axe murder of Lizzie Borden's father and step-mother in 1892, followed by Lizzie Borden's trial and acquittal, one still associated with the town to this day.[2]

Over the ensuing decades the expanding mill town encroached on the Durfee farm. During the Civil War, the Massachusetts state border moved south, making the farm officially part of the city of Fall River. When John Durfee died in 1867, the family sold the property to the city. The mill town hired renowned landscape architect Frederick Law Olmsted, designer of New York's Central Park, to draw up plans to convert the farm into a city park. South Park would run from South Main Street down to the Taunton River—the same ground that John Durfee tramped along on that cold December morning in 1832. The town disinterred all the graves from the Durfee family plot and moved them to the stately Oak Grove Cemetery across town.[3]

Although Ephraim Avery had been declared a free man, the outrage over the trial's outcome made it impossible for him to continue to live and preach in New England. Within a few years he resigned from the ministry and moved his family to the Berkshire hills of Massachusetts, on the New York border, where his father and mother had relocated from Connecticut more than a decade earlier. Other than a census taker, no one recorded anything about his time there. Earlier, when he had been rising to manhood, there was nothing that Ephraim wanted more than to avoid being confined as a landless, tenant farmer without an occupation or profession, yet there he was once more. Sometime during the 1840s he packed up his family and moved again, this time to Ohio, where he took up farming in a village five miles south of Oberlin College. He died there in 1869.

This would not be the last of the sex scandals involving clergymen and their churches. Hundreds of ministers and priests faced the consequences for their sexual dalliances or abuses throughout the nineteenth century. Ephraim Avery's career, as well as his trial, intersected with a handful of other scandals involving clergymen's sexual misconduct toward women. Soon after Avery's acquittal, another evangelical revivalist preacher in southern New England, Eleazer Sherman, faced the only documented church trial for allegedly making same-sex sexual advances during his travels as an itinerant preacher. Indeed, witnesses at that tribunal recounted that in late-night encounters in bed, Sherman voiced his opinion on Avery's guilt.[4]

Where did Americans' attentions go when they eventually lost interest in the stories about Maria Cornell and Ephraim Avery? It wasn't just a matter of a dwindling fascination with a provocative scandal. The reading public was also pulled by gravitational force toward a new national preoccupation with slavery, antislavery, and the nation's deepening divisions that would culminate in civil war.

The early signs were there when Fall River residents awoke to the news that one of their factory girls had been found dead. A year before Maria Cornell's death, Nat Turner's rebellion had broken out in Virginia, and William Lloyd Garrison began publishing his antislavery newspaper, *The Liberator*, in Boston, which launched a new phase of the abolitionist movement. Only days before the haystack crime, the Nullification Crisis, in which South Carolina provoked a constitutional and near-military conflict over the tariff—anathema to southern economies built on exporting products produced by the enslaved—had reached its apex. Men in Fall River taverns had been discussing Jackson's threats to send troops to enforce the law on the night when one of them heard a woman's screams in the dark near Durfee's farm.

In a stunning turn, the principal protagonists in Avery's trial found themselves engrossed in the nation's divisions over slavery. The prominent Methodists involved in defending Avery and their church almost immediately immersed themselves in the abolitionist struggle. Avery's peers, including George Storrs, Abraham Merrill, Orange Scott (who was on the investigation committee that exonerated Avery), and Timothy Merritt, now devoted their preaching and writing labors to the abolitionist cause. They insisted in an appeal to the conference that no one has "a right to hold a fellow man for one moment in bondage as a piece of merchantable property" and that whoever did so was guilty of a crime that "cannot be reconciled with the spirit of the Christian religion." But they ran directly into fierce opposition from other Methodists like Wilbur Fisk, Nathan Bangs, and the church's bishops, all supporters of the colonization society, who vehemently attacked abolitionists as troublemakers seeking to "create great excitement and alarm" and incite mobs throughout the country. Once the abolitionist faction began creating antislavery societies within the church, there was no turning back the divisive racial and sectional politics that would soon split the nation's largest church into two groups—a Methodist Episcopal Church, North and South—and would presage the kind of secessionist divisions that would later sever the Union.[5]

Trial reporters Richard Hildreth and Benjamin Hallett took opposing positions on the antislavery politics that consumed the nation. Even Nathaniel Borden, Antimason and Fall River mill owner, embraced the abolitionist cause. Yet the mill town found itself caught between cotton and conscience. Like manufacturers in Lowell, Fall River's textile capitalists became more deeply embedded with each passing year in a cotton economy that tied them inextricably to southern slavery, while at the same time the town's shopkeepers and factory workers filled the ranks of the several antislavery societies in the growing city. All of New England was racked by abolitionist agitation and anti-abolitionist riots that escalated in 1834 and continued through the coming of the Civil War.[6]

American theatergoers soon forgot the play *Sarah Maria Cornell* as they became infatuated with a new cultural phenomenon also rooted in the racial politics of slavery. The same year that Maria Cornell took her last breath, white performer Thomas D. Rice began an entertainment craze when he started dancing "Jumping Jim Crow" on the stage of New York's Bowery Theatre. Attracting working folks from the city and country, blackface minstrelsy would soon become the nation's pre-eminent form of popular culture, building a fantasy world of racist stereotypes and imagined slavery that would shape the thinking of white Americans for more than a century. Theater patrons could witness that transition before their very eyes: advertisements for the Richmond Hill play on the Avery scandal appeared side-by-side with ads for Rice's performances of Jim Crow in New York City papers.[7]

The social drama that erupted around the tragic encounter between Ephraim Avery and Sarah Maria Cornell, and the question of whether or not he murdered her, slowly played itself out. But even if people had moved on from the case, the troubles it provoked still mattered to them. They might no longer talk about Rev. Avery and the factory girl, but they conversed about women, work, religion, sex, and justice in the rapidly changing world ushered in during Maria Cornell's lifetime. At the height of public attention to this scandalous crime, people had somehow wished and expected that the trial of Ephraim Avery—both in a Newport courtroom and in the court of public opinion—might somehow produce a resolution to anxieties about the revolutions they were living through. Yet the point of a social drama is to expose the problems. It rarely promises to resolve the dilemmas.

Today the landscaped garden of Fall River's Oak Grove Cemetery is home to countless grave markers for Bordens and Durfees, as well as the family plots of doctors Wilbur and Hooper, and generations of John Durfee's descendants. But Maria Cornell's coffin, when re-interred, was separated from anyone's family plot. In her final resting place, among the graves of poorer mill town folk on Whitethorn Path, Maria was once again friendless.

ACKNOWLEDGMENTS

I am very grateful for the generous support that made possible the writing of this book, particularly a Eugene Lang Faculty Fellowship from Swarthmore College, a German Academic Exchange Service (DAAD) grant at the Department of North American History, University of Erfurt, a scholar-in-residence grant from the John F. Kennedy Institute for North American Studies at the Free University of Berlin, and a year-long fellowship at the Charles Warren Center for Studies in American History at Harvard University. Thank you, Robin Bernstein, Samuel Zipp, Nancy Cott, Lizabeth Cohen, Walter Johnson, Arthur Patton-Hock, and Larissa Kennedy for fostering and nurturing that amazing community, and a special thanks to my Warren Center cohort: Luiz Alvarez, Jayna Brown, Karen Hansen, Martha Hodes, David Jaffee, Ann Pellegrini, Kyla Wazana Tompkins, Sara Warner, and Harvey Young for your fearless inquiry and generous collegiality.

Thank you to everyone who assisted me with good cheer in finding the records necessary to tell the stories of the protagonists involved in this case at many archives and libraries across the United States: the staffs of the American Antiquarian Society, American Textile History Museum in Lowell, Center for Lowell History at the University of Massachusetts-Lowell, Connecticut Historical Society, Fall River Historical Society, Baker Library at Harvard Business School, Countway Library of Medicine at Harvard Medical School, Schlesinger Library on the History of Women in

America at Harvard University, The Huntington Library, John Hay Library at Brown University, Kheel Center for Labor-Management Documentation and Archives at Cornell University, Leffingwell House Museum in Norwich, Library Company of Philadelphia, Library of Congress, Massachusetts Historical Society, Newport Historical Society, New York Public Library, Pocumtuck Valley Memorial Association Library, Redwood Library in Newport, Rhode Island Historical Society, Town Clerk's Office in Rupert in Vermont, University of Connecticut Archives and Special Collections, Vermont Historical Society, Beinecke Rare Book and Manuscript Library and Manuscripts and Archives at Sterling Memorial Library at Yale University. Special thanks for answering all of my many requests and questions to Elizabeth Bouvier at the Massachusetts Supreme Judicial Court Archives, and Kara Jackman at the New England Conference of the Methodist Episcopal Church's Commission on Archives and History at Boston University.

Many people read, listened, and offered thoughtful questions and suggestions that improved this book: I am deeply grateful to Vaughan Booker, Joyce Chaplin, Karin Gedge, James Gilbert, Josh Greenberg, Grace Hale, Rodney Hessinger, Sebastian Jobs, Martha Jones, Nora Kreuzenbeck, Jürgen Martschukat, Silvan Niedermeier, Seth Rockman, Charles Rosenberg, Bryant Simon, Olaf Stieglitz, Sharon Ullman, Judith Weisenfeld, and the organizers and participants of the Writing History Seminar in New York City, as well as audiences at the University of Coimbra in Portugal, the University of Paderborn, the Halle American Studies Seminar in Wittenberg, the University of Erfurt, the University of Münster, and Free University of Berlin in Germany, the University of Vienna, Princeton University, Harvard University, Richard Stockton College, and Michael Zuckerman's salon at the McNeil Center for Early American Studies at the University of Pennsylvania. I offer special thanks to Kathleen Brown, Amy Greenberg, Nancy Hewitt, and Christine Stansell for being model historians as well as for their steadfast support for my journey toward this book.

My students at Brown University, the University of California-Santa Cruz, the University of Erfurt, and especially at Swarthmore College, where I began this project as a course of the same title, have contributed creative and analytical insights that shaped the storytelling in this book. Josh Greenberg, Cecilia Tsu, and Miriam Rich moved from students in that course to colleagues and friends, and I also wish to thank Miriam for her insightful and invaluable reading of Act II.

My agent, Deirdre Mullane, has been a writer's dream, believing that I could do justice to Maria Cornell's story and shine a spotlight on its meaning for Maria's lifetime and our own. Her enthusiasm for this book never wavered, beginning with our first conversation, and her encouragement continually inspired me. Freelance editor Susan Whitlock took seriously the book that I wanted to write and, with her skillful touch, pointed the way to get to there. Her editorial advice was spot-on across the entire manuscript. I wish to thank my Oxford editor, Susan Ferber, for her belief in this story and for her precise and brilliant editorial guidance.

James Goodman, the kind of writer—and friend—I aspire to be, read an early draft, and our two-person writers' workshop in Central Park one beautiful summer day guided my thinking to the very last day of writing. My story of Maria Cornell and Ephraim Avery would not be the same without his bountiful assistance. Naomi Lamoreaux believed in me long ago and invited me to assist in the initial design of a course on the Avery case. Years later, she gladly read an early draft and offered invaluable suggestions. For both of those gifts I will be forever grateful to her. Each of these many readers and guides deserve credit for the best parts of this book.

Along the way I have been blessed with friends who have graciously listened to me talk about Maria Cornell and the world she sadly departed. Thank you, Julie Berebitsky, Laurie Bernstein, Tim Burke, Katharina Dahl, Matthew Dennis, Konstantin Dierks, Michel Gobat, James Goodman, Laura Gotkowitz, Jessica Halem, Mary Huissen, Connie Hungerford, Sarah Knott, Jen Manion, Jürgen Martschukat, Jennifer McFeely, Shana Minkin, Michael Mullan, Fritz Read, Woody Register, Elizabeth Reis, Gigi Simeone, Sharon Ullman, Bob Weinberg, Ben Yagoda, and all my friends and colleagues at Swarthmore College. My family has sustained me in far too many ways to express. Thank you, Linda Hodes, Stephen Margolies, Stuart Hodes, Elizabeth Hodes, Tal Ben-David, Kevin Brady, Quinn Brady, Matthew Choi, Ryn Hodes, Holly Richardson, Danielle Abrams, Ken Tosti, David O'Keefe for all your love and good cheer at Hodes family gatherings. Thank you to my parents, David and Betty Dorsey, and to Connie Cashman, Ruth Purcell, Chris Purcell, Jon Dorsey, Stacy Dorsey, Katie and Jordan Hilbert, Danielle Dorsey, Evan Dorsey, Kailee Dorsey, Tyler Dorsey, Scott Kalousek and Hope Melton, Brian Kalousek and Holley Biroczky, for all of your love, and for every unforgettable moment when you joined me or indulged my passion to be near the surf in San Clemente.

A special word of gratitude to Woody Register for the deepest bonds of friendship and love: We set off on a journey together in (and by) Providence that will continue throughout our lifetimes. Thank you for every memorable meal, drink, conversation, and adventure, and all the loving words that we have shared and will continue to share.

I am so very grateful that Tim Dorsey and Sarah Dorsey are at the center of my life. Their love and companionship, and our joyful days and evenings spent together, have been treasured gifts for which I cannot thank them enough. (Thanks as well for introducing us to dear friends Jay and Kate Petel.) I am thankful too for Tim's artistry in designing the maps for this book. I will always recall the time when Tim accompanied me on a visit to Maria Cornell's grave and the Bristol Courthouse. We have also ascended many a mountain top together, my son, and raced down them on our snowboards with utter joy. I look forward to many more adventures ahead.

Martha Hodes heard me speak about this murder trial on the very first day we met, and yet she has never tired of listening to me describe this drama's plot twists. Graciously pausing her own writing to help me puzzle through a challenge or to offer a better word choice, Martha read scores of drafts at every stage, pondering every detail and turn of phrase with me, and her editorial guidance remains my lodestar forever. There are few greater joys in life that can compare with a long walk on a seemingly never-ending stretch of beach talking about writing—and life—with Martha. Her boundless love for me, and mine for her, has enriched my life and made me the happiest person in the world.

NOTES

To enhance readability, some minimal changes in spelling and punctuation have been made in quotations from original sources. Testimony from the trial has occasionally been rendered as a composite of what was recorded in the multiple trial reports for this case.

Abbreviations

AAS	American Antiquarian Society, Worcester, MA
AC	*The Arguments of Counsel in the Close of the Trial of Rev. Ephraim K. Avery*, ed. Benjamin F. Hallett (Boston, 1833)
AS	[Aristides], *Strictures on the Case of Ephraim K. Avery* (Providence, 1833)
AT	*American Traveler* (Boston)
ATP	Avery Trial Papers, Rhode Island Historical Society, Providence, RI
BCG	*Boston Commercial Gazette*
BDA	*Boston Daily Advocate*
BFH	Benjamin F. Hallett, *A Full Report of the Trial of Ephraim K. Avery, Charged with the Murder of Sarah M. Cornell*, 2nd ed. (Boston, 1833)
CA	*Christian Advocate; Christian Advocate and Journal and Zion's Herald* (New York)
CHS	Connecticut Historical Society, Hartford, CT
CSL	Connecticut State Library, Hartford, CT
CW	Catharine R. Williams, *Fall River: An Authentic Narrative* (Providence, 1833)
FRHS	Fall River Historical Society, Fall River, MA
FRM	*Fall River Monitor*
FRWR	*Fall River Weekly Recorder*

GW	[Gurdon Williams], *Brief and Impartial Narrative of the Life of Sarah Maria Cornell* (New York, 1833)
HBL	Baker Library, Harvard Business School, Harvard University
HCL	Countway Library, Harvard Medical School, Harvard University
HH	Harvey Harnden, *Narrative of the Apprehension in Rindge, N.H. of the Rev. E. K. Avery* (Providence, 1833)
HSE	Benjamin F. Hallett, *Avery's Trial [Supplementary Edition]* (Boston, 1833)
JHL	John Hay Library, Brown University
LD	Luke Drury, *A Report of the Examination of Rev. Ephraim K. Avery, Charged with the Murder of Sarah Maria Cornell* (Providence, 1833)
LFP	Leffingwell Family Papers, Manuscripts & Archives, Yale University Library
LJ	*Lowell Journal*
LM	*Lowell Mercury*
LO	*The Lowell Offering*
MB	*The Correct, Full and Impartial Report of the Trial of Rev. Ephraim K. Avery* (Providence, 1833), published by Marshall & Brown
NBC	*New Bedford Courier*
NBM	*New Bedford Mercury*
NECH	*New England Christian Herald* (Boston)
NEMA	New England Conference, Methodist Episcopal Church, Commission on Archives and History, Boston University School of Theology Library
NHT	*Newport Herald of the Times*
NM	*Newport Mercury*
NYCE	*New York Courier & Enquirer*
PJ	*Providence Journal*
PP	*Providence Patriot*
PRH	*Republican Herald* (Providence)
RAL	Richard Adams Locke, *Report of the Trial of the Rev. Ephraim K. Avery* (New York, 1833)
RH	Richard Hildreth, *A Report of the Trial of the Rev. Ephraim K. Avery, 2nd ed.* (Boston, 1833)
RIA	*Rhode Island American* (Providence)
RIR	*Rhode Island Republican* (Newport)
TAL	*The Trial at Large, of the Rev. Ephraim K. Avery, for the Wilful Murder of Sarah Maria Cornell* (New York, 1833)
TUM	*Trumpet & Universalist Magazine* (Boston)
UCA	University of Connecticut Archives & Special Collections, Storrs, CT
VIN	[Timothy Merritt et al.], *A Vindication of the Result of the Trial of Rev. Ephraim K. Avery* (Boston, 1834)
WS	William R. Staples, *A Correct Report of the Examination of Rev. Ephraim K. Avery* (Providence, 1833)
ZH	*Zion's Herald* (Boston)

Names

ACG	Albert C. Greene (Attorney General, RI, chief prosecutor)
CL	Christopher Leffingwell
EKA	Ephraim K. Avery
GR	Grindal Rawson
JC	James Cornell
JH	John Howe (Justice of the Peace, Bristol, RI)
LC	Lucretia Cornell (Maria's sister)
LCR	Lucretia Cornell Rawson (Maria's sister)
LLC	Lucretia Leffingwell Cornell
SMC	Sarah Maria Cornell
WL	William Leffingwell (Christopher's son)

Prologue

1. Walt Whitman [Velsor Brush], "City Photographs—No. VI," *New York Leader*, May 3, 1862, The Walt Whitman Archive: whitmanarchive.org.

2. For the Richmond Hill Theatre and Matilda Flynn, see Edwin Williams, *New-York, As It Is, in 1833* (New York, 1833); George C. D. Odell, *Annals of the New York Stage*, 15 vols. (New York: Columbia University Press, 1927-49), vol. 3; Joseph N. Ireland, *Records of the New York Stage, from 1750 to 1860*, 2 vols. (New York, 1867); *Evening Post* (New York), 1832–1833.

3. Mrs. M. [Mary Carr] Clarke, *Sarah Maria Cornell, or The Fall River Murder: A Domestic Drama, in Three Acts* (New York, 1833), 4.

4. This case has periodically piqued the curiosity of both fiction writers and historians. Previous histories include David Richard Kasserman, *Fall River Outrage: Life, Murder, and Justice in Early Industrial New England* (Philadelphia: University of Pennsylvania Press, 1986); William G. McLoughlin, "Untangling the Tiverton Tragedy: The Social Meaning of the Terrible Haystack Murder of 1833," *Journal of American Culture* 7 (1984): 75–84; Patricia Caldwell, "Introduction," in Catharine Williams, *Fall River: An Authentic Narrative* (New York: Oxford University Press, 1993); Ian C. Pilarczyk, "The Terrible Haystack Murder: The Moral Paradox of Hypocrisy, Prudery and Piety in Antebellum America," *American Journal of Legal History* 41 (1997): 25–60; Judith Barbour, "Letters of the Law: The Trial of E. K. Avery for the Murder of Sarah M. Cornell," *Law, Text, Culture* 2 (1995): 118–33; Kristin Boudreau, *The Spectacle of Death: Populist Literary Responses to American Capital Cases* (Amherst, NY: Prometheus Books, 2006). The case has inspired a few novels, including Mary Cable, *Avery's Knot* (New York: Putnam, 1981); Raymond Paul, *The Tragedy at Tiverton* (New York: Viking, 1984). Other outstanding examples of histories of sensational sex crimes and trials in this era include: Patricia Cline Cohen, *The Murder of Helen Jewett* (New York: Alfred A. Knopf, 1998); John Wood Sweet, *The Sewing Girl's Tale: A Story of Crime and Consequences in Revolutionary America* (New York: Henry Holt, 2022).

5. Herman Melville, *The Confidence-Man: His Masquerade* (London, 1857), 256. The social experience and performative participation of theater

audiences has been explored in Bruce A. McConachie, *Melodramatic Formations: American Theatre and Society, 1820–1870* (Iowa City: University of Iowa Press, 1992); Richard Butsch, *The Making of American Audiences: From Stage to Television, 1750–1990* (Cambridge: Cambridge University Press, 2000); David Grimsted, *Melodrama Unveiled: American Theater and Culture, 1800–1850* (Chicago, 1968; reprint, Berkeley: University of California Press, 1987); Rosemarie K. Bank, *Theatre Culture in America, 1825–1860* (Cambridge: Cambridge University Press, 1997).

6. Victor Turner in *Drama, Fields, and Metaphors: Symbolic Action in Human Society* (Ithaca, NY: Cornell University Press, 1974). For the importance of storytelling to social dramas, see Victor Turner, "Social Dramas and Stories about Them," *Critical Inquiry* 7 (1980): 141–68.

Chapter 1

1. On Tiverton, see Orin Fowler, *An Historical Sketch of Fall River, from 1620 to the Present Time* (Fall River, 1841); Richard M. Bayles, ed. *History of Newport County, Rhode Island* (New York, 1888). For the eighteenth-century farm economy, see Daniel Vickers, "The Northern Colonies: Economy and Society, 1600–1775," in *The Cambridge Economic History of the United States,* vol. 1, *The Colonial Era*, ed. Stanley L. Engerman and Robert E. Gallman (Cambridge: Cambridge University Press, 1996), 209–48; Daniel Vickers, *Farmers and Fisherman: Two Centuries of Work in Essex County, Massachusetts, 1630–1850* (Chapel Hill: University of North Carolina Press, 1994); Christopher Clark, *The Roots of Rural Capitalism: Western Massachusetts, 1780-1860* (Ithaca, NY: Cornell University Press, 1990); Daniel P. Jones, *The Economic and Social Transformation of Rural Rhode Island, 1780–1850* (Boston: Northeastern University Press, 1992).

2. Durfee's testimony: BFH, 18–23; LD, 6–7; RH, 11–13; weather: *NM*, January 5, 1833; Leonard Hill, *Meterological and Chronological Register . . .* (Plymouth, 1869), 162.

3. BFH, 19, 44–45, 50–51; RH, 11, 22, 25.

4. BFH, 24; RH, 14.

5. LD, 9. On coroners and inquest juries, see Paul F. Mellen, "Coroners' Inquests in Colonial Massachusetts," *Journal of the History of Medicine and Allied Sciences* 40 (1985): 462–72; Jeffrey M. Jentzen, *Death Investigation in America: Coroners, Medical Examiners, and the Pursuit of Medical Certainty* (Cambridge, MA: Harvard University Press, 2009).

6. LD, 7, 8. Later, at the Newport trial, Dr. Wilbur disclosed the limits of physicians' medical knowledge of pregnancy. "I took hold of her wrist and looked at her tongue," he said, to ascertain whether she was pregnant, but, he explained, "I did not come to any very definite conclusion." BFH, 35.

7. LD, 7–8; *RIR*, March 12, 1833.

8. BFH, 19. There was also a fourth letter in the trunk, in the woman's own hand, addressed to Rev. Ira Bidwell, informing him that she no longer wished to be connected with the Methodist church, since she no longer

enjoyed "any religion at all," and that "I have not seen a well or happy day since I left Thompson Camp-meeting ground." LD, 63; BFH, 189–90.

9. BFH, 189, 191.

10. *Philadelphia Repository*, February 7, 1801.

Chapter 2

1. CL Diary, February 9, 1805, LFP.

2. The life and work of Christopher Leffingwell and the history of Norwich, Connecticut, can be traced in Albert Leffingwell, *1637–1897: The Leffingwell Record* (Aurora, NY, 1897); Marvin G. Thompson, *Connecticut Entrepreneur: Christopher Leffingwell* (Hartford: American Bicentennial Commission of Connecticut, 1980); James P. Walsh, "'Mechanics and Citizens': The Connecticut Artisan Protest of 1792," *William and Mary Quarterly* 3rd ser., 42 (1985): 66–89; Frances Manwaring Caulkins, *History of Norwich, Connecticut, from Its Possession by the Indians to the Year 1866* (Hartford, 1874).

3. Leffingwell, *The Leffingwell Record*, 47. For mercantile trade within the British empire and its colonies, see John J. McCusker, "British Mercantilist Policies and the American Colonies," in *The Cambridge Economic History of the United States*, vol. 1, *The Colonial Era*, ed. Stanley L. Engerman and Robert E. Gallman (Cambridge: Cambridge University Press, 2008), 337–62; John J. McCusker and Russell R. Menard, *The Economy of British America, 1607–1789* (Chapel Hill: University of North Carolina Press, 1985); Jacob M. Price, "The Imperial Economy, 1700–1776," in *The Oxford History of the British Empire*, vol. 2, *The Eighteenth Century*, ed. P. J. Marshall (Oxford: Oxford University Press, 1998), 78–104. Ordinary laborers, on the other hand, experienced only the "bust" side of this mercantile boom. Prices skyrocketed, incomes diminished, and wartime casualties and widowhood escalated. Gary B. Nash, *The Urban Crucible* (Cambridge, MA: Harvard University Press, 1979).

4. CL to Unknown, December 26, 1765; CL to Nathaniel Greene, November 11, 1764, CL Letterbook, 1764–1767, LFP; "Memorial to the General Assembly," [October 1765], *Collections of the Connecticut Historical Society*, vol. 18 (Hartford: Connecticut Historical Society, 1920), 364–65; Thompson, *Connecticut Entrepreneur*, 21–22.

5. Caulkins, *History of Norwich*, 607–8; Thompson, *Connecticut Entrepreneur*, 19. On manufacturing in America before industrialization, see McCusker and Menard, *Economy of British America*; Lawrence A. Peskin, *Manufacturing Revolution: The Intellectual Origins of Early American Industry* (Baltimore: Johns Hopkins University Press, 2003).

6. Thompson, *Connecticut Entrepreneur*, 29; Henry P. Johnston, ed. *The Record of Connecticut Men in the Military and Naval Service during the War of the Revolution, 1775–1783* (Hartford, 1889), 629; "Papers Relating to the Expedition to Ticonderoga, April and May, 1775," *Collections of the Connecticut Historical Society*, vol. 1 (Hartford, 1860), 163–74.

7. Caulkins, *History of Norwich*, 368–69, 374, 380; Daniel Coit Gilman, *A Historical Discourse, Delivered in Norwich, Connecticut, September 7, 1859, at the Bi-Centennial Celebration of the Settlement of the Town* (Boston, 1859), 51–56; *Boston Gazette*, March 30, 1767.

8. Thompson, *Connecticut Entrepreneur*, 18–21; Christopher Leffingwell to John Chester, August 26, 1791, in *Industrial and Commercial Correspondence of Alexander Hamilton, Anticipating His Report on Manufactures*, ed. Arthur Harrison Cole (Chicago: A. W. Shaw, 1928), 15–17.

9. *Norwich Packet*, April 26, 1787; November 28, 1788; December 26, 1788.

10. *Norwich Packet*, November 3, 1791, January 3, 1792; GW, 4–5. On apprenticeship in the eighteenth century, see W. J. Rorabaugh, *The Craft Apprentice: From Franklin to the Machine Age in America* (New York: Oxford University Press, 1986); David Waldstreicher, *Runaway America: Benjamin Franklin, Slavery, and the American Revolution* (New York: Hill & Wang, 2004). On the hat-making craft, see John Thomson, *A Treatise on Hat-Making and Felting* (Philadelphia, 1868).

11. CL Diary, January 12, 1793; February 21, 1794; May 7, 1794, LFP.

12. White women's lives in the eighteenth century, including their education, household labor, economics, and invisibility, have been examined in Laurel Thatcher Ulrich, *Good Wives: Image and Reality in the Lives of Women in Northern New England, 1650–1750* (New York: Alfred A. Knopf, 1982); Laurel Thatcher Ulrich, *A Midwife's Tale: The Life of Martha Ballard, Based on Her Diary, 1785–1812* (New York: Alfred A. Knopf, 1990); Joan M. Jensen, *Loosening the Bonds: Mid-Atlantic Farm Women, 1750–1850* (New Haven, CT: Yale University Press, 1986); Karin Wulf, *Not All Wives: Women of Colonial Philadelphia* (Ithaca, NY: Cornell University Press, 2000); Serena R. Zabin, *Dangerous Economies: Status and Commerce in Imperial New York* (Philadelphia: University of Pennsylvania Press, 2009); Sara T. Damiano, *To Her Credit: Women, Finance, and the Law in Eighteenth-Century New England Cities* (Baltimore: Johns Hopkins University Press, 2021).

13. CL to Ezekiel Williams, September 5 and November 29, 1779, CL Letterbook, 1776–1801, LFP; "Extracts from the Diary of Dr. Mason Fitch Cogswell," *Connecticut Magazine* 5 (December 1899), 606–7. On widowed schoolteacher Margaret Hancock: Henry R. Stiles, *Families of Ancient Wethersfield, Connecticut* (1904; reprint, Westminster, MD: Heritage Books, 2007), 409.

14. CL to [Nathaniel Green], July 24, 1764; CL Letterbook, 1764–1767; WL to John L. Whiting, November 11, 1816, William Leffingwell's Letterbooks, 1816–1824; CL to Fanny Leffingwell, December 15, 1798, CL Letterbook, 1776–1801, all in LFP.

15. CL Diary, November 20, 1795; September. 12, 1795; October 28 and 29, 1795, LFP.

16. CL Diary, January 17, 1796, LFP.

17. Ulrich, *A Midwife's Tale*, 138–44; Philip J. Greven Jr., *Four Generations: Population, Land, and Family in Colonial Andover, Massachusetts* (Ithaca, NY: Cornell University Press, 1970); Daniel Scott Smith, "Parental Power and Marriage Patterns: An Analysis of Historical Trends in Hingham, Massachusetts," *Journal of Marriage and the Family* 35 (1973): 419–28.

18. Thomas Paine, *Common Sense* (Philadelphia, 1776), 26–27, 32. For new ideals of marriage for couples as well as the republic, see Jan Lewis, "The Republican Wife: Virtue and Seduction in the Early Republic," *William and Mary Quarterly* 3rd ser., 44 (1987): 689–721; Jay Fliegelman, *Prodigals and Pilgrims: The American Revolution Against Patriarchal Authority, 1750–1800* (Cambridge: Cambridge University Press, 1982); Richard Godbeer, *Sexual Revolution in Early America* (Baltimore: Johns Hopkins University Press, 2002); Anya Jabour, *Marriage in the Early Republic: Elizabeth and William Wirt and the Companionate Ideal* (Baltimore: Johns Hopkins University Press, 1998); Nancy F. Cott, "Eighteenth-Century Family and Social Life Revealed in Massachusetts Divorce Records," *Journal of Social History* 10 (1976): 20–43.

19. The sexual behavior of young people in the revolutionary era and the prevalence of premarital sex and pregnancy have been examined in Clare A. Lyons, *Sex among the Rabble* (Chapel Hill: University of North Carolina Press, 2006); Godbeer, *Sexual Revolution in Early America*; Laurel Thatcher Ulrich and Lois K. Stabler, "'Girling of It' in Eighteenth-Century New Hampshire," *Annual Proceedings of the Dublin Seminar for New England Folklife* 10 (1985): 24–36; Ulrich, *A Midwife's Tale*; Daniel Scott Smith and Michael S. Hindus, "Premarital Pregnancy in America, 1640–1971: An Overview and Interpretation," *Journal of Interdisciplinary History* 5 (1975): 537–70.

20. On manhood and manly independence in the new republic, see Anne S. Lombard, *Making Manhood: Growing Up Male in Colonial New England* (Cambridge, MA: Harvard University Press, 2003); Thomas A. Foster, *Sex and the Eighteenth-Century Man* (Boston: Beacon, 2006); Thomas A. Foster, ed., *New Men: Manliness in Early America* (New York: New York University Press, 2011); Mark E. Kann, *On the Man Question: Gender and Civic Virtue in America* (Philadelphia: Temple University Press, 1991); Mark E. Kann, *A Republic of Men* (New York: New York University Press, 1998).

21. CL to Samuel Capen, September 1, 1796; CL to Samuel Capen, October 27, 1796; WL to JC, March 10, 1802, LFP. The records refute Catharine Williams's assertion that James hatched a plan to "become a gentleman" and "repeatedly drew large sums" from Lucretia's "indulgent father," CW, 77.

22. Thompson, *Connecticut Entrepreneur*, 16–17; CL Diary, 1800–1802 [undated, pp. 1–2], LFP; CL to John Boardman, September 22, 1797; CL to JC, May 21, 1798; CL to Messrs. Boardman and Millhouse, May 21, 1798, CL Letterbook, 1776–1801, LFP; CL Diary, January 29, 1801, LFP.

23. Nathan Perkins, *A Narrative of a Tour through the State of Vermont from April 27 to June 12, 1789* (Woodstock, VT: Elm Tree Press, 1920), 19–20. Frontier migration of New Englanders in the early republic, and the life and work of Vermont women can be traced in Hal S. Barron, *Those Who Stayed Behind: Rural Society in Nineteenth-Century New England* (Cambridge: Cambridge University Press, 1984); Randolph A. Roth, *The Democratic Dilemma: Religion, Reform, and the Social Order in the Connecticut River Valley of Vermont* (Cambridge: Cambridge University Press, 1987). On Rupert, Naomi Sheldon Guibord, *A Glimpse of the Early History of Rupert, Vermont* (n.p., ca. 1940s). On women's household labor in the early republic: Jeanne Boydston, *Home and Work: Housework, Wages, and the Ideology of Labor in the Early Republic* (New York: Oxford University Press, 1990).

24. Cynthia Leffingwell to Mrs. Esther Williams, March 11, 1792, Williams Family Papers, Box 8, Folder 9; Cynthia Leffingwell to Mr. Ephraim Williams, November 17, 1794, Elizabeth Fuller Collection, Williams Family Papers, Box 9, Folder 1; Cynthia Leffingwell to Polly Ashley, November 8, 1800, Ashley Papers, Box 2, Folder 5, Cynthia Leffingwell to Mrs. Mary C. Ashley, February 1804, Ashley Family Papers, Box 2, Folder 5; Pocumtuck Valley Memorial Association Library, Deerfield, Massachusetts. Amelia F. Miller and A. R. Riggs, eds., *Romance, Remedies, and Revolution: The Journal of Dr. Elihu Ashley of Deerfield, Massachusetts, 1773–1775* (Amherst: University of Massachusetts Press, 2007), 17, 24, 49–71, 317.

25. CL to Samuel Capen, September 1, 1796; CL to Samuel Capen, October 27, 1796; CL to John Boardman, September 22, 1797; CL to JC, May 21, 1798; CL to John Boardman, May 21, 1798; CL to Elisha and Elias Kane, November 8, 1796; CL to Thomas and Samuel Mather, November 8, 1796; CL to WL, November 10, 1796, CL Letterbook, 1776–1801, LFP; CL to Samuel and Fanny Whiting, April 7, 1803; CL to Christopher Leffingwell Jr., July 5, 1803, CL Letterbook, 1803–1810, LFP; *Vermont Gazette* (Bennington), May 10, 1802; *Farmers' Register* (Troy), June 7, 1803.

26. Town of Rupert, Record of Deeds, Book 5, 1800–1801, p. 17–20, Rupert Town Clerk's Office, Rupert, VT; Town Meetings, Highways and Marks, 1789–??, 48, Rupert Town Clerk's Office, Rupert, VT.

27. Town of Rupert, Record of Deeds, Book 6, 1801–1803, 150–52, Rupert Town Clerk's Office, Rupert, VT; George S. Hibbard, *Rupert, Vt.: Historical and Descriptive, 1761–1898* (Rutland, VT, 1899), 132–33.

28. *Farmers' Register* (Troy), January 25, 1803, June 7, 1803.

29. Connecticut Superior Court, New London County, Divorce Papers, 1719–1865, State Archives, Hartford, CT, Family History Library Microfilm, reel 1638185; *Norwich Courier*, December 10, 1806. On divorce and desertion by husbands, see Nancy F. Cott, "Divorce and the Changing Status of Women in Eighteenth-Century Massachusetts," *William and Mary Quarterly* 3rd ser., 33 (1976): 586–614; Cornelia Hughes Dayton, *Women Before the Bar: Gender, Law, and Society in Connecticut, 1639–1789*

(Chapel Hill: University of North Carolina Press, 1995); Mary Beth Sievens, *Stray Wives: Marital Conflict in Early National New England* (New York: New York University Press, 2005).

30. CL Diary, June 4, 1805, LFP; Sievens, *Stray Wives*, 24. After the murder trial, Maria Cornell's two posthumous biographers concocted their own stories about her parents' divorce. Gurdon Williams, a family acquaintance hoping not to offend either the Leffingwells or the Cornells, interpreted James's departure as a selfless gesture. James simply believed Christopher better able to support Lucretia and her children. Missing was any mention of adultery or a husband's responsibility to support his own family; GW, 4–5. Catharine Williams, by contrast, cast James as a rogue and a scoundrel, acting on deceit and overwrought ambition, and once his plan to live off of the largesse of Lucretia's "indulgent father" failed, he "relieved himself forever from the task of supporting a woman he had probably married without the least sentiment of affection," CW, 77.

Chapter 3

1. BFH, 26.
2. BFH, 181, 26; RH, 14, 98.
3. *VIN*,10-11; HSE19; LD, 20; JH to ACG, December 25, 1832, ATP, Folder 2.
4. *Connecticut Gazette* (New London), September 30, 1774; Maude Gridley Peterson, *Historic Sketch of Coventry, Connecticut* (Coventry: [The Town], 1912), 28; John B. Porter, comp., "Notes on the Early History of Coventry," From Notes Made by Marvin Root in 1844), 1864, 27–30. Typescript. CSL, CHS.
5. William S. McFeely, *Grant: A Biography* (New York: W.W. Norton, 1981), 4–5; *The Record of Connecticut Men in the Military and Naval Service During the War of the Revolution, 1775–1783*, ed. Henry P. Johnston (Baltimore, 1889), 7. On Connecticut communities and the Revolutionary War, see Richard Buel Jr., *Dear Liberty: Connecticut's Mobilization for the Revolutionary War* (Middletown, CT: Wesleyan University Press, 1980).
6. Henry Phelps Johnston, *Nathan Hale, 1776: Biography and Memorials* (New Haven, CT: Yale University Press, 1914); M. William Phelps, *Nathan Hale: The Life and Death of America's First Spy* (New York: Thomas Dunne Books, 2008).
7. Johnston, *Record of Connecticut Men*, 254, 131. Amos's regiment traveled across the same landscape that Ephraim would claim to have covered more than fifty years later on the night of Maria Cornell's death. On the Battle of Rhode Island: Paul F. Dearden, *The Rhode Island Campaign of 1778: Inauspicious Dawn of Alliance* (Providence: Rhode Island Bicentennial Foundation, 1980); Patrick T. Conley, "The Battle of Rhode Island, 29 August 1778: A Victory for the Patriots," *Rhode Island History* 62 (2004): 51–65.
8. [J. Hector St. John de Crèvecoeur], *Letters from an American Farmer* (Philadelphia, 1793), 27–28.

9.   On the transition from the rural farm economy to market
      capitalism: Christopher Clark, *Roots of Rural Capitalism: Western
      Massachusetts, 1780–1860* (Ithaca, NY: Cornell University Press, 1990);
      Steven Hahn and Jonathan Prude, eds., *The Countryside in the Age of
      Capitalist Transformation* (Chapel Hill: University of North Carolina
      Press, 1985); Allan Kulikoff, "The Transition to Capitalism in Rural
      America," *William and Mary Quarterly* 3rd ser., 46 (1989): 120–44; James
      A. Henretta, *The Origins of American Capitalism* (Boston: Northeastern
      University Press, 1991); Naomi R. Lamoreaux, "Rethinking the Transition
      to Capitalism in the Early American Northeast," *Journal of American
      History* 90 (2003): 437–61; Winfred Barr Rothenberg, *From Market-
      Places to a Market Economy: The Transformation of Rural Massachusetts,
      1750–1850* (Chicago: University of Chicago Press, 1992); Charles Sellers,
      The Market Revolution (New York: Oxford University Press, 1991);
      Melvin Stokes and Stephen Conway, eds., *The Market Revolution in
      America* (Charlottesville: University Press of Virginia, 1996); John Lauritz
      Larson, *The Market Revolution in America* (Cambridge: Cambridge
      University Press, 2010); Scott C. Martin, ed., *Cultural Change and the
      Market Revolution in America, 1789-1860* (Lanham, MD: Rowman &
      Littlefield, 2005).
10.   George A. Calhoun, *A Historical Address Before the Church of Christ in
      North Coventry, Conn.* (Hartford, CT 1846), 14–15.
11.   Marion Root, "History &c of North Coventry," 1844, 9–10, ms., CHS;
      The Genealogy of the Descendants of Henry Kingsbury, ed. Mary Kingsbury
      Talcott (Hartford, CT: Hartford Press, 1905), 239–40, 286–90; Calhoun,
      Historical Address, 25–26.
12.   For the Avery family real estate and residences in Coventry, see probate
      auction for Amos Avery Sr. in *Times and Hartford Advertiser*, April 5, 1825;
      plus Root, "History &c of North Coventry," 39; Porter, "Notes," 64–65,
      111; Tax List, 1794, in Coventry Town Papers, 1723–1872; Joseph Kingsbury,
      Account Books, 1787–1808, all at CHS.

Chapter 4

1.   Thirty-four-year-old John Durfee wasn't asked to serve on the coroner's
      jury because his seventy-four-year-old father, Richard, was the owner of the
      family farm.
2.   LD, 7–8, 12–13, 28; BFH, 30–43; Dr. Foster Hooper to William R. Staples,
      February 4, 1833, ATP, Folder 6.
3.   LD, 7–8, 12–13; BFH, 30–43; RH, 16–21; on women witnesses: LD, 33–35;
      BFH, 47–49; RH, 23–24; on second inquest verdict: BFH, 191.
4.   CL Diary, February 10, 1805; February 19, 1805; February 21, 1805, LFP;
      U.S. Federal Census, 1810; *Vital Records of Norwich, 1659–1848*, vol. 1
      (Hartford: Society of Colonial Wars, 1913), 448.
5.   CL Diary, June 3 and 4, 1805, LFP; *True Republican* (Norwich), June
      12, 1805; *Genealogical and Biographical Record of New London County,*

Connecticut (Chicago: J. H. Beers, 1905), 664; Leffingwell, *The Leffingwell Record*, 64.

6. Letter No. 2 [SMC to LC], Norwich, May 6, 1819, in CW, 118; Letter No. 3 [SMC to LC], Norwich, August 26, 1820, in CW, 119.

7. Probate Court, Norwich District, vol. 11–12, October 10, 1809, in *Connecticut, Wills and Probate Records, 1609–1999,* online database, ancestry. com; Norwich Probate District. Vol. 11, CSL, Family History Library, Salt Lake City, Utah, microfilm reel #5059; Thompson, *Connecticut Entrepreneur*, 15; "Extracts from the Diary of Dr. Mason Fitch Cogswell," 606; Franklin Bowditch Dexter, *Biographical Sketches of the Graduates of Yale College*, 6 vols. (New York: Holt, 1907), vol. 4:488–90.

8. Letter No. 2 [SMC to LC], Norwich, May 6, 1819, in CW, 117.

9. On women's labor in the farm economy, see Ulrich, *A Midwife's Tale*; Jensen, *Loosening the Bonds*; Marla R. Miller, *Entangled Lives: Labor, Livelihood, and Landscapes of Change in Rural Massachusetts* (Baltimore: Johns Hopkins University Press, 2019).

10. For the "putting out" industry that predated factory production, see Thomas Dublin, *Transforming Women's Work: New England Lives in the Industrial Revolution* (Ithaca, NY: Cornell University Press, 1994); Jonathan Prude, *The Coming of Industrial Order: Town and Factory Life in Rural Massachusetts, 1810–1860* (Cambridge: Cambridge University Press, 1983); on school teaching, see Mary Kelley, *Learning to Stand and Speak: Women, Education, and Public Life in America's Republic* (Chapel Hill: University of North Carolina Press, 2006); Nancy F. Cott, *The Bonds of Womanhood: "Woman's Sphere in New England, 1780–1835* (New Haven, CT: Yale University Press, 1977); Martha Tomhave Blauvelt, *The Work of the Heart: Young Women and Emotion, 1780–1830* (Charlottesville: University Press of Virginia, 2007); on domestic service: Jeanne Boydston, "To Earn Her Daily Bread: Housework and Antebellum Working-Class Subsistence," *Radical History Review* 35 (1986): 7–25; Boydston, *Home and Work*; Faye E. Dudden, *Serving Women: Household Service in Nineteenth-Century America* (Middletown, CT: Wesleyan University Press, 1983).

11. Letter No. 4 [SMC to LC], Bozrahville, May 3, 1821, in CW, 120.

12. Letter No. 10 [SMC to LLC, GR & LCR], Dorchester, Sept. 25, 1827, in CW, 132; Letter No. 4 [SMC to LC], Bozrahville, May 3, 1821, in CW, 120. On the needle trades and seamstresses, see Marla R. Miller, "The Last Mantuamaker: Craft Tradition and Commercial Change in Boston, 1760–1845," *Early American Studies* 4 (2006): 372–424; Marla R. Miller, *The Needle's Eye: Women and Work in the Age of Revolution* (Amherst: University of Massachusetts Press, 2006); Wendy Gamber, *The Female Economy: The Millinery and Dressmaking Trades, 1860–1930* (Urbana: University of Illinois Press, 1997); Jo Anne Preston, "'To learn me the whole of the trade': Conflict between a Female Apprentice and a Merchant Tailor in Ante-bellum New England," *Labor History* 24 (1983): 259–73; Christine Stansell, *City of Women: Sex and Class in New York, 1789–1860*

(New York: Knopf, 1986); Mari Jo Buhle, "Needlewomen and the Vicissitudes of Modern Life: A Study of Middle-Class Construction in the Antebellum Northeast," in *Visible Women: New Essays on American Activism*, ed. Nancy A, Hewitt and Suzanne Lebsock (Urbana: University of Illinois Press, 1993), 145–65. On men's clothing trades, see Michael Zakim, *Ready-Made Democracy: A History of Men's Dress in the American Republic, 1760–1860* (Chicago: University of Chicago Press, 2003).

13.   Letter No. 2 [SMC to LC], Norwich, May 6, 1819, in CW, 117.

14.   On Calvinist religious beliefs, see E. Brooks Holifield, *Theology in America: Christian Thought from the Age of the Puritans to the Civil War* (New Haven. CT: Yale University Press, 2003); David W. Kling, *A Field of Divine Wonders: The New Divinity and Village Revivals in Northwestern Connecticut, 1792–1822* (University Park: Pennsylvania State University Press, 1993).

15.   Letter No. 4 [SMC to LC], Bozrahville, May 3, 1821, in CW, 120; Letter No. 3 [SMC to LC], Norwich, August 26, 1820, in CW, 119.

16.   Letter No. 3 [SMC to LC], Norwich, August 26, 1820, in CW, 119; Letter No. 4 [SMC to LC], Bozrahville, May 3, 1821, in CW, 121.

17.   Letter No. 3 [SMC to LC], Norwich, August 26, 1820, in CW, 118–19. Another woman (who later married the preacher who helped convert Maria Cornell) recalled that she always heard it preached during her Calvinist upbringing that "we could do nothing of ourselves," and that none "but the elect would be saved." Gilbert Haven and Thomas Russell, *Father Taylor, The Sailor Preacher* (Boston, 1872), 73.

18.   *Connecticut, Church Record Abstracts, 1630–1920*, vol. 9, *Bozrah, 1737–1845*, 20, Ancestry.com, originals at CSL; WL to Charles Lathrop, December 21, 1821, LFP. For religious revivals in Connecticut, and their relatively sedate nature, see Charles Roy Keller, *The Second Great Awakening in Connecticut* (New Haven, CT: Yale University Press, 1942); William G. McLoughlin, *Revivals, Awakenings, and Reform* (Chicago: University of Chicago Press, 1978); Kling, *A Field of Divine Wonders*.

19.   Letter No. 2 [SMC to LC], Norwich, May 6, 1819, in CW, 117. Quotations are from Harriet's journals and letters, reprinted in Miron Winslow, *A Memoir of Mrs. Harriet W. Winslow* (London, 1838), 6–19; see also *Memoir of Charles Lathrop Winslow* (Boston, 1834), 97–99; "The Missionary's Mother," *Presbyterian Magazine* (1851), reprinted in *Mrs. Whittelsey's Magazine for Mothers and Daughters* 2 (October 1851), 309–33; Caulkins, *History of Norwich*, 591, 693. On foreign missionaries in the early republic, see Barbara Welter, "She Hath Done What She Could: Protestant Women's Missionary Careers in Nineteenth-Century America," in *Women in American Religion*, ed. Janet Wilson James (Philadelphia: University of Pennsylvania Press, 1980), 111–25; Christine Leigh Heyrman, *Doomed Romance: Broken Hearts, Lost Souls, and Sexual Tumult in Nineteenth-Century America* (New York: Knopf, 2021); Ashley E. Moreshead, "'Beyond All Ambitious Motives': Missionary Memoirs and the Cultivation of Early

American Evangelical Heroines," *Journal of the Early Republic* 38 (2018): 37–60; Mary Kupiec Cayton, "Canonizing Harriet Newell: Women, the Evangelical Press, and the Foreign Mission Movement in New England, 1800–1840," in *Competing Kingdoms: Women, Mission, Nation, and the American Protestant Empire, 1812–1960*, ed. Barbara Reeves-Ellington et al. (Durham, NC: Duke University Press, 2010), 69–93; Emily Conroy-Krutz, *Christian Imperialism: Converting the World in the Early American Republic* (Ithaca, NY: Cornell University Press, 2015).

20. Letter No. 3 [SMC to LC], Norwich, August 26, 1820, in CW, 119–20. Maria followed her question ("why am I spared?) with the answer, "perhaps for some usefulness," and a promise to "devote the rest of my life to service of God." Letter No. 4 [SMC to LC], Bozrahville, May 3, 1821, in CW, 121.

21. David L. Dodge, *Memorial of Mr. David L. Dodge* (Boston, 1854), 96; see also, 81–98, 103–13; Caulkins, *History of Norwich*, 616.

22. CW, 79; GW, 6; Letter No. 4 [SMC to LC], Bozrahville, May 3, 1821, in CW, 121.

23. Dodge, *Memorial of Mr. David L. Dodge*, 63.

Chapter 5

1. On Fall River's ascent as a leading textile manufacturing town before the Civil War, see Fowler, *An Historical Sketch of Fall River*; Henry H. Earl, *A Centennial History of Fall River, Mass.* (New York, 1877); Frederick M. Peck and Henry H. Earl, *Fall River and Its Industries* (New York, 1877); Arthur Sherman Phillips, *The Phillips History of Fall River*, 3 vols. (Fall River: Dover Press, 1941); David Richard Kasserman, *Fall River Outrage: Life, Murder, and Justice in Early Industrial New England* (Philadelphia: University of Pennsylvania Press, 1986), 15–23.

2. HH, 34–35. That night an additional thirteen men were chosen to serve on a committee of vigilance, which would also help gather evidence and report to the committee. See bills and expenses paid by Nathaniel B. Borden, Avery Murder: Papers & Letters Folder, FRHS; and notes and letters in ATP, Folders 13, 14, and 18.

3. On new masculine ideals, men on the make, and the "go-ahead" ethos of masculine action in the nineteenth century, see Bruce Dorsey, *Reforming Men and Women: Gender in the Antebellum City* (Ithaca, NY: Cornell University Press, 2002); Charles E. Rosenberg in "Sexuality, Class and Role in 19th-Century America," *American Quarterly* 25 (1973): 131–53; E. Anthony Rotundo, *American Manhood: Transformations in Masculinity from the Revolution to the Modern Era* (New York: Basic Books, 1993); Brian P. Luskey, *On the Make: Clerks and the Quest for Capital in Nineteenth-Century America* (New York: New York University Press, 2010); Scott A. Sandage, *Born Losers: A History Failure in America* (Cambridge, MA: Harvard University Press, 2005).

4. Bozrah Manufacturing Company and Jewett City Cotton Manufacturing Company, U.S. Federal Manufacturing Census, 1820, manuscript,

microfilm, Family History Library, Salt Lake City, UT; Letter No. 5 [SMC to LC], Killingly, May 20, 1822, in CW, 123.

5. GW, 6.

6. "Letters from Susan," *Lowell Offering*, June 1844; Lucy Larcom, *A New England Girlhood* (Boston, 1889), 154; Lise Vogel, "'Humorous Incidents and Sound Common Sense': More on the New England Mill Women," *Labor History* 19 (1978), 282–83.

7. *Windham Herald* in November 1811, cited in Richard M. Bayles, *History of Windham County, Connecticut* (New York, 1889), 93; Samuel Batchelder, *Introduction and Early Progress of the Cotton Manufacture in the United States* (Boston, 1863), 57–59. For the history of early textile factories, Samuel Slater, and the Rhode Island system, see George S. White, *Memoir of Samuel Slater* (Philadelphia, 1836); Caroline F. Ware, *The Early New England Cotton Manufacture: A Study in Industrial Beginnings* (Boston: Houghton Mifflin, 1931); Gary Kulik et al., eds., *The New England Mill Village, 1790–1860* (Cambridge, MA: M.I.T. Press, 1982); Barbara M. Tucker, *Samuel Slater and the Origins of the American Textile Industry, 1790–1860* (Ithaca, NY: Cornell University Press, 1984).

8. Joseph Hollingworth to William Rawcliff, November 2, 1830; George Hollingworth to William Rawcliff, June 28, 1828, in *The Hollingworth Letters: Technical Change in the Textile Industry, 1826–1837*, ed. Thomas W. Leavitt (Cambridge, MA: MIT Press, 1969), 93, 27.

9. Batchelder, *Introduction and Early Progress*, 51–59; White, *Memoir of Samuel Slater*, 188; Joseph Brennan, *Social Conditions in Industrial Rhode Island, 1820–1860* (Washington, DC: Catholic University of America, 1940), 4, 8; Kulik, *New England Mill Village*, xxv, 156–64; *Report of the Secretary of State, of Such Articles Manufactured in the United States*, 18th Congress, 1st session, 1824, S. Rept. 90, 37, 19–26, 30; Caulkins, *History of Norwich*, 564.

10. Ware, *Early New England Cotton Manufacture*, 19. On the political economy of the new nation and disputes over manufacturing, see Thomas Bender, *Toward an Urban Vision: Ideas and Institutions in Nineteenth Century America* (Baltimore: Johns Hopkins University Press, 1975), 3–29; John F. Kasson, *Civilizing the Machine: Technology and Republican Values in America, 1776-1900* (New York: Grossman, 1976); Drew R. McCoy, *The Elusive Republic: Political Economy in Jeffersonian America* (Chapel Hill: University of North Carolina Press, 1980); John R. Nelson Jr., *Liberty and Property: Political Economy and Policymaking in the New Nation, 1789–1812* (Baltimore: Johns Hopkins University Press, 1987); Peskin, *Manufacturing Revolution*.

11. *Address of the American Society for the Encouragement of Domestic Manufactures, to the People of the United States* (New York, 1817), 12, 14. On the new American designs for manufacturing, see Bender, *Toward an Urban Vision*; Prude, *The Coming of Industrial Order*; David A. Zonderman, *Aspirations and Anxieties: New England Workers and the Mechanized Factory*

System, 1815–1850 (New York: Oxford University Press, 1992); Peskin, *Manufacturing Revolution.*

12. *PP*, October 1, 1814; see also: *PP*, August 16, 1820; January 23, 1822; *Dedham Gazette*, January 15, 1816; *The Times, and Hartford Advertiser*, November 18, 1823; Ware, *Early New England Cotton Manufacture*, 23, 26.

13. For family contracts, see Pomfret Manufacturing Company Records, Contract and Memorandum Books 1 and 2, reprinted in Kulik, *New England Mill Village*, 437–61; Jewett City Cotton Manufacturing Company, Labor Contracts, 1812–1815, Slater Company Records, Box 2, UCA; Tucker, *Samuel Slater*, 139–62; Daniel Webster, speech on the repeal of the Embargo in the House of Representatives, April 6, 1814, in *The Writings and Speeches of Daniel Webster*, 18 vols. (Boston: Little, Brown, 1903), vol. 14:44–45.

14. On single women in early textile manufacturing: Tucker, *Samuel Slater*, 145–46; Caroline Sloat, "Factory Girls in a 'Rhode Island System' Mill: The Pomfret Manufacturing Company, 1806–35," Old Sturbridge Village Research Library, 1978.

15. Jeanne Boydston, "The Woman Who Wasn't There: Women's Market Labor and the Transition to Capitalism in the United States," *Journal of the Early Republic* 16 (1996): 183–206.

16. There's no evidence that Maria's mother ever worked outside the home. On motherhood and the disparities between the working lives of single women and their mothers, see Cott, *Bonds of Womanhood*; Tucker, *Samuel Slater*; Nancy Folbre, "The Unproductive Housewife: Her Evolution in Nineteenth-Century Economic Thought," *Signs* 16 (1991): 463–84.

17. Maria worked from January to April 1822 at the Jewett City cotton factory; Jewett City Cotton Manufacturing Company, Laborers Time Book, 1812–1823, Slater Company Records, Box 2; Day Book, January 1, 1821–March 30, 1822, Slater Company Records, Box 10, UCA.

18. Daniel L. Phillip, *Griswold—A History* ([New Haven]: Turtle, Morehouse & Taylor, 1929), 100–107; Day Book, January 1, 1821–March 30, 1822, Slater Company Records, Box 10.

19. [Sarah Savage], *The Factory Girl* (Boston, 1814), 3–4. On the cultural history of the "factory girl" and the seduction of factory work: Boydston, The Woman Who Wasn't There"; Sylvia Jenkins Cook, *Working Women, Literary Ladies: The Industrial Revolution and Female Aspiration* (New York: Oxford University Press, 2008).

20. Seth Luther, *An Address to the Working Men of New England* (New York, 1833), 35.

21. Letter No. 5 [SMC to LC], Killingly, May 20, 1822, in CW, 122–23. For other examples of family opposition, see Sally Rice letter above; and Lura Currier to Harriet Hanson Robinson, December. 14, 1845, in Allis Rosenberg Wolfe, ed., "Letters of a Lowell Mill Girl and Friends: 1845–1846," *Labor History* 17 (1976), 100.

22. BFH, 127; *The Providence Directory* (Providence, 1824). Examples of successful tailoresses in New England cities in these years can be seen in the *Boston Daily Advertiser*, March 15, 1819; *Columbian Centinel* (Boston), February 9, 1822; *Concord Gazette* (Concord, NH), March 31, 1818; *Salem Gazette*, November 2, 1821; for the wretched conditions of impoverished seamstresses, see Mathew Carey, *Report on Female Wages* (1829) in *Miscellaneous Essays* (Philadelphia, 1830), 266–72; Mathew Carey, *Female Wages and Female Oppression, Nos. I–III* (Philadelphia, 1835).

23. For a taste of these advertisements, see *Providence Gazette*March 23, 1822; June 12, 1822; July, 6, 1822; *PP*, May 22, 1822; *RIA*, May 14, 1822, June 4, 1822; *The Providence Directory . . .* (Providence, 1824), 8, 14, 18, 25. On shops, shopping, and consumer goods, see Ellen Hartigan-O'Connor, *The Ties That Buy: Women and Commerce in Revolutionary America* (Philadelphia: University of Pennsylvania Press, 2009); Kate Haulman, *The Politics of Fashion in Eighteenth-Century America* (Chapel Hill: University of North Carolina Press, 2011).

24. BFH, 131; RH, 71; MB, 96.

25. Descriptions of Cornell: RH, 43, 69; MB, 92; CW, 83, 86–87; GW, 6.

26. George Wilkes, *The Lives of Helen Jewett, and Richard P. Robinson* (New York, 1849), 60. On store clerks, and the flirtations between clerks and women shoppers, see Luskey, *On the Make*; Cohen, *The Murder of Helen Jewett*.

27. RH, 70–71; BFH, 129–30; MB, 95–96. Jen Manion, *Liberty's Prisoners: Carceral Culture in Early America* (Philadelphia: University of Pennsylvania Press, 2015), 109–13.

28. GW, 6–10; CW, 79–84.

29. MB, 95; RH, 66; BFH, 122–23.

30. Sally Rice to Father and Mother, 1839, in Kulik, *New England Mill Village*, 388-89.

31. Letter No. 6 [SMC to GR & LCR], Slatersville, 1825 (misdated 1824), in CW, 125–26.

Chapter 6

1. *FRWR*, December 26, 1832. On Christmas rituals and traditions, see Leigh Eric Schmidt, *Consumer Rites: The Buying and Selling of American Holidays* (Princeton, NJ: Princeton University Press, 1995).

2. MB, 117; RH, 82; BFH, 77; *RIA*, December 28, 1832; January 25, 1833; HSE, 25–26 BFH, 163. For more on the meaning and significance of "crowds" and mobs in the working of American democracy in this era, see Act III.

3. JH to ACG, December 25, 1832, ATP, folder 2; *FRWR*, December 26, 1832.

4. Letter No. 9 [SMC to LLC], Mendon Mills, August 6, 1826, in CW, 130. Other references to James and his whereabouts, see Letter No. 2 [SMC to LC], Norwich, May 6, 1819, in CW, 118; Letter No. 3 [SMC to LC], Norwich, August 26, 1820, in CW, 118; Letter No. 4 [SMC to LC],

Bozrahville, May 3, 1821, in CW, 122; Letter No. 5 [SMC to LC], Killingly, May 20, 1822, in CW, 123; Letter No. 6 [SMC to GR & LCR], Slatersville, 1825 (misdated 1824), in CW, 126; Letter No. 7 [SMC to LCR], Slatersville, September 6, 1825, in CW, 127; Letter No. 8 [SMC to LLC], Slatersville, December 18, 1825, in CW, 128; Letter No. 16 [SMC to LLC], Lowell, July 4, 1830, in CW, 142.

5. MB, 96; BFH, 142–43; RH, 77–78. On Slatersville, see White, *Memoir of Samuel Slater*; William R. Bagnall, *The Textile Industries of the United States* (Cambridge, MA, 1893); Walter A. Nebiker, *The History of North Smithfield* (North Smithfield, RI: North Smithfield Bicentennial Commission, 1976); Tucker, *Samuel Slater*.

6. RH, 66, 69–70, 77; MB, 84, 91–93, 110–11; BFH, 122, 127, 142.

7. Letter No. 6 [SMC to GR & LCR], Slatersville, 1825 (misdated 1824), in CW, 124, 126.

8. This scene draws on the journal of Rachel Stearns, who recalled Methodist meetings she passed (or first attended) at night. Rachel Willard Stearns Journal, April 24, 1835, October 23, 1835, Sarah Ripley Stearns Papers, microfilm M–59, reel 992, Schlesinger Library, Harvard University, Cambridge, MA.

9. Letter No. 6 [SMC to GR & LCR], Slatersville, 1825 (misdated 1824), in CW, 124–25; Letter No. 14 [SMC to LCR], Lowell, May 3, 1829, in CW, 138.

10. On anti-Calvinism and a new democratic theology: Nathan O. Hatch, *The Democratization of American Christianity* (New Haven, CT: Yale University Press, 1989); David Hempton, *Methodism: Empire of the Spirit* (New Haven, CT: Yale University Press, 2005); Bruce Dorsey, "Friends Becoming Enemies: Philadelphia Benevolence and the Neglected Era of American Quaker History," *Journal of the Early Republic* 18 (1998): 407–10.

11. Rachel Willard Stearns Journal, 1834–1835. Although ten years younger, Rachel's early Methodist experiences occurred at roughly the same age as Maria's. Their lives have certain other parallels: both were setting out in search of work (Rachel as a schoolteacher, Maria as a factory worker) when Methodism captivated their imaginations; both came from Calvinist Congregational families who expressed disapproval and ridicule. Their spirituality was markedly similar, as evidenced in the language they used to write about their conversions; Rachel wrote, "I *know* I am not what I once was . . . I the chief of sinners am,/ But Jesus dy'd for *me*." January 1, 1835.

12. Rachel Willard Stearns Journal, October 15, 1834; March 31, 1835; Letter No. 6 [SMC to GR & LCR], Slatersville, 1825 (misdated 1824), in CW, 125.

13. *A Memoir of Ralph Waldo Emerson*, ed. James Elliot Cabot, 2 vols. (Boston, 1887), vol. 2: 393. A critic of Methodist camp meetings remarked that he heard a preacher use "the pronoun *I* 180 times before he resumed his seat." "Farmington Camp Meeting," *Christian Intelligencer and Eastern Chronicle*, October 1, 1830.

14. CW, 116.

15. Rachel Willard Stearns Journal, October 18, 23, 1834; see also October 15, 17, 19, and 20, 1834; January 25, 1835; May 5, 1835; August 1, 1835; Letter No. 6 [SMC to GR & LCR], Slatersville, 1825 (misdated 1824), in CW, 125; "The Advantages of Class Meetings, and the Best Means of Rendering Them Profitable," CA, June 4, 1830.

16. Rachel Willard Stearns Journal, January 25, 1835. On Methodist spirituality and theology, see John H. Wigger, *Taking Heaven by Storm: Methodism and the Rise of Popular Christianity in America* (New York: Oxford University Press, 1998); A. Gregory Schneider, "Heart Religion on the Divide," in *"Heart Religion" in the Methodist Tradition and Related Movements*, ed. Richard B. Steele (Lanham, MD: Scarecrow Press, 2001), 127–73. On Methodist women and spirituality: Candy Gunther, "The Spiritual Pilgrimage of Rachel Stearns, 1834–1837: Reinterpreting Women's Religious and Social Experiences in the Methodist Revivals of Nineteenth-Century America," *Church History* 65 (1996): 577–95; Rhonda D. Hartweg, "All in Raptures: The Spirituality of Sarah Anderson Jones," *Methodist History* 45 (2007): 166–79.

17. Letter No. 6 [SMC to GR & LCR], Slatersville, 1825 (misdated 1824), in CW, 125; Letter No. 14 [SMC to LCR], Lowell, May 3, 1829, in CW, 138; Letter No. 15 [SMC to LLC], Lowell, January 17, 1830, in CW, 140. For the contrast between the spirit-filled Methodist and the "Formalist," in Methodist spirituality and hymns, see Charles A. Johnson, *The Frontier Camp Meeting* (Dallas: Southern Methodist University Press, 1955); Ann Taves, *Fits, Trances, and Visions: Experiencing Religion and Explaining Experience from Wesley to James* (Princeton, NJ: Princeton University Press, 1999).

18. Rachel Willard Stearns Journal, May 3, 1835.

19. Letter No. 14 [SMC to LCR], Lowell, May 3, 1829, in CW, 138; Rachel Willard Stearns Journal, January 1, 1835; December 18, 1834; December 5, 1834; see also: April. 30, 1835; May 16, and 31, 1835.

20. Rachel Willard Stearns Journal, April 30, 1835. On family hostility toward Methodist converts: Christine Leigh Heyrman, *Southern Cross: The Beginnings of the Bible Belt* (New York: Alfred A. Knopf, 1997), 118–27.

21. Letter No. 14 [SMC to LCR], Lowell, May 3, 1829, in CW, 138; Letter No. 6 [SMC to GR & LCR], Slatersville, 1825 (misdated 1824), in CW, 125. Maria made a similar statement in her last, undelivered letter to the Rev. Ira Bidwell: "The methodists are my people when I enjoy any religion—To them I was indebted under God for my spiritual birth." BFH, 189–90.

22. Rachel Willard Stearns Journal, May 7, 1835; CW, 116.

23. Robert Drew Simpson, ed., *American Methodist Pioneer: The Life and Journals of the Rev. Freeborn Garrettson, 1752–1827* (Rutland, VT: Academy Books, 1984), 49.

24. Rachel Willard Stearns Journal, July 19, 1835; Letter No. 14 [SMC to LCR], Lowell, May 3, 1829, in CW, 138. On Methodist class meetings: Wigger, *Taking Heaven by Storm*; Philip F. Hardt, "The Evangelistic and

Catechetical Role of the Class Meeting in Early New York City
Methodism," *Methodist History* 38 (1999): 14–26.

25. BFH, 110, 135–36; LD, 46. On class meetings, see *CA*, November 9, 1827;
August 22, 1828; April 23, 1830; June 4, 1830; James Porter, *A Compendium
of Methodism* (Boston, 1853), 458–60.

26. *ZH*, September 20, 1826.

27. Letter No. 6 [SMC to GR & LCR], Slatersville, 1825 (misdated 1824), in
CW, 125; Letter No. 12 [SMC to LLC], Dorchester, [Month not given] 28,
1828, in CW, 135; also: Letter No. 7 [SMC to LCR], Slatersville, September
6, 1825, in CW, 127; Letter No. 9 [SMC to LLC], Mendon Mills, August 6,
1826, in CW, 129; Letter No. 10 [SMC to LLC, GR & LCR], Dorchester,
September 25, 1827, in CW, 131–32.

28. Letter No. 6 [SMC to GR & LCR], Slatersville, 1825 (misdated 1824), in
CW, 125; Letter No. 14 [SMC to LCR], Lowell, May 3, 1829, in CW, 137;
Letter No. 8 [SMC to LLC], Slatersville, December 18, 1825, in CW, 128;
Letter No. 7 [SMC to LCR], Slatersville, September 6, 1825, in CW, 127.

Chapter 7

1. Letter No. 7 [SMC to LCR], Slatersville, September 6, 1825, in CW,
126–27.

2. Letter No. 6 [SMC to GR & LCR], Slatersville, 1825 (misdated 1824), in
CW, 124; Letter No. 8 [SMC to LLC], Slatersville, December 18, 1825, in
CW, 128.

3. Letter No. 6 [SMC to GR & LCR], Slatersville, 1825 (misdated 1824), in
CW, 124.

4. Nathan Appleton, *Introduction of the Power Loom, and Origin of Lowell*
(Lowell, 1858), 14; Bagnall, *The Textile Industries of the United States*,
546–550. By 1826, about a third of Rhode Island mills had power looms;
Brennan, *Social Conditions*, 17. On power looms and the new Waltham-
Lowell system of textile manufacturing: Gail Fowler Mohanty, "Putting Up
with Putting-Out: Power Loom Diffusion and Outwork for Rhode Island
Mills, 1821–1829," *Journal of the Early Republic* 9 (1989): 191–216; Thomas
Dublin, *Women at Work: The Transformation of Work and Community in
Lowell, Massachusetts, 1826–1860* (New York: Columbia University Press,
1979); Zonderman, *Aspirations and Anxieties*.

5. Letter No. 6 [SMC to GR & LCR], Slatersville, 1825 (misdated 1824), in
CW, 124; N. B. Gordon, "Diary (1829–1830)," January 23, 1829, in Kulik,
New England Mill Village, 284; Joseph Hollingworth to William Rawcliff,
September 5, 1830, in *Hollingworth Letters*, 88; Zonderman, *Aspirations and
Anxieties*, 37, 42–43.

6. N. B. Gordon, Diary, Nathaniel Batchelder Gordon Business Papers,
HBL; N. B. Gordon, "Diary (1829–1830)," in Kulik, *New England Village*,
283–307; *Hollingworth Letters*, 66; Gary Kulik, "Pawtucket Village and the
Strike of 1824: The Origins of Class Conflict in Rhode Island," *Radical
History Review* 17 (1978), 5–37.

7. *Hampshire Gazette* (Northampton, MA), July 3, 1833; Letter No. 7 [SMC to LCR], Slatersville, September 6, 1825, in CW, 126.

8. *AT*, February 3, 1826; *PP*, February 4, 1826; *Boston Weekly Messenger*, February 9, 1826.

9. *Massachusetts Spy* (Worcester), January 25, 1826.

10. BFH, 128, 127, 122; MB, 93; *National Aegis* (Worcester), June 19, 1833.

11. Catharine Williams later declared that Maria departed because she disliked weaving wool instead of cotton, ignoring her expulsion by the Methodists. CW, 130–31.

12. *Essex Register* (Salem), October 9, 1826; *RIA*, October 3, 1826; *AT*, October 3, 1826; Letter No. 11 [SMC to LLC], Dorchester, 2 March 1828, in CW, 134.

13. Letter No. 10 [SMC to LLC, GR & LCR], Dorchester, September 25, 1827, in CW, 131; CW, 130; *Village Register and Norfolk County Advertiser* (Dedham), December 21, 1826; January 18, 1827. Maria might have been fleeing from those in Rhode Island who knew her reputation as much as distancing herself from her birth family; see Thaddeus Bruce testimony, RH, 69; BFH, 127.

14. Letter No. 10 [SMC to LLC, GR & LCR], Dorchester, September 25, 1827, in CW, 131.

15. Letter No. 8 [SMC to LLC], Slatersville, December 18, 1825, in CW, 128.

16. Letter No. 10 [SMC to LLC, GR & LCR], Dorchester, September 25, 1827, in CW, 131.

17. Letter No. 10 [SMC to LLC, GR & LCR], Dorchester, September 25, 1827, in CW, 131.

18. Letter No. 11 [SMC to LLC], Dorchester, March 2, 1828, in CW, 133. The average daily wage for women in the Dorchester factory was forty-four cents per day, so Maria's experienced tending of four looms made her one of the higher paid women workers in that factory. Louis McLane, *Documents Relative to the Manufactures in the United States* (Washington, DC, 1833), 380–81.

19. Letter No. 11 [SMC to LLC], Dorchester, March 2, 1828, in CW, 133–34.

20. John R. Chaffee, *The History of the First Methodist Episcopal Church, Dorchester, Massachusetts* (Boston: Pilgrim Press, 1917), 147, 29; Dorchester Antiquarian and Historical Society, *History of the Town of Dorchester, Massachusetts* (Boston, 1859), 632–34.

21. Chaffee, *History of the First Methodist Episcopal Church, Dorchester*, 145; Letter No. 10 [SMC to LLC, GR & LCR], Dorchester, September 25, 1827, in CW, 132, 133.

22. RH, 64, 70; BFH, 117–18, 128; MB, 80, 93–94; *National Aegis* (Worcester), June 12, 1833.

23. "Moral Influences of Factories—No. 1," *Christian Watchman,* September 6, 1833; Elisha Bartlett, *A Vindication of the Character and Condition of the Females Employed in the Lowell Mills* (Lowell, 1841), 11; Henry A. Miles, *Lowell, as It Was, and as It Is,* 2nd ed. (Lowell, 1846), 129.

24.   Letter No. 14 [SMC to LCR], Lowell, May 3, 1829, in CW, 137–38.

Chapter 8

1.   *PJ,* December 25, 1832; *FRWR*, December 26, 1832; February 6, 1833; *LM,*
       January 4, 1833; *BCG*, February 7, 1833.
2.   *FRWR*, December 26, 1832; *TUM*, January 5, 1833.
3.   Lorenzo Dow, *History of Cosmopolite; or, the Four Volumes of Lorenzo's
       Journal Concentrated in One* (New York, 1814), 48. On Lorenzo Dow's life
       and career, see Hatch, *Democratization of American Christianity*; Charles
       Coleman Sellers, *Lorenzo Dow: The Bearer of the Word* (New York: Minton,
       Balch & Co., 1928).
4.   Well over 200 boys were given the first and middle name of Lorenzo
       Dow at birth between 1800 and 1830; see records on Ancestry.com. On
       the impact of a print revolution on religion, see Hatch, *Democratization*;
       R. Laurence Moore, *Selling God: American Religion in the Marketplace
       of Culture* (New York: Oxford University Press, 1994); Candy Gunther
       Brown, *The Word in the World: Evangelical Writing, Publishing, and Reading
       in America, 1789–1880* (Chapel Hill: University of North Carolina Press,
       2004); David Paul Nord, *Faith in Reading: Religious Publishing and the
       Birth of Mass Media in America* (New York: Oxford University Press, 2004).
       On personal narratives and self-published memoirs, see Ann Fabian, *The
       Unvarnished Truth: Personal Narratives in Nineteenth-Century America*
       (Berkeley: University of California Press, 2000).
5.   Dow, *History of Cosmopolite*, 356–57; Lorenzo Dow, *Analects, or Reflections
       upon Natural, Moral, and Political Philosophy*, 3rd ed. (New York, 1813),
       12, 72–73; see also 14, 18, 44–45, 47, 76, 90; [Lorenzo Dow,] *The Chain of
       Lorenzo; By the Request of His Friends, as His Farewell to Georgia* (Augusta,
       GA, [1803]), 8. Dow's and early Methodism's egalitarian and antislavery
       ideas have been addressed by Hatch, *Democratization of American
       Christianity*; Donald G. Mathews, *Slavery and Methodism* (Princeton,
       NJ: Princeton University Press, 1965); Cynthia Lynn Lyerly, *Methodism and
       the Southern Mind, 1770–1810* (New York: Oxford University Press, 1998);
       Dee E. Andrews, *The Methodists and Revolutionary America, 1760–1800*
       (Princeton, NJ: Princeton University Press, 2000).
6.   George A. Calhoun, *A Historical Address Before the Church of Christ in
       North Coventry, Conn.* (Hartford, 1846).
7.   *Connecticut Evangelical Magazine and Religious Intelligencer* 8 (January
       1815); Connecticut Church Records, 2nd Cong. Church at North Coventry,
       1740–1917, CSL, 1959, 3–4, Ancestry.com; Calhoun, *Historical Address*, 29.
8.   BFH, 169, 179; RH, 91, 97; LD, 38; *VIN*, 24.
9.   "Revival of Religion in the Tolland Circuit, Connecticut," *Methodist
       Magazine* 5 (March, 1822); "Revival of Religion in New-Haven," *Methodist
       Magazine* 4 (June 1822); John E. Risley, *Some Experiences of a Methodist
       Itinerant, in a Ministry of Half a Century* (Boston, 1882), 24–27; Abel
       Stevens, *Memorials of the Introduction of Methodism into the Eastern States*

(Boston, 1848), 256–58; Abel Stevens, *Memorials of the Early Progress of Methodism in the Eastern States* (New York, 1854), 362; Robert E. Cray Jr., "High Style and Low Morals: John Newland Maffitt and the Methodist Church, 1794–1850," *Methodist History* 45 (2006): 31–42.

10. Risley, *Some Experiences of a Methodist Itinerant*, 18–19.

11. Dan Young, *Autobiography of Dan Young, A New England Preacher of the Olden Time* (New York, 1860), 291. On the process of becoming a Methodist circuit rider, see Andrews, *The Methodists and Revolutionary America*, 207; Heyrman, *Southern Cross*, 86–94; Wigger, *Taking Heaven by Storm*, 48–79; Peter Feinman, "Itinerant Circuit-Riding Minister: Warrior of Light in a Wilderness of Chaos," *Methodist History* 45 (2006): 43–53; Frederick V. Mills Sr., "Mentors of Methodism, 1784–1844," *Methodist History* 12 (1973): 43–57; Frederick V. Mills Sr., "Methodist Preaching, 1798–1840: Form and Function," *Methodist History* 43 (2004): 3–16.

12. Cited in W. M. Gewehr, "Some Factors in the Expansion of Frontier Methodism, 1800–1811," *Journal of Religion* 8 (1928), 103.

13. Billy Hibbard, *Memoirs of the Life and Travels of B. Hibbard, Minister of the Gospel* (New York, 1825), 145; other examples: Mary Orne Tucker, *Itinerant Preaching in the Early Days of Methodism* (Boston, 1872), 46; Risley, *Some Experiences of a Methodist Itinerant*, 36, 55–56; James Mudge, *History of the New England Conference of the Methodist Episcopal Church, 1796–1910* (Boston; The Conference, 1910), 301.

14. *Minutes of the Annual Conferences of the Methodist Episcopal Church, for the Years 1773–1828*, vol. 1 (New York, 1840), 5–7; *Minutes of the Annual Conferences of the Methodist Episcopal Church, for the Years 1829–1839*, vol. 2 (New York, 1840), 74, 114; *The American Almanac and Repository for Useful Knowledge, for the Year 1845* (Boston, 1844), 199. On early Methodism in America, see Wigger, *Taking Heaven by Storm*; Andrews, *The Methodists and Revolutionary America*; Heyrman, *Southern Cross*; Russell E. Richey, *Early American Methodism* (Bloomington: University of Indiana Press, 1991); Hempton, *Methodism: Empire of Spirit*; Anna M. Lawrence, *One Family Under God: Love, Belonging, and Authority in Early Transatlantic Methodism* (Philadelphia: University of Pennsylvania Press, 2011). On the competitive religious marketplace in this era, see Moore, *Selling God*; Hatch, *Democratization of American Christianity*.

15. On Methodism in New England: Mudge, *History of the New England Conference*; George Claude Baker Jr., *An Introduction to the History of Early New England Methodism, 1789–1839* (Durham, NC: Duke University Press, 1941).

16. Stevens, *Memorials of the Early Progress of Methodism*, 360–63; *Minutes of the Annual Conferences . . . 1773–1828*, 365, 384.

17. See the many obituaries in *Minutes of the Annual Conferences*; S. G. Goodrich, *Recollections of a Lifetime, or Men and Things I Have Seen* (New York, 1857), 197; John C. Kilgo in *Journal of the Twenty-Fourth Delegated General Conference of the Methodist Episcopal Church* (New York,

1904), 566; Mudge, *History of the New England Conference*, 85–86; *Autobiography of Dan Young*, 88.

18. Mudge, *History of the New England Conference*, 68; Risley, *Some Experiences of a Methodist Itinerant*, 60–61; Young, *Autobiography of Dan Young*, 234–35. When Ephraim joined this traveling fraternity, preachers still regularly traveled far from home, but by the time of Maria Cornell's death, many more Methodist ministers in southern New England were stationed in a single large town or city, like Lowell, Bristol, Fall River, or Newport.

19. Abel Stevens, *Essays on the Preaching Required by the Times* (New York, 1855), 125; for "heart" more than "head," *Sketch of Rev. Philip Gatch*, ed. John M'Lean (Cincinnati, 1854), 102.

20. Tucker, *Itinerant Preaching in the Early Days of Methodism*, 77; Risley, *Some Experiences of a Methodist Itinerant*, 93; for ministers' salaries in Ephraim's day, see *The Doctrines and Discipline of the Methodist Episcopal Church*, 22nd ed. (New York, 1824), 171–72. For descriptions of Avery, see *Lowell Evangelist*, March 22, 1833; *BDA*, May 9, 1833; *Nantucket Inquirer*, May 11, 1833.

21. *The Doctrines and Discipline of the Methodist Episcopal Church in America*, 10th ed. (Philadelphia, 1798), 83, 52; "Camp-Meeting at Marshfield," *Christian Watchman*, August 31, 1822; see also *Boston Daily Advertiser*, August 20, 1822; *Boston Weekly Messenger*, August 23, 1822; *New England Galaxy*, August 29, 1823.

22. Heyrman, *Southern Cross*, 94–98; On sexuality and evangelical religion, including Methodists: Susan Juster, "The Spirit and the Flesh: Gender, Language, and Sexuality in American Protestantism," in *New Directions in American Religious History*, ed. Harry S. Stout and D. G. Hart (New York: Oxford University Press, 1997), 334–61; Henry Abelove, *The Evangelist of Desire: John Wesley and the Methodists* (Stanford, CA: Stanford University Press, 1990); Cynthia Lynn Lyerly, "Passion, Desire, Ecstasy: The Experiential Religion of Southern Methodist Women, 1770–1810," in *The Devil's Lane: Sex and Race in the Early South*, ed. Catherine Clinton and Michele Gillespie (New York: Oxford University Press, 1997), 168–86; Lawrence, *One Family Under God*; Hartweg, "All in Raptures"; Aaron Spencer Fogleman, *Jesus Is Female: Moravians and the Challenge of Radical Religion in Early America* (Philadelphia: University of Pennsylvania Press, 2007); Bruce Dorsey, "'Making Men What They Should Be': Male Same-Sex Intimacy and Evangelical Religion in Early Nineteenth-Century New England," *Journal of the History of Sexuality* 24 (2015): 345–77; Rodney Hessinger, *Smitten: Sex, Gender, and the Contest for Souls in the Second Great Awakening* (Ithaca, NY: Cornell University Press, 2022).

23. The other was Elisha Frink, charged with "indecorous and unchristian conduct towards certain females" and removed from his appointment as a preacher. Minutes of the New England Conference of the Methodist Episcopal Church, From Its Beginning in New York, in 1766 to the

beginning of the unbroken series of Conference Minutes in 1845," 1826
Minutes, vol. 2: 51, typescript, NEMA.

24. T. L. Nichols, *Forty Years of American Life*, 2nd ed. (London, 1874),
     248; Charles T. Congdon, *Reminiscences of a Journalist* (Boston, 1880),
     46–47; Abel Stevens, *A Compendious History of the American Methodism*
     (New York, 1867), 561; *Charleston Courier*, reprinted in *Salem Gazette*,
     February 4, 1823; *Charleston Courier*, November 4, 1824; *Christian
     Philanthropist*, January 28, 1823; *Hallowell Gazette* (Maine), June 28, 1826;
     *Theological Pretenders, or, An Analysis of the Character and Conduct of the
     Rev. J. N. Maffit, Preacher in the Methodist Episcopal Society* (New York,
     1830), 8, 10; Cray, "High Style and Low Morals."

25. *Rhode Island Religious Intelligencer*, June 7 and 21, 1822; September 27,
     1822; October 11, 1822; November 22, 1822; *Providence Gazette*, June 12, 19,
     and 29, 1822. On the pamphlet war: *Rhode Island Religious Intelligencer*,
     June 28, 1822; December 27, 1822; *New Hampshire Gazette*, August 2,
     1825; *RIA*, May 31, 1822; the rival pamphlets included *Epitome of Mr.
     Maffitt's Discourse, Taken Down Verbally and Literally* (Providence, 1822);
     [Demens Egomet], *The Greatest Sermon, That Ever Was Preached*, 2nd ed.
     (New England, 1825); *An Answer to the Greatest Falsehood Ever Told by a
     Providence Lawyer, alias 'Demens Egomet.' Published as a Warning to All
     Notorious Liars* ([Providence], 1822); *Theological Pretenders*.

26. *Trial: Commonwealth vs. J. T. Buckingham, On an Indictment for a Libel,
     before the Municipal Court of the City of Boston, December Term, 1822*
     (Boston, 1822), 6.

27. *Report of the Trial of Mr. John N. Maffitt, before a Council of Ministers, of the
     Methodist Episcopal Church, Convened in Boston, December 26, 1822* (Boston,
     1823), 14, 24; *ZH*, January 9, 1823.

28. *Minutes of the Annual Conferences . . . 1773–1828*, 391, 410; Bagnall, *The
     Textile Industries of the United States*, 416–23; David R. Meyer, *The Roots
     of American Industrialization* (Baltimore: Johns Hopkins University Press,
     2003), 101–5.

29. Written testimony by Mrs. Sylvester Stanley, Providence, April 5, 1833, ATP,
     Box 11, Folder 12; Connecticut, U.S. Wills and Probate Records, 1609–
     1999, Ancestry.com.

30. Written testimony by Mrs. Sylvester Stanley; [Nancy N. (Stanley)
     Truesdell], *The Trials and Sufferings of an Afflicted Widow, Who Once Resided
     at Pomfret Manufacturing Village, 1833*, broadside, [Thompson, 1833], JHL.

31. Written testimony by Mrs. Sylvester Stanley.

32. Gilbert Haven and Thomas Russell, *Father Taylor, the Sailor
     Preacher: Incidents and Anecdotes of Rev. Edward T. Taylor, for over Forty
     Years Pastor of the Seaman's Bethel, Boston* (New York, 1881), 86–93;
     E. Waldo Long, ed., *The Story of Duxbury* (Duxbury, MA: Duxbury
     Tercentenary Committee, 1937), 48, 53, 120–22, 129–30; Samuel Deane,
     History of Scituate, Massachusetts, from Its First Settlement to 1831 (Boston,
     1831), 58–59; CW, 102.

33. All the evidence and quotations for this and the next few paragraphs can be found in CW, 102–8.

34. Horace H. Atherton, Jr., *History of Saugus, Massachusetts* (Saugus: Citizen Committee, 1916), 31–34; D. Hamilton Hurd, *History of Essex County, Massachusetts*, 2 vols. (Philadelphia, 1888), vol. 2: 399, 402; CW, 108.

35. *Mutual Rights, Etc.* (Baltimore) (later *Mutual Rights & Christian Intelligencer; Mutual Rights and Methodist Protestant*), 1824–1834; "Seceding Methodists," *Hampden Whig* (Springfield), October 6, 1830; *Hampshire Gazette* (Northampton, MA), August 4, 1830; *TUM*, January 10, 1829, October 16, 1830. The Universalists openly cheered for the Reformed Methodists in their battle against the "monied and sectarian" aristocracy of the Methodist Church. *TUM*, October 16, 1830; "Seceding Methodists," *Religious Intelligencer* (Boston), February 13, 1830; *Mutual Rights and Methodist Protestant* 1.9 (March 4, 1831), 69. On the history of Reformed Methodists, see T. H. Colhouer, *Sketches of the Founders of the Methodist Protestant Church, and its Bibliography* (Pittsburgh, 1880); Ancel H. Bassett, *A Concise History of the Methodist Protestant Church* (Pittsburgh, 1877); Edward J. Drinkhouse, *History of Methodist Reform,* 2 vols. (n.p., 1899).

36. T. F. Norris and Wm. Granville, "An Address to Local Preachers," *ZH*, April 24, 1823; Colhouer, *Sketches of the Founders*, 393–94; Drinkhouse, *History of Methodist Reform*, vol. 2: 254, 303, 325, 345, 364; *Star of Bethlehem* 2 (October 18, 1828), 142–43.

37. Thomas Norris v. Ephraim K. Avery, Court of Common Pleas, Middlesex Division, September Term, 1831, Record Book, Massachusetts Supreme Judicial Court Archives, Boston; CW, 109.

38. Thomas Norris v. Ephraim K. Avery; Thomas Norris, "To the Public," broadside, [n.p., 1833], ATP, Folder 8; *RIR*, July 3, 1833.

Chapter 9

1. Jay Coughtry, *The Notorious Triangle: Rhode Island and the African Slave Trade, 1700–1807* (Philadelphia: Temple University Press, 1981); Christy Clark-Pujara, *Dark Work: The Business of Slavery in Rhode Island* (New York: New York University Press, 2016).

2. By February 1833, two reports were published on Avery's pre-trial hearing in Bristol: Luke Drury, *A Report of the Examination of Rev. Ephraim K. Avery, Charged with the Murder of Sarah Maria Cornell* (Providence, 1833); William R. Staples, *A Correct Report of the Examination of Rev. Ephraim K. Avery* (Providence, 1833).

3. *RIA*, December 28 and January 1, 1833; *TUM*, January 5 and 12, 1833.

4. *FRWR*, January 2, 1833.

5. LD, 11; BFH, 180–81.

6. *NBC*, January 22, 1833.

7. Harriet H. Robinson, *Loom and Spindle: Or Life Among the Early Mill Girls* (New York, 1898), 63.

8. For the history of Lowell and its workers, see Dublin, *Women at Work*; Kasson, *Civilizing the Machine*; Teresa Anne Murphy, *Ten Hours' Labor: Religion, Reform, and Gender in Early New England* (Ithaca, NY: Cornell University Press, 1992); Zonderman, *Aspirations and Anxieties*; William Moran, *The Belles of New England* (New York: Thomas Dunne Books, 2002); Cook, *Working Women, Literary Ladies*; Lori Merish, *Archives of Labor: Working-Class Women and Literary Culture in the Antebellum United States* (Durham, NC: Duke University Press, 2017). The two classic accounts of former mill workers are Lucy Larcom, *A New England Girlhood* (New York, 1889); Robinson, *Loom and Spindle*.

9. Miles, *Lowell, As It Was*, 40–41, 59; Bartlett, *Vindication of the Character*, 9; William Scoresby, *American Factories and Their Female Operatives* (Boston, 1845), 11, 37; Benjamin Floyd, *The Lowell Directory* (Lowell, 1832), 5–6.

10. Robinson, *Loom and Spindle*, 63.

11. Robinson, *Loom and Spindle*, 64; Caroline Stone Gun to Mathias and Judith Stone, November 17, 1831; "Tales of Factory Life. No. 2," *LO*, April 1, 1841; "Leisure Hours of the Mill Girls," *LO*, January 1, 1842; Hamilton Registers, vol. 481: July 16, 1830—December 31, 1830, vol. 482: December 30, 1830–June 2, 1832, Hamilton Manufacturing Company Collection, HBL. On homesickness in American culture: Susan J. Matt, *Homesickness: An American History* (New York: Oxford University Press, 2011).

12. Letter No. 13 [SMC to LLC], Lowell, January 11, 1829, in CW, 136; Letter No. 14 [SMC to LCR], Lowell, May 3, 1829, in CW, 139; BFH, 79.

13. Letter No. 15 [SMC to LLC], Lowell, January 17, 1830, in CW, 139.

14. BFH, 121; Letter No. 14 [SMC to LCR], Lowell, May 3, 1829, in CW, 139; Letter No. 16 [SMC to LLC], Lowell, July 4, 1830, in CW, 142.

15. "The Factory Girl," broadside [ca. 1830–1860], JHL.

16. Abigail Lovering to Abram and Susan Guptill, April 27, 1834, Lowell Mill Girl Letters, University of Massachusetts, Lowell, https://libguides.uml.edu/c.php?g=542883&p=3735176, accessed August 1, 2018.

17. Robinson, *Loom and Spindle*, 84. On labor conflict and the erasure of memories of slavery in New England: Dublin *Women at Work*, 86–107; Joanne Pope Melish, *Disowning Slavery: Gradual Emancipation and "Race" in New England, 1780–1860* (Ithaca, NY: Cornell University Press, 1998); Margot Minardi, *Making Slavery History: Abolitionism and the Politics of Memory in Massachusetts* (New York: Oxford University Press, 2010).

18. Huldah B. Currier to Abram and Susan Guptill, April 27, 1834, Lowell Mill Girl Letters, University of Massachusetts, Lowell, https://libguides.uml.edu/c.php?g=542883&p=3735176, accessed August 1, 2018; "Moral Influences of Factories—No. 1," *Christian Watchman* (September 6, 1833); Scoresby, *American Factories and Their Female Operatives*, 31, 33, 62; Michael Chevalier, *Society, Manners and Politics in the United States* (Boston, 1839), 128.

19. Bartlett, *Vindication of the Character*, 19.

20. Bartlett, *Vindication of the Character*, 19.
21. Miles, *Lowell, As It Was*, 133–34.
22. Scoresby, *American Factories and Their Female Operatives*, 84, 89; *AT*, July 4, 1828; Bartlett, *Vindication of the Character*, 19; A Factory Girl, "Factory Girls," *LO*, December 1840, 18; Miles, *Lowell, As It Was*, 146–59; 162–91.
23. Hamilton Registers, vol. 481: July 16, 1830–December 31, 1830; vol. 482: December 30, 1830–June 2, 1832.
24. Bartlett, *Vindication of the Character*, 19, 20; Miles, *Lowell, As It Was*, 187.
25. Letter No. 14 [SMC to LCR], Lowell, May 3, 1829, in CW, 138; also Letter No. 16 [SMC to LLC], Lowell, July 4, 1830, in CW, 142.
26. RAL, 23; BFH, 135–36, 116–18; LD, 46; MB, 77–80, 106; RH, 63–64.
27. Letter No. 15 [SMC to LLC], Lowell, January 17, 1830, in CW, 140–41; *CA*, August 21, 1829; *AT*, August 18, 1829.
28. Letter No. 14 [SMC to LCR], Lowell, May 3, 1829, in CW, 138; Letter No. 16 [SMC to LLC], Lowell, July 4, 1830, in CW, 142.

Chapter 10

1. Mudge, *History of the New England Conference*, 221; Risley, *Some Experiences of a Methodist Itinerant*, 78–79; Leonard A. Morrison, *The History of the Morison or Morrison Family* (Boston, 1880), 98–99; *ZH*, 22 August 1827.
2. "Lowell, Mass.," *NECH*, January 12, 1831; "Revivals. Lowell, Mass.," *NECH*, May 18, 1831.
3. RH, 62–63; BFH, 115–16; MB, 76–77; *VIN*, 12.
4. "Revivals. Lowell, Mass.," *NECH*, May 18, 1831.
5. "Revivals," *NECH*, July 27, 1831; "Revivals. Lowell, Mass.," *NECH*, May 18, 1831; *Minutes of the Annual Conferences of the Methodist Episcopal Church, for the Years 1829–1839*, vol. 2 (New York, 1840), 149.
6. Caroline Sloat, "The Dover Manufacturing Company and the Integration of English and American Calico Printing Techniques, 1825–29," *Winterthur Portfolio* 10 (1975): 51–68.
7. 61st Congress, 2nd Session, Senate Document No. 645, *Report on Condition of Woman and Child Wage-Earners in the United States*, 19 vols. (Washington, DC: GPO, 1910), vol. 10:23–24.
8. BFH, 126; RH, 69.
9. Payroll Records, Mill No. 3, January 1830 to March 1834, Cocheco Manufacturing Company Records, 1821–1879, HBL.
10. BFH, 129, 126; MB, 90–91.
11. MB, 89; BFH, 125; LD, 44; *VIN*, 13–14.
12. HSE, 20.
13. Evidently Methodist church members in Somersworth insisted that Maria's name be removed from the class meeting book, indicating that rumors about her conduct and dismissal at Lowell had traveled to other Methodist meetings in the region's mill towns. RAL, 25.
14. MB, 88; Payroll Ledger, vol. 91: September 25, 1830 to August 27, 1831; Boston Manufacturing Company Records, 1813–1930, HBL.

15. BFH, 113–14, 128; RH, 61.
16. Letter No. 17 [SMC to LLC], Taunton, March 10, 1832, in CW, 142–43.
17. BFH, 86–87; Fall River Manufactory, Accounts of Sheeting Woven, 1827–1835, FRHS.

Chapter 11

1. LD, 14; WS, 7.
2. BFH, 67; *NBC*, January 22, 1833.
3. BFH, 66–67; LD, 14–15; MB, 35–36; WS, 7–8.
4. MB, 21–22; LD, 28–29; BFH, 53–54.
5. BFH, 67, 72; LD, 18.
6. LD, 62, 15; BFH, 66.
7. It got dark on December 20 in 1832 about fifty minutes later than it would today. Almanacs recorded sunset at 4:30 P.M., fifteen minutes later than in 2022, and twilight lasted about thirty minutes. But keep in mind, too, that the Fall River factories might have set their time intentionally slow to garner more labor from the mill workers. *New England Anti-Masonic Almanac for the Year of our Lord 1832* (Boston, 1831), 30; LD, 14–15, 18; WS, 9; BFH, 65–66, 72; MB, 35–36, 40; William F. Reed, *The Descendants of Thomas Durfee of Portsmouth, R. I.*, vol. 1 (Washington, DC: Gibson Brothers, 1902), 518.
8. LD, 13.
9. SMC to LCR and GR, November 18, 1832, in *NBC*, January 22, 1833.
10. *RIR*, March 12, 1833; SMC to Rev. [Ira] Bidwell, no date, BFH, 189–90.
11. LD, 14, 15; WS, 8.

Chapter 12

1. LD, 53, 55, 59, 61. On Howe: *The Biographical Cyclopedia of Representative Men of Rhode Island* (Providence, 1881), 206; *RIA*, June 20, 1817; August 9, 1831.
2. LD, 55.
3. LD, 56–57.
4. *FRWR*, January 9, 1833; *FRM*, reprinted in *NBC*, January 15, 1833.
5. HH, 5.
6. On Edgar Allan Poe and detective fiction: Martin Priestman, *Crime Fiction: From Poe to the Present*, 2nd ed. (Devon, UK: British Council, 2013); Peter Goodwin, "The Man in the Text: Desire, Masculinity, and the Development of Poe's Detective Fiction," in *Edgar Allan Poe: Beyond Gothicism*, ed. James M. Hutchisson (Newark: University of Delaware Press, 2011), 49–68; Heather Worthington, *The Rise of the Detective in Early Nineteenth-Century Popular Fiction* (New York: Palgrave Macmillan, 2005).
7. HH, 6.
8. *Nantucket Inquirer*, January 23, 1833; *NBM*, January 25, 1833; HH, 5.
9. HH, 10–12.

10. HH, 14–19. On the self-made man and its narratives: John Cawelti, *Apostles of the Self-Made Man* (Chicago: University of Chicago Press, 1965); Irvin G. Wyllie, *The Self-Made Man in America: The Myth of Rags to Riches* (New York: Free Press, 1966); Sandage, *Born Losers*.
11. HH, 23.
12. HH, 24, 25.
13. HH, 26.
14. *RIA*, January 25, 1833; *RIR*, January 22, 1833.
15. HH, 32.
16. *FRWR*, February 20, 1833; *NHT* (reprinted from *PJ*), February 14, 1833.
17. *RIA*, January 22, 1833.

Chapter 13

1. This account of Avery's walk from the jailhouse to the courthouse, led by Newport's jailkeeper William Allen, is based, in part, on my own observations on an early May morning in 2017 with nearly identical weather, and based on my reading of the May 1833 weather record in *NM*, June 8, 1833.
2. Richard M. Bayles, ed. *History of Newport County, Rhode Island* (New York, 1888).
3. *VIN*, 20.
4. *BDA*, May 9, 1833.
5. Charles H. Bell, *The Bench and Bar of New Hampshire* (Boston, 1894), 506. On Richard Randolph: Genealogies of Randolph Family, Box 142, Randolph Family Papers, 1844–1884, Newport Historical Society, Newport, RI. On Jeremiah Mason: *Proceedings in Massachusetts and New Hampshire on the Death of the Hon. Jeremiah Mason* (Boston, 1849); G. J. Clark, *Memoir, Autobiography and Correspondence of Jeremiah Mason* (Kansas City: Lawyers International, 1917); G. S. Hillard, *Memoir and Correspondence of Jeremiah Mason* (Cambridge, MA, 1873); Francis N. Stites, "Mason, Jeremiah," *American National Biography Online*, https://www.anb.org, accessed July 10, 2020.
6. *RIA*, August 7, 1829; *The Complete Works of the Hon. Job Durfee* (Providence, 1849), 521–22; *The Biographical Cyclopedia of Representative Men of Rhode Island* (Providence, 1881), 86–87; *BDA*, May 17, 1833.
7. MB, 6–8, RH, 5; *TAL*, 4, RAL, 3.
8. RH, 6.
9. *FRWR*, December 26, 1832; January 2, 1833; quotation in February 6, 1833; *NYCE*, reprinted in *Charleston Courier*, May 16, 1833; *Nantucket Inquirer*, May 11, 1833; *BDA*, May 9, 1833; *RIA*, January 1, 15, & 25, 1833; *RIR*, January 8, 1833; *NHT*, January 17, 1833; *New-York Commercial Advertiser*, February 1, 1833; *Philadelphia Album and Ladies' Literary Portfolio*, February 2, 1833; *BCG*, February 7, 1833; March 14, 1833; *Philadelphia Inquirer*, April 19, 1833; *Essex Gazette* (Haverhill, MA), April 27, 1833.

10. Charles H. Dow, *Newport: The City by the Sea. Four Epochs in Her History* (Newport, 1880), 53; see also Elaine Forman Crane, *A Dependent People: Newport, Rhode Island, in the Revolutionary Era* (New York: Fordham University Press, 1985); Lynne Withey, *Urban Growth in Colonial Rhode Island: Newport and Providence in the Eighteenth Century* (Albany: State University of New York Press, 1984); Peter J. Coleman, *The Transformation of Rhode Island, 1790–1860* (Providence: Brown University Press, 1963).

11. *Southern Patriot*, reprinted from *Boston Morning Post*, May 22, 1833.

12. BFH, 5; *FRWR*, May 15, 1833; *Norfolk Advertiser* (Dedham), May 11, 1833; *PJ*, June 11, 1833; On Towndrow, see *AT*, February 22, 1833, May 14, 1833; *BCG*, April 11, 1833; *American Mercury* (Hartford), February 4, 1833; *Eastern Argus* (Portland, ME), February 6, 833; T. Towndrow, *A Complete Guide to Stenography, or An Entirely New System of Writing Short Hand* (Boston, 1831). My best guess for the identity of "Mr. Wheeler," the New York *Journal of Commerce* reporter, is Jacob D. Wheeler, a New York City attorney and author of *Reports of Criminal Law Cases Decided at the City-Hall of the City of New-York* (1823–1854).

13. RH 6; BFH, 5; MB, 5; *AT*, May 10, 1833; *NM*, May 11, 1833; *NHT*, May 23, 1833 *PJ*, May 9, 1833.

14. In all, eleven men were dismissed because of their objection to capital punishment. Many Quakers had resided in Newport since its founding, and their pacifist principles led them to have conscientious objections to capital punishment. On the antebellum movement against capital punishment, see Louis P. Masur, *Rites of Execution: Capital Punishment and the Transformation of American Culture, 1776–1865* (New York: Oxford University Press, 1989), 117–59.

15. BFH, 5–6. See also ATP, Folders 33 and 34.

16. *VIN*, 26.

17. RAL, 3.

18. BFH, 11–12.

19. *TAL*, 4.

20. BFH, 6–13.

21. *NM*, June 8, 1833; *BDA*, May 11, 1833.

22. *BDA*, May 11, 1833. Several trial reports agreed on this exact wording: RH, 9; BFH, 15; MB, 9; *TAL*, 7.

23. Pearce was certainly glossing over the actual uncertainties that Tiverton residents had expressed in the first few days after Cornell's body was discovered about whether her death was a suicide.

24. My composite reconstruction of Pearce's statement, with his original wording from the trial reports, yet in some parts replaced by my more succinct wording of his basic points. BFH, 15–16; *TAL*, 8–9. Pearce, for example, used the euphemism "her situation" to refer to Cornell's pregnancy.

25. BFH, 16.

26. Again, composite reconstruction of Pearce's statement from the trial reports: *TAL*, 10; MB, 11; RH, 10; BFH, 18.
27. *BDA*, May 11, 1833.
28. On criminal trials, storytelling, and the scholarship on law and literature, see W. Lance Bennett and Martha S. Feldman, *Reconstructing Reality in the Courtroom: Justice and Judgment in American Culture* (New Brunswick, NJ: Rutgers University Press, 1981); Laura Hanft Korobkin, "Narrative Battles in the Courtroom," in *Field Work: Sites in Literary and Cultural Studies*, ed. Marjorie Garber et al. (New York: Routledge, 1996), 225–37; Laura Hanft Korobkin, *Criminal Conversations: Sentimentality and Nineteenth-Century Legal Stories of Adultery* (New York: Columbia University Press, 1998); Paul Gewirtz, "Narrative and Rhetoric in the Law," in *Law's Stories: Narrative and Rhetoric in the Law*, ed. Peter Brooks and Paul Gewirtz (New Haven, CT: Yale University Press, 1996), 2–13; Robert A. Ferguson, "Untold Stories in the Law," in Brooks and Gewirtz, eds., *Law's Stories*, 84–98; Robert A. Ferguson, *The Trial in American Life* (Chicago: University of Chicago Press, 2007); Jerome Bruner, *Making Stories: Law, Literature, Life* (New York: Farrar, Straus and Giroux, 2002); Karen Halttunen, *Murder Most Foul: The Killer and the American Gothic Imagination* (Cambridge, MA: Harvard University Press, 1998).
29. BFH, 18; RH, 11.

Chapter 14

1. BFH, 19; MB, 11–12.
2. BFH, 21–22.
3. Clark, *Memoir, Autobiography and Correspondence of Jeremiah Mason*, 377.
4. BFH, 22.
5. One didn't have to throw a stick too far to hit a Durfee (or a Borden) in Tiverton and Fall River. Williams Durfee was not related to the Durfees on whose farm Cornell was found.
6. BFH, 23–24; RH, 13; RAL, 5; *TAL*, 13.
7. BFH, 24; RAL, 5.
8. BFH, 45–46, 49; RH, 23.
9. BFH, 25; RH, 14; RAL, 6; MB, 60. The Rawsons cooperated with the prosecution from the start; Grindal even helped search for evidence against Avery.
10. Based on a sample of forty-three murder trials with published trial reports (hence even more sensational than other capital trials) between 1801 and 1819 in the database *Early American Imprints: Shaw and Shoemaker*. Forty-one, or 95 percent, of the trials lasted between one and three days, nearly three-fourths took only a day. *Nantucket Inquirer* (reprint of *Boston Atlas*, Richard Hildreth reporting), May 11, 1833.
11. BFH, 66–67, 72, 78.
12. BFH, 69.
13. BFH, 73–75, 75–76; RAL, 12.

14. BFH, 76–77.
15. *RIA*, January 4, 1833; RH, 36; BFH, 77; *TAL*, 34; RAL, 12–13.
16. *American Mercury* (Hartford), May 14, 1833; *New York Spectator*, May 13, 1833; RAL, 3; *BDA*, May 14, 1833; May 9, 1833.
17. Janet Malcolm, "The Side-Bar Conference," in *Law's Stories: Narrative and Rhetoric in the Law*, ed. Peter Brooks and Paul Gewirtz (New Haven, CT: Yale University Press, 1996), 106–9:
18. RH, 38; RAL, 13.
19. RAL, 14; RH, 38; BFH, 79–80; *TAL*, 36.
20. BFH, 80.
21. BFH, 189; *A Fac-simile of the Letters Produced at the Trial of the Rev. Ephraim K. Avery* (Boston, 1833).
22. BFH, 164, 178.
23. RH 41–42; BFH, 82–83; RAL, 14; Thomas Starkie, *A Practical Treatise on the Law of Evidence*, 3 vols. (Boston, 1826), vol. 1:370.
24. BFH, 90.
25. RH, 48; BFH, 90.
26. BFH, 91–93.

Chapter 15

1. *TAL*, 19; BFH, 47; RH, 23.
2. On women's customs of burial and healing: Mary E. Fissell, "Introduction: Women, Health, and Healing in Early Modern Europe," *Bulletin of the History Medicine* 82 (2008): 1–17; Laurel K. Gabel, "Death, Burial, and Memorialization in Colonial New England: The Diary of Samuel Sewall," *Markers* 25 (2008): 8–43; Laurel Thatcher Ulrich, *A Midwife's Tale: The Life of Martha Ballard, Based on Her Diary, 1785–1812* (New York: Alfred A. Knopf, 1990).
3. RAL, 8. Likely these women also gathered at local childbirths; they also shared direct ties to the First Congregational Church that Richard Durfee had founded at that farmhouse sixteen years before: *The Confession of Faith and Covenant of the First Congregational Church, Fall River* (Fall River, 1838), 18–24.
4. LD, 33.
5. LD, 33–34; also: WS, 17–18; BFH, 47–49; 52–53; RH, 23–24, 26; RAL, 7–8.
6. BFH, 31; the cloth had been placed there by the women when they prepared her for burial. LD, 35; J. P. Maygrier, *Midwifery Illustrated* (New York, 1833).
7. Ulrich, *A Midwife's Tale*, 46–47; Bernard Capp, *When Gossips Meet: Women, Family, and Neighbourhood in Early Modern England* (Oxford: Oxford University Press, 2003), 267–319; *The Art of Midwifery: Early Modern Midwives in Europe*, ed. Hilary Marland (London: Routledge, 1993).
8. RAL, 7; BFH, 47, 52–53; RH, 26; MB, 20.
9. BFH, 47, MB, 15.
10. BFH, 47, 52–53; RAL, 7–8.

11. BFH, 47; RH, 23; LD, 33.
12. MB, 16; RAL, 8; BFH, 48.
13. BFH, 47; MB, 15; RAL, 7; RH, 23.
14. LD, 34.
15. BFH, 47; RH, 24; *TAL*, 20; RAL, 8.
16. BFH, 48. On women's reticence to testify about rape, see Ulrich, *A Midwife's Tale*, 115–27; Sharon Block, *Rape and Sexual Power in Early America* (Chapel Hill: University of North Carolina Press, 2006), 1–125; Dayton, *Women Before the Bar*, 231–84; Anna Clark, *Women's Silence, Men's Violence: Sexual Assault in England, 1770–1845* (London: Pandora, 1987).
17. LD, 9.
18. MB, 61; RAL, 6; BFH, 29, 183; RH, 16; see also *Boston Statesman*, May 25, 1822.
19. Henry H. Earl, *A Centennial History of Fall River, Mass.* (New York, 1877), 241; *FRM*, March 6 and 20, 1830; August 21, 1830; July 11, 1832; *FRWR*, March 20, 1833; *American Quarterly Review* 13, no. 4 (May 1841), 475.
20. BFH, 30, 32; MB, 63.
21. BFH 32.
22. BFH, 34.
23. For the pro-Avery reports, see RH, 17; TAL, 16–17; *Boston Statesman*, May 25, 1822. For anti-Avery reports, see BFH, 32; MB, 62; RAL, 6.
24. RAL, 7; RH, 18.
25. BFH, 37.
26. BFH, 40.
27. RAL, 7; RH, 21; BFH, 42–43.
28. *BDA*, May 13, 1833.

Chapter 16

1. BFH, 99; RAL, 19; MB, 66.
2. BFH, 107, 105.
3. RH, 52; BFH, 95.
4. Steven Shapin, *The Scientific Revolution* (Chicago: University of Chicago Press, 1996); Leigh Eric Schmidt, *Hearing Things: Religion, Illusion, and the American Enlightenment* (Cambridge, MA: Harvard University Press, 2000); Jonathan Crary, *Techniques of the Observer: On Vision and Modernity in the Nineteenth Century* (Cambridge, MA: M.I.T. Press, 1990); James Delbourgo, *A Most Amazing Scene of Wonders: Electricity and Enlightenment in Early America* (Cambridge, MA: Harvard University Press, 2006).
5. BFH, 53.
6. LD, 33, 12–13.
7. BFH, 99; RH, 56.
8. BFH, 104, 106; see also: RAL, 19–21; MB, 66–72.
9. Susan H. Brandt, *Women Healers: Gender, Authority, and Medicine in Early Philadelphia* (Philadelphia: University of Pennsylvania Press, 2022);

Rebecca J. Tannenbaum, *The Healer's Calling: Women and Medicine in Early New England* (Ithaca, NY: Cornell University Press, 2002).

10.   On the efforts of elite male physicians to establish an exclusive medical profession, see Barnes Riznik, "The Professional Lives of Early Nineteenth-Century New England Doctors," *Journal of the History of Medicine and Allied Sciences* 19 (1964): 1–16; Joseph F. Kett, *The Formation of the American Medical Profession* (New Haven, CT: Yale University Press, 1968); Charles E. Rosenberg, "Prologue: The Shape of Traditional Practice, 1800–1875," in *The Structure of American Medical Practice, 1875–1941*, ed. George Rosen (Philadelphia: University of Pennsylvania Press, 1983); John Harley Warner, *The Therapeutic Perspective: Medical Practice, Knowledge, and Identity in America, 1820–1885* (Cambridge, MA: Harvard University Press, 1986); John C. Burnham, *Health Care in America: A History* (Baltimore: Johns Hopkins University Press, 2015); Paul Starr, *The Social Transformation of American Medicine*, rev. ed (1982, New York: Basic Books, 2017). On alternative medical practitioners, see James C. Whorton, *Nature Cures: The History of Alternative Medicine in America* (New York: Oxford University Press, 2002); Norman Gevitz, ed., *Other Healers: Unorthodox Medicine in America* (Baltimore: Johns Hopkins University Press, 1988); John S. Haller Jr., *The People's Doctors: Samuel Thomson and the American Botanical Movement, 1790–1860* (Carbondale: Southern Illinois University Press, 2000).

11.   Dr. Walter Channing, Harvard Professor of Obstetrics, wrote that physicians' increased role in childbirths "ensures to them the permanency and security of all their other business." [Walter Channing], *Remarks on the Employment of Females as Practitioners in Midwifery* (Boston, 1820), 19. On physicians' aspirations to encroach on midwives' practice and their steadily rising presence at childbirth, see Judith Walzer Leavitt, *Brought to Bed: Childbearing in America, 1750–1950* (New York: Oxford University Press, 1986); Catharine M. Scholten, "'On the Importance of the Obstetrick Art': Changing Customs of Childbirth in America, 1760 to 1825," *William and Mary Quarterly* 3rd ser., 34 (1977): 426–45; Laurel Ulrich, *The Life of Martha Ballard, Based on Her Diary, 1785–1812* (New York, Knopf, 1990).

12.   RH, 102; BFH, 196.

13.   BFH, 200.

14.   Channing, *Remarks on the Employment of Females as Practitioners in Midwifery*, 7, 4.

15.   BFH, 94, 95; RH, 52, 56; RAL 17.

16.   MB, 66; BFH, 99.

17.   BFH, 99–100.

18.   BFH, 107, 102; see also 105, 108–9.

19.   BFH, 107, 100, 105, 108; RAL, 19–21; MB, 67–72; RH, 56–58.

20.   BFH, 109. Ironically, medical witnesses' preferences for book knowledge rather than empirical learning runs against the trend toward sensory experience they garnered from much-praised Parisian modes of medical

learning; see John Harley Warner, *Against the Spirit of System: The French Impulse in Nineteenth-Century American Medicine* (Princeton, NJ: Princeton University Press, 1998).

21. BFH, 198, 104.

22. On medical jurisprudence, see James C. Mohr, *Doctors and the Law: Medical Jurisprudence in Nineteenth-Century America* (New York: Oxford University Press, 1993); Michele Rotunda, *A Drunkard's Defense: Alcohol, Murder, and Medical Jurisprudence in Nineteenth-Century America* (Amherst: University of Massachusetts Press, 2021).

23. BFH, 104. In a post-trial article, the *Boston Medical and Surgical Journal* tried to convince the public that all physicians at Avery's trial (prosecution and defense witnesses) essentially agreed about the basic medical facts in the case. The article was a confusing jumble of contradictions that no one (except a few embattled members of the state medical society) would think demonstrated agreement and professional reliability among the region's physicians. "Medical Evidence in the Trial of the Reverend E. K. Avery for the Murder of Sarah M. Cornell," *Boston Medical and Surgical Journal* (July 3, 1833), 333–40.

Chapter 17

1. I have recreated William Graves's story from his testimony at Avery's trial; BFH, 110–12; RH, 60–61; *MB*, 72–73; RAL, 21–22; and his letter published in LD, 63–64, as well as Mrs. Lucy B. Howe's testimony: BFH, 121. He named the men, but trial reports excised them.

2. I have recreated Maria's story through the recollections of Caroline Tibbitts, a co-worker and fellow Methodist, and the testimony of a few other witnesses at Avery's trial: BFH, 123–24; MB, 86–88; RH, 67–68; RAL, 25–26. For other witnesses, BFH, 116–17, 121–22, 126, 128–29; MB, 78–80, 83–84, 90–91, 94–95; RH, 63–66, 69–70; RAL, 24–27.

3. On the concept of the historically possible (or "critical fabulation"): Saidiya Hartman, *Wayward Lives, Beautiful Experiments: Intimate Histories of Social Upheaval* (New York: W.W. Norton, 2019); Dorsey, " 'Making Men What They Should Be,' " 345–46.

4. William Buchan, *Domestic Medicine* (Boston, 1813), 327. On the history of venereal disease and its treatment, see Jon Arrizabalaga et al., *The Great Pox: The French Disease in Renaissance Europe* (New Haven, CT: Yale University Press, 1997), 1–19; Claudia Stein, "'Getting' the Pox: Reflections by an Historian on How to Write the History of Early Modern Disease," *Nordic Journal of Science & Technology Studies* 2 (2014): 53–60; Kevin P. Siena, *Venereal Disease, Hospitals and the Urban Poor: London's "Foul Wards," 1600–1800* (Rochester: University of Rochester Press, 2004); Kevin P. Siena, "'The Venereal Disease,' 1500–1800," in *The Routledge History of Sex and the body, 1500 to the Present*, ed. Sarah Toulalan and Kate Fisher (London: Routledge, 2013), 463–78; Kevin P. Siena, "The 'Foul Disease' and Privacy: The Effects of Venereal Disease and Patient Demand on the

Medical Marketplace in Early Modern London," *Bulletin of the History of Medicine* 75 (2001): 199–224; Mary Spongberg, *Feminizing Venereal Disease: The Body of the Prostitute in Nineteenth-Century Medical Discourse* (New York: New York University Press, 1997); Olivia Weisser, "Treating the Secret Disease: Sex, Sin, and Authority in Eighteenth-Century Venereal Cases," *Bulletin of the History of Medicine* 91 (2017): 685–712; W. F. Bynum, "Treating the Wages of Sin: Venereal Disease and Specialism in Eighteenth-Century Britain," in *Medical Fringe and Medical Orthodoxy, 1750–1850,* ed. W. F. Bynum and Roy Porter (London: Croom Helm, 1987), 5–28; Thomas P. Lowry, *Venereal Disease and the Lewis and Clark Expedition* (Lincoln: University of Nebraska Press, 2004).

5. RAL, 22; BFH, 111; Buchan, *Domestic Medicine*, 327, 343.

6. MB, 72.

7. MB, 72; RH, 60; BFH, 110; James C. Mohr, *Abortion in America: The Origins and Evolution of National Policy, 1800–1900* (New York: Oxford University Press, 1978), 7.

8. Benjamin Floyd, *Lowell Directory* (Lowell, 1832), 69, 29, 47; *AT*, November 13, 1829; *Hampshire Gazette*, March 3, 1830; *BCG*, August 27, 1829; "Swaim's Panacea," Broadside, Philadelphia, February 1825, American Broadsides and Ephemera database; "Beware of Imposition . . . Swaim's Panacea is in Round Bottles . . . ," Broadside, Philadelphia, 1830, American Broadsides and Ephemera database; James Harvey Young, *The Toadstool Millionaires: A Social History of Patent Medicines in America Before Federal Regulation* (Princeton, NJ: Princeton University Press, 1961), 37, 63, 87.

9. BFH, 112; RAL, 22; MB, 73; RH, 61; Buchan, *Domestic Medicine*, 328–31; Lowry, *Venereal Disease and the Lewis and Clark Expedition*, 27.

10. BFH 111, 116; RAL, 22, 23; *National Aegis* (Worcester), June 12, 1833.

11. Graves couldn't appear at the Bristol pre-trial hearing, but he sent in a letter that had the same gossipy tone: LD, 63–64. Graves never once mentioned in court that he had an adversarial relationship with Cornell nor that he threatened to sue her for unpaid medical bills.

12. RAL, 26; BFH, 124; MB, 72; RH, 60; BFH, 110. On the history of secrecy and medical ethics: Robert Baker, "The History of Medical Ethics," *Companion Encyclopedia of the History of Medicine*, 2 vols., ed. W. F. Bynum and Roy Porter (London: Routledge, 1993), vol. 2:864–70.

13. *Boston Medical Police* (Boston, 1808), 4; see also Thomas Percival, *Medical Ethics; or, A Code of Institutes and Precepts, Adapted to the Professional Conduct of Physicians and Surgeons* (Manchester, 1803); "Medical Improvement—No. XIII," *Boston Medical and Surgical Journal* 9 (January 1, 1834), 327.

14. *New Hampshire Sentinel*, October 12, 1837.

15. Block, *Rape and Sexual Power*.

16. *Examination of Dr. William Graves, before the Lowell Police Court, from Sept. 25 to Sept. 29, 1837, for the Murder of Mary Anne Wilson, of Greenfield, N.H., by Attempting to Produce an Abortion* (n.p., [1837]), 1–2, 5–6, 10, 15;

Supreme Judicial Court, Middlesex County, Record Books, 1838 October, Commonwealth v. Graves, Massachusetts Supreme Judicial Court Archives, Massachusetts Archives, Boston. Hereafter: Commonwealth v. Graves.

17. The indictment against Graves in Docket and Record Books, Commonwealth v. Graves; *Examination of Dr. William Graves*, 21, 36.

18. *New Hampshire Patriot and State Gazette* (Concord), December 31, 1838. Physicians for Lowell corporations, key agents of Lowell's "moral police," made appearances at Graves's trial, and even Walter Channing was subpoenaed, though he did not ultimately testify. *Examination of Dr. William Graves*, 6–11, 17–21, 27–31; Certificates of Witnesses, Witness Fees, and Subpoenas, Commonwealth v. Graves.

19. *BDA*, May 24, 1833.

Chapter 18

1. *Rhode Island and Pawtucket, Massachusetts, U.S., Birth Index, 1800–1855*, online database, Ancestry.com; US Federal Census, 1850, 1880, BFH, 122.

2. *BDA*, May 21, 1833; May 18, 1833.

3. BFH, 110; CW, 81.

4. BFH, 122; MB, 84; RAL, 25; RH, 66. Miriam Libby also testified that Maria told her she had expected to marry Rawson, and when he married her sister, "it was a great disappointment to her." BFH, 123.

5. On rape trials and feminist rape reform from 1970s through the 1990s, see Lisa M. Cuklanz, *Rape on Trial: How the Mass Media Construct Legal Reform and Social Change* (Philadelphia: University of Pennsylvania Press, 1996); Aviva Orenstein, "No Bad Men!: A Feminist Analysis of Character Evidence in Rape Trials," *Hastings Law Journal* 49 (1998): 663–716.

6. *BDA*, May 21, 1833; see also CW, 60.

7. BFH, 142–43; see also, MB, 110–11; RH, 77.

8. BFH, 139–40.

9. BFH, 127. One witness testified that Cornell told her that "she said she had lived a lewd life ever since she was 15" while another person reported that her conduct "was as becoming as that of any female he ever was acquainted with." BFH, 118; CW, 97; see also RH, 66.

10. BFH, 114–15; *BDA*, May 21, 1833.

11. *BDA*, May 14, 1833.

12. BFH, 110, 112; RH, 61.

13. BFH, 117; MB, 83.

14. BFH, 123–24; RH, 68; BFH, 126, 129.

15. On the shifting of sexual controls in the early republic, see Richard Godbeer, *Sexual Revolution in Early America* (Baltimore: Johns Hopkins University Press, 2002); Clare A. Lyons, *Sex among the Rabble* (Chapel Hill: University of North Carolina Press, 2006); Cornelia Hughes Dayton, "Taking the Trade: Abortion and Gender Relations in an Eighteenth-Century New England Village," *William and Mary Quarterly* 3rd ser., 48 (1991): 19–49; John D'Emilio and Estelle B. Freedman, *Intimate Matters: A*

History of Sexuality in America (New York: Harper & Row, 1988); Nancy
F. Cott, "Passionlessness: An Interpretation of Victorian Sexual Ideology,
1790–1850," in *A Heritage of Her Own*, ed. Cott and Elizabeth H. Pleck
(New York: Simon and Schuster, 1979), 162-81; April R. Haynes, *Riotous
Flesh: Women, Physiology, and the Solitary Vice in Nineteenth-Century
America* (Chicago: University of Chicago Press, 2015); Kara M. French,
Against Sex: Identities of Sexual Restraint in Early America (Chapel
Hill: University of North Carolina Press, 2021).

16. MB, 76, 111; BFH, 115, 142–43, 111. John Wood Sweet, *The Sewing
Girl's Tale: A Story of Crime and Consequences in Revolutionary America*
(New York: Henry Holt, 2022).

17. Sally Rice to Father and Mother, 1839, in *The New England Mill Village,
1790–1860*, eds. Gary Kulik et al. (Cambridge, MA: M.I.T. Press, 1982),
388–89.

18. See Dr. Graves's statement about "passion or insanity." BFH, 111.

19. BFH, 110–12, 115–16. Historians have yet to explore the history of male
cultures of gossip with the same rigor as women's gossip; see David
S. Shields, *Civil Tongues and Polite Letters in British America* (Chapel
Hill: University of North Carolina Press, 1997); Kathleen M. Brown, *Good
Wives, Nasty Wenches, and Anxious Patriarchs: Gender, Race, and Power in
Colonial Virginia* (Chapel Hill: University of North Carolina Press, 1996);
Karen V. Hansen, *A Very Social Time: Crafting Community in Antebellum
New England* (Berkeley: University of California Press, 1994).

20. For more on male sex talk in early America, see Bruce Dorsey, "'Making
Men What They Should Be': Male Same-Sex Intimacy and Evangelical
Religion in Early Nineteenth-Century New England," *Journal of the History
of Sexuality* 24 (2015): 345–77; Lyons, *Sex Among the Rabble*, 244–48;
Thomas A. Foster, *Sex and the Eighteenth-Century Man* (Boston: Beacon,
2006), 26–30, 77–89. On male sexual and political privilege in the public
sphere in revolutionary America, see Christine Stansell, *City of Women: Sex
and Class in New York, 1789–1860* (New York: Alfred A. Knopf, 1986); Dana
D. Nelson, *National Manhood: Capitalist Citizenship and the Imagined
Fraternity of White Men* (Durham, NC: Duke University Press, 1998);
Thomas A. Foster, *Sex and the Founding Fathers* (Philadelphia: Temple
University Press, 2014).

21. CW, 61; *RIR*, June 12, 1833.

Chapter 19

1. BFH, 123; MB 86; RH 66–67; RAL, 25.
2. BFH, 123; RH 66–67; MB 86.
3. BFH, 121; RAL, 25.
4. CW, 61.
5. BFH, 125, 121, 120; MB, 89; LD, 44.
6. Jenny Franchot, *Roads to Rome: The Antebellum Protestant Encounter with
Catholicism* (Berkeley: University of California Press, 1994); Bruce Dorsey,

Reforming Men and Women: Gender in the Antebellum City (Ithaca: Cornell University Press, 2002); Rodney Hessinger, *Smitten: Sex, Gender, and the Contest for Souls in the Second Great Awakening* (Ithaca, NY: Cornell University Press, 2022), 65-67.

7.   BFH, 118, 121, 117; MB, 82.
8.   Henry Abelove, *The Evangelist of Desire: John Wesley and the Methodists* (Stanford: Stanford University Press, 1990); Richard O. Johnson, "The Development of the Love Feast in Early American Methodism," *Methodist History* 19 (1981): 67–83.
9.   Hibbard, *Memoirs*, 111; Rachel Willard Stearns Journal, Sarah Ripley Stearns Papers, microfilm M-59, reel 992, Schlesinger Library, Harvard University, Cambridge, Mass..
10. *CA*, January 10, 1834; March 17, 1827.
11. Christine Leigh Heyrman, *Southern Cross: The Beginnings of the Bible Belt* (New York: Alfred A. Knopf, 1997), 21–22; *The Doctrines and Discipline of the Methodist Episcopal Church in America*, 10th ed. (Philadelphia, 1798), 73; "Love Feast," *ZH*, February 21, 1827; BFH, 135–36; MB, 106; LD, 46.
12. BFH, 124; RH, 67. On evangelicals and confessional self-narratives: Susan Juster, "'In a Different Voice': Male and Female Narratives of Religious Conversion in Post-Revolutionary America," *American Quarterly* 41 (1989): 34-62; Heyrman, *Southern Cross*.
13. BFH, 116; RH, 63.
14. BFH, 121.
15. BFH, 121.

Chapter 20
1.   *AC*, 25.
2.   BFH, 110.
3.   BFH, 111.
4.   BFH, 113–14; MB, 74; RAL, 22; also RH, 61.
5.   BFH, 114, 116, 117; MB, 77, 79. Ellen Griggs testified that Maria's "face and eyes were red—she seemed to have been weeping." RH, 64.
6.   BFH, 114–28; RH, 62–70; MB, 74–94; RAL, 23–27.
7.   Letter No. 11 [SMC to LLC], Dorchester, March 2, 1828, in CW, 134.
8.   *AC*, 66.
9.   Juster, "'In a Different Voice,'" 38; Heyrman, *Southern Cross*; Richard Bell, *We Shall Be No More: Suicide and Self-Government in the Newly United States* (Cambridge, MA: Harvard University Press, 2012). On religion and mental illness: Julius H. Rubin, *Religious Melancholy and Protestant Experience in America* (New York: Oxford University Press, 1994); John Owen King III, *The Iron of Melancholy: Structures of Spiritual Conversion in America from the Puritan Conscience to Victorian Neurosis* (Middletown, CT: Wesleyan University Press, 1983).
10. *BCG*, March 7, 1833; *AC*, 67–68.

11. BFH, 118.
12. Residents of Bristol, Rhode Island, remembered a similar figure in their history but spoke of him only as an "eccentric character"; Charles O. F. Thompson, *Sketches of Old Bristol* (Providence, RI: Roger Williams Press, 1942), 23–28. On the history of insanity and mental illness in early America, see Mary Ann Jimenez, *Changing Faces of Madness: Early American Attitudes and Treatment of the Insane* (Hanover, NH: University Press of New England, 1987); David J. Rothman, *The Discovery of the Asylum: Social Order and Disorder in the New Republic* (Boston: Little, Brown, 1971); Gerald N. Grob, *The Mad Among Us: A History of the Care of America's Mentally Ill* (New York: Free Press, 1994); Lynn Gamwell and Nancy Tomes, *Madness in America: Cultural and Medical Perceptions of Mental Illness Before 1914* (Ithaca, NY: Cornell University Press, 1995); Andrew Scull, *Madness in Civilization: A Cultural History of Insanity from the Bible to Freud, from the Madhouse to Modern Medicine* (Princeton, NJ: Princeton University Press, 2015); Brenna Holland, "Mad Speculation and Mary Girard: Gender, Capitalism, and the Cultural Economy of Madness in the Revolutionary Atlantic," *Journal of the Early Republic* 39 (2019): 647–75.
13. BFH, 94, 96, 122; RAL, 24.
14. RH, 52.
15. BFH, 117–18, 122, 123, 125.
16. Benjamin Hallett carefully recorded the Methodists' influence. When prosecutors asked Elizabeth Shumway, for example, "Who applied to you, respecting your testimony?" She replied, "A gentleman come for me, his name was Palmer." This was Methodist clergyman, Rev. Samuel Palmer, Hallett informed his readers. BFH, 122; see also, 113–15, 119, 125–29, 140. Palmer had only been admitted as a probationary preacher six months before Cornell's death (Hallett described him as "quite a young man"), yet he apparently attended the entire trial, appeared as an alibi witness for Avery's whereabouts at the Thompson camp meeting and Providence four-day meeting, and interviewed two witnesses who lived thirty miles apart. BFH, 139, 153.
17. BFH, 125.
18. RH, 54; BFH, 122.
19. BFH, 96.
20. BFH, 129–30; RAL, 28.
21. Buchan, *Domestic Medicine*, 289.
22. Elaine Showalter, *The Female Malady: Women, Madness, and English Culture, 1830–1980* (New York: Pantheon, 1985), 11. For critics of Showalter's thesis, see Joan Busfield, "The Female Malady? Men, Women and Madness in Nineteenth Century Britain," *Sociology* 28 (1994): 259–77; Peter McCandless, "A Female Malady? Women at the South Carolina Lunatic Asylum, 1828–1915," *Journal of the History of Medicine and Allied Sciences* 54 (1999): 543–71; R. A. Houston, "Madness and Gender in the

Long Eighteenth Century," *Social History* 27 (2002): 309–26. Also Ellen Dwyer, "A Historical Perspective," in *Sex Roles and Psychopathology*, ed. Cathy Spatz Widom (New York: Plenum Press, 1984), 19-48; Helen Small, *Love's Madness: Medicine, the Novel, and Female Insanity, 1800–1865* (Oxford: Clarendon Press, 1996); Holland, "Mad Speculation and Mary Girard"; Mark S. Micale, *Hysterical Men: The Hidden History of Male Nervous Illness* (Cambridge, MA: Harvard University Press, 2008).

23. On women, insanity, and suicide in fiction: Small, *Love's Madness*; Karen A. Weyler, *Intricate Relations: Sexual and Economic Desire in American Fiction, 1789–1814* (Iowa City: University of Iowa Press, 2004).

24. BFH, 112–13.

25. On passion: Nicole Eustace, *Passion Is the Gale: Emotion, Power, and the Coming of the American Revolution* (Chapel Hill: University of North Carolina Press, 2008); Cynthia Lynn Lyerly, "Passion, Desire, Ecstasy: The Experiential Religion of Southern Methodist Women, 1770-1810," in *The Devil's Lane: Sex and Race in the Early South*, ed. Catherine Clinton and Michele Gillespie (New York: Oxford University Press, 1997), 168–86.

26. *AC*, 22, 27.

27. *AC*, 27.

28. It is impossible, of course, to compare rates of mental illness from one era to the next. They have likely remained constant across time. For the history of suicide in early America, see Bell, *We Shall Be No More*; Howard I. Kushner, *American Suicide: A Psychocultural Exploration* (New Brunswick, NJ: Rutgers University Press, 1991); Terri L. Snyder, "What Historians Talk About When They Talk About Suicide: The View from Early Modern British North America," *History Compass* 5 (2007): 658–74; Michael MacDonald and Terence R. Murphy, *Sleepless Souls: Suicide in Early Modern England* (Oxford: Clarendon Press, 1990).

29. *FRWR*, May 15, 1833; *BDA*, May 15, 1833. This was a recurring theme throughout the antebellum era: "Statistics of Suicides in the United States," *American Journal of Insanity* 1 (January 1845), 234; "On Monomania Induced Through Imitation," *American Journal of Insanity* 1 (October 1844), 119–21; "The Alarming Increase in Suicide," *New York Times*, August 3, 1859.

30. Managers of the State Lunatic Asylum, Utica, New York, "Annual Report," *Documents of the Assembly of the State of New-York* 1, no. 29 (1845), 24; Tennessee Hospital for the Insane, *Fifth Biennial Report* (Nashville, 1861), quoted in Rothman, *The Discovery of the Asylum*, 111.

31. Amariah Brigham, *Remarks on the Influence of Mental Cultivation and Mental Excitement upon Health*, 2nd ed. (Boston, 1833), 82, 85, 81; see also 36, 78.

Chapter 21

1. *BDA*, May 21, 1833.

2. MB, 27–28; BFH, 56, 58; RH, 27.

3. MB, 30; RH, 28; BFH, 61–62. Although Lawton testified that he'd "never seen Avery's face before," he picked out Avery among a group of three men at the pre-trial hearing in Bristol. Lawton had a strong emotional feeling that the man he seen on December 20 had been Avery: "It looked so much like the man, I had seen on the bridge, I had quite a serious feeling . . . it was more like the man that crossed the bridge than I could describe." BFH, 61.

4. BFH, 21, 45–46, 49–50; MB, 13–14, 17–18, 25–26. Not everyone, though, had a faceless encounter with a tall stranger in dark clothing. Peleg Cranston, tollkeeper at the Stone Bridge, talked briefly with a man who crossed the bridge a little before three o'clock, and "thought from his appearance he was a minister, doctor, or lawyer," RH, 28; MB, 29; BFH, 58. Annis Norton, whose father's house was on the Tiverton side of the bridge, saw the man's face, and "suspected it was the Methodist minister from Portsmouth or Bristol": BFH, 62.

5. RH, 26–27; BFH, 54–55; MB, 22–23.

6. BFH, 89.

7. LD, 29–31, 49; BFH, 82–83. Avery told others that his walk had been sparked by his father's battlefield experiences there during the Revolutionary War.

8. BFH, 172–74.

9. HSE, 26.

10. BFH, 171–72, 175–76.

11. BFH, 65; LD, 41; BFH, 186–87; HSE, 30–31. It was later revealed by Methodists who defended Avery that Jane Gifford had been expelled for being "in the habit of illicit intercourse with men"; *VIN*, 60.

12. The other key fact of Jane Gifford's testimony was her claim that Avery told her the next morning that he'd been on the Island on December 20 on business at Brother Cook's. When both of the Methodists named Cook denied they'd seen Avery that day, it then seemed that the Bristol preacher had been caught in a lie. LD, 41; BFH, 65.

13. On changing perceptions of time in antebellum America: Michael O'Malley, *Keeping Watch: A History of American Time* (New York: Viking, 1990); Martin Bruegel, "'Time That Can Be Relied Upon': The Evolution of Time Consciousness in the Mid-Hudson Valley, 1790–1860," *Journal of Social History* 28 (1995): 547–64; Alexis McCrossen, *Marking Modern Times: A History of Clocks, Watches, and Other Timekeepers in American Life* (Chicago: University of Chicago Press, 2013); David M. Henkin, *The Week: A History of the Unnatural Rhythms That Made Us Who We Are* (New Haven, CT: Yale University Press, 2021).

14. BFH, 51–52.

15. "Letters from Susan," *Lowell Offering*, June 1844. On factories, industrial time, and resistance to mill owners' control of time: Gary Kulik, "Pawtucket Village and the Strike of 1824: The Origins of Class Conflict in Rhode Island," *Radical History Review* 17 (1978): 5–37; David Brody,

"Time and Work During Early American Industrialism," *Labor History*
30 (1989): 5–46; Paul B. Hensley, "Time, Work, and Social Context in
New England," *New England Quarterly* 65 (1992): 531–59; Murphy, *Ten
Hours' Labor*.

16. BFH, 89; HSE, 5.
17. Caroline F. Ware, *The Early New England Cotton Manufacture: A Study
in Industrial Relations* (Boston: Houghton Mifflin, 1931), 250; *Pawtucket
Chronicle*, October 18, 1828; Kulik, "Pawtucket Village and the Strike of
1824," 28.
18. On the origins of clocks, clock time, and public clocks: Carlo M. Cipolla,
Clocks and Culture, 1300–1700 (London: Collins, 1967); David S. Landes,
Revolution in Time: Clocks and the Making of the Modern World, rev. ed.
(Cambridge, MA: Harvard University Press, 2000); Gerhard Dohrn-van
Rossum, *History of the Hour: Clocks and Modern Temporal Orders*, trans.
Thomas Dunlap (1992; reprint, Chicago: University of Chicago Press,
1996); McCrossen, *Marking Modern Times*. On clock ownership in the
United States: Chris H. Bailey, *Two Hundred Years of American Clocks &
Watches* (Englewood Cliffs, NJ: Prentice-Hall, 1975); Brooke Hindle and
Steven Lubar, *Engines of Change: The American Industrial Revolution, 1790–
1860* (Washington, DC: Smithsonian Institution Press, 1986).
19. BFH, 21, 53, 54; HSE, 8.
20. BFH, 64, 84, 170. On the mass-produced clock industry and clock
peddlers: David Jaffee, *A New Nation of Goods: The Material Culture of
Early America* (Philadelphia: University of Pennsylvania Press, 2010);
Kenneth D. Roberts and Snowden Taylor, *Eli Terry and the Connecticut
Shelf Clock*, 2nd ed. (Fitzwilliam, NH: Ken Roberts, 1994); O'Malley,
Keeping Watch, ch. 1; Henry Terry, *American Clock Making, Its Early History
and Present Extent of the Business* (Waterbury, CT, 1870); Chauncey Jerome,
History of the American Clock Business for the Past Sixty Years (New Haven,
CT, 1860).
21. Harriet Martineau, *Society in America*, 2 vols. (New York, 1837), vol. 2: 27;
G.W. Featherstonhaugh, *Excursion through the Slave States*, 2 vols. (London,
1844), vol. 2: 27; HSE, 8–9; also Thomas C. Haliburton, *The Clockmaker;
or the Sayings and Doings of Sam Slick of Slicksville* (Philadelphia, 1837).
22. HSE, 5.
23. RAL, 15; BFH, 86; MB, 54; *AC*, 29.
24. BFH, 137–38.
25. Nathan Bangs, *A History of the Methodist Episcopal Church*, 2 vols., 3rd ed.
(New York, 1839), vol. 2:266–68.
26. BFH, 141.
27. On the historical rise of time discipline, see E. P. Thompson's pioneering
article: "Time, Work-Discipline, and Industrial Capitalism," *Past
and Present* 38 (1967): 56–97; and reconsiderations and critiques of
Thompson: Michael O'Malley, "Time, Work and Task Orientation: A
Critique of American Historiography," *Time and Society* 1 (1992): 341–58;

Paul Glennie and Nigel Thrift, "Re-working E. P. Thompson's 'Time, Work-Discipline and Industrial Capitalism,'" *Time and Society* 5 (1996): 275–99; Michael J. Sauter, "Clockwatchers and Stargazers: Time Discipline in Early Modern Berlin," *American Historical Review* 112 (2007): 685–709.

28. *ZH*, August 25, 1824; August 31, 1825. For the Methodists' emphasis on decorum and order at camp meetings, see *ZH*, June 23, 1824; January 14, 1824; September 15, 1824; September 22, 1824; September 29, 1824; *New York Evangelist*, September 11, 1830.
29. Bangs, *A History of the Methodist Episcopal Church*, vol. 2:274.
30. BFH, 137; also, 134, 131–32, 139.
31. BFH, 140; also BFH, 137–39; RAL, 30.
32. RH, 100; MB, 148; RAL, 40; BFH, 183.
33. BFH, 146, 148, 153.
34. *BDA*, June 1, 1833; *NM*, May 25, 1833.
35. *BDA*, May 29, 1833; *Newburyport Herald*, May 31, 1833; *AT*, June 4, 1833.
36. BFH, 184; HSE, 3–5, 6–7; RH, 104, 110, 113; *PRH*, October 23, 1833.
37. HSE, 20, 14–16; *AC*, 79.
38. HSE, 11–13.

Chapter 22

1. *AC*, 5, 7. On Mason's speaking style: Charles H. Bell, *The Bench and Bar of New Hampshire* (Boston, 1894), 507.
2. *AC*, 8, 9.
3. *AC*, 12, 13, 14.
4. *AC*, 24.
5. *AC*, 50.
6. *AC*, 26, 34.
7. *AC*, 26, 24, 32–33.
8. *AC*, 25, 53, 54, 30.
9. *AC*, 55–56.
10. *AC*, 56-57.
11. *AC*, 60-61.
12. *AC*, 65, 69.
13. *AC*, 70–73.
14. *AC*, 67.
15. *AC*, 76.
16. *AC*, 74.
17. *AC*, 77. Greene revealed an interesting fact about the white letter, dated December 8 from Fall River; he noticed that at the beginning the author had started to write a "B" for the place, as he might have been in the habit of writing, then checked himself and wrote "Fall River."
18. *AC*, 78–80.
19. *AC*, 89–90.
20. *AC*, 92, 91, 93.

21. *PJ*, June 8, 1833; *NM*, June 8, 1833; *PRH*, July 3, 1833.
22. HSE, 36–37; *AC*, 54.

Chapter 23

1. Newport's Jews (who met in the oldest synagogue in the United States) and Sabbatarian Baptists gathered on Saturdays.
2. "The Closing Scene of the Rev. E. K. Avery's Trial," *CA*, June 14, 1833.
3. Jeremiah Mason had returned to Boston the day after delivering his closing remarks to the jury.
4. *PJ*, June 5, 1833; RH, 143.
5. *PJ*, June 6, 1833; *BCG*, June 10, 1833; *RIR*, June 24, 1833.
6. *FRWR*, June 5, 1833.
7. *FRWR*, June 26, 1833.
8. *NHT*, May 23, 1833; *BDA*, May 24, 1833. For leadership roles of the seven committee members, see James Mudge, *History of the New England Conference of the Methodist Episcopal Church, 1796-1910* (Boston; The Conference, 1910), 171–72, 459–60, 463–64.
9. *BCG*, June 10, 1833; *New York American*, June 10, 1833; *Hampshire Gazette* (Northampton), June 12, 1833.
10. *Report of a Committee of the New England Annual Conference of the Methodist Episcopal Church, on the Case of Rev. Ephraim K. Avery, Member of Said Conference* (Boston, 1833), 12, 6, 9, 11, 3.
11. *AT*, June 14, 1833; *Salem Gazette*, June 7, 1833.
12. *Evening Post* (New York), June 10, 1833; *AT* (reprint of *PJ*), June 4, 1833; *NECH*, June 12, 1833; *RIR*, June 12, and 19, 1833.
13. *New England Galaxy*, June 15, 1833; *Christian Intelligencer and Eastern Chronicle* (Gardiner, ME), June 21, 1833; *TUM*, July 6, 1833; *NM*, June 22, 1833; June 29, 1833; *Episcopal Recorder* (Philadelphia), July 20, 1833.
14. *BCG*, June 10, 1833; *PRH*, June 6, 1833; *Religious Inquirer* (Hartford), July 13, 1833.
15. *Boston Transcript*, reprint in *Eastern Argus* (Portland, ME), June 17, 1833; *NBM*, June 21, 1833; *FRWR*, June 19, 1833; *LJ*, June 19, 1833; *NM*, June 22, 1833.
16. Pope's Day marked the anniversary of the foiled plot in 1605 to blow up Parliament and the King, known in Britain as Guy Fawkes Day. On popular shaming rituals and crowd actions in early modern Europe and colonial America, see David Underdown, *Revel, Riot, and Rebellion: Popular Politics and Culture in England, 1603–1660* (Oxford: Oxford University Press, 1985); E. P. Thompson, "'Rough Music' or English Charivari," *Annales* 27 (1972): 285–312; E. P. Thompson, *Customs in Common* (New York: W.W. Norton, 1993); Alfred F. Young, "English Plebeian Culture and Eighteenth-Century American Radicalism," in *The Origins of Anglo-American Radicalism*, ed. Margaret D. Jacob and James R. Jacob (London: Allen & Unwin, 1984), 185–212; William Pencak, Matthew Dennis, and Simon P. Newman, eds., *Riot and*

Revelry in Early America (University Park: Pennsylvania State University Press, 2002).

17. There is an enormous scholarly literature on crowds, rioting, and the American Revolution, including Paul A. Gilje, *The Road to Mobocracy: Popular Disorder in New York City, 1763–1834* (Chapel Hill: University of North Carolina Press, 1987); Peter Shaw, *American Patriots and the Rituals of Revolution* (Cambridge, MA: Harvard University Press, 1981); Alfred F. Young, ed. *The American Revolution: Explorations in the History of American Radicalism* (DeKalb: Northern Illinois University Press, 1976); Alfred F. Young, ed., *Beyond the American Revolution* (DeKalb: Northern Illinois University Press, 1993); Alfred F. Young, *Liberty Tree: Ordinary People and the American Revolution* (New York: New York University Press, 2006); Pencak et al., *Riot and Revelry in Early America.*

18. *Providence City Gazette*, reprint in *Newburyport Herald*, June 18, 1833; *LJ*, June 26, 1833.

19. *RIR*, June 19, 1833.

20. *AT*, July 9, 1833; *Norfolk Advertiser* (Dedham), July 13, 1833; *TUM*, July 20, 1833; *New Hampshire Sentinel* (Keene, NH), July 11, 1833; *NBM*, June 12, 1833; *Philadelphia Inquirer*, August 7, 1833; *FRWR*, August 28. 1833.

21. *Providence City Gazette*, reprint in *Alexandria Gazette*, July 11, 1833; *Farmers' Cabinet* (Amherst, NH), July 19, 1833; July 26, 1833; *PJ*, reprinted in *Evening Post* (New York), July 22, 1833; also *FRWR*, July 31, 1833; *Hampden Whig* (Springfield), August 7, 1833; *Family Pioneer and Juvenile Key* (Brunswick, ME), August 10, 1833.

22. "Newport's Liberty Tree in New Ground," July 4, 1920, newspaper clippings, FRHS; Young, *Liberty Tree*, 561–72.

23. On mobs in the early nineteenth-century United States, see Gilje, *Road to Mobocracy*, 123–282; Susan G. Davis, *Parades and Power; Street Theatre in Nineteenth-Century Philadelphia* (Philadelphia: Temple University Press, 1986); Bryan D. Palmer, "Discordant Music: Charivaris and Whitecapping in Nineteenth-Century North America," *Labour/Le Travail* 3 (1978): 5–62; David Grimsted, *American Mobbing, 1828–1861* (New York: Oxford University Press, 1998).

24. On criminal justice and vigilantism in a popular democracy: Richard Maxwell Brown, *Strains of Violence: Historical Studies of American Violence and Vigilantism* (New York: Oxford University Press, 1975).

25. *Providence City Gazette*, reprint in *Jamestown Journal* (NY), July 24, 1833; PRH, July 17, 1833; for the opposing view that public opinion should never devolve into "mob law," see *Boston Patriot*, reprint in *Norfolk Advertiser* (Dedham), June 22, 1833.

26. *Evening Post* (New York), June 17, 1833; *Philadelphia Inquirer*, June 18, 1833; *Alexandria Gazette*, July 11, 1833; *New Hampshire Sentinel* (Keene, NH), July 11, 1833.

27. *Columbian Register* (New Haven, CT), July 13, 1833; see also *PRH*, September 25, 1833.

28. *RIR*, September 18, 1833; *PRH*, September 14, 1833.
29. *Lynn Record*, reprint in *Gloucester Telegraph*, December 21, 1833; *TUM*, December 21, 1833; *ZH*, December 25, 1833.
30. *LM*, December 27, 1833; *TUM*, January 4, 1834.
31. The *New York Standard* and *U.S. Gazette* (Philadelphia) were the most vocal in deeming the trial reports "entirely unfit for the public eye." *National Gazette* (Philadelphia), June 6, 1833; *Alexandria Gazette* (VA), June 7, 1833; *Southern Patriot* (Charleston, SC), June 15, 1833; *Philadelphia Inquirer*, June 3, 1833; *Eastern Argus* (Portland), June 3, 1833; *BCG*, June 20, 1833.
32. This total includes the *Boston Morning Post*'s report that appeared only in newspapers as well as the two reports created after the pre-trial examination in Bristol.
33. The trial report as a new print genre and the changing cultural understandings of murder are explored in Halttunen, *Murder Most Foul*; Daniel A. Cohen, *Pillars of Salt, Monuments of Grace: New England Crime Literature and the Origins of American Popular Culture, 1674–1860* (New York: Oxford University Press, 1993); and Bruce Dorsey, "Changing Representations of Scandalous Murders in the United States," in *Violence and Visibility in Modern History*, ed. Jürgen Martschukat and Silvan Niedermeier (New York: Palgrave Macmillan, 2013), 57–72.
34. *Utica Sentinel*, reprinted in *NM*, June 22, 1833; *Rome Telegraph*, reprinted in *Vermont Gazette* (Bennington), June 25, 1833; *Utica Observer*, reprinted in *RIR*, June 26, 1833; "Male Inmates Discharged," New York, Auburn Prison Records, 1816–1942, New York State Archives, Albany, Ancestry.com.
35. *Report of the Trial of Abraham Prescott, on an Indictment for the Murder of Mrs. Sally Cochran, Before the Court of Common Pleas, Holden at Concord, in the County of Merrimack* (Concord, 1834), 10.
36. *Report of the Trial of Abraham Prescott*, 12, 59, 61–62.
37. *Report of the Trial of Abraham Prescott*, 54. The earliest news accounts had erroneously reported that after the attack Prescott returned to the farmhouse, sat down at the backdoor, and began to read the Avery trial report. *BCG*, June 27, 1833; *New Hampshire Sentinel* (Keene, NH), June 27, 1833; *NM*, June 29, 1833.
38. *Report of the Trial of Abraham Prescott*, 138–41.
39. *New York American*, September 17, 1833.

Chapter 24

1. On the Morgan murder and the origins of Antimasonry: Whitney R. Cross, *The Burned-Over District: The Social and Intellectual History of Enthusiastic Religion in Western New York, 1800–1850* (Ithaca, NY: Cornell University Press, 1950); Lee Benson, *The Concept of Jacksonian Democracy: New York as a Test Case* (Princeton, NJ: Princeton University Press, 1961); Ronald P. Formisano and Kathleen Smith Kutolowski, "Antimasonry and Masonry: The Genesis of Protest, 1826–1827," *American*

Quarterly 29 (1977): 139–65. The best history of the Freemasons in early America is Steven C. Bullock, *Revolutionary Brotherhood* (Chapel Hill: University of North Carolina Press, 1996).

2. *Rochester Telegraph*, March 6, 1827.

3. *RIA*, January 25, 1833; February 1, 1833; *NHT*, January 24, 1833; *Eastern Argus* (Portland, ME), January 25, 1833; *Boston Masonic Mirror*, January 26, 1833; *LJ*, January 30, 1833; *National Gazette* (Philadelphia), January 31, 1833; *New-York Commercial Advertiser*, February 1, 1833; *New York Spectator*, February 18, 1833.

4. On Antimasonry as a reform movement and political party, especially in New England, see Paul Goodman, *Towards a Christian Republic: Antimasonry and the Great Transition in New England, 1826–1836* (New York: Oxford University Press, 1988); Randolph A. Roth, *The Democratic Dilemma* (Cambridge: Cambridge University Press, 1987); Donald J. Ratcliffe, "Antimasonry and Partisanship in Greater New England, 1826–1836," *Journal of the Early Republic* 15 (1995): 199–239; Ronald P. Formisano and Kathleen Smith Kutolowski, "Antimasonry and Masonry: The Genesis of Protest, 1826–1827," *American Quarterly* 29 (1977): 139–65; Kathleen Smith Kutolowski, "Antimasonry Reexamined: Social Bases of the Grass-Roots Party," *Journal of American History* 71 (1984): 269–93; Kathleen Smith Kutolowski, "Freemasonry and Community in the Early Republic: The Case for Antimasonic Anxieties," *American Quarterly* 34 (1982): 543–61.

5. *Jamestown Journal* (NY), June 10, 1829; *NM*, March 6, 1830; *Boston Masonic Mirror*, March 20, 1830; *BCG*, April 1, 1830; "*Masonry Is the Same All Over the World:* ANOTHER MASONIC MURDER," Broadside, [Boston], 1830, broadside, American Broadsides and Ephemera database.

6. *Vermont Luminary* (East Randolph, VT), January 10 and 24, 1829, or February 25, 1829, quoted in Roth, *The Democratic Dilemma*, 152; William Preston Vaughn, *The Antimasonic Party in the United States, 1826–1843* (Lexington, KY: University of Kentucky Press, 1983), 15.

7. Richard Rush, Letter from York, PA, May 4, 1831, in *RIA*, May 20, 1831; *RIA*, March 30, 1832; *An Abstract of the Proceedings of the Antimasonic State Convention of Massachusetts* (Boston, 1831), 24, 52; *Proceedings of the Rhode-Island Anti-Masonic State Convention* (Providence, 1831), 5, 16; David Bernard, *Light on Masonry* (Utica, NY, 1829), x; *Christian Register* (Boston), January 17, 1829; *The Proceedings of the United States Anti-Masonic Convention* (Philadelphia, 1830), 120; James C. Odiorne, *Opinions on Speculative Masonry* (Boston, 1830), 224.

8. *Proceedings of the Rhode-Island Anti-Masonic State Convention*, 6; *Antimasonic Republican Convention of Massachusetts* (Boston, 1832), 18.

9. *NHT*, January 31, 1833; *Boston Masonic Mirror*, January 26, 1833; *New-York Commercial Advertiser*, February 1, 1833; *PJ*, January 19, 1833; *RIA*, February 1, 1833; *BDA*, January 7, 10, 11, and 24, 1833. A Newport paper cried out: shame on those who exploited this crime for partisan purposes;

if guilty, Avery deserved to be hanged whether he was a Mason or an Antimason. *NHT*, January 24, 1833.

10. BFH, 33–34.

11. HSE, 10; *FRWR*, July 11, 1832; November 14, 1832; *Antimasonic Republican Convention, of Massachusetts* (Boston, 1833), 46. I borrow this phrase "hotbed of Antimasonry" from Goodman, *Towards a Christian Republic*, 177.

12. HSE, 10–11.

13. On conspiracy politics in the early republic, see David Brion Davis, "Some Themes of Counter-Subversion: An Analysis of Anti-Masonic, Anti-Catholic, and Anti-Mormon Literature," *Mississippi Valley Historical Review* 47 (1960): 205–24; David Brion Davis, *The Fear of Conspiracy: Images of Un-American Subversion from the Revolution to the Present* (Ithaca, NY: Cornell University Press, 1971); Gordon S. Wood, "Conspiracy and the Paranoid Style: Causality and Deceit in the Eighteenth Century," *William and Mary Quarterly* 3rd ser., 39 (1982): 401–41; Richard Hofstadter, *The Paranoid Style in American Politics* (New York: Alfred A. Knopf, 1965); Seymour Martin Lipset and Earl Raab, *The Politics of Unreason: Right-Wing Extremism in America, 1790–1970* (New York: Harper & Row, 1970).

14. *New-York Commercial Advertiser*, February 1, 1833; *NHT*, May 23, 1833; *RIR*, July 17, 1833; June 19, 1833; *BCG*, July 11, 1833.

15. *RIR*, June 12, 1833.

16. *RIR*, June 19, 1833; July 10, 1833. Critics of fast-growing evangelical churches often fixated on the fundraising of their missionary and philanthropic societies as examples of how ordinary folk's money helped build the power of the church. As the Methodists began attracting wealthier, middle-class members, part of their movement toward respectability, the attacks on "moneyed" churches and priests grew. On longer history of "priestcraft," see Peter Harrison, *"Religion" and the Religions in the English Enlightenment* (Cambridge: Cambridge University Press, 1990).

17. *RIR*, July 10, 1833; June 19, 1833; also July 3, 1833; June 19, 1833; BFH, 6–13; TAL, 5–6.

18. *RIR*, June 26, 1833; July 3, 1833; July 24, 1833.

19. *RIR*, June 19, 1833.

20. AS, 9, 32; see also *BCG*, June 24, 1833.

21. AS, 16.

22. AS, 18, 60, 31.

23. AS, 9, 61.

24. *TUM*, September 21, 1833; *Traveller, Family Journal, Spirit of the Times & Life in New York*, August 10, 1833; *New Hampshire Gazette*, October 1, 1833; *PRH*, July 20, 1833; August 3 & 10, 1833; *RIR*, October 2, 9, and 23, 1833; *Charleston Courier*, November 15, 1833. For evidence that Frieze was Aristides, see *RIR*, October 23, 1833. A genealogical account recalled of Frieze that "in the days when pamphlets were one of the main instruments in political warfare, he was somewhat noted in Rhode Island for his skill

as a pamphleteer." James B. Angell, "Obituary Notice of Henry Simmons Frieze," *Proceedings of the American Philosophical Society* 28, no. 132 (1890), 59. On Universalists, see Ann Lee Bressler, *The Universalist Movement in America, 1770–1880* (New York: Oxford University Press, 2001); Russell E. Miller, *The Larger Hope: The First Century of the Universalist Church in America, 1770–1870* (Boston: Unitarian Universalist Association, 1979).

25. AS, 27–29, 40–41, 55–58, 35, 76.
26. AS, 11.
27. AS, 14; also 6, 11, 33, 81.
28. AS, 92.
29. AS, 90, 62, 45, also 80, 94.
30. AS, 92.
31. AS, 93; *PRH*, October 16 and 30, 1833; AS, 95.
32. *PRH*, October 16, 1833; AS, 96.
33. AS, 92.

Chapter 25

1. Portsmouth Methodist Episcopal Church, List of Preachers, 1792–1891, NEMA; Samuel Foster, "History of the Methodist Episcopal Church, Bristol, R.I.," 1891, 82–83, ms. NEMA; see also Wilfred H. Munro, *The History of Bristol, R.I.* (Providence, 1880), 265–66; Lucius D. Davis, *History of the Methodist Episcopal Church, in Newport, R. I.* (Newport, 1882), 53–54, 57; *History of Newport County, Rhode Island*, ed. Richard M. Bayles (New York, 1888), 683–86; Abel Stevens, *Memorials of the Early Progress of Methodism in the Eastern States* (New York, 1854), 419. The Methodists reported only minor declines in local memberships in these years, perhaps an indication that they weren't counting the empty pews but holding onto memberships: *Minutes of the Annual Conferences of the Methodist Episcopal Church, for the Years 1829–1839*, vol. 2 (New York, 1840), 28, 65, 103, 149, 199, 259, 324, 384.
2. *Gloucester Telegraph*, January 14, and February 5, 1834; *NM*, January 18, 1834.
3. Merrill and Merritt testified about Avery's character in court in Bristol and Newport, respectively. For biographical information on the authors of the *Vindication*, see Mudge, *History of the New England Conference*, 51–52, 64, 77, 197; G. F. Cox, "Timothy Merritt," in *Annals of the American Pulpit*, vol. 7, ed. William B. Sprague (New York, 1859), 273–76; George Prentice, *Wilbur Fisk* (Boston, 1890), 228–29.
4. The *Christian Advocate*, where Merritt was one of the editors, had the largest circulation (at 25,000 subscribers) of any paper in the country. Abel Stevens, *Life and Times of Nathan Bangs, D.D.* (New York, 1863), 244. On the Methodists' movement toward respectability by the 1830s: Nathan O. Hatch, *The Democratization of American Christianity* (New Haven: Yale University Press, 1989); John H. Wigger, *Taking Heaven by Storm: Methodism and the Rise of Popular Christianity in*

America (New York: Oxford University Press, 1998); Roger Robins, "Vernacular American Landscape: Methodists, Camp Meetings, and Social Respectability," *Religion and American Culture* 4 (1994): 165–91; Roger Finke and Rodney Stark, *The Churching of America, 1776–1990* (New Brunswick, NJ: Rutgers University Press, 1992).

5. *VIN*, 15; also 9–22.

6. *VIN*, 10, 20.

7. *VIN*, 18, 19, 11.

8. *VIN*, 15, 18, 19.

9. *VIN*, 22.

10. *VIN*, 24–25.

11. *VIN*, 26, 31, 25. On opposition to and persecution of early Methodists, see Eric Baldwin, "'The Devil Begins to Roar': Opposition to Early Methodists in New England," *Church History* 75 (2006): 94–119; Richard D. Shiels, "The Methodist Invasion of Congregational New England," in *Methodism and the Shaping of American Culture*, ed. Nathan O. Hatch and John H. Wigger (Nashville, TN: Abingdon Press, 2001), 257–80.

12. *VIN*, 33, 28. They also conflated the immoral reputation of the theater where plays about the murder were performed with Cornell's depraved character.

13. *VIN*, 39, 29, 30, 50.

14. *VIN*, 51, 56, 31, 58, 38. Seventeen times in the pamphlet they used the term "conspiracy" itself. Avery's supporters were already promulgating this conspiracy theory months before the publication of the *Vindication*. A Methodist leader in upstate New York, calling himself "Vindicator," wrote: "We believe that there has been a plot, artfully contrived and artfully executed" to charge Avery with a crime of which he had no knowledge. *PRH*, September 25, 1833.

15. *VIN*, 37, 38, 51, 52, 56, 55.

16. *VIN*, 38, 26–27.

17. *VIN*, 56, 58.

18. *AT*, March 28, 1834.

19. *PRH*, February 26, 1834.

20. Davis, "Some Themes of Counter-Subversion," 223–24.

Chapter 26

1. *Explanation of the Circumstances Connected with the Death of Sarah Maria Cornell; by Ephraim K. Avery* (Providence, 1834), 3, 5, 6.

2. *Explanation . . . by Ephraim K. Avery*, 6, 7, 5, 13.

3. *Explanation. . . by Ephraim K. Avery*, 9, 12, 13.

4. *ZH*, February 5, 1834; *Boston Saturday Morning Transcript*, February 1, 1834; *CA*, February 21, 1834; *Free Enquirer*, January 26, 1834.

5. *RIR*, June 26, 1833; July 3, 1833; *New York Evening Post*, June 26, 1833; *Newburyport Herald* (MA), July 2, 1833; *Hampshire Gazette* (Northampton, MA), July 3, 1833.

6. *CA*, July 26, 1833; AS, 23; *VIN*, 43–51; *NBM*, July 19, 1833; *NM*, July 20, 1833; *RIR*, July 24, 1833.

7. *A Fac-simile of the Letters Produced at the Trial of the Rev. Ephraim K. Avery* (Boston, 1833).

8. *VIN*, 31, 51, 53–55; *Norwich Republican*, February 19, 1834; *AT*, January 10, 1834; *TUM*, December 14, 1833. David Melvill must not have "traced" Maria Cornell's December 20 note because the wording and spelling do not match the version recorded by trial reporters and newsmen who saw and heard the note being read at both the trial and examination. The transcription of the letters allegedly written by Avery, however, do match the text in the trial reports.

9. On a rapidly expanding print culture in the early republic, see Richard D. Brown, *Knowledge Is Power: The Diffusion of Information in Early America, 1700–1865* (New York: Oxford University Press, 1989); Robert A. Gross and Mary Kelley, eds., *A History of the Book in America*, vol. 2, *An Extensive Republic: Print, Culture, and Society in the New Nation, 1790–1840* (Chapel Hill: University of North Carolina Press, 2010); Trish Loughran, *The Republic in Print: Print Culture in the Age of U.S. Nation Building, 1770–1870* (New York: Columbia University Press, 2007); Richard R. John, *Spreading the News: The American Postal System from Franklin to Morse* (Cambridge, MA: Harvard University Press, 1995); Ronald J. Zboray, *A Fictive People: Antebellum Economic Development and the American Reading Public* (New York: Oxford University Press, 1993).

10. On the penny press in antebellum America, see Michael Schudson, *Discovering the News: A Social History of American Newspapers* (New York: Basic Books, 1978); Dan Schiller, *Objectivity and the News* (Philadelphia: University of Pennsylvania Press, 1981); Isabelle Lehuu, *Carnival on the Page: Popular Print Media in Antebellum America* (Chapel Hill: University of North Carolina Press, 2000); John D. Stevens, *Sensationalism and the New York Press* (New York: Columbia University Press, 1991); Donald K. Brazeal, "Precursor to Modern Media Hype: The 1830s Penny Press," *Journal of American Culture* 28 (2005): 405–14; Andie Tucher, *Froth and Scum: Truth, Beauty, Goodness, and the Ax Murder in America's First Mass Medium* (Chapel Hill: University of North Carolina Press, 1994); Andie Tucher, *Not Exactly Lying: Fake News and Fake Journalism in American History* (New York: Columbia University Press, 2022).

11. *New York Sun*, September 3, 1833.

12. The moon hoax series ran in the *New York Sun* from August 21 to December 17, 1835. Quotations from Richard Adams Locke, *The Moon Hoax; or, A Discovery that the Moon has a Vast Population of Human Beings* (New York, 1859), 37. See also Lehuu, *Carnival on the Page*; Ulf Jonas Bjork, "'Sweet Is the Tale': A Context for the *New York Sun*'s Moon Hoax," *American Journalism* 18 (2001): 13–27; David A. Copeland, "A Series of Fortunate Events: Why People Believed Richard Adams Locke's 'Moon

Hoax,'" *Journalism History* 33 (2007): 140–50; Mario Castagnaro, "Lunar Fancies and Earthly Truths: The Moon Hoax of 1835 and the Penny Press," *Nineteenth-Century Contexts* 34 (2012): 253–68.

13. [Richard Hildreth], *The Slave: or the Memoirs of Archy Moore*, 2 vols. (Boston, 1836); Hallett, quoted in Richard Hildreth, *Archy Moore, the White Slave; or, Memoirs of a Fugitive* (New York, 1856), xi. See also Lara Langer Cohen, *The Fabrication of American Literature: Fraudulence and Antebellum Print Culture* (Philadelphia: University of Pennsylvania Press, 2012).

Chapter 27

1. On theater as popular entertainment in early nineteenth-century America, see David Grimsted, *Melodrama Unveiled: American Theater and Culture, 1800–1850* (Chicago, 1968; reprint, Berkeley: University of California Press, 1987); Bruce A. McConachie, *Melodramatic Formations: American Theatre and Society, 1820–1870* (Iowa City: University of Iowa Press, 1992); Lawrence W. Levine, *The Unpredictable Past: Explorations in American Cultural History* (New York: Oxford University Press, 1993); Rosemarie K. Bank, *Theatre Culture in America, 1825–1860* (Cambridge: Cambridge University Press, 1997); Butsch, *The Making of American Audiences*; *The Cambridge History of American Theatre*, vol. 1, *Beginnings to 1870*, ed. Don B. Wilmeth and Christopher Bigsby (Cambridge: Cambridge University Press, 1998).

2. *NM*, August 31, 1833.

3. Clark Jillson, *Sketch of M'Donald Clarke* (Worcester, 1878); "M'Donald Clarke, 'The Mad Poet': A Reminiscence by James Linen," *Providence Evening Press*, October. 9, 1866; William Sidney Hillyer, "McDonald Clarke, 'The Mad Poet,'" *Monthly Illustrator and Home and Country* 12 (May 1896): 357–67; Charles Hemstreet, *Literary New York: Its Landmarks and Associations* (New York: G. P. Putnam's Sons, 1903); William L. Stone, "Reminiscences of McDonald Clarke, The Mad Poet," in *History of New York City from Its Discovery to the Present Day* (New York, 1872); David S. Reynolds, *Walt Whitman's America: A Cultural Biography* (New York: Knopf, 1995).

4. *RIR*, September 4, 1833; *NHT*, September 5, 1833.

5. *NHT*, September 5, 1833; *RIR*, September 4, 1833.

6. *NHT*, September 5, 1833; *NM*, September 7, 1833.

7. McDonald Clarke, *Poems of M'Donald Clarke* (New York, 1836), 276–79. All quotations in the following paragraphs are from this text.

8. *Nantucket Inquirer*, September 11, 1833; *BCG*, September 16, 1833.

9. Oscar Wilde, "The Decay of Lying: A Dialogue," *Nineteenth Century* 25 (1889), 47.

10. Mrs. M. Clarke, *Sarah Maria Cornell, or the Fall River Murder: A Domestic Drama in Three Acts* (New York, 1833), 10, 25.

11. Mary Carr Clarke's life can be traced in Susan Branson, *Dangerous to Know: Women, Crime, and Notoriety in the Early Republic* (Philadelphia: University of Pennsylvania Press, 2008); Amelia Howe

Kritzer, "Mary Carr Clarke's Dramas of Working Women, 1815–1833," *Journal of American Drama and Theatre* 9 (1997): 24–39; her autobiographical accounts can be found in M. Clarke, *The Memoirs of the Celebrated and Beautiful Mrs. Ann Carson*, 2nd ed., 2 vols. (Philadelphia, 1838); and Mary Clarke, *A Concise History of the Life and Amours of Thomas S. Hamblin, Late Manager of the Bowery Theatre* (Philadelphia, 1838).

12. Carr Clarke was more than a bystander, though, having invited Carson into her home while they worked together on the memoir, which entangled Carr Clarke in Carson's never-ending associations with the criminal underworld. Clarke, *The Memoirs of the Celebrated and Beautiful Mrs. Ann Carson*, 2nd ed.

13. Matilda Flynn's believable performance as the title character also raised familiar concerns about independent young women. She had, after all, tried to give up an acting career, hoping to attain a married woman's respectability and beat back the dubious reputation accorded female actors, but she was lured back to the stage when her husband became manager of the Bowery Theatre for the 1832–33 season. Joseph N. Ireland, *Records of the New York Stage, from 1750 to 1860*, 2 vols. (New York, 1867), vol. 1:455.

14. Clarke, *Sarah Maria Cornell*, 27, 35.

15. Clarke, *Sarah Maria Cornell*, 8, 9. On anticlerical criticisms of evangelical philanthropic enterprises, see Bruce Dorsey, "Friends Becoming Enemies: Philadelphia Benevolence and the Neglected Era of American Quaker History," *Journal of the Early Republic* 18 (1998): 410–11; Bertram Wyatt-Brown, "Prelude to Abolitionism: Sabbatarian Politics and the Rise of the Second Party System," *Journal of American History* 58 (1971): 316–41.

16. Clarke, *Sarah Maria Cornell*, 29–30.

17. *Lines in Commemoration of the Death of Sarah M. Cornell* (Philadelphia, 1833), broadside, Library of Congress; *Lines Written on the Death of Sarah M. Cornell* (n.p., 1833), broadside, JHL; see also *Death of Sarah M. Cornell* (Boston, 1833), broadside. JHL.

18. *Factory Maid, and the Clove-Hitch Knot* ([Boston?], 1833), broadside, AAS, American Broadsides and Ephemera database.

19. *Factory Maid, and the Clove-Hitch Knot*; *RIR*, August 7, 1833; *VIN*, 31.

20. *Philadelphia Inquirer*, September 26, 1833; *New-York Commercial Advertiser*, September 7, 1833; *New-York Mirror*, September 21, 1833.

21. *New-York Commercial Advertiser*, September 7, 1833; *Nantucket Inquirer*, September 25, 1833; *Atkinson's Saturday Evening Post* (Philadelphia), September 7, 1833; *New York Echo, and the Spirit of the Age*, September 21, 1833; *Emancipator* (New York), November 13, 1833; *Philadelphia Inquirer*, September 18, 1833; *New-York Mirror*, September 21, 1833.

22. *New-York Commercial Advertiser*, September 7, 1833; *Boston Courier*, September 30, 1833; *New-York Mirror*, October 19, 1833; *A Very Bad Man* (New York, 1833); *A Minister Extraordinary Taking Passage & Bound on a Foreign Mission to the Court of His Satanic Majesty!* (New York, 1833), both broadsides, Library of Congress. See also Donna Dennis, *Licentious*

Gotham: Erotic Publishing and Its Prosecution in Nineteenth-Century New York (Cambridge, MA: Harvard University Press, 2009), 20–22, 130–35.

23. *Philadelphia Inquirer*, September 6, 1833; *Boston Courier*, September 30, 1833.

Chapter 28

1. On women writers and female readership, including magazines like *Godey's Lady's Book*: Anne C. Rose, *Voices of the Marketplace* (New York: Rowman & Littlefield, 2004); Mary Kelley, *Private Woman, Public Stage* (New York: Oxford University Press, 1984); Mary Kelley, *Learning to Stand and Speak: Women, Education, and Public Life in America's Republic* (Chapel Hill: University of North Carolina Press, 2006); Heidi Brayman Hackel and Catherine E. Kelley, eds., *Reading Women: Literacy, Authorship, and Culture in the Atlantic World, 1500–1800* (Philadelphia: University of Pennsylvania Press, 2008).

2. April R. Haynes, *Riotous Flesh: Women, Physiology, and the Solitary Vice in Nineteenth-Century America* (Chicago: University of Chicago Press, 2015); Bruce Dorsey, "'Making Men What They Should Be': Male Same-Sex Intimacy and Evangelical Religion in Early Nineteenth-Century New England," *Journal of the History of Sexuality* 24 (2015): 345–77.

3. Catharine R. Williams, "Memoir," ms., 1859, Sidney S. Rider Collection on Rhode Island History, JHL; Sidney S. Rider, *Biographical Memoirs of Three Rhode Island Authors* (Providence, 1880); Patricia Caldwell, "Introduction," in Catharine Williams, *Fall River: An Authentic Narrative*, ed. Patricia Caldwell (New York: Oxford University Press, 1993), xi–xxi.

4. Williams, "Memoir." Williams was married by Rev. Benjamin Onderdonk, later Bishop of New York, who afterward faced his own sex scandal for improperly fondling women. Patricia Cline Cohen, "Ministerial Misdeeds: The Onderdonk Trial and Sexual Harassment in the 1840s," *Journal of Women's History* 7 (1995): 34–57.

5. CW, 3.

6. CW, 5, 81, 115.

7. CW, 86, 87.

8. CW, 3–4, 17.

9. CW, 90, 91, 92.

10. CW, 22, 58.

11. CW, 170–71.

12. CW, 171, 172.

13. CW, 178. Camp meetings were key sites for the dilemma of religious and sexual excess in the early republic; see Wigger, *Taking Heaven by Storm*; Catherine A. Brekus, *Strangers and Pilgrims: Female Preaching in America, 1740–1845* (Chapel Hill: University of North Carolina Press, 1998); Christine Leigh Heyrman, *Southern Cross: The Beginnings of the Bible Belt* (New York: Alfred A. Knopf, 1997).

14. CW, 189, 188, 192, 191.
15. CW, 189, 177, 178, 168, 188.
16. CW, 176, 177, 169.
17. CW, 84, 98.
18. *AC*, 27.

Chapter 29

1. Susanna Rowson, *The Inquisitor: or, Invisible Rambler* (Philadelphia, 1793), 154. On seduction stories and tales of ruin for fallen women, see Clare A. Lyons, *Sex among the Rabble* (Chapel Hill: University of North Carolina Press, 2006); Cathy N. Davidson, *Revolution and the Word: The Rise of the Novel in America* (New York: Oxford University Press, 1986); Donna R. Bontatibus, *The Seduction Novel of the Early Nation* (East Lansing: Michigan State University Press, 1999); Elizabeth Barnes, *States of Sympathy: Seduction and Democracy in the American Novel* (New York: Columbia University Press, 1997).

2. William Hill Brown, *The Power of Sympathy: or, The Triumph of Nature, Founded in Truth*, 2 vols. (Boston, 1789), vol. 2:54. For examples of Marias in seduction fiction, see "Maria; or, The Seduction," *New York Magazine*, October. 26, 1796; "Fatal Effects of Seduction: A Tale," *Weekly Visitor, or Ladies' Miscellany*, May 11, 1805; "A Tale Without a Name," *The Eye*, April 7, 1808; "Domestic Misery; or the Victim of Seduction," *The Lady's Miscellany*, October 17, 1812; "Maria—A Sentimental Fragment," *Juvenile Port-Folio*, September 4, 1813; "Seduction," *Philadelphia Album and Ladies' Literary Portfolio*, January 26, 1833.

3. *FRWR*, January 2, 1833, emphasis added; *Lowell Weekly Compend*, January 24, 1833; *LJ*, January 30, 1833; *LM*, January 4, 1833; *RIR*, June 12, 1833; June 19, 1833; July 31, 1833; AS, 13, 58–59; *PRH*, August 3, 1833; November 2, 1833; *VIN*, 35–39, 73; see also *Baltimore Gazette and Daily Advertiser*, June 13, 1833; *New York Spectator*, June 13, 1833; *RIR*, June 26, 1833; July 17, 1833; September 4, 1833; *Providence Gazette*, reprint in *Jamestown Journal* (NY), July 24, 1833; *National Banner and Daily Advertiser* (Nashville), January 21, 1834.

4. Dr. Thomas Wilbur's deposition, published in *RIR*, March 12, 1833.

5. RH, 100; *RIR*, March 12, 1833; Block, *Rape and Sexual Power in Early America*.

6. *RIR*, March 12, 1833; BFH, 86.

7. Before the trial, prosecutors, with help from Grindal Rawson and the Fall River Committee, tried to track down credible witnesses who could confirms many of the rumors that circulated about Avery having a past history of ruining young women and acquiring abortions to cover his actions. GR to William R. Staples, January 24, 1833, ATP, Folder 5; GR to William R. Staples, March 19, 1833, ATP, Folder 11; Nathaniel B. Borden to William R. Staples, April 8, 1833, ATP, Folder 13. None of these rumored accusations ever met the public's eyes.

8. The portrait of Avery appeared in two different trial reports: an abridged version of Jacob Wheeler's report for *New York Journal of Commerce*: *The Trial of the Rev. Ephraim K. Avery, for the Murder of Sarah Maria Cornell, at Tiverton, in the County of Newport, R.I. on the Evening of the 20th of December, 1832* (New York, 1833); and MB, frontispiece. Both of these reports, in the minds of the Methodists, should have been sympathetic to evangelical Christians. The latter trial report was prepared by Providence attorney George Rivers, initially hired by the Methodists, and it was published by the city's leading evangelical publishers, William Marshall and Hugh H. Brown.

9. *Lowell Evangelist*, March 22, 1833; *BDA*, May 9, 1833; *Nantucket Inquirer*, May 11, 1833.

10. *VIN*, 30.

Epilogue

1. CW, 163.

2. On Fall River's mill operations throughout the nineteenth century, see Mary H. Blewett, *Constant Turmoil: The Politics of Industrial Life in Nineteenth-Century New England* (Amherst: University of Massachusetts Press, 2000).

3. After John F. Kennedy's assassination in 1963, the town named the park after the fallen, Massachusetts-born president.

4. Bruce Dorsey, " 'Making Men What They Should Be': Male Same-Sex Intimacy and Evangelical Religion in Early Nineteenth-Century New England," *Journal of the History of Sexuality* 24 (2015): 345-377; see also Karin E. Gedge, *Without Benefit of Clergy: Women and the Pastoral Relationship in Nineteenth-Century American Culture* (New York: Oxford University Press, 2003); Robert E. Cray, Jr., "High Style and Low Morals: John Newland Maffitt and the Methodist Church, 1794-1850," *Methodist History* 45 (2006): 31-42; Patricia Cline Cohen, "Ministerial Misdeeds: The Onderdonk Trial and Sexual Harassment in the 1840s," *Journal of Women's History* 7 (1995): 34-57.

5. *An Appeal on the Subject of Slavery; Addressed to the Members of the New England and New Hampshire Conferences of the Methodist Episcopal Church* (Boston, 1835), 6; *Christian Advocate and Journal* (Chicago), October 11, 1833. On Methodists and abolitionism, see Donald G. Mathews, *Slavery and Methodism* (Princeton, NJ: Princeton University Press, 1965); Ben Wright, *Bonds of Salvation* (Baton Rouge: Louisiana State University Press, 2020).

6. On the abolitionist controversy and violence, see Manisha Sinha, *The Slave's Cause: A History of Abolition* (New Haven, CT: Yale University Press, 2016); Kate Masur, *Until Justice Be Done: America's First Civil Rights Movement, from the Revolution to Reconstruction* (New York: W. W. Norton, 2021); W. Caleb McDaniel, *The Problem of Democracy in the Age of Slavery* (Baton Rouge: Louisiana State University Press, 2013); Leslie M. Harris, "From

Abolitionist Amalgamators to 'Rulers of the Five Points': The Discourse of Interracial Sex and Reform in Antebellum New York City," in *Sex, Love, Race: Crossing Boundaries in North American History*, ed. Martha Hodes (New York: New York University Press, 1999); Linda K. Kerber, "Abolitionists and Amalgamators: The New York City Race Riots of 1834," *New York History* 48 (1967): 28-39.

7. *New York Evening Post*, September 20, 1833; *New-York Mirror*, October 26, 1833.

INDEX

―――∞∞∞――――

For the benefit of digital users, indexed terms that span two pages (e.g., 52–53) may, on occasion, appear on only one of those pages.

Pearce, William, Jr., 103
penny press, 258–59, 260
peremptory challenges, 124, 125, 242
Pervere, Lydia, 188, 189
Philadelphia, Pennsylvania, 32, 164, 210–11, 265, 268–69
physicians and "regular" doctors, 137, 147–55, 163, 164–65, 166
piece work, 32, 44. *See also* "putting out" work
Poe, Edgar Allan, 109
poems featuring crime and trial, 263. *See also* songs featuring crime and trial
political citizenship, 19, 20–21
Pomfret, Connecticut, 77, 78
Pope's Day, 228–29
Portsmouth, Rhode Island, 23–24, 103, 104–5, 119–20, 198–200, 203–4, 229, 245–46, 248–49, 250
power looms, 57–58, 59f, 61, 63–64, 89
Power of Sympathy, The (Brown), 278–79
predestination, 33. *See also* Calvinism
preliminary hearing (examination), 24, 49, 83–85, 107–8, 128, 131, 139, 140, 141, 143, 148–49, 200, 204–5, 238–39
premarital pregnancy, 18, 28, 77–78
Presbyterians, 72, 228
Prescott, Abraham, 234–35
press coverage of case
    and conspiracy theories, 238
    and jury selection process, 124–25
    and public audience at trial, 121–23
    and reactions to verdict, 231–33
    and scope/length of trial, 196, 210–11
    and trial's closing arguments, 218–19
    See also news media
print media, 4, 69, 232, 233–34, 251, 272–77. *See also* press coverage of case
privacy, patients' rights to, 165–67. *See* doctor-patient confidentiality
probable cause, 107
prostitution and prostitutes, 12, 90, 97, 107–8, 163, 175, 193–94, 215, 272–73, 280

Proteus (essayist), 241–43
Providence, Rhode Island, 30–31, 44, 45, 46–47, 49–50, 62, 74, 76, 78, 109, 122, 169–70, 194, 209, 229–30
Providence Journal, 68, 113, 218–19, 227
public opinion, 122, 230, 231, 232–33, 238, 241, 242, 243
Puritanism, 33, 180, 188–89
"putting out" work, 32, 40, 63

quickening, 167
Quinebaug River, 77

racism and racial dynamics, 174, 277, 283. *See also* abolitionism; antislavery sentiment
railroads, 205
Randolph, Richard
    background, 119–20
    and character issues at trial, 168, 170–72
    and conspiracy theories surrounding case, 239–40
    and defense's reliance on expert witnesses, 147, 148, 152
    and handwriting testimony, 211
    and medical testimony, 141, 143–45
    and mental illness/suicide testimony, 185, 189, 190
    and physical evidence at trial, 129, 133, 134–35
    and timeline of crime, 205
    and verdict of trial, 223–24
rape, 3, 140–41, 166, 208–9, 275, 279–80
Rawson, Grindal
    and character issues at trial, 169
    and conspiracy theories surrounding case, 214, 253
    and Cornell's embrace of Methodism, 93–94
    and Cornell's employment troubles, 100
    and Cornell's estrangement from family, 50, 62, 88–89